BROTHERS OR ENEMIES

The Ukrainian National Movement and Russia, from the 1840s to the 1870s

Ко за к.

Козак.

М

Мо ска л́.

Моска́л.

"Moskal." Mykola Hatchuk, Ukrainska abetka. Moscow: Universytetska drukarnia, 1861. Courtesy of the National Library of Finland, Slavic collection.

JOHANNES REMY

Brothers or Enemies

The Ukrainian National Movement and Russia, from the 1840s to the 1870s

UNIVERSITY OF TORONTO PRESS
Toronto Buffalo London

Toronto Buffalo London
www.utppublishing.com

ISBN 978-1-4875-0046-7

Library and Archives Canada Cataloguing in Publication

Remy, Johannes, 1962–, author
Brothers or enemies : the Ukrainian national movement and Russia, from the 1840s to the 1870s / Johannes Remy.
Includes bibliographical references and index.

ISBN 978-1-4875-0046-7 (cloth)

1. Nationalism – Ukraine – History – 19th century. 2. Ukrainian literature – Censorship – History – 19th century. 3. Imperialism – History – 19th century. 4. Ukraine – History – 19th century. 5. Ukraine – Politics and government – 19th century. 6. Ukraine – Relations – Russia – History – 19th century. 7. Russia – Relations – Ukraine – History – 19th century. I. Title.

DK508.772.R44 2016 947.708 C2016-904895-0

This book has been published with the help of a grant from the Federation for the Humanities and Social Sciences, through the Awards to Scholarly Publications Program, using funds provided by the Social Sciences and Humanities Research Council of Canada.

The Kowalsky Program for the Study of Eastern Ukraine at Canadian Institute of Ukrainian Studies has assisted the publication of this book.

University of Toronto Press acknowledges the financial assistance to its publishing program of the Canada Council for the Arts and the Ontario Arts Council, an agency of the Government of Ontario.

Canada Council for the Arts
Conseil des Arts du Canada

Funded by the Government of Canada
Financé par le gouvernement du Canada

To Eelis, Filip, and Misael

Contents

Group of students volunteering as teachers at Sunday schools. Beginning of 1860s. Courtesy of university museum of Taras Shevchenko University of Kyiv.

Acknowledgments

This book is a result of long work. I began to work on the nineteenth-century Ukrainian movement in 1999. At first, I worked in the Academy of Finland research project "Imperial Self and Other in Modern Russia," which was led by Elena Hellberg-Hirn. In addition to the project leader, I especially profited from my discussions with Chris Chulos who worked on the same project. Later, I received a postdoctoral grant from the Academy of Finland to continue my research on Ukrainian nationalists. I continued the work at the University of Helsinki as a lecturer at first in Russian and East European Studies, and then in History. I am especially indebted to the former head of the former Department of History, Hannes Saarinen. At the University of Helsinki, I am also and especially indebted to the staff of the Slavic department of the university library, without which this book would hardly have been possible. After moving to Canada in 2009, I worked as a sessional lecturer at the University of Saskatchewan, St Thomas University, Brock University, Carleton University, and Glendon College of York University. This book has been written at all those universities.

Aleksei Miller gave me useful advice during my archival trips to Moscow, and we also had fruitful discussions at several conferences. In Kyiv, I am especially indebted to Viktor Pylypenko, who did all what he could to make my research trips successful. Also in Kyiv, Andrii Katrenko and Volodymyr Ulianovsky helped with their advice in the early stage of my work. Liudmyla Kruhlova, director of the university museum of Taras Shevchenko University of Kyiv, generously provided the second illustration. During my two stays at the Harvard Ukrainian Research Institute in 2000 and in 2007, in the latter period as Eugene and Daymel Shklar Fellow, I received useful guidance and encouragement from Roman Szporluk and George G. Grabowicz. I am also indebted to Zenon Kohut and Heather Coleman at the University of Alberta. In Britain, my contact with David Saunders has been most fruitful. In the final stage of the work, Anton Kotenko read the manuscript and gave a number of very useful remarks. Heather Lunergan and Marta Olynyk did the proofreading of the manuscript. Since I have revised it even after their work, they can by no means be held responsible for the final result.

Originally, the title had a question mark: *Brothers or Enemies?* It has been necessary to drop the question mark, because it would have caused technical difficulties in marketing this book on the web.

Johannes Remy
College of Europe Natolin (Warsaw), Poland,
17 February 2016

BROTHERS OR ENEMIES

The Ukrainian National Movement and Russia, from the 1840s to the 1870s

Chapter One

Introduction

> Even those Little Russian patriots in whose actions … there are no criminal political ideas involved, work for the enemies of Russia, although unconsciously, cannot be found innocent in a careful investigation (na strogom sude). They are positively guilty in their lack of … caring love for our common fatherland, which [love] in the present conditions should have guided them to special caution and understanding and revealed to them that their actions are dangerous.[1]
>
> Chief Procurator of the Holy Synod Aleksei Akhmatov to Petr Valuev, 24 December 1864

> Times are different today; gone is the time of ruling over others by physical force. If such force is needed, it emerges only as a consequence of the homogeneity of the population. Nations now strive for decentralization, large states decay [and break] into their constituent parts. The same fate will befall Russia.[2]
>
> Ukrainian activist Petro Iefymenko in his letter to unidentified "Ivan Alekseevich," 1861

In the period from the 1840s to the 1870s, mutual antagonism emerged between the Ukrainian national movement and Russian imperial government. Many national activists set either political autonomy or even independence as their long-term goal, while the authorities increasingly came to perceive all Ukrainian cultural work as subversive. This period was in many ways formative of both Ukrainian nationalism and the imperial policies regarding that nationalism. The activities of the Slavic Society of St Cyril and St Methodius in the years 1845–7 marked the beginning of Ukrainian political nationalism and sparked the first wave of government repressions that targeted it. The Ems Decree of

18 May 1876, which severely restricted the printing and distribution of Ukrainian-language publications within the Russian Empire, marks the end of the period under study: by choosing outright repression, the imperial government put an end to the internal fluctuations in its Ukrainian policy. Because the goals of national activists and imperial politicians differed rather radically from each other, the emergence of antagonism between them is hardly surprising. While most Ukrainian activists wanted to dismantle the hierarchic society based on birthright and expand the functions of their language, the imperial politicians stuck to autocracy and preferred to promote the all-Russian national identity, in which all East Slavs were deemed Russians. A non-antagonistic outcome to the contest was not impossible, but it would have required more political wisdom from both sides than people normally have.

From the 1840s to 1870s, the nationally oriented Ukrainian intelligentsia developed a wide range of activities that included the organization of semi-public groups of adherents, research from a national point of view, publishing, popular education, and even lobbying of the government on the part of some sympathetic functionaries. Although the national activists numbered only a few hundred people, almost all of whom belonged to the intelligentsia, this period was important for the shaping of national mythology. Many of the ideas that later became enshrined in the Ukrainian national mythology were first expressed in the late 1840s and early 1860s. These included the often stereotypical ideas about the differences between the Ukrainian and Russian national characters, Ukrainian–Russian relations in history, and the relationship between the two languages.

In this study, I examine Ukrainian national activism, its relation to Russia and Russians, and the imperial government's policies on the Ukrainian question. With regard to the former, the main attention is focused on seeking answers to the following questions: (1) How was the relationship between Ukrainians ("Little Russians") and Russians ("Great Russians") perceived? (2) How was the relationship between Ukrainians and the Russian Empire perceived? The "Russian question" affected practically all the various fields of national activism, and different solutions were proposed. Most activists perceived their Ukrainian identity as exclusive; that is, they did not deem it possible to be a Ukrainian and Russian at the same time. To be sure, some activists adhered to the inclusive Ukrainian-Russian identity. Creation of negative stereotypes of Russians was an important aspect of Ukrainian nation building. Concerning the second question, I claim that full separation from Russia was indeed widely discussed in the national movement. Several national activists mentioned as a desirable long-term goal either independence or joining a federation of nations from which Russia would be excluded. My thesis is that the idea of independence did not enter the Ukrainian national discourse in the end of the nineteenth century, but in the late 1850s and early 1860s. In addition, however, Ukrainian autonomy either within the Russian Empire or in a federation which would include Russia was proposed, and this goal probably had more adherents.

As regards the imperial government's policies, I examine variations of the policy in relation to the Ukrainians and the motivations behind the differing opinions of various government agencies, such as the Ministry of Internal Affairs, the Third Section of His Imperial Majesty's Chancellery (political police), the Ministry of Public Enlightenment, the governor-general of Kyiv, and local governors. For a long time, the Russian government was unable to formulate a consistent policy on the Ukrainian question that would be implemented by all agencies. Nevertheless, for most of the time – and even during more liberal periods – the majority of the empire's political figures and agencies which dealt with this question had a negative attitude to the Ukrainian movement. With Petr Valuev's circular of 1863, repression was established as the long-term policy of the central imperial administration regarding the Ukrainian national movement. Valuev banned all Ukrainian literature except fiction. However, even after the circular, some governors-general of Kyiv practised more flexible policies regarding Ukrainian activities. Alexander II enacted the Ems Decree of 1876 in order to force all authorities to follow the imperial centre's policies regarding the Ukrainian question.

This study is focused on the relations between the Ukrainian nationally minded intelligentsia and Russia, broadly understood. General perceptions of Russia and the Russian Empire, ideas about the relation between and functions of the Ukrainian and Russian languages, probing the limits of censorship, occasional cooperation with the imperial authorities, and revolutionary activities are examined. However, this is not a general history of the Ukrainian national movement during the studied period; rather, the focus is on the relation between Ukrainians and Russia. I do not limit my enquiry to the recognized leaders of the national movement. Sometimes the views of rank-and-file activists tell us more about the orientation of a political movement than the programmatic publications of its leaders. The ideological leaders of any political movement direct their message not only to the participants of the movement but also to the public outside of it. That is why their message is often more moderate than that of rank and file participants who, to a lesser extent, take into account the need to evoke goodwill outside the movement. I therefore focus attention not only on the leaders, but also on the ideas of ordinary Ukrainian activists. Special attention is also paid to those ideas of Ukrainian–Russian relations that did not become part of the established national mythology.

The study is organized chronologically. In this introduction, I provide background material on the emergence of the Ukrainian national movement. The latter part of the introduction consists of an overview of the development of the national movement before the 1840s. Its purpose is to introduce to our topic those readers who are not familiar with it. Readers with knowledge of the early Ukrainian national movement may want to proceed directly to chapter 2, which deals with the St Cyril and Methodius Society, discusses the government's response to it, and describes Ukrainian activism in the last years of Nicholas I's reign, which ended in 1855. Chapter 3 examines the views on Russia and Russians in Ukrainian publications that appeared in the latter half of 1850s, the liberal beginning of Alexander II's reign. The chapter also includes a discussion of the censorship policies regarding Ukrainian publications in those years. Chapter 4 discusses Ukrainian publishing, including periodicals and the books intended for popular enlightenment, at the beginning of the 1860s. Until 1863,the imperial censors tolerated Ukrainian nationalism, but only within certain limits. Chapter 5 describes clandestine and semi-clandestine Ukrainian activities from 1856–64, between the beginning of the reign of Alexander II and the end of the Polish January insurrection. Ukrainian subversion was not a product of the imagination of the political police, as it indeed existed. Among other ideas disloyal to the imperial rule, Ukrainian independence was discussed. On the question of the Polish uprising, the Ukrainian movement was split, most activists in Kyiv cooperating with the government, while some sympathizing with the insurgents. There were important contacts and negotiations between the Ukrainians and the Polish underground state.

The clandestine and semi-clandestine Ukrainian activities form part of the background of the Valuev circular, a secret instruction issued on 18 July 1863 by Minister of Internal Affairs Petr Valuev, banning all Ukrainian-language publications except belles-lettres. Although only literature intended for the lower social classes was ostensibly forbidden, Chapter 6 will show that between 1863 and 1870 the authorities were reluctant to authorize the publication of any books in Ukrainian. In the 1870s many Ukrainian books began to be published, but this may be explained by the benevolent attitude of the local authorities in Kyiv and even corruption rather than by a conscious change of policy in St Petersburg. The notorious Ems Decree of 1876 essentially reinforced the Valuev circular of 1863 and re-established uniformity in the actions of the different government agencies.

Chapter 7 contains an analysis of the perception of Russia and Russians among the Ukrainian activists in the 1870s. While in the early part of this decade many Ukrainian authors tried to avoid repressions by emphasizing their loyalty to the empire, at the same time the first clandestine Ukrainian publications with an explicit revolutionary message were printed abroad and smuggled into the Russian Empire. Ukrainians were skilled in using all the available opportunities for public and lawful activities. Chapter 8 consists of my conclusions. I find the exclusive Ukrainian national identity dominant in the national movement, although some influential individuals supported the inclusive identity in which it was possible to be a Ukrainian and Russian at the same time. Ukrainian independence was the long-term political goal for some national activists, but different federal arrangements were more popular. I claim that the exposure of the St Cyril and Methodius Society in 1847 did not lead to a radical reorientation in the government's policy regarding the Ukrainian question. Until the Valuev circular, opportunities to publish in Ukrainian were relatively good. However, the change that took place in 1863 was rather significant: Valuev did not intend his circular as a temporary measure for the period of the Polish uprising but as a long-term solution of the Ukrainian question. After 1863 the government's attitude on the level of the central administration was consistently hostile to all Ukrainian activities, even cultural ones. To be sure, government repressions were not unprovoked, as Ukrainian "subversion" did exist in the 1860s and 1870s. In addition, as an aspect of the construction of Ukrainian nationhood, some Ukrainians formed a negative and stereotypical perception of Russians.[3] Compared to the 1860s, in the 1870s Ukrainians were much more circumspect in what they wrote about Russia and Ukrainian–Russian relations, but by that time government policy was already entrenched. However, the negative stereotype of Russians among Ukrainians is only one part of the story: an inclusive identity, in which it was deemed possible to be a

Ukrainian and a Russian at the same time, persisted in the 1870s even among the nationally oriented intelligentsia.

The national activities of the Ukrainian Greek-Catholic population of Eastern Galicia in the Austrian empire, today's western Ukraine, are discussed inasmuch as they had an impact on what happened in the Russian Empire. Since this work is primarily focused on the Ukrainians, I use the Ukrainian spelling of place names pertaining to the territory of Ukraine. A few additional terminological explanations are necessary. In the nineteenth century, the Russian word *russkii* had a different meaning from the current one, because at that time Russians and Ukrainians were not fully defined as distinct nationalities separate from each other. Some Ukrainians attempted to give the term a multi-ethnic meaning that would have facilitated the existence of two or more languages and/or nationalities under this general term. Nowadays, many Ukrainian historians write "Rus'" in their English texts as an adjective where this kind of concept is concerned. They are correct in claiming that this term is different from what we call "Russian" today. However, when referring to the use of *russkii* in this sense, I prefer to write "Russian" since this word in the multi-ethnic and multilingual sense was a homonym of the term that denoted simply a unified Russian people with no internal ethnic differences. A nineteenth-century reader could only fathom what was meant from the context, and using "Rus'" now would conceal the very ambiguity of the term, which was often intentional. Thus, contemporary readers must be prepared to encounter the word "Russian" in different meanings.[4] Furthermore, although I use the words "Ukraine" and "Ukrainian" in the general narrative, I have not "corrected" other terms when I refer to discussions about Ukraine and Ukrainians. Thus, when I deal with a text in which the author writes about the "Little Russian" (*malorossiiskii, malorusskii*) language, I use the same word.[5] All dates are given according to the Julian calendar, officially used in the Russian Empire, which was twelve days behind the Gregorian calendar in the nineteenth century.

The most important sources of the study are archival materials located in Russia and Ukraine. Among these, the most important are documents of the central administration of censorship, which are located in the Russian State Historical Archive (*Rossiiskii Gosudarstvennyi Istoricheskii Arkhiv*, RGIA) in St Petersburg; the Third Section of His Imperial Majesty's Own Chancellery, located in the State Archive of the Russian Federation (*Gosudarstvennyi Arkhiv Rossiiskoi Federatsii*, GARF) in Moscow; the Special Section (*osoboe prisutstvie*) of the Ruling Senate in the same archive; and documents of the governor-general of Kyiv in the Central State Historical Archive of Ukraine in Kyiv. All the Russian authorities mentioned above produced documents related to the policies practised in relation to the Ukrainian question. The documents of censorship also contain materials related to banning and permitting publications in Ukrainian, while the Third Section arrested and repressed several Ukrainian activists. The governor-general of Kyiv was responsible for the administration of Right-bank Ukraine west of the river Dnipro. The archival sources also include important documents produced by the Ukrainian national activists, like those of the Chernihiv Hromada found in the possession of Stepan Nis, who was arrested in 1863. They are now located among the documents of the Special Section of the Senate in GARF. The Special Section contains also Ukrainian revolutionary activist Ivan Andrushchenko's correspondence. The Russian State Military Historical Archive in Moscow contains the case file of a Ukrainian activist, Andrii Krasovsky, which includes the handwritten journals which circulated in the Kyiv Hromada from 1861–2.

Apart from the archival materials, the study is based on published sources and existing research literature. Most of the relevant published sources were published either in the 1920s and 1930s, or after Ukraine gained its independence. In the research literature, Fedir Savchenko's *Zaborona ukrainstva*[6] (Ban on Ukrainism) is still useful. In the more recent literature, especially relevant are Alexei Miller's *The Ukrainian Question: The Russian Empire and Nationalism in the Nineteenth Century*[7] and Serhiy Bilenky's *Romantic Nationalism in Eastern Europe: Russian, Polish, and Ukrainian Imaginations.*[8] Savchenko based his work on extensive archival materials, many of which he published in full. Savchenko did not perceive the imperial policies as monolithic, but wrote also about substantial disagreements among the imperial politicians on the Ukrainian question. Miller's valuable book was originally published in Russian in 2000. The author is well learned in theories of nationalism and ways of politics among the highest layers of the imperial bureaucracy. He perceives the Ukrainian question as a contest between all-Russian and Ukrainian national identities. The all-Russian identity meant that Great Russians, Ukrainians, and Belarusians were deemed to form a single nation. This identity was promoted by the government, while the exclusive Ukrainian national identity emerged in opposition to it. Miller's work has a broad source basis which includes many unpublished documents not consulted by Savchenko. While Miller studies both imperial policies and Ukrainian activities, he pays more attention to the first. This book differs from Miller's in that I systematically analyse the Ukrainian national activists' perception of Russia and Great Russians and bring to light archival materials which he did not use. The most important of these documents are those of Krasovsky's and Nis's cases, the Kyiv governor-general's chancellery in the early 1860s, and many of the documents of the central institutions of censorship. Together, these materials broaden and deepen the perception of the imperial policies and the ideas and strategies of the Ukrainian national activists. Sometimes, I make conclusions which are different from Miller's, considering the imperial policies in the Ukrainian question more repressive than he does. However, the old saying about standing on the shoulders of giants applies to this book's relation to Savchenko's and Miller's works.

Serhiy Bilenky's book is an in-depth analysis of Polish, Russian, and Ukrainian nationalism in the 1830s and 1840s up to 1847, the time of the Cyrillo-Methodian Society. Bilenky analyses the perceptions of geographic scope of the three nations and what different thinkers considered the most essential aspects or, in Bilenky's language, "idioms" of nationality: historical tradition, folklore, language, national identity, mentality, political order. Bilenky's work brings light on both all-Russian and Ukrainian identities. One of his achievements is to highlight the great variety which existed within both Russian and Ukrainian nationalism. Because of its chronologic scope, Bilenky's book has been especially useful for chapter 2 of this book. While Bilenky's book is a study of ideas, this book is a study of events and ideas in the context of those events. Except for his analysis of the so-called Official Nationality, the government ideology which sought to reconcile Russian nationalism and autocracy, Bilenky does not research government policies either in the promotion of Russian nationality or regarding the Ukrainian national movement. The interaction and practical encounters between the government and Ukrainian national activists are outside the scope of Bilenky's *Romantic Nationalism*.

Faith Hillis's *Children of Rus': Right-Bank Ukraine and the Invention of the Russian Nation*[9] is a study of the development of Russian national identity in the nineteenth and early twentieth century up to 1917. My approach to and conclusions regarding Ukrainian national movement differ from hers. According to Hillis, a coherent Little Russian lobby which adhered to the all-Russian identity existed until the late 1870s, and the Ukrainian national movement emerged only after Ems Decree of 1876 as a result of the split in the Little Russian lobby. Thus, in her view, the Kyiv Hromada and its activities in 1860s and most of 1870s belong to the history of Russian and not Ukrainian nationalism. Hillis finds that the coherent Little Russian lobby was influential and in the authorities' favour especially in 1860s and 1870s. However, as will become evident in this book, Ukrainian activists' tendency to distance themselves from Russians is discernible already in the activities of the Cyrillo-Methodians in 1845–7. Furthermore, Ukrainian independence was discussed at the end of the 1850s and beginning of the 1860s. That is why I disagree with Hillis regarding the existence of a united Little Russian lobby and the time of the emergence of the Ukrainian national movement. To be sure, on several occasions, Ukrainian national activists cooperated with those conservative adherents of the all-Russian identity who considered local Little Russian identity permissible and compatible with Russian identity. This does not mean that the two orientations formed one movement or a Little Russian lobby. Since the uncovering of the Cyrillo-Methodian Society in 1847, the imperial government certainly perceived the existence of a Ukrainian national movement.

It is now fairly widely accepted that nationalism and national identity are connected with the modernization process that began in Western Europe some two hundred years ago and spread from there to other parts of the world.[10] However, some theorists of nationalism, most notably Anthony D. Smith and Miroslav Hroch, emphasize pre-modern and early modern roots of nationalism.[11] Their approach is relevant for Ukraine, where the early modern Little Russian local patriotism of the Cossack upper class of the left bank of the Dnipro offered building blocks for modern Ukrainian national identity. However, from the 1840s to the 1870s the Ukrainian nation existed in the minds of nationalists as a goal to be achieved, rather than as a reality in the consciousness of the entire Ukrainian-speaking population or its majority. The territory of what is now Ukraine belonged to two empires, the Austro-Hungarian and Russian, and it was further divided into lesser units, in which administrative practices differed from each other. The history of various regions differed from each other, and the Ukrainian literary language was just beginning to emerge. Even among the intelligentsia the Ukrainian national orientation was only one of the projects proposed, the others being all-Russian and Polish identities. Miller has emphasized the persistence and importance of the so-called Little Russian orientation, in which distinctively Ukrainian characteristics were accommodated within the larger all-Russian identity,[12] and Bilenky has studied in detail some of the representatives of this orientation in the 1830s and 1840s.[13] Since the all-Russian national identity had a sizeable following even in the Austrian empire, a subject that has been studied by Nina Pashaeva[14] and Anna Weronika Wendland,[15] it cannot be viewed as a mere anomaly caused by imperial Russian policies. Andreas Kappeler sees the existence of non-exclusive multiple identities and loyalties as the initial situation in Ukraine before the process of nation building, while the exclusive Ukrainian identity only emerged in the course of that process.[16] Following Hroch, Kappeler views the situation of Ukrainians in the light of the completeness of their social structure. In this light, Ukrainians were certainly an incomplete nation in the second half of the nineteenth century. According to Kappeler, over 90 per cent of participants in the national movement in 1860–1914 belonged to the intelligentsia. However, if one takes the spoken language rather than national consciousness as the basis of identity, Ukrainians seem to be much closer to completeness: their language was spoken by the bulk of the peasantry and some of the nobility. To be sure, the geographic limits of the language were as yet undefined: it was not clear whether Galicians and Belarusians spoke the same language which was spoken along the Dnipro.

In the early part of the nineteenth century, the territory of what is now Ukraine shared only one element in its past: it had all belonged to medieval Rus', a principality, or group of principalities, which had existed from the ninth to the thirteenth centuries. The most important political centre of Rus' was once located in Kyiv, and the ancestors of the Ukrainians had created a high literary culture since the tenth century. However, Rus' extended far north, beyond the limits of the Ukrainian linguistic territory as it was in the nineteenth century. Great Russians and the Russian Empire, too, claimed the Kyivan heritage as their own.[17] Luckily for Ukrainian nation building, the relatively short period of Mongol-Tartar rule in southern Rus' meant that its history was different from its northern neighbour's. The difference in historical development between what were to become Ukraine and Russia was further augmented when the former passed to Poland-Lithuania in the fourteenth century, and the latter was united under the principality of Moscow in the fifteenth and sixteenth centuries. However, Poland-Lithuania also extended far past the limits of Ukrainian linguistic territory, which was located rather in the periphery than in the centre of the polity. There was a well-established Polish high culture, and the claim of Poles as the rightful successors of the Polish-Lithuanian Commonwealth was difficult to contest. Furthermore, the various areas in which Ukrainian was spoken had belonged to Poland-Lithuania in different periods. In Lviv, Polish rule began in the fourteenth century and lasted until the partitions of Poland-Lithuania (1772–95), but Sloboda Ukraine (today, the Kharkiv region) had belonged to Lithuania only very briefly in the fifteenth century.[18] For these reasons, the Polish-Lithuanian period was not very suitable as the basis of Ukrainian national historical mythology.

The building blocks of modern Ukrainian national identity were most often sought in the period of the Cossack wars from the sixteenth to the eighteenth centuries. The Ukrainian Cossacks had initially protected the Polish-Lithuanian Commonwealth as a semi-independent force on its southern borderlands, then rose up against the Commonwealth because of social and religious grievances. Finally, with the signing of the Treaty of Pereiaslav in 1654 the Cossacks, under the leadership of Hetman Bohdan Khmelnytsky had submitted themselves to Tsar Alexis II of Russia, while retaining their autonomy. After Khmelnytsky's death, the Cossacks divided into various groups that were loyal to various suzerains: the Russian tsar, the Polish-Lithuanian Commonwealth, or the Ottoman sultan, and these groups fought frequently against each other. In 1709 Hetman Ivan Mazepa sided with the Swedes against Russia, but ended up suffering a disastrous defeat and going into exile. Nevertheless, autonomous Cossack territories populated by Ukrainian speakers remained in the Russian Empire until the second half of the eighteenth century. These were the Hetmanate (or Little Russia, as contemporaries called it) on the left bank of the Dnipro until 1781,[19] Sloboda Ukraine in the Kharkiv region until 1765, and the famous Zaporozhian Host until 1775.

Typical of the Cossack administrative system was the combination of civilian and military administration under Cossack leaders with troops assigned to a specific area. Originally, the administration contained an element of archaic democracy in the form of elections of leaders by all the Cossacks. Votes were not counted: an election was conducted by shouting, the same procedure by which the king of Poland-Lithuania was elected after 1569. During the period of autonomy serfdom did not exist in a legally confirmed form, but was introduced only in the late eighteenth century, with the incorporation of autonomous territories into the Russian administrative system. Among the nobility in Left-bank Ukraine, the memory of past autonomy persisted in the form of Little Russian identity and regrets over the loss of that autonomy.[20] This identity differed from modern national identity in that it concentrated exclusively on the previously autonomous territories and the

Cossack upper class with their privileges, ignoring the bulk of Ukrainian linguistic territory and other social estates. However, the Ukrainian national identity was constructed on the pre-existing material of the Little Russian identity.

As a rule, Ukrainians were not discriminated against in state service, which offered the most relevant job opportunities to the Ukrainian intelligentsia. However, the fact that the Ukrainian language lacked official status and was not used in administration and education certainly promoted linguistic and cultural assimilation to imperial Russian culture. Although government circles perceived as new Ukrainian linguistic demands, such as the introduction of Ukrainian into elementary education, national activists felt that they were in a defensive struggle against ongoing Russification. Both sides felt threatened by the other.

Beginnings of the National Movement

Books dealing with the history of the region began to appear in the 1770s. Many of them were written with the aim of defending the status of the Cossack upper class in the Russian Empire as a hereditary nobility. There was indeed a danger that the Cossack upper class, or a significant part of it, might be denied noble status in the process of unification with the rest of Russia.[21] During the first half of the nineteenth century three important general histories of Little Russia were published in Russian. Dmitri Bantysh-Kamensky's *Istoriia Maloi Rossii* (*History of Little Russia*) appeared in three printings, the first in 1822.[22] It begins from the earliest times, but concentrates mainly on the period of the Cossack wars and the Hetmanate. Although the author was very loyal to the Russian monarchs, the work still presented Little Russia as a unit with its own distinct history. Mykola Markevych, whose *Istoriia Malorossii* (*History of Little Russia*) appeared in 1842–3, contrasted here and there Little Russia with Great Russia. The author called the Great Russians "younger brothers," thereby emphasizing that the main heritage of ancient Rus' belonged to the Little Russians.[23] Markevych was influenced by an important work called *Istoriia Rusov ili Maloi Rossii* (*History of the Rus' or Little Russia*), a work written most likely in the Starodub region between 1809 and 1818, and which in Markevych's time circulated in manuscript form. The *History of the Rus'* is an apocryphal text of unknown authorship. It was attributed to Heorhii Konysky (Georgii Koniskii), archbishop of Mogilev in the eighteenth century.[24] The text, which is written in Russian with a large admixture of Ukrainian words, depicts the history of Ukraine from Kyivan Rus' to 1769, focusing mostly on the period of the Cossacks. To a great extent, the *History of the Rus'* is a work of fiction, as it is filled with deliberate distortions of the historical past, including fictitious sources and citations from them. It is one of the last expressions of Little Russian ideas. The local language is mentioned only in passing. The author's chief aim is to defend the noble dignity of the Cossack upper class, as the imperial government did not unequivocally recognize it. He also defended Cossack autonomy. According to *History of the Rus'*, Cossacks were an ancient noble estate with privileges established long before they joined the Russian Empire. They formed the nobility of Rus', a state that, according to the anonymous author, belonged to the Polish Commonwealth on an equal footing with Poland and Lithuania. The Cossacks fought against Poland only because it violated all traditional privileges and through the church union tried to destroy the Orthodox faith. Thus, the Cossacks were not at all rebels of humble origin who rose up against their lawful sovereign, but nobles who defended their traditional rights and liberties against unlawful incursions. For the author, the acme of the Cossacks' development coincided with their life under Poland before the Poles began to violate their rights, that is, before the end of the sixteenth century and, later, the Khmelnytsky era. After that period, Cossack liberties were curtailed.

Despite the importance of historical mythology for the Ukrainian nation-building project, language was the litmus test that defined, in the minds of most national activists, the limits of the prospective nation. Ukraine consisted of Ukrainian speakers. There were plenty of them, but the language lacked a literary standard and its literary use was rather limited. Although most Ukrainian speakers were peasants, Ukrainian was also spoken among the nobility, especially in the province of Poltava on the left bank of the Dnipro. However, the language was generally accorded low social status. The literate strata of society most often used either Russian or Polish for writing. The geographic limits of the Ukrainian language were still not defined. Nevertheless, literature in modern Ukrainian began in 1798 with the publication of Ivan Kotliarevsky's *Eneïda*, a travesty of Virgil's *Aeneid* in which the Trojan heroes were recast in a Cossack cultural setting. Although the poem contains some passages in a more serious tone, Kotliarevsky most often intended the language to produce a comic effect.

However, Ukrainian-language publications written in a more serious tone began to appear in the following decades. Mykhailo

Maksymovych, an adjunct professor of botany at the University of Moscow, published *Ukrainskie narodnye pesni* (*Ukrainian Folk Songs*) in 1827, including many epic songs about the Cossack wars.[25] In his foreword, written in Russian, Maksymovych claimed that Ukrainian was a language and not a dialect. He compared Little Russian songs with Great Russian ones and found many differences:[26] Little Russian songs expressed a more active spirit, a struggle against fate, whereas Great Russian songs were marked by an attitude of resigned submission to it. Great Russian songs were good at depicting nature, since it was only in this field that their authors could express themselves freely. In contrast, Little Russian songs depicted human action often in a dramatic form, expressing bursts of passion and strength of feeling. In Great Russian songs one could discern melancholy and absent-mindedness (*zabivchivost'*), whereas in Little Russian songs there was anger and yearning. Although depiction of nature was more developed in Great Russian songs, Little Russian ones also showed their authors' closeness to nature: in love songs, there were often comparisons taken from nature, since the as yet undeveloped spirit could not otherwise express its feelings. According to Maksymovych, analogous comparisons in Great Russian songs were more artificial and expressed a tendency to unnecessary decoration. Maksymovych's comparison betrays a conscious tendency to emphasize the difference between Little Russians and Great Russians as distinct cultural groups. Implicit in the comparison was the claim that Little Russians tended to struggle for their freedom, whereas Great Russians were passive and did not care about their liberty.

Maksymovych's collection inspired Izmail Ivanovich Sreznevskii to publish his collection *Zaporozhskaia starina* (*Zaporozhian Antiquities*) in 1833–8.[27] The publication combined fiction and non-fiction: it included both a history of the Cossacks from the sixteenth century to the beginning of the eighteenth and epic songs, ostensibly from the same period. Although Sreznevskii claimed they were all authentic folk songs, many were of recent vintage, possibly his own creations. The deception was uncovered only forty years later. Despite its shortcomings, *Zaporozhian Antiquities* demonstrated that it was possible to express in the Ukrainian language more than just humour and that the language itself was not a joke. Furthermore, *Zaporozhian Antiquities* was the first publication in the Russian Empire that expressed an exclusive Ukrainian national identity. Sreznevskii consistently used the words "Ukrainian" and "Russian" as mutually exclusive concepts. For example, he writes: "In the Ukrainian chronicles the Polish nation is often called *liatskii, liadskii* ... In the Russian chronicles too."[28] Sreznevskii did not hide the fact that the Cossacks had sometimes warred against Muscovy: one of the fake folk songs in *Zaporozhian Antiquities* describes the readiness of the sixteenth-century Cossacks to wage war against the Muscovites together with the Polish king Stefan Batory on condition of being granted "liberty."[29] On the whole, however, Sreznevskii described Russia's role in Ukraine as positive, since Russia helped the Ukrainians liberate themselves from the Polish yoke.

Another pioneer of Ukrainian studies was Osyp Bodiansky (Osip Maksimovich Bodianskii), professor of Slavic studies at the University of Moscow.[30] In 1835, when he was still a graduate student, Bodiansky published a review of a collection of Slovak poetry that contained his ideas on the difference between North and South Russians.[31] Two years later he included them, in a greatly mitigated form, in his master's thesis on the poetry of the Slavic nations.[32] Bodiansky described the North Russians as the "others," which the South Russians were not: "Of all the Slavic tribes, the North and South Rus' are the most different from each other."[33] Bodiansky made explicit the political subtext of the stereotypes that Maksymovych had expressed. He found in North Russian folk poetry a passive melancholy without any attempt to influence one's surroundings or improve one's lot. According to Bodiansky, this was due to the hard climate as well as the political conditions, which demanded of the population only obedience but no active participation. These writings of Bodiansky appeared before the epic songs (*byliny*) were discovered in the northernmost areas of European Russia, which explains why he was able to emphasize the insignificant role of historical themes in North Russian oral poetry. His North Russians were interested only in real things in their immediate vicinity, and then only in the present. The usual contents of the North Russian's songs, he declared, are "the Tsar's tavern, a beautiful girl, the concerns of crude love, the simple jealousy of the common people, comparisons with a birch tree, pine, dove, and duck."[34] Most often the North Russian wants to "forget himself, wants to disappear (*rasteriat'sia*) into his lengthy sounds and the stretching of his voice."[35] In contrast, South Russian folk songs were full of drama, describing the active political struggle for liberty. The ideal of liberty (*volia*) had become most deeply rooted in the memory of the people in the Cossack wars of the sixteenth and seventeenth centuries. The incorporation of the Cossack territories in the Russian Empire had been a practical necessity, not an optimal choice:

> The Sons of Ukraine had gradually to submit themselves and become part of the system of the White Tsar; to be sure, not willingly, since they had already understood their own power. We see here mainly a necessity ... and so they accepted their fate, although for a long time after 8 January 1654 they cultivated the idea of [i.e., that this was] a misfortune.[36]

As a result, South Russian folk songs most often expressed the individual's dissatisfaction with the present situation and described attempts to overcome it. Such an identification of North Russia with autocracy and South Russia with liberty did not cause any problems for the author, perhaps because it was combined with a sharp condemnation of the Polish political and social system before the partitions of Poland.

Hryhorii Kvitka-Osnovianenko's *Malorossiiskie povesti* (Little Russian Stories) appeared in 1834 and became rather popular. Encouraged by his success, Kvitka wrote several other Ukrainian works before his death in 1843. Most of them depict contemporary peasant life in Sloboda Ukraine, in the Kharkiv region. Some stories are humorous and feature a supernatural aspect taken from local folk beliefs. Others are more serious in tone and treat their heroes with empathy and respect. Kvitka explicitly defended the capability of the Little Russian language to convey serious and abstract ideas. Despite their moral didacticism and ethnographic descriptiveness, his stories make enjoyable reading even today. Politically, Kvitka was an ardent adherent of the existing social and political order. Although Kvitka sometimes portrayed Russians in a negative light, as being prone to greed and dishonesty, there are also positive Russian personages in Kvitka's Ukrainian stories. His play *Shel'menko-denshchik* (Shelmenko the Orderly) has a Ukrainian-Russian marriage as its happy ending. On the whole, Kvitka contributed to the Ukrainian national movement by developing the language and literature rather than disseminating stereotypes about Russians.

Taras Shevchenko (1814–61) published his first collection of poems in 1840. Shevchenko's poetry was the highest achievement of Ukrainian literature by the beginning of the period that is the subject of this book. For nation-building purposes, Shevchenko's choice of subject matter is most important: his poems on historical themes are mainly about the Cossacks, and Shevchenko ignores peaceful times.[37] His poetic depiction of Ukraine's past has some elements in common with the *History of the Rus'*, which he read in manuscript before its publication.[38] Both the anonymous author of the *History of the Rus'* and Shevchenko posit the idea of Ukraine's decline from its previous, better, state. However, for Shevchenko this decay is both political and moral. His general scheme of Ukraine contains at first oppression, then liberation and the thriving of freedom, then decline and a return to slavery. The Cossacks of yesteryear were ready to defend their liberty, a state of affairs that contrasted sharply with the present situation: the descendants of the Cossacks had become serfs or had acquiesced to Russian rule in return for wealth and high status in society. Although Shevchenko's poetry does not provide clear-cut ideas of the relations between various social classes among the Ukrainians, he most often describes the role of Cossack officers negatively.[39] Thus, Ukraine is a victim not only of Russia but also of its own leaders. However, in Shevchenko's views the past shows a path to the future: Ukraine will rise from the dead and return to its previous Cossack liberty.[40] This will come about through violent upheaval aided by divine intervention. In his poetic works the future political system remains unclear, for his vision was as much religious as it was political, and he expected the appearance of divinely inspired leaders. George Grabowicz has emphasized this otherworldly aspect of Shevchenko's poetry. He even claims that Shevchenko cannot be called a nationalist for he was opposed to any kind of state.[41] This is true only if we accept a narrow definition of nationalism as an ideology that demands the establishment of a national state. However, for Shevchenko a nation was unquestionably a relevant political entity that should be liberated from foreign political domination.

The absence of a proper name for Ukraine reflected the fragmented history of its various territories. Kotliarevsky, Kvitka-Osnovianenko, and the other early writers in modern Ukrainian most often used the term "Little Russia" (*Malorossiia*) and "Little Russian" (*Malorossiiskii*). In the historical context, the name of the relevant autonomous territory was frequently used.[42] "Little Russia" was a term manifestly not suited to be the name of an emerging nation. Although it retained the connotation of the region's previous distinct administrative status, it also gave the impression of a younger brother closely related and inferior to the supposed older brother, (Great) Russia. In addition, the term was ambiguous in its territorial meaning. Sometimes, it could mean only the territory of the former Hetmanate, and sometimes the entire perceived Ukrainian ethnographic and linguistic territory. The term "Ukraine," as applied to the Cossack territory in the seventeenth century, was in fairly wide use, but it had a somewhat vague and poetic connotation. In the eighteenth century "Little Russia" was used more often for the Hetmanate, while "Ukraine" occurred in the official name of Kharkiv region, that is, "Sloboda Ukraine" (*Slobodskaia Ukraina*). After the abolition of the autonomous status of Sloboda Ukraine in 1765, the word "Ukraine" remained, until 1835, in the official name of the province that succeeded it: the "Sloboda Ukrainian Gubernia" (*Slobodska-ukrainskaia guberniia*).[43] Thus, it was natural the word "Ukrainian" was used in the titles of two Russian-language journals, *Ukrainskii vestnik* (*Ukrainian Messenger*) and *Ukrainskii zhurnal*, which were published in Kharkiv in 1816–19 and 1824–5, respectively. In the latter journal "Ukraine" was considered a part of "South Russia" (*Iuzhnaia Rossiia*).[44] Neither of the terms was defined in the journal, but it seems that "Ukraine" denoted the Kharkiv region, while "South Russia" approached the concept of Ukraine in its current understanding. In his letter to the Galician historian Denys Zubrytsky, Maksymovych wrote about "ancient Ukrainian and Red Russian (*chervonorusskikh*, that is, Galician) texts" and thus excluded Galicia from "Ukraine," by which he meant only the part of the country that belonged to the Russian Empire.[45] To be sure, Maksymovych perceived a kind of unity between Galicia and Ukraine, but he called the language "South Russian" (*iuzhnorusskii*) and the country – "South Rus'" (*Iuzhnaia Rus'*). However, Sreznevskii reintroduced in *Zaporozhian Antiquities* the term "Ukraine" in the sense of all Ukrainian ethnographic territories on both banks of the Dnipro. Shevchenko wrote most often about "Ukraine," but even he occasionally used "Little Russia."[46] The Slavic Society of St Cyril and St Methodius adopted Shevchenko's terms and preferred "Ukraine" in most of its documents, even though in the organization's rules the country's inhabitants were called "South Russians."[47] In the private correspondence of the members, the term "Little Russia" also occurred.[48] Henceforward, "Ukraine" became increasingly more established in the discourse of national activists, but outside the movement "Little Russia" was still the most widespread name. Thus, the use of "Ukraine" was closely connected with the national movement and had a definite political subtext. However, even national activists often used the term "Little Russia" and some other variants that emphasized the special relationship with Russia, for example, "South Rus'" (*Iuzhnaia Rus'*) and "South Russian" (*Iuzhnorusskii*).

The lack of unity with regard to religious confession presented a problem for the national movement, at least if Galicia in the Austrian empire were to be included in the projected Ukraine. In the Russian Empire practically all Ukrainian-speakers were Orthodox. The Greek-Catholic (Uniate) Church, in communion with Rome, existed on the right bank of the Dnipro until 1839, when the government abolished this confession altogether, forcing its adherents to join the Russian Orthodox Church. Although in 1860 the governor-general of Kyiv still complained about the weak adherence of the Volhynian clergy and peasants to Orthodoxy,[49] Greek Catholicism had no influence on the nascent national movement, which generally was anti-Catholic. This does not mean that it was Orthodox: Shevchenko and the Cyrillo-Methodians to a great extent identified Christianity with the political struggle for liberty and equality. Shevchenko's attitude to the established church hierarchy was rather negative. He admired Jan Hus, about whom he wrote a poem, and in general was an adherent of national political messianism rather than traditional Christianity. Although Shevchenko depicted the struggle between the Orthodox and Roman Catholics during the Cossack era, for him these religious confessions were practically only markers that separated the two nationalities from each other. The author of the *History of the Rus'* also revealed a somewhat anti-clerical tone, while condemning the church union as an unsuccessful Polish trick. Thus, belonging to the Orthodox Church, rather than doctrinal adherence, was the key distinguishing factor that separated the early national activists from their western neighbours. Nevertheless, materialist and atheist ideas were not expressed in the movement until the reign of Alexander II. Although adherence to the Orthodox Church as opposed to Roman Catholicism was probably in accord with the mood of the peasantry, it was problematic for the national movement: there existed religious unity with the Great Russians, but not with the East Slavic speakers of Galicia, who were all Byzantine-rite Greek Catholics in union with Rome.

The challenges that the pre-existing building blocks of nationhood – history, folk culture, language, and religious confession – presented to Ukrainian nation building were quite similar to those that the other early Eastern European nationalists from non-dominant nations encountered in the course of their work. In the long run, the national project that the Cyrillo-Methodians launched in 1845–7 was a viable one.

Chapter Two

From the Cyrillo-Methodian Society to the Death of Nicholas I, 1845–55

The Slavic Society of St Cyril and St Methodius[1] was denounced to the authorities in March 1847. The most prominent persons involved were the historian and adjunct professor Mykola Kostomarov, the civil servant Mykola Hulak, the recent university graduate Vasyl Bilozersky, the poet and artist Taras Shevchenko, and the secondary-school teacher Panteleimon Kulish. In the end, punishment was meted out to nine people, although the number of persons involved in the society was probably higher.The goal of the society was to establish a pan-Slavic republican federation with Ukraine as one of the constituent states. Ukrainian conspirators viewed political questions in religious terms and identified Christianity with political liberty and social equality, at least in the sense of the abolition of estate privileges.[2] The document entitled *Zakon Bozhyi* (*God's Law*), written in both Ukrainian and Russian, was a creative reinterpretation of the ideas contained in Adam Mickiewicz's *Books of the Polish Nation*.[3] Both texts include the image of the crucifixion of a Christ-nation, Poland or Ukraine, respectively, which inaugurates a second resurrection and the complete regeneration of social life on earth. However, whereas in Mickiewicz's *Books* only Poland has a special place in the divine plan to reorder the world, the Ukrainian document presents a Hegelian transfer of divine mercy from the Jews to the Romance nations, then to the Germanic nations, and finally to the Slavs. Although in *God's Law* Ukraine occupies a special status, all the Slavs are relevant to the regeneration of the world. However, Mickiewicz emphasized the importance of all Slavs in his other work, a collection of lectures on Slavic literature that he gave at the Collège de France in 1840–4.[4] The members of the society were acquainted with both of Mickiewicz's works, but formed their own ideas. One of the most important differences between the Ukrainian activists and the

Polish poet was the evaluation of the Great Russian nation. Mickiewicz found in the Great Russians positive, Slavic, traits as well as negative, Finnish-Turkic, ones. The Cyrillo-Methodians accepted the Great Russians as Slavs. As the statute of the secret society stipulated, Russia was to be one of the constituent republics of the Slavic federation, placed on an equal footing with the others. The Cyrillo-Methodians wanted to separate Ukraine and Poland from Russia within the federation and make Kyiv the capital of all the Slavs.The borders of Ukraine, Poland, and Russia were left unspecified, but Belarus was to be included in the same state with Russia.[5]

The basic political principles of the society were incompatible with Russian autocracy. Proclaiming the establishment of a republican federation as its goal, it declared that this arrangement was in accordance with the Slavic character. According to *God's Law*, even before their conversion to Christianity, the Slavs had no tsars or lords; all were equal. It followed that at least legal, and perhaps also social, inequality was introduced into the Slavic world by foreigners, inequality being fundamentally alien to the Slavs. Indeed, one of the two textual variants of *God's Law* states that the despot (i.e., emperor Nicholas I) and his officials are not Slavs but Germans. Thus, the imperial government was not only a political opponent but a foreign invader – even of Great Russia.[6]

God's Law was predominantly negative in its evaluation of the history of Ukrainian–Russian relations. God had punished all the Slavs for introducing kings and inequality by letting them fall under foreign rule: the Czechs and Polabian Slavs to the Germans, and the Serbs and Bulgarians to the Turks. The two versions of *God's Law* evaluated Lithuanian rule in Ukraine differently: whereas in the text that was found among Mykola Kostomarov's papers it was considered a foreign occupation,[7] in the other version, found among Mykola Hulak's papers, it was written only that Moscow fell under foreign Tatar rule, while foreign rule in Ukraine was not mentioned at all.[8] However, according to both versions, God's wrath did not last forever, for there soon emerged three independent Slavic states: Poland, Lithuania, and Muscovy (*Moskovshchyna*). The Muscovite tsar consolidated his position with the aid of the Muslim Tatars and rid the Muscovite people of liberty. He cheated the Muscovite people, who fell into idolatry because they called the tsar "god on earth."[9] *God's Law* perceives the historical Polish-Lithuanian union as a Polish-Ukrainian union and evaluates it positively. The Hulak version considers the union a precursor of the future union of all Slavic nations. However, since the Poles had tried to convert Ukrainians to Roman Catholicism, oppressed the peasants, and committed atrocities against the population, Ukraine wanted to unite as equals with Muscovy. This union between the two Slavic nations is another precursor of future Slavic unity, although later, according to *God's Law*, it led to Ukraine's oppression under the tsar. The text disapproves of Ukraine's partition between Russia and Poland in the seventeenth century. The Hulak version places responsibility for the partition on Polish lords and the tsar of Muscovy,[10] whereas Kostomarov's version speaks about Muscovites and Poles in general.[11] *God's Law* criticizes Peter I for killing hundreds of thousands of people, including Zaporozhian Cossacks, during the construction work to build channels in St Petersburg. Catherine II, who is called here "a famous, manifestly godless whore" (*kurva vsesvitna, bezbozhnytsia iavna*),[12] completed the destruction of Cossacks, making some of them lords and submitting the remainder to them. Both versions mention the Russian Decembrist uprising in 1825 and describe the punishments meted out to its participants. The Kostomarov version states that the Decembrists deserved their fate because they did not know that their ideas derived from Ukraine, but the Hulak version lacks these harsh words about the Russian revolutionaries.[13]

Thus, according to *God's Law*, the Russian state had played a negative role in the history of Ukraine. There seems to have been disagreement among the members of the society about the extent to which the Russian nation could be held responsible for this: the Hulak text places the responsibility solely on the rulers and lords, but evaluates the Decembrist revolutionaries positively, whereas the Kostomarov text finds all Russians responsible and displays less sympathy for the Decembrists. The idea that the entire Russian nation bears responsibility for Ukraine's fate is also expressed in the proclamation to the "Great Russian and Polish Brothers," written by Kostomarov's hand.[14] Here both Poles and Russians are blamed for the partition of Ukraine. However, the proclamation also states that Ukraine is ready to shed blood for the liberty of Poles and Great Russians, who are called to put aside their mutual enmity. Although this document evaluates the historical role of the Russian nation negatively, it does not consider the situation irredeemable nor national reconciliation impossible.

George Luckyj has emphasized the peaceful character of the society: "It is clear that the society was non-violent and that it aimed at education and indoctrination," he wrote.[15] I find it necessary to qualify his statement: although there were not any actual plans to use violence, an armed insurrection was indeed discussed among the members, and some of them approved of it in principle. Aleksei Petrov, who denounced the society to the authorities, claimed to have heard a discussion concerning the possible use of the Kyiv fortress as the base for the launch of an insurrection, as well as comparisons to the plans of the Decembrists.[16] When Petrov claimed that Hulak had principally accepted a violent insurrection, the latter did not deny this, but gave an evasive answer.[17] Under interrogation, another member, Iurii Andruzky put it simply: "The means follow from the principles: the year 1825 was to be repeated."[18] Andruzky testified also about having discussed the possibility of armed resistance against Russia with Ivan Posiada. He had reached the conclusion that he might fight against the Russians in Ukraine, but not outside of it.[19] Thus, although the Cyrillo-Methodians were not taking up arms in the nearest future, not all of them were convinced pacifists, either.

The other documents that the authorities found among the members' papers indicate the members' diverse opinions concerning Russia and Russians. In a private letter Panteleimon Kulish wrote to Mykola Kostomarov that since Peter I had Germanized some of the Russians, only those who remained untouched by this change were close to Christianity.[20] Kulish's Russian-language work *Povest' ob ukrainskom narode* (*The Story of the Ukrainian People*), published in St Petersburg in 1846, contained a negative evaluation of Russia's role in the history of Ukraine, finding hardly anything positive to be said about the political connection between what the author perceived as two separate nations.[21] The book describes how Ukrainians united with Moscow under conditions that guaranteed special rights and a distinct administration. However, in time the Cossack upper class became morally degraded and destroyed the peasants' freedom, in cooperation with the Russian government and Russian administrators. In this context, Kulish lamented the defeat of "the democratic party"[22] and the abolition of the practice of deciding matters by a majority of votes with the participation of the common people. If the political order that Hetman Bohdan Khmelnytsky established had been continued, Kulish speculated, civilization in Ukraine would have continued on a domestic basis, as it did in Western Europe. He identified Ukraine with the common people and with those Cossacks who defended their rights and Ukraine's distinct status. In his estimation, the most important trait of the Ukrainian national character was love of liberty.

Kulish evaluated favourably the actions of several hetmans who had fought against Russia, like Ivan Vyhovsky, who united Ukraine with Poland-Lithuania by the Treaty of Hadiach (1658), or Petro Doroshenko, who in turn sided with the Poles and the Turks. The description of Ivan Mazepa, who had sided with Sweden against Russia in 1709, was rather neutral in tone, but Kulish mentioned that the independence of Ukraine had been his aim. He also hinted that independence had been Khmelnytsky's aim, too.[23] Russians were described as guilty of atrocities, general high-mindedness, and disrespect for Ukraine. However, Kulish wrote negatively about Russians only by describing concrete acts that were sometimes committed by named persons, sometimes by a collective unit, like a "host" (*voisko*); nowhere in the book is there a single sentence with any negative evaluation of Russians in general. In Kulish's two other works that the authorities noticed during the investigation, Russians were mentioned rarely, but in a negative light. In *Ukraine*, his history of the country before Khmelnytsky, written in the form of epic poetry, Kulish reproduces Sreznevskii's poem about the Cossacks receiving a message from the king of Poland, who wants them to wage war against the Tatars and Muscovites. They answer that they will gladly go against both, if the king first grants them liberty.[24] In a Russian-language novel, *Mikhailo Charnyshenko, ili Malorossiia vosemdesiat let nazad* (*Mykhailo Charnyshenko, or Little Russia Eighty Years Ago*), which described the events of 1762, the abolition of Cossack autonomy was mentioned as a frightening and gloomy prospect. Kulish's positive Cossack heroes praised Hetman Petro Doroshenko and recalled the fate of Pavlo Polubotok, who had died in jail after having expressed Ukrainian grievances to Peter I. Furthermore, Kulish made his heroes utter proverbs that contained stereotypical evaluations of Russians: "To bring a Muscovite," meaning "to lie"; "Escape from a Muscovite, even though you will rip your coat [while making your escape]"; "Make friends with a Russian, but keep a stone in your bosom"; "A Muscovite is not your brother"; "If the devil or a Muscovite have stolen something, you won't get it back."[25] However, these proverbs contain the only negative generalizations of Russians that can be found in Kulish's works of the 1840s, and even they are uttered by fictional characters. Taken together, Kulish's works of purported non-fiction, *The Story of the Ukrainian People* and *Ukraine*, as well as his correspondence, show his political, rather than cultural, antipathy to Russia: he found positive aspects in Russian culture, although, for the time being, none in the state. Kulish's private correspondence shows that he held the Russian writers Alexander Pushkin and Vasilii Zhukovskii in high esteem and found that Ukrainian writers could learn from them.[26] On the personal level, Kulish got along well with Russians, and even preferred St Petersburg to Kyiv as his place of residence.[27]

In the last few years before the society was exposed, Taras Shevchenko wrote a number of poems that express a negative and stereotypical image of Russians. Perhaps the most famous is "Son" (*Dream*, 1844), in which the emperor and the high-ranking Russian officials are ridiculed and condemned, and the poet describes the Russian monarchy as some kind of madness of morally degraded people. In his palace the tsar hits a senior official, who hits his junior, who transmits the imperial blow all the way down the social hierarchy. To be sure, the target of the criticism here is the autocracy, the Russian upper classes, and the Russified Ukrainian nobility in the imperial service. Such antipathy does not necessarily imply any antipathy against Russians in general. However, in a couple of verses the poet hints that he does not absolve the Russian common people of responsibility: when the imperial blow is transmitted down the social hierarchy, even the humblest Orthodox inhabitants of St Petersburg get their share of it, and they receive it with enthusiasm:

> Then those began to screech
> And holler fit to wake the dead:
> "Our royal father deigns to play!
> Hoorah, hoorah, hoorah, 'ray, 'ray!"
> I laughed most heartily and left;[28]

Shevchenko, too, perceived Russia's historical role as detrimental to Ukraine: "There were Poles, they drank blood! But the Muscovites have put the whole of God's world in chains!"[29] As Myroslav Shkandrij has pointed out, Shevchenko criticized Russian imperialism not only in Ukraine but also in the Caucasus and elsewhere.[30] A couple of times Shevchenko points to the German character of Russian autocracy, and possibly even of Russians in general.[31] Although most of his negative verses about Russians, which are expressed without limitations, can arguably be read as being directed against state officials and the upper classes. The poems that Shevchenko wrote between the years 1843 and 1847 contain only a single positive statement about anything Russian: a mention of the Decembrists as the victims of evil forces, that is, the autocracy.[32] He expressed his opinion of Russians in the most explicit form in his foreword to the planned second edition of *Kobzar*, which was written in 1847, before his arrest:

> They shout: why do we not write in Russian? But why do the Russians themselves write nothing in their own language, but only translate, and

> even then the devil knows into which language ... They shout about fraternity, but fight all the time like mad dogs. They shout about the one Slavic literature, but they do not want even to glance over what the Slavs are doing! Have they studied but one Polish, Czech, Serbian, or even our book? For we are not, glory to God, Germans! No, they have not studied ... If they happen to come across our book, they repeat and praise that which is the worst in its contents. And our village-patriots (*patrioty khutoriany*) follow suit. Most *charming* are: Jews, pubs, swine, and drunken women. For their *refined* taste that may really be good. But in our peasant view, it is very bad.[33]

Further, Shevchenko states that Ukrainians, Russians, and even Germans look alike, if they are described in a pub or fulfilling their labour obligations to a landlord, implying that there is no point in laughing at Ukrainian commoners. He defends the dignity of the Ukrainian language that was evident in the epic songs. He accuses the Ukrainian lords who have abandoned their language: "They traded their own good mother for an obscene drunkard."[34] Here, it is noteworthy that Russians represent the upper classes, while Shevchenko claims that he himself represents the peasant view. The strong polemical tone may perhaps be explained by the fact that the text was written as a defence of the Ukrainian language against the sceptical views of its literary worth. However, Shevchenko's private correspondence also contains negative statements about Russians in general, and he often uses the derogatory expression *katsapy* to denote them.[35] To be sure, as George Grabowicz has pointed out, there is a duality between Shevchenko as expressed in his Ukrainian poetry and in his other works: the poetry does not even hint of his life as a successful artist and writer associating with the members of intellectual circles in St Petersburg, and with many admirers and social contacts among both Russians and Ukrainians.[36] A hint to Shevchenko's everyday positive experiences of Russian culture can be found in his letters: he enjoyed Ivan Glinka's opera *Ruslan and Liudmila* and, despite his expressed antipathy to Russians, he had friends among them.[37]

Harsh, stereotypical images of Russia and Russians can also be found in the student Iurii Andruzky's sketches on poetry and language. Andruzky wrote his sketches in Russian. Possibly under Shevchenko's influence, he identified Russia with noble landowners and Ukraine with the peasantry. "Where is poetry to be found? In the simple peasant life that is close to the nature? Or the past, dirty nobleman's life? The first type is nobler (*blagorodnee*) in Little Russia, the latter thrives in Russia."[38] Andruzky despaired that Russian landowners' interests did not rise higher than the conservative journal *Otechestvennye zapiski* (*Notes of the Fatherland*) and that the poetry of Alexander Pushkin or Mikhail Lermontov was absolutely incomprehensible to them. Landowners were focused exclusively on corporal interests. However, the peasants had a natural inclination to abstract thought: "What is there in the stars? What is it like in the other world?"[39] Andruzky found the peasant naturally inclined to religion, and the folk songs presented evidence of strong emotions and richness of life. Little Russia's rich historical past was expressed even by the crudest landowners. For Andruzky, it was the existence of Russian literature that was in doubt. If one excluded the Little Russian writers who wrote in Russian, Russia had only three writers who were able to write articles: Osip Senkovsky, Faddei Bulgarin, and Vissarion Belinsky. All three were rather mediocre, and the first two were Poles. Moreover, the Russian language lacked the vocabulary to express abstract ideas, because in Russian all such words were borrowed from the French.[40]

Of course, it was a rather fantastic idea to identify both Little Russia and Great Russia with certain social classes.[41] Andruzky's Ukrainian-language poems and short stories described Russian rule in Ukraine in highly negative colours:[42] the Muscovites were perceived as oppressors who had called Ukrainians to themselves as brothers, but then, like non-Christians, had chained them, while the tsar himself was perpetrating evil. Here and there, the Muscovites were blamed for having committed atrocities, and no difference was made between the actual culprits and Russians in general. Andruzky used the derogatory expression *po-katsaps'ky* (in the *katsap* language) about the Russian language. According to him, the Cossack glory had been buried in the battlefield of Poltava, which indicates that his sympathies were on the side of Mazepa, a topic that was not raised in *God's Law* or other documents that contained the general principles of the society. However, during his interrogation Andruzky testified that Mazepa had indeed been discussed, and opinions for and against him had been voiced: Shevchenko had praised Mazepa, Ivan Posiada had criticized him, while Kostomarov found in him both good and bad sides.[43] In a short story entitled "The Last Zaporozhian" Andruzky positively evaluated the mass defection of Zaporozhian Cossacks to the Ottomans after the Russian government destroyed the Sich in 1775.[44] A poem entitled "Dear Pole," described Polish and Muscovite atrocities in Ukraine, but rated contemporary Poland's struggle for liberty as a positive phenomenon. Ukrainians and Poles should embrace each other and begin the armed struggle.[45] Naturally, in his poetry Andruzky could express radical ideas that he not necessarily intended to put into practice.

Finally, and perhaps most strikingly, a plan of a federation uniting Ukraine, Poland, Lithuania, Moldova, the Baltic region (i.e., today's Estonia and Latvia), as well as the Don River region, Bulgaria, and Serbia, but excluding Russia, was found among Andruzky's papers in Petrozavodsk, his place of deportation, in March 1850.[46] In his diary, which was confiscated when he was arrested, Andruzky wrote: "In order to create Ukraine, Russia must be pulled down."[47] Cyrillo-Methodian ideas could indeed lead to the wish to break with Russia altogether.

However, other, more positive, ideas about Russians also circulated among the Cyrillo-Methodians, and they were expressed in the general pan-Slavic context: Vasyl Bilozersky was enthusiastic about Petr Pavlovich Dubrovskii's *Slovianskie dela* (*Slavic Affairs*), a series of articles that appeared in Mikhail Pogodin's journal *Moskvitianin* (*The Muscovite*) in 1846.[48] This work described the cultural activities of all Slavic nations and cooperation between them. Kostomarov's poem "Children of Glory, Your Era Is Dawning" granted a special, albeit not exclusive, role to Russia in the creation of a pan-Slavic federation:

> Love each other, children of glory
> Love will save us!
> Glory, honour to you forever,
> Our double-headed eagle!
>
> For you will pull us from slavery
> By your talons
> From long neglect you will bring to light
> The Slavic destiny (*dolia*)![49]

This is hardly a poem that anyone considering himself an enemy of Russia and Russians would write. Here, even the political symbol of Russian monarchy, the double-headed eagle, is depicted as a liberator. These ideas are congruent with Kostomarov's notes on pan-Slavism, in which the "granting" (*darovat'*) of autonomous development (*sobstvennoe razvitie*) to each Slavic nation is mentioned; the wording implies some kind of imperial agent.[50] To be sure, the poem cited above also predicts woe to those who claim that their power derives from God. The emphasis on Russia's positive role is lacking in the programmatic documents of the society, and reflects Kostomarov's own thoughts.

Another rank-and-file member, the student Ivan Posiada, had vague ideas about Russia. The authorities found a fragment of his letter to the emperor and another letter to an unidentified high-ranking imperial politician, in which he complained about how the landowners and the government were oppressing the Ukrainian peasants. Posiada himself was of peasant origin. Such letters indicate that the author considered the possibility of appealing to the existing state power, at least in principle. He wrote that one who obeys the tsar in heaven will not be guilty of disobeying the tsar on earth. Although his main idea was that duty to God surpasses obligations to the monarch, Posiada's text demonstrates that he found disobedience to the earthly tsar as something morally suspect. Some passages of the fragment indicate that Posiada identified with the "Russian land." However, in another sentence he used the word Russia (*Rossiia*), clearly excluding Ukraine from it. Posiada's identity in relation to Russia was neither exclusive nor inclusive, but ambiguous.[51]

The society's programmatic documents and the correspondence among the members show that the Slavic Society of St Cyril and St Methodius aimed to overthrow Russian autocracy and to establish a pan-Slavic republican federation in its place. Although the members looked to God's help in their great task, they planned to contribute their own efforts to realizing this goal. This means that they were revolutionaries.[52] The members were in agreement that the short-term method of activity was to be the dissemination of popular enlightenment in the spirit of the society's general principles, but some of them found an armed uprising in an unspecified future acceptable. Russia was to be one of the member states of this pan-Slavic federation, even though its historical role was considered detrimental to Ukraine. The Russian monarchy, government, and, in Kulish's perception, all the privileged classes were deemed un-Slavic.

The discussions within the society did not take place outside the framework of Russian culture. Most of the programmatic documents were written in Russian, which was the literary language to which the members were most accustomed. In their private correspondence, the Russian language was even more predominant, although Ukrainian was used as well. Shevchenko was an exception: he used Ukrainian more than Russian in his private correspondence.[53] All the members were educated in the Russian high culture, which was, to a great extent, also their own culture. Even Kulish wrote about "us, Russians" in a letter to Mykola Hulak, without specifying what he meant by that word.[54] To be sure, this expression can be balanced with comments made in another letter, such as "To me, Russian seems to be a foreign language."[55] Although the members broke radically with Russian national identity in their program, some discrepancy between their political thought and everyday private life remained. This was a rather usual pattern in the early phase of the nationalisms of Eastern European non-dominant ethnic groups.

Ukrainian activities with a connection to the Cyrillo-Methodians also took place in Moscow. The periodical *Chteniia v Imperatorskom Obshchestve Istorii i Drevnostei pri Moskovskom Universitete* (*Readings in the Imperial Society of History and Antiquities at the University of Moscow*) published important historical sources on Ukraine. The importance of Ukrainian themes in the *Readings* was the result of the activities in 1846–8 of its editor, Osyp Bodiansky, now a professor of Slavic philology at the University of Moscow.[56] The Imperial Society of History that published the journal benefited from the general privilege of universities, which had the right to censor their own publications. Thus, the *Chteniia* were not subject to any form of censorship; at most, to self-censorship. In 1846 the journal published the first edition of *Istoriia Rusov*.[57] Its author emphasized how Little Russia had joined the Russian Empire through a mutually binding treaty that guaranteed the Cossacks their traditional privileges. Although he criticized Ivan Mazepa's alliance with Sweden against Russia in 1709, he praised the hetman to such an extent that his criticism lost all its force. Serhii Plokhy has observed that the author seems loyal to the Russian monarchy, but hostile to (Great) Russian people.[58] Indeed, the image of the Great Russian people in *The History of the Rus'* is definitely negative. The author portrays the Muscovites as crude and ignorant people. For instance, the dissatisfaction of the Muscovite clergy with liturgical practices in Little Russia is characterized as "peasant delusions" (*bred muzhichii*).[59] Most of the criticism of Great Russians is somewhat distanced from the author and placed in fictitious quotations of various Cossacks and, in one passage, even the khan of Crimea. To the author, the main problem with Muscovites is their slavery. He uses the word in a broad sense, denoting both the relationship between the Muscovite upper class and their tsar, and the relationship between peasants and their lords, serfdom. In the context of the negotiations between the Cossacks and the representatives of Tsar Alexis, the Cossack officer Bohun argues: "The most unconditional (*nekliuchimoe*) slavery dominates among the Muscovite people. In their country no one has nor can have anything of his own, for everything belongs either to God or the tsar. According to their ideas, human beings purportedly come into the world only in order to have nothing and to be slaves."[60]

Thus, for the author, Muscovite slavery emerges from ideas deeply rooted in the minds of Muscovites, rather than from any specific historical circumstances. According to the opinion of the Crimean khan in the *History of the Rus'*, another Muscovite flaw is their arrogance, which is evident in their claims of ancestry in Greece, Rome, and the Kyivan Rus' period, whereas they are actually descended from the Scythians. In addition, the Khan points out, the Muscovite government lacks stability: many of their tsars were killed and one was even sold to be slaughtered by the Poles.[61] The khan concludes that the Muscovites lack good morals and deep religious convictions (*postoiannoi religii*).[62] Hetman Pavlo Polubotok's speech, which contains criticism of the policies of Peter I in Little Russia, mentions that to subjugate nations by slavery is the cause characteristic of an Asiatic tyrant rather than of a Christian monarch.[63] Thus, in the *History of the Rus'* Polubotok casts doubt on the European character of the Russian ruler.

To summarize, the *History of the Rus'* singles out five purported negative traits of Great Russians: (1) inclination to slavery; (2) expansionist mentality; (3) lowly barbarian ancestry; (4) immorality and lack of religion, expressed in political instability and regicide; and (5) Asiatic character. The author perhaps did not realize the inherent tension in the postulated inclination to slavery, on the one hand, and to regicide, on the other. Some of the ideas expressed in this work were outdated by the time of its publication. Indeed, it is interesting to note how the *History of the Rus'* negatively assessed the lowly origins of the Great Russians, while Andruzky, writing some thirty years later, found nobility the most typical representative of the entire Great Russian nation. This was because the author of the *History of the Rus'* wrote in the framework of the traditional values of the Cossack nobility, whereas the Cyrillo-Methodians were republicans, who criticized all privileges based on ancestry. However, the politically radical Ukrainians could apply some ideas of *History of the Rus'*, like the critique of slavery, to the situation in the 1840s. At least Shevchenko, Kulish, and Kostomarov had read the *History of the Rus'* in manuscript form before its publication, and at least Posiada and Andruzky after it appeared.[64] At the time of its publication in 1846, the *History of the Rus'* was not of academic interest only. Its use for the purposes of Ukrainian nationalism is congruent with Anthony D. Smith and Miroslav Hroch's emphasis on the importance of pre-existing ethnic identity for modern nation building.

The publication of another Cossack history, *Litopys samovydtsia* (*Samovydets Chronicle*) followed on the heels of the *History of the Rus'*.[65] This publication was directly linked to the activities of the Cyrillo-Methodians: Kulish obtained one of the manuscripts that served as the basis of the publication.[66] The *Samovydets Chronicle* was a history of the Cossack wars written in the early eighteenth century by an anonymous author, possibly a Cossack-turned-Orthodox priest, Roman Rakushka-Romanovsky.[67] The author was loyal to the political union of Cossack Ukraine with Muscovy. The chronicle and the documents published at the same time with it gave the impression of a settlement that was reached following the negotiations between the two parties, without, however, the formal character of a mutually binding treaty between equal participants. Although the author criticized certain details and incidents connected with Muscovite policies in Ukraine, he did not perceive any inherent antagonism between the interests of Ukraine and Muscovy. The author condemned the Cossack disobedience to the tsar in strong words.[68] He did not express any antipathy against Muscovites, and he praised a number of individuals among them.[69]

To the end of the *Samovydets Chronicle*, Bodiansky appended a short comment on the fact that "Konysky," as the author of the *History of the Rus'*, had relied on the *Samovydets Chronicle* as a source. He emphasized that this enhanced the latter's reliability. In Bodiansky's words, perceptive readers could find an argument that favoured the *Samovydets* version of the enactment of the Ukrainian-Russian union of 1654 over that of the *History of the Rus'*. However, the editor did not state explicitly that the two texts were mutually contradictory in their accounts of that event.[70]

In addition to these two Cossack histories, Bodiansky regularly published materials on Ukrainian history in *Chteniia*. Not a single issue of the journal in 1846–7 lacked a publication on Ukraine. Ukrainian topics constituted more than half of the contents of four out of the six issues that appeared in the first half of 1847.[71] Kulish's notes reveal his close cooperation with Bodiansky in the distribution of publications on Ukrainian history and preparations for Kulish's journey abroad.[72] In a private letter Ivan Posiada indicated that Bodiansky was involved in the activities of the Society of St Cyril and St Methodius: "Moscow itself is paying attention to us, as is evident from the fact that Bodiansky has taken to this so energetically, and, indeed, any Little Russian, if only he has not killed nobility, morality, and nationality in himself, will not refuse his contribution to the common cause."[73]

Kostomarov and Hulak, too, were in contact with Bodiansky while the society was still active.[74] In the light of these facts, it is noteworthy that in the final issue of 1846 *Chteniia* published a short biography of Saints Cyril and Methodius, written by Filaret (Gumilevskii), bishop of Riga.[75] It is unlikely that the publication was a coincidence: at the very least, Bodiansky knew about the existence of the Cyrillo-Methodian society.

From the Cyrillo-Methodians to the End of the Reign, 1847–55

The ideas and activities of the Society of St Cyril and St Methodius surprised government circles. The government agencies that were tasked with monitoring and suppressing political subversion – the Third Section of His Imperial Majesty's Own Chancellery and the Ministry of Internal Affairs – did not find out about the society on their own. A student named Aleksei Mikhailovich Petrov denounced it to his superior, Superintendent of the Kyiv school district Aleksandr Semenovich Traskin.[76] The Third Section had no previous information on the members, and it had not paid attention to Ukrainian cultural activities. However, the chief of gendarmes, Aleksei Fedorovich Orlov, immediately understood the gravity of the matter and gave the order to arrest Mykola Hulak. Other arrests soon followed.

In a book published in 1959, the Soviet historian Petr Zaionchkovskii focused attention on the contradictions between Orlov's initial reports to Nicholas I and his final report on the results of the investigation: whereas the first report presented the society as hostile to the imperial government and emphasized the subversive nature of its members' ideas, the final report concluded that the members wanted to establish a pan-Slavic federation under the Russian emperor. Furthermore, some of the members initially offered testimonies pointing to the existence of a secret society that was directed against the government, but they later modified their statements, claiming that they either knew nothing about any society, or that there was a monarchist society that pursued the loyalist aim mentioned above. In both cases, their modified testimonies were accepted, and no further questions about subversion were posed. At Mykola Kostomarov's request, the Third Section even consented to destroy his first testimonies, an extraordinary action in any criminal investigation. Zaionchkovskii concluded that the Third Section was perfectly aware of the society's true radical orientation, but pretended not to notice it. The government found a secret monarchist instead of a republican society because that was preferable. The documents of the investigation, which were published in Kyiv in 1990, confirm Zaionchkovskii's thesis.[77]

Why were the imperial authorities interested in diminishing the subversive aspect of the Cyrillo-Methodian society? Zaionchkovskii explained the Third Section's deliberate distortion of the society's aims by the need to demonstrate Russia's might to a foreign audience: admitting the existence of a Ukrainian anti-government, national movement would have exposed a previously unknown weakness in the government. In addition, the lesser guilt was necessary in order to hand down milder sentences to those involved. By its relative leniency, the government wanted to avoid giving too bad an impression of itself to foreign pan-Slavs, with whom it had been in contact.[78] Finally, the same leniency was deemed expedient for the Little Russian audience, too.[79] As proposed in a memorandum written by the Third Section, the government wished to avoid sparking in Little Russia the same kind of strong irritation against it as was widespread in the kingdom of Poland:

> One must be even more cautious [than regarding the Slavophiles] in relation to Little Russia. To be sure, the ideas about separate existence that originate from young Ukrainophiles, like Shevchenko and Kulish, may be circulating even among the public which is more sedate than those Ukrainophiles themselves are. However, harsh measures are making the forbidden ideas ever dearer to them and may lead the hitherto obedient Little Russians to a state of resentment against the government similar to the one [that exists] in the Kingdom of Poland, especially after the rebellion.[80]

The quotation above must be balanced with another passage in the same text:

> The government cannot permit ... Ukrainophile ideas about the re-establishment of their native land (*vosstanovlenii ikh rodiny*), since it will lead the Little Russians and, following them, the other subject peoples (*narody*) as well to the desire for independent existence (*zhelaniiu sushchestvovat' samobytno*).[81]

In other words, the Third Section sought to prevent Ukrainian political nationalism without banning all Ukrainian cultural work.[82] It was also concerned about the possible domino effect that Ukrainian attempts to establish autonomy or independence might have on the other minority nationalities of the Russian Empire. It is worth noting that the political police did not find the Cyrillo-Methodians to be hotheads isolated from the rest of the society, but considered it likely that their ideas had a somewhat wider backing among the educated classes.

Only two members of the Cyrillo-Methodian society received harsh sentences according to the standards of the time: Taras Shevchenko, who was sentenced to serve as an army conscript without the right to write or draw, and Mykola Hulak, whose sentence was three years of confinement in the Schlüsselburg Fortress, followed by deportation to a distant province for an indefinite period. All the other sentences were considerably milder: even Kostomarov was imprisoned for only one year and then deported to a Great Russian province; Oleksandr Navrotsky received a six-month sentence combined with deportation; and Panteleimon Kulish and Bilozersky got only four months' imprisonment, followed by deportation to a Great Russian province. Ivan Posiada, Opanas Markovych, and Iurii Andruzky avoided prison altogether, although they had to face deportation to a Great Russian province. A Kharkiv teacher, whose letter to Kostomarov indicated that he knew about the society and was organizing a collection of funds, was not investigated.[83]

The Cyrillo-Methodians were sentenced according to an irregular administrative procedure. Instead of the proper legal criminal procedure, Orlov referred the decision on the case to Emperor Nicholas and forwarded his own suggestions. No law was cited. This was not due to the lack of an appropriate article in criminal law: according to the criminal code,[84] an attempt to form a secret society with the aim of dethroning the emperor or even failure to denounce such a society to the authorities was tantamount to an actual attempt to dethrone the ruler of Russia. All such acts were punishable by death only, although the emperor could use his prerogatives to mitigate the sentence. Thus, compared to the regular procedure, the irregular procedure did not result in arbitrary severity. An irregular administrative procedure was not exceptional in the processing of political cases. In the case of the Cyrillo-Methodians, this path was most likely chosen in order to avoid the publicity that the authorities did not desire for Ukrainian nationalism: in the regular legal process, the sentences would have been made public.

Orlov justified Hulak's harsh sentence with the explanation that he was the main leader of the Society of St Cyril and Methodius, that he had not made a full confession, and that he was still dangerous to the government.[85] The perceived lack of gratitude was the explicit reason for Shevchenko's exceptionally severe punishment, although his humble birth background may also have played a role.[86] Shevchenko's freedom had been purchased with funds raised in a lottery conducted in the imperial family. In 1849 Orlov supported Shevchenko's petition to be allowed to draw, but the emperor rejected his proposal to that effect,[87] seeming to bear a personal grudge against the poet. Individual emotions apart, Shevchenko's poetry was certainly offensive to the supporters of Russian autocracy. The Third Section's memorandum considered the poems "Chyhryn, Chyhryn" and "Dream" to be the most noteworthy ones in this sense. About "Dream" the political police wrote: "His slanders are nowhere as impertinent and insolent as in the description of the meeting in the [imperial] court ... Everyone tried to approach the Emperor in order to get a slap in the face from him ... In another passage, he has the Cossacks shouting: "Oh, the bad tsar, oh the damned tsar, oh the evil tsar, the insatiable demon!"[88]

What the gendarmes found insulting was not only the desecration of the emperor's person but also the denial of honour to those who served him. In the cultural code of the nobility, a slap in the face destroyed the honour of the man receiving it, unless he responded in the appropriate way and demanded a duel. It was all the worse that this mocking came from a person who was born a serf. However, there was an additional cause for the severity with which the poet was treated. The same memorandum stated that "Shevchenko uses all the available insulting and libellous expressions when describing the Emperor, and Russians in general ... He curses Russians and says among other things: 'We changed our good native land and took an obscene drunkard (Russia)!'"[89] Here, an anonymous staff member of the Third Section, either intentionally or unintentionally, altered the sense of Shevchenko's sentence by claiming that it referred to "Russia" instead of the Russian language.[90] The Third Section was sensitive to the image of and attitude towards the titular ethnic group of the Russian Empire. This approach was similar to that which was sometimes practised in relation to Polish national activists, for whom the proven hatred of Russians was considered a factor that aggravated their guilt.[91] Despite the cosmopolitan old-regime character of the empire, its leading functionaries displayed their national identity in that they disapproved of manifestations of antipathy towards Russians.

The fate of some Cyrillo-Methodians was mitigated in the last years of Nicholas's reign. This, too, was somewhat exceptional compared to the treatment of the participants of the Decembrist uprising in 1825 and the members of Nikolai Butashevich-Petrashevskii's socialist group that was uncovered in 1849. As a rule, their punishments were not mitigated after their sentences were handed down, and those deported for an indefinite period could not return home until Alexander II was on the throne. Most of the Cyrillo-Methodians were treated in a more lenient manner: Panteleimon Kulish was released from prison in August 1847, before the end of his four-month sentence;[92] in April 1850 Opanas Markovych was released from deportation;[93] in November 1850 Kulish, Oleksandr Navrotsky, and Ivan Posiada were allowed freedom of movement within the empire;[94] Vasyl Bilozersky was released from deportation in July 1853;[95] and police supervision over Mykola Hulak was lifted at the very end of the reign, in February 1855,[96] which decision restored his freedom of movement as well. However, Iurii Andruzky's situation deteriorated after he was sentenced: in April 1850 he was imprisoned in the Solovetsky Monastery after the authorities found additional subversive texts in his possession.[97] Andruzky was punished for his perseverance in Ukrainian political nationalism, which the government was seeking to uproot. In his case, the relatively soft policy had not produced the desired results, and the government's reaction was severe. Andruzky was released from prison in September 1854, after volunteering for the defence of the monastery against the British fleet, but he remained in exile in Arkhangelsk for the rest of Nicholas's reign.[98] Of the prominent members of the Cyrillo-Methodian Society, Shevchenko and Kostomarov were not significantly pardoned under Nicholas I.

During the last years of the reign, 1847–55, there were no additional political prosecutions of Ukrainian activists. Government control over Ukrainian activism was exercised through censorship: secular matters fell under the jurisdiction of the Ministry of Public Enlightenment, and religious matters under the Holy Synod. In 1833–49, the minister of public enlightenment was Sergei Semenovich Uvarov, famous for his triune formula of the government's leading ideology: Orthodoxy, Autocracy, and Nationality. Uvarov had favoured Ukrainian activists as a useful counterweight to Polish claims for Right-bank Ukraine, which had been incorporated into the empire only during the partitions of Poland, 1772–93.

The first five university professors of Slavic studies included two prominent Ukrainian cultural activists, Izmail Sreznevskii and Osyp

Bodiansky, although only Bodiansky continued to pursue his Ukrainian orientation to the end of his career. Another Ukrainian activist who worked in higher education in the end of the 1840s was Amvrosii Lukianovych Metlynsky, professor of Russian literature at the Kharkiv University. Most of the prominent Cyrillo-Methodians also worked in the field of education: Kostomarov taught at St Vladimir's University, Shevchenko had just been appointed as a teacher at the same university,[99] and Kulish was on his way abroad to study the Slavic nations outside Russia on a grant from the Academy of Sciences.[100] Kulish's instructions, probably written mainly by Kulish himself, included a study of the relationship between the Galician Ruthenian dialect (*rusinskii*) and the Little Russian language that was spoken in the Russian Empire. Considering that Kulish's education was limited to five classes of secondary school, it was remarkable that he taught Russian to non-native speakers at the University of St Petersburg and was being groomed to hold the chair of Slavic studies in both the university and the Academy of Sciences. To cap it all, his *Ukraine* and *Story of the Ukrainian People* had been printed by the Kyiv university press on credit, although the Third Section does not seem to have been aware of this fact.[101] After the Slavic Society of St Cyril and St Methodius was exposed, the possible dangers implicit in Ukrainian and other Slavic studies became evident to the highest government circles. Furthermore, the Cyrillo-Methodian case forced the Third Section to focus attention on the work of censors, who had sanctioned the first edition of Shevchenko's *Kobzar*, Kulish's works *Ukraine, Story of the Ukrainian People*, and *Mikhailo Charnyshenko*, and Kostomarov's *Ukrainskie ballady* (*Ukrainian Ballads*) and *Vitka* (*Branch*).[102] Orlov saw danger in Kulish's works: "He [Kulish] … described with enthusiasm the spirit of the former Cossacks, depicted the *haidamak* [eighteenth-century Ukrainian social bandits] attacks as knighthood, presented the history of that nation (*narod*) as the most remarkable of all … included Ukrainian songs in which the love of liberty is expressed, and hinted that this mood has not calmed down and still exists hidden among the Little Russians; he described the acts of Peter I and his successors on the throne as oppression and suppression of national rights (*prav narodnykh*)."[103]

However, Orlov specified that Kulish had expressed his opinions "with decency, unlike Shevchenko," and claimed that the political harm that might be inflicted by his works was unintentional. Nevertheless, the circumstance that increased the potential dangers of Kulish's books was that they had been written for adolescents. Orlov's statement was not quite exact, since only *Story of the Ukrainian People* was definitely aimed at schoolchildren, while *Ukraine* targeted uneducated people in general. His remarks indicate that the government was more concerned about works which were aimed at a wider audience than about those that circulated only among the intelligentsia. As a general policy which applied to all publications, not only to those in Ukrainian, the texts for wider audiences were censored more severely than those for the educated. The authorities' perception of Kostomarov's works as harmful originated with Governor-General Bibikov, who compelled the Third Section to focus attention on them.[104] In the collection *Ukrainian Ballads*, Bibikov flagged the following four poems as dangerous: "Maksim Perebiinos," "The Plain Truth," "The Old Beekeeper," and "The Singer." The first poem described the Cossacks' revenge against the Polish lords for Ukraine's dismal fate. It contained a detailed description of Cossack atrocities perpetrated against Polish lords and Jews, which was written in an approving tone. The second poem, "The Plain Truth," depicted two Polish friends during Khmelnytsky's insurrection: one thinks that it is crucial to remain loyal to the Polish king, while the other wants to be faithful to the truth, and sides with the insurgents. Both fall victim to their respective convictions. Although the poem contains the somewhat dangerous idea that the truth may oblige people to rise against the monarch, Bibikov's interpretation was even more radical: "The conclusion can be reached that one should neither speak the truth nor be faithful to one's duty."[105] "The Old Beekeeper" was a romantic summary of Ukrainian history, in which Kostomarov expressed many ideas about Ukrainian–Russian relations in condensed form: he mentioned in a favourable light the Muscovite tsar (Alexis), who had defended the Ukrainians against the Poles; he described Hetman Petro Doroshenko as an evil leader who wrecked Khmelnytsky's achievements; his generally negative description of Mazepa hinted that all the choices available to him had been bad ones. Inspired by *History of the Rus'*, Kostomarov praised Hetman Pavlo Polubotok for the bravery with which he purportedly had openly expressed Ukraine's grievances to Peter I. Kostomarov called Polubotok, who died in jail, "the last Ukrainian."[106] "The Singer"expressed sorrow for the native language that was disappearing. Although this poem did not contain anything explicitly political, Bibikov paraphrased its contents, turning them into dangerous material. While the banning of *Ukrainskie ballady* is understandable in the Russian imperial context, Bibikov also perceived subversion in the rather harmless *Vitka*. He noted the emphasis on all Slavs in one poem and nostalgia for the ancient Cossack glory in another. Furthermore, the governor-general noticed that the poet used the Latin letter (hard) *g*, thus distancing Ukrainian orthography from Russian. The verses were mild in any political sense, and the censors could hardly have been blamed for permitting them, if Kostomarov had not been involved in the case of the Cyrillo-Methodian society.[107] Nicholas I heeded Bibikov and severely reprimanded the censors who had approved these Kostomarov works.[108]

With the vigilance of censors and the utility of Slavic studies under doubt, Uvarov was forced to defend his policy.[109] In May 1847 he wrote a memorandum to Nicholas I concerning the Society of St Cyril and St Methodius. He claimed that both pan-Slavism and Ukrainian local patriotism were compatible with the interests of the Russian Empire. Pan-Slavism could be interpreted either in a pro-Russian or anti-Russian way. Uvarov predicted that the first of these would prevail, thanks to the attraction of Russia among the other Slavs. Further, Uvarov wrote that during his visit to Prague he had assured the local Slavs of Russia's support for their cultural activities, at the same time advising them not to get involved in politics. Proceeding to analyse the membership of the society, Uvarov denied that the Slavic idea had been dear to them at all:

> The word "Slavdom" (*slavianstvo*) was insincerely used as a mere cover to conceal ideas of another kind. Those ideas could have taken any other form as well, but the Slavic one was chosen because it has an especially strong effect on the Russian heart. This is demonstrated by the strong presence of the Ukrainian viewpoint in all the confiscated documents, including the most remarkable of them, *God's Law*. The first half of this subversive and dangerous work … is almost word for word taken from Lamennais, Mickiewicz, and other authors of that type who combine revolutionary ideas with mystical nonsense. The second half is about Ukraine. Here, the heart of the author, so to speak, begins to tremble, his style becomes livelier, and all the force of the mad raving is revealed on those pages on which he describes his own land in its purported oppressed state … Against the dominant Slavic orientation, we see here the results of a blind striving of a provincial spirit to disunity, contrary to the Slavic idea which … strives to unite all the parts into one.[110]

The minister claimed that no Moscow-based Slavophiles would ever have joined such a society, possibly alluding to Bodiansky. He blamed the Cyrillo-Methodians for having compromised the Slavic idea, which was "indispensable and holy."[111] Furthermore, Uvarov claimed that the ideas of the Cyrillo-Methodians were not typical even of normal

Little Russian local patriotism: "Little Russia, faithful to the Throne, unswerving in the Faith, does indeed cultivate in its memory the idea of its past. In spare time, she regrets the loss of the previous independence, her own Hetman, the riotous Cossack life, the enserfment of her free inhabitants, loss of local privileges; perhaps, the loss of the free sale of vodka. However, the Ukrainian spirit cannot be blamed for the criminal plans of a few madmen, with which … the highest rank, the local clergy, and even less so the large majority of peaceful and obedient inhabitants have nothing in common."[112]

In short, Uvarov did not consider all Ukrainian cultural activity to be subversive. His interpretation left a niche for such Ukrainian activity that was acceptable from the government's point of view. He did not propose any restrictions on Ukrainian activities in general. Two days before submitting his memorandum, Uvarov sent a circular to the censors, which was in accord with the memorandum. The circular warned about political ideas in journal articles on Russian history. Such ideas were to be permitted only if they were moderate. "Here special attention must be paid to some authors' strivings to evoke in the reading public uncontrolled bursts of patriotism, either general or provincial. This tendency sometimes becomes if not dangerous, then at least not sensible because of the consequences to which it may lead."[113] The circular did not mention either the Ukrainians or the Slavophiles. Although the Third Section, too, wished to avoid provoking Ukrainians into support for political nationalism, Uvarov's position was even more moderate.

However, Uvarov's defence of loyal Slavophiles and Little Russian patriots did not impress Nicholas I. On 27 May the minister sent an additional circular to all school districts that bore responsibility for censorship. The circular advised against any pan-Slavic orientation: even in the cultural field, concentration mainly on Russia was desirable, although other Slavic languages could be studied insofar as they aided research on the Russian language.[114] The circular was written explicitly at the emperor's behest, and it expressed a more negative view of the Slavophiles than Uvarov's previous memorandum. Apart from the core text that was sent in exactly the same wording to all school districts, the circular contained a section that differed from district to district. Ukrainian tendencies were hinted at only in the versions that were forwarded to Kharkiv and Kyiv. To Kharkiv, Uvarov wrote: "The university, through its wise influence, removes all thoughtless bursts of a provincial spirit that might sometimes lead to overstepping the limits of what is appropriate and permissible."[115] The version sent to Kyiv called for the faculty of St Vladimir University to be alert because, under the Slavic guise, the rebellious Polish spirit could be hidden.[116] Despite such warnings, the abstract nature of the circulars is striking. They did not contain practical guidelines with regard to what was going to be permitted or not. This omission may have meant that superintendents and censors were empowered to act according to their own discretion, or that Uvarov wished the practical effect of the circular to be as minimal as possible. I am inclined to interpret the circular in the latter sense. As I noted above, it did not reflect Uvarov's own ideas but rather those of Nicholas I. Uvarov either did not consider the Cyrillo-Methodians to be representative of Ukrainian opinion in general, or he found their ideas too abstract to be dangerous.

On 2 June Uvarov distributed another circular to school districts on the same topic. It is highly probable that the short interval between the two circulars indicates that Nicholas I was not satisfied with the text of the first one. The 2 June circular specifically mentioned those publications that were deemed harmful during the investigation of the Society of St Cyril and St Methodius. Uvarov now specified that in those texts the authors tried to present Ukraine's past in an idealized light and as one that was better than its present, thus invoking regret for the lost liberty. That was why he forbade re-editions and reprints of those publications and called upon censors to pay closer attention to literary works in general. Thus, in a third circular Uvarov decreed, with reluctance, specific restrictions on Ukrainian literature, limiting them to the historical aspect of Ukrainian nationalism.[117]

The repressions against the members of the society did not spell the end of all Ukrainian activities in the Russian Empire. The journal *Chteniia* continued to pursue its Ukrainian orientation. In the May 1847 issue, immediately after the sentences were handed down, the journal published an important collection of documents about Pylyp Orlyk, Mazepa's successor as hetman in exile, who in 1710–11 waged war against Russia on the side of Sweden and the Ottoman empire.[118] The documents included Orlyk's famous "constitution," a charter of the Zaporozhian host, which was enacted in 1710. The passage below demonstrates the political sensitivity of the publication:

> After the death of Hetman Bohdan Khmelnytsky of blessed memory, the Muscovite tsardom attempted by many ingenious means to weaken and utterly destroy the liberties of the Zaporozhian Host that it itself had confirmed and to place the yoke of slavery on the free people whom it itself

> had never subdued by the force of arms. Then, whenever the Zaporozhian Host suffered that violence, it was forced to defend the integrity of its laws and liberties with its own blood and courage ... Finally, in recent years, during the tenure of His Highness Hetman Ivan Mazepa of blessed memory, the aforementioned Muscovite tsardom, intent on carrying out its evil designs and repaying good with evil, instead of with gratitude and esteem for the many loyal services the Cossacks had been forced to perform at an utterly ruinous cost and number of losses, and for innumerable acts of heroism and bloody military exploits, wanted to transform them into a regular militia, to place their towns under its sovereignty, to destroy their rights and liberties, to eradicate the Zaporozhian Host on the Lower Dnipro, and to extinguish its name for ever.[119]

The charter envisioned transferring the Zaporozhian host under perpetual Swedish protection, an alliance with Crimea, and switching ecclesiastic allegiance from Moscow to the patriarch of Constantinople. In addition, the published documents included a letter from Orlyk to his rival, Hetman Ivan Skoropadsky, who served the Russian Empire. In it, Orlyk warned Skoropadsky that allegiance to Moscow "will become the poison that will kill the entire fatherland and doom it for good."[120] Bodiansky had received Orlyk's documents from Kulish before the latter's arrest.[121] As a precaution, the documents were not translated from their original Latin, and Kulish was not mentioned in the context of the publication. However, since Latin lessons were obligatory in Russian secondary schools, there were plenty of readers who understood the text.

Uvarov's first circular of 27 May sparked a sequence of events that led to Bodiansky's official fall from favour and the cessation of his activities as the editor of *Chteniia*. The version of the circular that Uvarov sent to the school district of Moscow called upon the local university to "uproot by its influence the thoughtless outbursts of some of its previous students (*pitomtsev*) who have separated themselves from the commonly shared historical opinions, not so much motivated by any conviction, but rather due to light-mindedness and well-meaning fantasies."[122] Who were these former students? It is unlikely that Uvarov was referring to the Cyrillo-Methodians: of them, only Kostomarov had studied briefly in Moscow, but he had taken his degrees in Kharkiv.[123] It seems that Uvarov, contrary to the ideas that he had previously expressed to the emperor, was characterizing Bodiansky and the other Moscow Slavophiles. To the circular that he sent to Sergei Grigorevich Stroganov, superintendent of the Moscow school district, the minister added a brief explanation in French, in which he called the circular a "preventive"[124] measure, which shows how uneasy he felt while admonishing the Slavophiles. However, Stroganov refused to read the circular to the professors, as requested.[125] He mentioned Uvarov's illogical behaviour, but did not give any other grounds for his refusal. However, as the chairman of the Society of History and Antiquity that published the *Chteniia*, Stroganov probably felt insulted by the admonition contained in the circular.[126] He did not hesitate to argue with Uvarov about Kostomarov's *Ukrainskie ballady*: in another letter he explained that he did not understand the admonition given to the censor, since the book did not contain anything harmful.[127] Nicholas I ultimately cancelled the admonition, but the book remained banned.[128] Because of his conflict with Uvarov, Stroganov had to resign as superintendent, but he continued as the chairman of the Society of History and Antiquity. Uvarov found a suitable occasion for Stroganov's dismissal even from his post as chairman when Giles Fletcher's description of Russia in the sixteenth century was published in *Chteniia* in the first issue of 1848. Some of Fletcher's critical statements about the Russian clergy were too much for Uvarov, who personally decreed the confiscation of the issue and closed down the journal. At the same time, he gave the order to transfer Bodiansky to the University of Kazan, but the latter preferred to retire altogether. Although Uvarov most likely acted out of personal animosity towards Stroganov, anti-Ukrainian sentiment may have been behind the denunciation that was submitted to the minister about the publication of Fletcher's work. Some Moscow professors disliked Bodiansky for his Ukrainian sympathies. In a private letter Professor Aleksei Mikhailovich Kubarev strongly disapproved of the publication of Ukrainian materials in *Chteniia*, ending his letter with these words: "Such a *khokhol*!"[129] *Khokhol* is a Russian derogatory expression for a Ukrainian. Professor Mikhail Petrovich Pogodin, on his part, characterized Bodiansky as "Mazepa" in his private letter to Stepan Petrovich Shevyrev in 1848.[130] However, Bodiansky was restored to his chair in December 1849, after one year of disfavour. The publication of *Chteniia* was revived the same year, appearing under a new title, *Periodical of the Imperial Society of History and Antiquities at the University of Moscow*, and new editorship.[131]

In the late 1840s Uvarov was falling into disgrace with the emperor. The revolutions in Western and Central Europe in 1848 and the discovery of the Petrashevskii group, whose members were arrested in St Petersburg in April 1849, put an end to the minister's political career. In

March 1848 Nicholas I appointed a committee to oversee publications that had passed censorship, which for all practical purposes supervised censors and their ministry.[132] In October 1849 Uvarov requested permission to submit his resignation, and the emperor immediately granted it.[133] He was succeeded by his deputy, Platon Aleksandrovich Shirinskii-Shikhmatov, and in 1854 Avraam Sergeevich Norov succeeded Shirinskii-Shikhmatov after the latter's death. Under these ministers the volume of Ukrainian publishing slightly increased compared to the years preceding the exposure of the Slavic Society of St Cyril and St Methodius.[134] First of all, these numbers indicate that the case of the Cyril and Methodius society did not lead to a dramatic change in the government's policy regarding Ukrainian publications; and second, that Ukrainian cultural activism had a broad enough base to survive the arrests. Nine of the sixteen books in the Ukrainian language in 1847–54 appeared in St Petersburg, the rest in what is now Ukraine.

Number of titles published in Ukrainian or partly in Ukrainian in the Russian Empire, 1840–54 (by year)

1840: 5;	1841: 5;	1842: 2;	1843: 2;	1844: 1;	1845: 1;	1846: 0;	
1847: 1;	1848: 3;	1849: 4;	1850: 0;	1851: 3;	1852: 3;	1853: 1;	1854: 2

Perhaps the most important Ukrainian books published in 1848–55 were Father Vasyl Hrechulevych's three books of sermons that were aimed at both the clergy and the common people.[135] The first collection appeared in 1849 and was authorized by the Holy Synod's censorship committee in St Petersburg. It was an important achievement in two ways: it extended the use of Ukrainian to a new sphere that had a direct bearing on the general perception of the worth of the language, thus elevating its status;[136] and it was the first book in Ukrainian aimed at the common people since the banning of Panteleimon Kulish's *Ukraine*. Indeed, Hrechulevych's modest works were used as an argument even in 1905 for obtaining permission for a Ukrainian translation of the Bible.[137] The author dedicated his book and addressed its foreword to member of the Holy Synod Gedeon, archbishop of Poltava and Pereiaslav. The foreword indicates that the author's aim was, apart from religious instruction, the defence of the Little Russian language. He argued that millions of Orthodox Christians spoke Little Russian, but they were preached to in a language that was not easily comprehensible to them. During his twenty-nine years of service in Podillia,

Hrechulevych was "fully convinced of the great use to our parishioners of preaching the word of God in the Little Russian language,which is comprehensible to them."[138] He had sought a powerful individual who would support the publication and thus give "the Little Russian language ... some kind of importance and dignity (*vazhnost' i znachimost'*), as not unworthy of communicating high Christian truths."[139] To Hrechulevych's satisfaction, he found such a person in Gedeon. His second collection of sermons, which appeared in 1852 and specifically explained the Sermon on the Mount and the Ten Commandments, was dedicated to Evsevii, bishop of Podillia.[140]

Other important publications in Ukrainian in the last years of the reign of Nicholas I included collections of Ukrainian folk songs compiled by Mykhailo Maksymovych (1849)[141] and Amvrosii Metlynsky (1854),[142] the *Iuzhnyi russkii zbornyk* (*South Russian Collection*) of modern poetry and prose edited by Metlynsky (1848),[143] and Levko Borovykovsky's *Baiky i prybaiutky* (*Fables and Tales*, 1852), a book of poetry.[144] Metlynsky, who was a professor of Russian literature, had known about the Cyrillo-Methodian society before the arrests of its members, but he advised Kostomarov to establish an officially authorized society and practice all-Russian official-sounding rhetoric: "Then [you should mention] something about the nationality that is indissolubly bound with Orthodoxy and autocracy, following the example of the Geographic Society and the like (you understand that it is necessary to leave something for the reader to comprehend and to follow not only national but also official forms)."[145]

Metlynsky put these ideas into practice in his *South Russian Collection*. The precarious status of Ukrainian literature was evident in his foreword. In a previous publication in 1839, Metlynsky had emphasized how South Russian had been spoken in all social classes and how it could be used to express any type of information.[146] By 1848, however, his tone had changed: he now tried to demonstrate the usefulness of publications in South Russian to the general Russian language and Russian ethnographic studies. He referred to the circular of the Imperial Geographic Society, which called for the gathering of geographic, statistical, and ethnographic information. The circular paid specific attention to local dialects, recommending the creation of dictionaries for them. Metlynsky now wrote about South Russian as a dialect of the Russian language and about South Russians as a subspecies of Russians. However, when he presented his proposal for the creation of a South Russian orthography, Metlynsky characterized the South

Russian language as a fully distinct entity, providing in parentheses the following alternative terms: Little Russian, or Ukrainian; and Red Russian or Galician.[147] The book included different kinds of works: Metlynsky's own poems contained Cossack romanticism. However, Mykhailo Makarovsky's tale "Harasko, or Good Luck Even in Captivity" was the success story of a peasant who becomes a wealthy merchant, adopts the habits of the lords and even some words from their language, that is, Russian, and all of this is depicted without any moralizing nationalism. The plot of the story was characteristic of the genre of personal success story, which was becoming popular among peasants in Russia.[148]

The publication of Maksymovych's *Sbornik ukrainskikh piesen* (*Collection of Ukrainian Songs*) was permitted four years before it appeared in 1849. It contained mainly epics describing events that took place during the Cossack era, but some lullabies and women's songs were also included. In his Russian-language foreword, Maksymovych mentioned the difference in verses between Ukrainian and Russian songs, and emphasized how the entire Ukrainian nation (*narod*) authored the songs. The songs did not contain anything subversive: only Tatars, Turks, and Poles figured as enemies in them. In one song, Mazepa's uprising against Peter I was condemned. Maksymovych commented that this was how the Ukrainian common people perceived that historical event.[149]

Maksymovych's *Nachatki ruskoi filologii* (*Beginnings of Russian Philology*, 1848) was another important Russian-language contribution to Ukrainian studies.[150] The Kyiv censors sanctioned this work two years before its publication. Although Maksymovych upheld the idea of Ukrainian as a separate language, his linguistic thought contained elements of all-Russian patriotism, too. In differentiating twelve Slavic languages and nations, Maksymovych opposed the idea of an all-Slavic language and nation existing in the present day, as had been proposed by the Slovak linguist Pavol Šafarik. The difference between the two scholars was mainly a terminological one, for Šafarik, too, acknowledged substantial differences among various Slavic dialects, of which he identified fourteen. According to Maksymovych, since language expressed the individuality of a nation, the classification of languages had to correspond to the classification of nations.These ideas precluded the possibility of a single nation with more than one language or a single language spoken by different nations. Maksymovych identified South Russian and North Russian as two separate languages, which, however, were very closely related to each other. He divided the Slavic languages into Russian (*ruskuiu*) or Eastern and Western sections (*udel*). These sections were analogous with the Russian and West Slavic "tribes" (*plemena*). The Russian section consisted of the South Russian (*iuzhnoruskii*) and North Russian (*severnoruskii*) languages, each of which was divided further into two dialects (*narechiia*). Identifying Belarusian as a dialect of North Russian, Maksymovych considered its distance from Great Russian equal to the distance of the Galician dialect from Little Russian. In this scheme, it turned out that South Russian was a language, but Great Russian was merely a dialect.[151] Maksymovych supposed that the two languages and nations had separated from each other in the prehistorical period. To be sure, the author emphasized that Christianity and government had strengthened "the unity of the Russian spirit"[152] at the time of St Volodymyr (Vladimir) in the tenth century.

Maksymovych's emphasis on the importance of the mutually related languages to each other somewhat softened his identification of Ukrainian as a separate language and Ukrainians as a nation. However, the same was true of all nations that had relatives: Maksymovych claimed that all the Slavic languages should be studied in the context of the whole Slavic group. Furthermore, they could even be developed in light of the comparative knowledge thus gained. After presenting his classification of Slavic languages, Maksymovych contradicted himself by using the term "Russian language" (*iazyk ruskii*) to denote specifically Great Russian. He credited it with a special place within the entire Slavic world: "The Russian language, which emerged from the Muscovite dialect under the influence of the Old Slavonic language, is the main representative of not only Russian but of the entire Slavic subgroup (*rechi*). By its brave force and richness of sound, it surpasses all others that belong to the same tribe."[153]

Maksymovych found that both South Russian and North Russian were closer to the proto-Slavic than was Old Slavonic. The supposed antiquity of North and South Russian entailed, for him, a positive normative judgment. Indeed, Maksymovych used Russian and Ukrainian words as the norm against which he evaluated the vocabularies of the West Slavic languages.[154] The theoretical foundation of such an approach was the assumption of the qualitative superiority of the more ancient linguistic forms to the more recent ones, which, for Maksymovych, was analogous to the superiority of original species of animals and plants to more recent and lower ones. Such a view, incompatible with the idea of progress, shows Maksymovych as a rather conservative thinker in the context of the nineteenth century. However, the combination of language and nation with each other was an aspect of his thought that certainly belonged to the era of nationalism.[155]

Levko Borovykovsky's *Fables and Tales* consisted of poems depicting village life, most often with a moral message. He referred to Russians only once, in a poem that describes a Russian lord as fairly stupid.[156] However, Metlynsky's foreword to the book contained his opinions on the relationship between Ukrainians and Russians. Again, Metlynsky used the official vocabulary to convey the Ukrainian national message. Metlynsky's innovation notionally separated Great Russian and literary Russian from each other. This approach made it possible for him to write about "dialects, like Great Russian and Little Russian, which have been spoken by millions of people since time immemorial."[157] The division of the Russian language into Little Russian and Great Russian dialects was not new: Izmail Sreznevskii had proposed it in 1843.[158] However, by defining Great Russian as something different from the "language of the upper, educated stratum,"[159] Metlynsky placed the former on an equal footing with Little Russian. This was the first appearance of an idea that later became more prominent: in the 1870s Ukrainian national activists often expressed the idea of literary Russian as separate from Great Russian.[160] However, Metlynsky combined his innovation with a cautious proposal for rather limited status for Little Russian:

> Nowadays it has become strange to mistake the literary, standard, general Russian for any one of the popular dialects, or to wonder whether one should write in a local dialect or not to understand that everything is good in its proper place; one cannot replace the other, like all cannot wear similar dress, like the flower cannot exist without its petals, and petals without roots. Nowadays seldom does anyone think that those who have written well in any popular dialect would benefit literature more by writing in the literary language. Those writers will always number but a few, and that is why their works are especially useful for the study of vernacular and for the common people to read.[161]

Thus, Metlynsky now accorded literary Little Russian a limited social function in linguistic studies and among the common people. Taking into account his advice to Kostomarov in 1847, as mentioned above, it is likely that Metlynsky's caution was motivated by tactical political considerations and the wish to avoid repressions.

Metlynsky's 1854 collection of folk songs included, apart from epic historical songs, many other types of songs, like those connected with different feasts, seasons, and events in human life. The publication included some inauthentic epics, too, but Metlynsky published them in good faith.[162] He was now even more cautious in his emphasis on the local nationality. In the Russian-language foreword Metlynsky avoided speaking explicitly about a distinct language, but explained that all dialects were necessary in the Russian language: "The literary creations of all the Russian tribes include in themselves and reveal a part of the common, great national spirit."[163] He explained his focus on the folk literature of South Russia by the fact that he had lived there all his life and was not acquainted with the other branches of Russian folk culture. He dedicated his work to "my mother, Russia."[164] The term that he now used for the language was "the Ukrainian dialect of the Russian language, or the language of the common people of the southern region of Russia."[165] Referring to the Cossack period, he mentioned "Ukraine's struggle against the West for Christianity and Orthodoxy."[166] This was appropriate in the last years of Nicholas's reign, which were marked by an exceptional atmosphere of xenophobia in official circles. Metlynsky's caution was expressed by the fact that he placed the historical epics, essential to the creation of Ukrainian identity, almost at the end of the book, after more than three hundred pages of the most politically harmless songs. Most of the epics depicted as enemies Poles, Tatars, and Jews, and, in several poems imperial rule was referred to in a favourable tone. However, one song lamented the destruction in 1775 of the Zaporozhian Sich, the centre of the autonomous Cossack host.[167] To be sure, the Russian government was not explicitly mentioned as the cause of the destruction.

After the cessation of Bodiansky's activities in *Chteniia*, the Provisional Commission for the Study of Ancient Documents continued to publish important sources on Ukrainian history. The main task of this government agency, established in Kyiv in 1843, was to publish historical documents primarily in order to counteract Polish claims to its previous eastern borderlands of Poland-Lithuania, which now belonged to the Russian Empire (present-day Lithuania, Belarus, and part of Ukraine west of the Dnipro).[168] Some of the published historical sources served as inspiration for Ukrainian nationalists. In 1848–55 the commission published the chronicles of Velychko and Hrabianka, two of the most important Cossack chronicles written at the beginning of the eighteenth century.[169] On the whole, both authors supported the Cossacks' allegiance to Russia. At the same time, however, they expressed strong Little Russian/Ukrainian identity (both terms were used) and support for the region's autonomous status. Both authors also criticized the Muscovite government or its individual representatives for some of their actions. This criticism was consistent with the emerging national mythology, in which the curtailment of the original autonomy was emphasized. Nationally oriented Ukrainians received the chronicles with interest, and these works continued to provide material for national aspirations well into the twentieth century.[170] The work of editing Velychko's chronicle was begun by Kostomarov before his arrest.[171] It was written by Samiilo Velychko, who had worked as a scribe in the hetman's chancellery. Like the *History of the Rus'*, Velychko's chronicle described the Pereiaslav agreement of 1654 between the Cossacks and Muscovites as a mutually binding treaty and claimed that the tsar's representatives had sworn an oath to maintain Cossack autonomy.[172] Velychko recounted that many Cossack officers were dissatisfied with the changes made to the original terms of the Pereiaslav agreement under Hetman Iurii Khmelnytsky, and he explicitly criticized the additional curtailment of autonomy under Hetmans Ivan Briukhovetsky and Demko Mnohohrishny. The author sympathized with Hetman Petro Doroshenko, who swore allegiance to the Ottoman empire rather than to Muscovy: since Muscovy had abandoned Ukraine west of the Dnipro to the Poles in the Treaty of Andrusovo in 1667, Doroshenko had no other choice. Velychko did not hesitate to criticize even Peter I for breaking his promise of granting greater Cossack liberty, which he had given during the Great Northern War against Sweden. The Kyiv censor D. Matskevich wanted to excise from the chronicle the rumour that the Russian commander of the 1689 campaign against Crimea, Vasilii Golitsyn, had been bribed by the Crimean khan, as well as some information about Mazepa.[173] Golitsyn's possible corruption was a sensitive question in Ukrainian–Russian relations, since it was Hetman Ivan Samoilovych who had been deposed and deported for the failure of the Crimean campaign. However, after Deputy Superintendent of the school district Mikhail Iuzefovich appealed to Minister Shirinskii-Shikhmatov, Velychko's chronicle was published without cuts.

Hrabianka's chronicle, a history of the Cossacks to the year 1709, was written in 1710 by Hryhorii Hrabianka, a Cossack officer.This publication also had a connection to the Cyrillo-Methodians: one of the manuscripts that served as the basis for the publication was presented to the commission by Opanas Markovych.[174] Ivan Samchevsky's foreword contained cautious but explicit expressions of the distinct Ukrainian identity: he repeated, with sympathy, Hrabianka's opinion that the Cossacks descended from the ancient Khazars; found "a feeling of national pride" among the Cossacks; elevated Khmelnytsky to heroic status; and displayed interest in the local vernacular.[175] Hrabianka evaluated Ukrainian–Russian relations in a more positive light than Velychko and disapproved of those hetmans, like Vyhovsky, Doroshenko, and Mazepa, who after 1654 sided with any other powers against Russia.[176] However, he disapproved of the introduction of direct taxation of the local population by the Muscovite government under Hetman Ivan Briukhovetsky, a reform that was later repealed.[177] Furthermore, Hrabianka criticized the Muscovite government for its support of Briukhovetsky. This and some passages in the foreword were, once again, too much for the censor Matskevich, who wanted to remove them, but the commission opposed any abridgment of the text.The controversy was referred to the Main Administration of Censorship in St Petersburg, which sided with Matskevich on the main points. Accordingly, part of the description of events that had taken place during Briukhovetsky's reign was removed. That passage included the mention that the Little Russian delegation which was sent to Moscow with many complaints in 1667 did not receive any answer there; a long citation from Hetman Petro Doroshenko's letter to his rival Briukhovetsky, in which he accused the latter of voluntarily submitting the free people to the Muscovite *voevodas* (governors), and favoured Polish rather than Russian rule in the country; as well as a description of how Briukhovetsky rose up against Muscovite rule, had many of the Russian *voevodas* killed, and invited the Crimean Tatars to help him against Muscovy. From the foreword was excised a sentence that indicated how Hrabianka had concentrated on describing events in the seventeenth century, since he found the eighteenth century much less remarkable in the history of his country. The Main Administration of Censorship inserted a couple of expressions into the foreword, which emphasized the enmity towards Poles and union with Russia.[178]

As Miroslav Hroch has written, cultivation of a national history by national activists was one of the means of politicizing the non-dominant ethnic groups in nineteenth-century Europe.[179] The disputes over censoring these eighteenth-century chronicles indicate that the Russian authorities of the 1850s understood this, too. Other incidents also indicate that the authorities were now alert to the dangers of "provincial patriotism," as it was called in Uvarov's circular of 27 May 1847. Ukrainian publications received their share of the conservative vigilance that prevailed in the above-mentioned committee of 2 April that supervised censorship. The committee took note of a small collection of Little Russian historical proverbs that were collected by Oleksandr Lazarevsky and published in the *Chernigovskiia gubernskiia vedomosti* (*Chernihiv Provincial News*) in September 1853. The proverbs contained such lines as: "Make friends with a Russian (*moskal'*), but keep a stone in your bosom," which was published earlier in Kulish's *Mikhailo Charnyshenko*; "When the devil starts praying to God, the Russian may stop stealing"; "Who's there? The devil. Good, as long as it's not a Russian"; "Between Bohdan and Ivan [Mazepa] there was no hetman."[180] The censor who sanctioned the publication of this issue of the newspaper was Oleksandr Danylovych Tulub, who had been involved in the investigation of the Cyrillo-Methodian society and may very likely have been one of its members.[181] The committee of 2 April found that the proverbs were apt to promote animosity between Little Russians and Great Russians. Nicholas agreed and ordered Shirinskii-Shikhmatov to issue an official reprimand to Tulub.[182] The reprimand led to greater vigilance on the part of the other censors: a month later the Main Administration of Censorship in St Petersburg discussed the case of Hrabianka's chronicle. In rendering its decision, it relied on Uvarov's circular about patriotism and referred to the recent incident with the Little Russian proverbs in the *Chernihiv Provincial News*. In this connection, Shirinskii-Shikhmatov sent a circular requesting that all texts of local folklore be submitted to the Kyiv Censorship Committee before they could be published in provincial newspapers. Since provincial newspapers were normally censored by a local person who resided in the provincial capital, the Shirinskii-Shikhmatov circular meant that publications on Ukrainian folklore were subjected to a special procedure reserved for politically sensitive materials.[183]

The new works by the sentenced Cyrillo-Methodians constituted a special case for the censors, which they were permitted to resolve only in cooperation with the Third Section. To be sure, only Shevchenko's and Kulish's sentences explicitly mentioned that they were forbidden to write, but none of the sentenced actually published anything in Ukrainian during the rest of the reign. Kulish petitioned for the general right to publish, and mentioned in particular the manuscript of his novel *Chorna rada* (*The Black Council*) in November 1847, almost immediately after arriving at his place of deportation in Tula.[184] Although his petition was rejected as premature, the director of the Third Section, Leontii Vasilevich Dubelt, wrote to Kulish informing him that it was indeed desirable for him to continue writing.[185] By referring to future literary works, Dubelt hinted that *Black Council* would not be the first work to be permitted. The prospect of publishing again would be decided on the basis of the texts that the Third Section received from Kulish. Dubelt gave no instructions on the language in which Kulish should write.

Why was Kulish's right to publish reconsidered so soon? The official version, that he had never been a member of the society, is highly implausible: Andruzky named Kulish as a member, and Kulish was arrested in Warsaw together with his close relative, Vasyl Bilozersky, who confessed his membership. Moreover, Kulish's papers contained financial notes on raising funds "for good causes," in which the only donors were Kulish, Hulak, and Bilozersky. Orlov later stated that Bilozersky's guilt was lesser than Kulish's. Indeed, the Third Section knew that Kulish was a member of the Slavic Society of St Cyril and St Methodius, although he later denied it.[186]

One possible explanation is the hatred of Poles that even Kulish's forbidden works expressed. Passages like this may have been deemed potentially useful to the government:

> The impious Poles wanted to destroy the Orthodox Church,
> Introduce the Union into Ukraine,
> Uproot the Orthodox faith,
> Turn the Christian people into the Catholic faith.
> But our people did not agree to that,
> They defended by sword their ancient faith from the Poles and
> The Catholic priests ...[187]

> Cossacks cut them [Poles] like beets,
> Swiped them like husk along the field
> Drowned many thousands of them in the Trubizh and Alta,
> Dammed the rivers with Polish corpses.
> They gave the Poles a good lesson.[188]

In the light of such verses, it is not altogether surprising that the Third Section was somewhat open-minded about Kulish's future publications. To be sure, the government's inconsistency is evident in that this was the very same ethos that had been found subversive in Kostomarov's *Maksim Perebiinos*. Kulish himself was not averse to such literary cooperation. In this connection, it is noteworthy that in 1849 Kulish became a close friend of a local gendarme captain named Petr Gusev, and moved his family into his home. Ievhen Nakhlik has discovered an uncompleted manuscript of a novel written by Kulish and Gusev.[189] The correspondence between Dubelt and Kulish indicates that the leaders of the Third Section most likely knew about and approved of such cooperation. However, despite the shared anti-Polish interest, in the end literary cooperation between the political police and Panteleimon Kulish turned out to be untenable, to the disappointment of both sides.

In August 1848 Kulish sent his first new Russian-language work *Istoriia Borisa Godunova i Dmitriia Samozvantsa* (*History of Boris Godunov and Dmitrii the Pretender*) to the Third Section, requesting funds on credit to publish the book as well.[190] Instead of evaluating the manuscript themselves, the political police sent it to Uvarov and asked him to arrange a scholarly evaluation of the book in order to determine whether "it deserve[s] special promotion."[191] This is understandable in light of the fact that Kulish was asking for funding from the Third Section. Otherwise the book might have been forwarded to Uvarov, then to be passed on to the ordinary censorship.The scholarly evaluation was entrusted to Nikolai Gerasimovich Ustrialov, professor of Russian history at St Petersburg University. The reviewer knew the author's identity. Ustrialov was the architect of the historical concept that integrated pre-partition Lithuania into the history of Russia. His works promoted the all-Russian concept of nationality, but they also emphasized the historical importance of "West Russia" as another component of the country and nation.[192] According to Ustrialov, the limits of Russia had been defined in the Kyivan period. After that, the West Russians desired to unite with their countrymen in Russia, but this took place only with the partitions of Poland in 1772–95.

Professor Ustrialov roundly disliked Kulish's manuscript. Although his critique was scholarly, it also revealed his Russian patriotism: "The author's point of departure is that the murder of Prince Dmitri of Uglich was not committed by Boris Godunov alone but by the whole Muscovite government. In his words, 'since the first autocrats, the government many times used both public and secret acts of violence in order to prevent the ambitions of the lesser princes' (p. 35). However, the author does not know who instigated the murderers, and how. To solve this unclear case he refers to Shakespeare (p. 37). But the laws of historiography do not permit slandering the entire government without any evidence."[193] Ustrialov was upset that the author took negative evaluations by foreigners of seventeenth-century Russia at their face value. Finally, he pointed to several factual errors. The Third Section returned the manuscript to Kulish.[194]

In June 1850 Kulish sent the first part of his historical novel *Severiaki* (*Northerners*) to the Third Section. He explained that he could not complete the book without additional historical research, but he could not purchase the necessary books owing to a lack of funds. If he could publish the first part in a journal, he would then have money to complete the work. Orlov replied that it was more desirable to evaluate the entire book, not just part of it. However, he asked for the titles of the books that Kulish needed; the Third Section would pay for and send them. Orlov advised Kulish to send the completed novel to the Third Section. In response, Kulish sent a list of forty-three titles which may indeed have been sent to him. The following November, Kulish was released from exile, but he remained under police supervision and his books still had to pass censorship via the Third Section.[195]

The Third Section's final disappointment in Kulish was connected to his manuscript *Petr Ivanovich Berezin*. In January 1851 Dubelt received it from a member of the State Council, Senator Aleksandr Vasilevich Kochubei, who asked him to permit the manuscript to proceed to the ordinary censorship.[196] The Third Section reviewed the book and found it impermissible. The anonymous reviewer listed in detail numerous passages that, in his opinion, merited banning. It is difficult to understand exactly what was deemed subversive in some of the passages, such as a call to love all mankind. However, what was worst in the reviewer's opinion was that Kulish criticized the inequality of estates: he argued that any inequality should be based on education and moral character, and described peasants as morally superior to noblemen. A police officer and a noble landowner were presented in a negative light. The landowner beat his peasants until they told him that the lords would be tortured in the afterlife, and he suddenly wanted to become a peasant. The reviewer also disapproved of a passage with a hint of nationalism: "Little Russians lie with their head in Europe, but their feet in Asia: they are quite capable of rising above engrained ignorance to all the subtlety of enlightenment."[197] However, the reviewer emphasized that Kulish evidently did not want to go against the government, and even presumed, mistakenly, that it shared many of his ideas. The reviewer found that this showed the author to be out of touch with reality, not even comprehending how dangerous his book was. Because Kulish had submitted the manuscript to the Third Section, he could not be considered guilty. The manuscript was destroyed. Dubelt then wrote Kulish a strongly worded letter: "Your novel is full of Communist and social [i.e., socialist] ideas, it is permeated by those harmful doctrines that undermine all the holy foundations of well-structured societies and which have caused and still cause so many calamities in Western Europe ... Do you really think that happiness is in Western Europe? Do you not see that there is no faith in God there, no respect for rulers, no order, no tranquillity, and those governments have been brought to that abyss by the very routes that you open up in your novel?"[198] According to Dubelt, the novel demonstrated that Kulish still clung to his earlier ideas. Dubelt communicated Orlov's command to Kulish to forget his harmful ideas. If that were not possible, it would be better if Kulish did not write anything at all. The Third Section's reaction indicates that its leaders clearly understood the modern character of the Cyrillo-Methodian ideas and did not perceive in them mere old-fashioned patriotism.[199] How angry they were at Kulish is evident from his next publishing attempt in April 1851. He sent two Russian translations of English-language religious texts, in which the section's reviewer did not find anything harmful. Dubelt rejected them with the words: "[He] must serve and try to be forgotten, and then he will be remembered."[200] Kulish now made a risky choice and began to publish under a pseudonym.[201] He would be allowed to publish works under his own name only during the reign of Alexander II.

The documents of the Third Section do not contain a formal ban on Mykola Kostomarov's future publications. In August 1849 Kostomarov's scholarly notes and manuscripts were returned to him in Saratov, his place of deportation. He could thus resume work as a historian, but he managed to publish his new scholarly works only during the next reign. Despite this, Kostomarov was briefly the editor of *Saratovskie gubernskie vedomosti* (*Saratov Provincial News*), the local official newspaper.[202]

By the standards of the Russian Empire, the repressions against the Society of St Cyril and St Methodius were not very severe. The authorities deemed it expedient to downplay in their conclusions the society's revolutionary goals. No general ban on Ukrainian literature was enacted, and Ukrainian publishing indeed somewhat expanded during the final years of Nicholas I's reign, the most important achievement being religious publications in Ukrainian. However, after the uncovering of the society, the authorities became alert to the danger that Ukrainian nationalism presented to the empire, which impacted a number of decisions in the field of censorship. The new findings in this chapter include the existence of substantial differences between the known two versions of *God's Law*, statistical information about Ukrainian publishing from 1847–54, Amvrosii Metlynsky's notional separation of literary Russian from Great Russian, Shirinskii-Shikhmatov's 1854 circular on publications of Ukrainian folklore, and Panteleimon Kulish's abortive attempt at literary cooperation with the Third Section.

Chapter Three

Ukrainian Literature and Censorship, 1855–9

Alexander II ascended the imperial throne in March 1855, after the sudden death of his father Nicholas I. The defeat in the Crimean War (1853–6), the emperor's own intentions, and the general intellectual atmosphere among the educated public and imperial bureaucracy marked the early years of the reign as a period of liberalization. Buturlin's committee, overseeing regular censorship, was abolished and censorship returned to the ordinary regime, which had existed before the European revolutions of 1847–9. Censors now permitted many topics and opinions that had not been tolerated earlier. The relaxing of censorship was part of the preparation for the abolition of serfdom, which was finally enacted in February 1861. Beginning that year, the unrest in Poland became serious enough to attract the attention of both the imperial government and the Ukrainian national movement. The Polish movement for independence concerned Ukraine, inasmuch as the Poles were demanding the restoration of the pre-partition borders, which included almost all of Right-Bank Ukraine west of the Dnipro River. The armed insurrection in Poland in 1863–4 expanded to Right-Bank Ukraine. An additional factor that had an impact on the situation of Ukrainian national activists was the emergence of a Russian revolutionary movement and the government's repressions of it. The first arrests for distributing subversive Russian texts took place in the summer of 1861, and the first organized group, called Land and Liberty, was founded at the end of that year.

Ukrainian activists profited from the political turnabout in the first years of the reign and soon expanded their activities to an unprecedented scope. Those Cyrillo-Methodians who were still serving their sentences, Kostomarov, Shevchenko, and Andruzky, were pardoned and allowed to return from exile.[1] Better conditions for Ukrainian publishing in the late 1850s and early 1860s are apparent in the number of publications. In 1855–63, 130 Ukrainian-language books appeared in the Russian Empire:[2] 1855: 5; 1856: 5; 1857: 10; 1858: 7; 1859: 5; 1860: 20; 1861: 28; 1862: 36; and 1863: 14. Compared to the output in 1846–54, Ukrainian publishing increased sevenfold. The drop in 1863 is due to the Valuev circular. The centre of Ukrainian publishing was still St Petersburg, where 87 titles appeared, most of them from the press that Panteleimon Kulish acquired in 1857 with the help of donations from wealthy Ukrainian landowners.[3]

Perhaps the most important change that occurred in the 1850s was the expansion of the use of the Ukrainian language in the religious sphere. Vasyl Hrechulevych published six additional collections of sermons in the Little Russian language, as he called it, including expanded editions of the two first ones published during the previous reign.[4] The books passed the Holy Synod's censorship in St Petersburg. They covered the Sermon of the Mount, the Ten Commandments, the Lord's Prayer, the sacraments, and the Creed, thus constituting a whole course of elementary religious instruction. Hrechulevych dedicated his sermons on the Creed, which appeared in 1856, to Evsevii, bishop of Bratslav and Podillia, stating that in the whole diocese the priests were preaching in the language that was comprehensible to their parishioners.[5] This shows that the author had perceived an expansion in vernacular-based preaching since 1849, when he had complained that no one tried preaching in Little Russian.[6] Hrechulevych even published a version of the Lord's Prayer in Church Slavonic, which contained words that were modified according to the vernacular.[7] These changes were minor, but their symbolic meaning was important, since it was not customary to say this prayer even in Russian, only in Church Slavonic. Only a few of the sermons contained a social or political message, and that was traditional: the tsar and the Fatherland – by implication the Russian Empire – must be venerated, and Christians must be satisfied with their place in the social hierarchy. In Hrechulevych's books one could find religiously motivated, anti-Semitic statements that were, however, softened by the definition of the Jews and other people of non-Orthodox and non-Christian faiths as neighbours whom Christ had called his followers to love.[8]

Hrechulevych published the second edition of his general collection of sermons in collaboration with Kulish, informing readers that the first edition was completely sold out. The foreword was a revised version of the one that appeared in the first 1849 edition. The changes may be due either to Kulish's influence on Hrechulevych or heavy editing by Kulish. Referring to Pavol Šafarik, Hrechulevych now claimed that 13 million Orthodox Christians spoke Little Russian. The language in the book was modified according to the Poltava-Chyhyryn dialect that, as claimed in the foreword, was spoken by the majority of Little Russian speakers. The orthography was also modified according to Kulish's model, excluding the letter ы, which purportedly did not correspond to any sound in Ukrainian, thus strengthening the distance of the language from literary Russian. According to the foreword, the Little Russian language was an expression of the unique national character, and it derived from the entire past of the nation (*narod*). Hrechulevych and Kulish supposed that, as a result of the Little Russian nation's suffering in past centuries and its struggle for the truth and faith, it had developed a special capacity to understand the great truths of Revelation. This statement echoed Mickiewicz's ideas about Poles. Kulish did not hesitate to make essential revisions to the text of the book: in this particular edition "Ukraine" was the community, whose benefit parishioners had to keep in mind in all their undertakings.[9] Hrechulevych was not alone in his use of Ukrainian in religion-based functions. Shevchenko's translations of a couple of psalms were published in his *Kobzar* in 1860, but also as a separate edition, and thus a small part of the Ukrainian Bible had entered the market.[10] Mykhailo Maksymovych included his translation of some psalms into the "Ukrainian dialect" in his collection of miscellaneous works entitled *Ukrainets* (*The Ukrainian*).[11]

In fiction, the most important publishing events included Kulish's *Chorna Rada, khronika 1663 roku* (*The Black Council, a Chronicle of the Year 1663*) (1857).[12] Marko Vovchok (Maria Vilinska) marked her debut with her *Narodni opovidannia* (*Folk Tales*, 1858),[13] and a new and expanded edition of Shevchenko's *Kobzar* appeared in 1860.[14] *The Black Council*, a romantic novel in the style of Walter Scott, was the first novel in modern Ukrainian. It depicted the struggle for power among the various candidates for the hetmancy on the Left Bank of the Dnipro in the early period of Muscovite suzerainty. Ivan Briukhovetsky, who came to power by gaining the support of the lower social classes, was portrayed as a villain. Through his depiction of Briukhovetsky, Kulish distanced himself from violent and revolutionary politics. Hetman Briukhovetsky later turned against Muscovy, which made him a safe object of criticism. Kulish did not include the war against Muscovy in *The Black Council*, but ended the plot shortly after Briukhovetsky's ascent to power. While

Russia and Russians remained in the background in the novel, they are described as foreigners who backed Briukhovetsky's candidacy and thus contributed to Ukraine's misfortune. Kulish explicitly presented corruption and the urge to curtail Cossack autonomy as the motives underlying Muscovite policies. His heroes, who were opposed to Briukhovetsky, wanted to bargain and negotiate with Muscovy about the extent of Cossack autonomy, whereas Kulish's Briukhovetsky submitted to Muscovy without any conditions. Nevertheless, Kulish's heroes supported the Muscovite suzerainty as the best of the existing alternatives compared to Polish or Ottoman rule: "Whether it is good or not, we need to live together with the Muscovite."[15] Rather revealing of Kulish's tactics is the difference between the Ukrainian and Russian texts at the end of the book. While the Ukrainian text granted everlasting glory to the historical heroes who fell in their struggle against Briukhovetsky, the Russian text merely noted that they were executed, and added a negative evaluation of the Cossack system and contemporary Cossack nostalgia. Kulish thus reserved his national, romantic message for Ukrainian readers and ostensibly distanced himself from the same message to his Russian readers.[16]

The Russian edition of *The Black Council* included an epilogue entitled "On the Relationship between Little Russian Literature and General Russian Literature." Its central message was that literature in South Russian, or Little Russian, had a right to exist, but Southern and Northern Russian literatures should develop in close interaction with each other. Kulish rejected any possible claims that he was creating a separate literature to the detriment of general Russian literature. As an example of the all-Russian viewpoint that he found desirable, he indicated Gogol's works, which were written in Russian but influenced by the author's Little Russian background. However, according to Kulish, Kvitka-Osnovianenko was superior to Gogol in his description of the South Russian common people. Kulish argued that Kvitka's works were untranslatable into Great Russian because the Great Russian common people were so different in their culture from Little Russians. Kulish claimed that he had written *The Black Council* in Little Russian for the same reason: the seventeenth-century Cossack setting did not translate easily into Russian. That was also why the Russian edition of the novel was a separate book rather than a mere translation. Further, Kulish wrote that pre-Mongol Rus' had spoken one language, which was most developed in the Kyiv region. Later, as the political centre had shifted north, the Northern language began to diverge from the language of the South. Kulish pointed out that the inhabitants of the Northern provinces usually did not know South Russian, but those of the South were fluent in Great Russian. He argued that Northerners should pay more attention to Southern literature and language, otherwise they would be guilty of narrow provincialism. Finally, Kulish claimed that in *The Black Council* he sought to demonstrate the necessity of the union of South Russians with North Russians into one state.[17]

It took the censors ten months to approve *The Black Council*. The censor Ivan Lazhechnikov did not interfere with the contents of the novel, but he hesitated to permit the epilogue. He found that the relationship between the two tribes was too important a subject for him to issue a decision on his own. The director of the Main Administration of Censorship, Deputy Minister of Public Enlightenment Petr Aleksandrovich Viazemskii, read the manuscript and suggested several changes. Meanwhile, the procurator general of the Holy Synod, Aleksandr Petrovich Tolstoi, the highest functionary in ecclesiastical matters, lobbied vigorously for permission. Viazemskii, too, did not find the epilogue contrary to the rules of censorship, and permission was ultimately granted to publish it in a revised form. Unfortunately, documents of the Main Administration of Censorship do not reveal any additional information about the changes that were made to the text.[18]

In the first years of the new reign, it was Kulish who produced most of the important publications of non-fiction in Ukrainian. The first of these was *Zapiski o Iuzhnoi Rusi* (*Notes on Southern Rus'*) (1856–7), two volumes of ethnographic and historical materials and some fiction that he edited in their original Ukrainian, intertwined with his own observations in Russian. As a precaution, he continued his practice of presenting political opinions in discussions about history and by publishing suitable source texts. Although he edited his materials in anticipation of censorship, many politically sensitive passages on Ukrainian–Russian relations remained in the published text. In some of them, Russians were depicted as enemies, and Catherine II was criticized for the destruction of Sich, the centre of the Zaporozhian Cossacks: "Our mother, the great light, caused much sorrow: she destroyed the glorious Zaporozhian host!"[19] Perhaps the most remarkable of these materials was "Ochakivska bida" (Trouble in Ochakiv), a humorous story about the Cossacks' participation in a Russo-Turkish battle in 1788. A Cossack company is patrolling the no-man's land when they suddenly notice the advance of a huge Turkish army. Rather than raising the alarm or facing the Turks, the Cossacks hide for the duration of the great battle that ensues. By arresting some wounded Turks after the battle, the Cossacks pretend to have participated in it. In the story, the Russian commander Grigorii Aleksandrovich Potemkin is depicted as a crude individual, hostile to Ukrainians. Whether it was a piece of genuine folklore or not, "Trouble in Ochakiv" definitely fit well with the image of crude Muscovites previously promoted by the author of the *History of the Rus'* and Osyp Bodiansky. In his commentary, Kulish presented the story as an example of Ukrainians' humility: to boast about their bravery was alien to them. However, there was another, more obvious, subtext to the story: the war was not the Cossacks' own, but one that was fought between two foreign powers: "Brothers, I say, let us hide ourselves nearby! Let the devils fight; we'll sit here through the bad time and return home alive."[20] Several years later "Trouble in Ochakiv" was published as a small book.[21] To be sure, in all the materials published in *Notes*, Poles and Jews were most often mentioned as enemies. Except for "Trouble in Ochakiv," Kulish did not comment on anti-Russian episodes in his materials, and he included ones in which Mazepa was depicted as a villain. However, a folk legend about Mazepa's treason recounted that at one time Peter I had decided to behead all the local inhabitants, but changed his mind in the end. Such a passage cast the emperor in a rather ambiguous role.

In *Notes on Southern Rus'* Kulish introduced his new Little Russian orthography, which included the letters є and ґ, which did not exist in the Russian alphabet, but removed э and ы, which did. Although some of the differences lay in the differences of the two sound systems, others were clearly motivated by the tendency to increase the difference between the two languages.[22] Kulish also republished Galician scholar Ioann Mohyliansky's article "On the Ancient Origin and Originality of the South Russian Language," which had appeared in the *Journal of the Ministry of Public Enlightenment* in 1837, when Sergei Uvarov's policy was favourable for Ukrainian studies. Mohyliansky emphasized how in past centuries South Russian had been used in government offices and among the upper classes of society. He argued for the status of South Russian as a distinct language by citing references to ancient texts in which it had clearly been perceived as different from Great Russian. Kulish's publication of Mohyliansky's article served the same purpose as his orthography: distancing Ukrainian from Great Russian. In the historical opinions that Kulish presented in his own text, perhaps the most significant was his interpretation of the aims of the *haidamak* rebellion of the 1770s against Polish rule in Right-Bank Ukraine: "While being wild robbers of their brothers, they risked their own lives for the dreamed independence of their tribe."[23] At the time, the word "tribe" (*plemia*) was often used to denote an "ethnic group" or "nationality." The *haidamaks* had fought against Polish rule. To which tribe was Kulish referring? He did not specify. However, in his letter which the Third Section intercepted a year later, in 1858, he referred to the prospect of Little Russia's separation from Russia in a distant future, after his own lifetime.[24]

In his *Notes* Kulish presented a number of opinions that were untraditional for a Ukrainian national activist: he strongly criticized the autonomous administration of the Hetmanate in the eighteenth century and wrote favourably both about the Polish nobility and government in Right-Bank Ukraine. His criticism of the Hetmanate was included in the foreword to Grigorii Nikolaevich Teplov's memorandum to Empress Elizabeth, written in the latter half of the 1750s. Teplov emphasized arbitrariness and the general misuse of power in the Hetmanate, criticizing especially the local Lithuanian law code for its incompatibility with the autocracy. In 1775, during the reign of Catherine II, Teplov had been instrumental in the abolition of the Hetmanate. Kulish agreed with Teplov's criticism, especially his remarks about the oppression of lower-ranking Cossacks by the Cossack upper class. This position served two purposes: ostensibly, it displayed Kulish's loyalty to the empire, and it distanced him from the old Little Russian patriotism. For Kulish, the crux of Ukrainian nationality was not in the historical privileges of the nobility but in the language and folk culture. He also emphasized his opposition to estate privileges in his writings on Right-Bank Ukraine. However, Kulish's perception of Polish rule in the eighteenth century was relatively positive. Although he acknowledged the class antagonism between the peasants and nobles and the religious controversy between the Uniates (Greek Catholics) and Orthodox, he admitted that the peasants' obligations to their landlords had not been excessively onerous, and the nobles had done good work by encouraging settlement to the area.

In *Notes* Kulish published Michał Grabowski's article arguing the Polish nobility's beneficial role in the region's history, but paired it with his own critical response that rejected some of Grabowski's propositions. Grabowski, who was a personal friend of Kulish's, was a landowner on the Right Bank and ardent local patriot, who combined political loyalty to the Russian Empire with a defence of Polish culture. In his answer to Grabowski, Kulish criticized the Polish nobility for not having recognized the human dignity of non-nobles. Moreover, as Kulish claimed, noble rule and privileges had been incompatible with South Russian civil concepts. This was a masterful use of the available limited freedom of expression: polemics against a Polish opponent was the most convenient method of expressing those egalitarian opinions that the Third Section had deemed "communist" only a few years earlier.

The censors did not pay attention to the anti-Russian episodes or egalitarian ideas in *Notes*, but they reacted to Grabowski's article. Because of it, the Moscow Censorship Committee hesitated to permit the second volume of the book and referred the matter to the Main Administration of Censorship. The Moscow censors argued that the article contained "new ideas on the history of Little Russia [and] its relation to Poland, not fully coherent with the works of our historiography ... The Committee does not know to what extent these new opinions may fit together with the views of our government."[25] Kulish softened a number of Grabowski's passages according to the instructions he received from Petr Viazemskii. He also added a foreword, in which he further distanced himself from Grabowski's opinions. Kulish then appealed to the Main Administration of Censorship, emphasizing Grabowski's widely known loyalty. Viazemskii was convinced, and Grabowski's article was published in a revised form.[26]

Kulish's *Hramatka*, which appeared in 1857, was the first primer in modern Ukrainian, and it contained an unequivocal nationalist message. The book was authorized for publication by both censorships, secular and synodal. It began with biblical citations and their explanations. However, beginning with lesson 7, the texts to be explained were no longer from the Bible but from purportedly Ukrainian folk songs that described the Cossack wars against the Poles. Many of these folk songs were actually forgeries that were first published in Sreznevskii's *Zaporozhian Antiquities* in 1833–8.[27] To some extent, this was the same material that Kulish had used in his *Ukraine*. The arrangement of the lessons in his *Hramatka* elevated the historical songs to the status of sacred texts equal to the Holy Scripture. In order to demonstrate the tolerance of censorship regarding Ukrainian nationalism during this period, it is useful to quote the following passage:

> From ancient times our Ukraine suffers from great misfortunes, mainly because of other countries. She consists of flatland, and on her borders there are no high mountains or deep rivers or sea that would allow a

defence against foreigners who attempt to plunder the country. It was God's will that our beautiful, fertile land would stand unprotected from neighbours. How strange! A Pole ruled over our country, the Tatar and the Turk made raids here, how many Christian people fell from the swords of enemies! How many departed into slavery with Tatar raiders! How many humiliations our forefathers had to bear! How many of our families and generations converted to an alien faith and alien habits! But to this day Ukraine stands as a country separate from all the neighbours ... In those unhappy days, about which the present epic song recounts, God did not forget us; He helped us live through plagues and wars for He was sparing us for a great task, for regeneration. We needed a great effort in order to get rid of the Polish yoke; we needed great spirits in order to give a response to the proud lords who, having converted to an alien faith and habits, considered us mindless cattle. The merciful God knew why he sends misfortune to the Ukrainian land. He did not want to leave her to be insulted by neighbours, but wanted to elevate her to a struggle for liberty and faith, sending all kinds of misfortune. The hearts of Ukrainians strengthened under misfortune, and they rose above all turmoil, the whole country arose like one soul against the Polish unrighteous force – and soon not a single traitor or foreigner remained in Ukraine. From that emerged the idea: there is no one who can beat us, for a nation that rises up for its faith and rights is invincible in its strength. Poland was a great realm; it stretched from the Black Sea to the Baltic Sea. Now look what is left of her! ... Today Poland is a great cemetery of ancient glory, and in that cemetery the living weep for the dead. It is no one but we who have done this. The Poles exhausted our patience with their insults: we shook ourselves and Poland quaked. It quaked until the neighbours made it fall altogether. Thus, God punishes earthly kingdoms by those same hands that once defended them![28]

Kulish's primer demonstrates how Ukrainian activists in the 1850s were beginning to implement plans for disseminating their ideas among the common people, which had first been proposed and attempted by the Cyrillo-Methodians. The book reached a considerable number of peasants. In late 1860 Kulish mentioned in a letter that he had sold out the entire edition of 5000 copies. The fact that a second edition of 8000 copies was printed in 1861 indicates that this was true.[29]

Hramatka did not pass unnoticed. A number of Ukrainian nobles stopped supporting Kulish and refused to distribute the book because they disapproved of its anti-noble social ethos. The governor-general of

Kyiv, Ilarion Ilarionovich Vasilchikov, immediately banned the book in the area under his administration, which included all of the Right Bank with its Polish nobility. Vasilchikov reported to the Third Section that the Polish nobles who had informed him about the primer were afraid that its dissemination among the common people might strengthen the peasants' national hatred of their Polish lords. The governor-general accepted this view unequivocally, adding that most of his region consisted of "the previous Ukraine, the indigenous population of which (peasants and the common people in general) has always felt hatred for the Poles, who form the majority of noble landowners."[30] In Vasilchikov's hierarchy of values, the social stability of the Right Bank was evidently most important, and for the time being he did not see that the government had anything to gain from antagonism between the two nationalities. However, Vasilchikov did not want to ban the book altogether, having realized that it might even be useful. He was concerned only about his own area with its Polish nobility, but he was not against the book being circulated elsewhere. He specified the four pages that should be removed in any future reprinting of the book. They contained the fragment cited above and a few sentences for exercises, like "the yoke and misfortune fall on the poor," "liberty is the Cossack's lot," and "oh, how beautiful the lord's wife is." It was, of course, inappropriate for peasant men to look at noblewomen in this way. Immediately after receiving the information about Kulish's *Hramatka*, Vasilchikov also wanted to ban Maksymovych's publications insofar as they contained anti-Polish texts, but he soon dropped the idea.[31]

Vasilii Andreevich Dolgorukov, the chief of gendarmes, submitted Vasilchikov's proposals to Alexander II, who approved them. Only then did Dolgorukov inform Evgraf Petrovich Kovalevskii, the minister of public enlightenment, who was responsible for censorship.[32] Kovalevskii admonished the censors and added a passage at the end of the book to those that were to be banned in future editions because it was written "in the spirit of tribal exclusivity as opposed to the common Russian [identity]."[33] It contained four pages in which Kulish informed readers that the Ukrainian land stretched across the border to Austria up to the Carpathians.[34] He called the borders between states "transitory," whereas borders between nations (*plemena*) were God's creation and lasted for a much longer period. Everyone had an obligation to venerate his own language that was given him by God. Those who were forsaking their language were at the same time expelling themselves from the Ukrainian land.[35] By directing attention to these pages,

Kovalevskii brought a sanction against Ukrainian national agitation to the case that had started solely as an act against undesirable anti-Polish agitation.

The first public Ukrainian-Russian polemics over history concerned Kyivan Rus' and took place in 1856 between Mykhailo Maksymovych and Mikhail Petrovich Pogodin, professor of Russian history at the University of Moscow. Pogodin began the debate by claiming that the inhabitants of Kyiv and the Dnipro region had spoken Great Russian in the period before the Mongol conquest in 1240. According to Pogodin, Great Russian was closely related to and emerged from Church Slavonic. Pogodin also denied the continuity of the population from the pre-Mongol period to modern days. He found that the whole Dnipro region had been entirely depopulated as a result of the Mongol conquest, for the inhabitants had either died or migrated to the north. Little Russians were not descendants of the inhabitants of pre-Mongol Kyiv, for they had moved from what is now Western Ukraine between the fourteenth and sixteenth centuries. Thus, only Russians were the true descendants of the population of pre-Mongol Kyiv. However, Pogodin did not deny the possibility that the Little Russian language had existed in the western regions of Rus' even in the pre-Mongol period. He explicitly acknowledged that Little Russian was now a language separate from Great Russian.[36]

Maksymovych responded to Pogodin with a series of articles under the general title of *Philological Letters* that were published in *Russkaia beseda* (*Russian Discussion*), the organ of the Slavophiles, of which he was the editor.[37] Maksymovych defended the dignity of Little Russians as the direct descendants of pre-Mongol Kyiv, and found that a close and special relationship existed between Little Russians and Great Russians. One of his main arguments was that Pogodin had erred in exaggerating the distance between the two groups. He wrote: "You break the close relatedness between the Russian dialects. The Little Russian and Great Russian dialects, or, to be more precise, the South Russian and North Russian languages, are brothers, sons of one Russian subgroup (*rechi*) ... However, if I had to choose the lesser of two evils, I prefer to admit the absence of any differences between North and South Rus' in the pre-Mongol period, rather than to separate them and break their close relatedness to the extent that this is done in your present system."[38]

Maksymovych found that the difference between South Russian and North Russian existed already in the pre-Mongol period, and that during this period the inhabitants of the Kyiv region had been South Russian speakers. This made South Russians the proper owners of the pre-Mongol heritage: in the pre-Mongol period it had been Little Russia that had been called the "Russian land" and the southern dialect, the "Russian language." Implicitly, Maksymovych questioned the moral right of the Northerners to use these terms to denote only their own land and language. With his idea of the special, close relationship between the two Russias, Maksymovych can hardly be called a Ukrainian nationalist. Nevertheless, his defence of the right of South Russians to the heritage of pre-Mongol Kyiv was relevant to the national movement and earned the sympathies of later nationalists.

Oleksiy Tolochko has challenged the traditional Ukrainian interpretation of the debate as one between national Ukrainian and Russian viewpoints.[39] Tolochko emphasizes Maksymovych's emphasis on Russian unity and Pogodin's greater emphasis on the differences between Great Russians and Little Russians, claiming that Pogodin's viewpoint was more favourable to Ukrainian nation building than Maksymovych's. According to Tolochko, Little Russians at this time did not as yet consider the medieval Kyiv period part of their own history, and thus Pogodin's opinion was fully in accordance with the Little Russian views. Tolochko perceives Maksymovych as a pre-national thinker who did not see any linkage between language, ethnicity, and history. While Tolochko is right in refuting the interpretation of Maksymovych as a Ukrainian nationalist, his emphasis on the pre-nationalist traits in Maksymovych's thought goes too far. Although not a nationalist, Maksymovych was not a fully pre-national thinker, either. First, by the time of the debate, Ukrainians were already claiming the Kyiv period as belonging to their own history rather than the Great or North Russian history. As we have seen, Mykola Markevych wrote about Great Russians as "younger brothers" of Little Russians.[40] Furthermore, *History of the Rus'* explicitly rejected the Muscovites' claim to the heritage of Kyiv Rus', granting them only the status of the descendants of Scythians.[41] Second, far from being ignorant of the linkage between language and nationality, Maksymovych explicitly endorsed the idea that language defines nationality, as we have seen in chapter 2. Perceiving South Russian speakers but no Great Russian speakers in medieval Kyiv, he was fully aware of the national and political connotations of the debate. This became even more evident in the second phase of the debate, Maksymovych's "New Letters to M.P. Pogodin," which were published in Slavophile newspaper *Den* (*Day*) in 1863. Despite the title, Maksymovych now criticized Petr Lavrovskii's theory, according to which neither Little Russian nor Great Russian languages existed before they began to separate from each other in the fourteenth century. According to Maksymovych, both languages had existed in the pre-Mongol period, when Great Russian was spoken in the north-east corner of Rus'. He rejected the Great Russian claims to Kyiv, writing: "Even without Kyiv there is enough space in North Russia to accommodate everything that sounds absolutely Great Russian: "'All land is ours, great and wealthy!'"[42]

Even in the new liberal atmosphere, censorship continued to present obstacles to Ukrainian publishing. Local censors found several Ukrainian publications dubious and referred them to the Main Administration of Censorship in St Petersburg. Most often, the issue that censors found sensitive was the description of relations between social classes, but sometimes it was Ukrainian nationalism. The books that were referred to the central censorship administration included Kostomarov's works on Cossack and Russian history. Although Kostomarov wrote and published in Russian, many of his works contained a strong Ukrainian national message.

In 1855 Kostomarov published a work entitled *Ivan Svirgovsky* without encountering any problems with censorship.[43] However, he faced some obstacles when he submitted his work *Vek tsaria Alekseia Mikhailovicha. Bogdan Khmelnitskii i vozvrashchenie Iuzhnoi Rusi k Rossii* (*The Age of Aleksei Mikhailovich: Bogdan Khmelnitsky and the Return of Southern Rus' to Russia*) to the censors in St Petersburg in January 1856. Kostomarov intended to publish his work in the journal *Otechestvennye zapiski* (*Notes of the Fatherland*). This was the first monograph published in Russia on Bohdan Khmelnytsky's insurrection. The author viewed the war between the Cossacks and Polish-Lithuanian Commonwealth as essentially a national and social conflict between Ukrainian commoners and the Poles: "Khmelnytsky wanted to be the enemy of the lords, but not at all the enemy of the Polish nation and government. However, his trouble was that the lords governed the Polish nation!"[44] For Kostomarov, the best period during Polish-Lithuanian rule was before the reign of King Stefan Batory (1576–86). He claimed that before Batory, Ukraine had only nominally belonged to Poland-Lithuania. Batory tried to bring the country closer to the commonwealth and thus sparked hostilities that lasted for a hundred years. Kostomarov perceived the ecclesiastical Union of Brest as simply a Catholic trick devised in order to proselytize among the Orthodox. Polish nobility and Jewish leaseholders oppressed Ukrainian peasants, and thus exacerbated national grievances by social ones. Kostomarov called Jews by the derogatory word 'Yid' (*zhid*).

The historian inserted "Khmelnytsky's speeches" into his work without indicating his sources. The use of this stylistic device, which was widespread in earlier centuries, was a rather bold move for a nineteenth-century historian. There was a purpose to Kostomarov's idiosyncratic methodology, for the speeches contained important evaluations of the neighbouring powers. In a speech, Kostomarov indicated that Khmelnytsky, who originally allied himself with the Crimean Tatars, would have preferred an alliance with Muscovy all along. However, it was hardly possible to gain the Muscovites for such an alliance since they were still weak after their unsuccessful wars against Poland-Lithuania. Kostomarov claimed that the first Muscovite envoys to Khmelnytsky disliked his simple and informal manner of communicating with the common people. Thus, the historian was able to paint a picture of an encounter between plebeian Ukraine and hierarchical Russia. Relying on the Velychko chronicle, Kostomarov perceived the Pereiaslav agreement of 1654 as a mutually binding treaty that both sides had confirmed by sworn oaths. A number of times Kostomarov wrote about independence as Khmelnytsky's political aim, but the exact meaning of this term remained vague.

At first, the censor Freigang argued that all Kostomarov's publications were forbidden. The author then sought help from the Third Section, arguing – correctly – that his future publications had never been banned, only those that had been found harmful during the investigation in 1847. The director of the Third Section, Leontii Dubelt, agreed and informed the censor that Kostomarov was allowed to publish his works. However, the Third Section still demanded strict censorship of Kostomarov's works.[45] Freigang continued in his refusal to permit the publication, but after an appeal from the editor of *Notes of the Fatherland*, he referred the case to the decision of the regional St Petersburg Censorship Committee.[46] The censor was not concerned over nationalism, but rather antagonism between social classes in the book. It was Freigang's view that the description of the seventeenth-century Ukrainian peasants' hatred of and atrocities against their lords during the Khmelnytsky rebellion was potentially dangerous. In addition, he vacillated about permitting a part of the description of other atrocities committed by the Cossacks against [presumably Roman and Greek Catholic] churches, including the torture of priests and raping of women. Freigang indicated the suspect pages, which numbered no fewer than 109. However, the censor found that in general the author had merely described events, almost always backing his accounts with references to published sources, without presenting any of his own views. Of course, if this was Freigang's genuine opinion, he was mistaken.[47]

Like Freigang, the St Petersburg Censorship Committee was reluctant to make an independent decision. Its evaluation of Kostomarov's work was mixed. On the one hand, the committee found the study important and valuable, but on the other, it found that some events in the text were harshly depicted. The committee emphasized that the work was intended for publication in a periodical, implying that it would have a relatively large audience. It referred the case to the Main Administration of the Censorship,[48] which permitted the publication, but stipulated that at least three chapters of the book should be published in each issue of the journal, and all passages containing a "subversive orientation" (*neblagonamerennogo napravleniia*) were to be excluded.[49] Thus, the explicit concerns of the censors were about the possible socially subversive impact of a book that described an uprising of peasants against their lords. What might have been included in a learned treatise could not be permitted in a journal, among whose readers were some common people. As Stephen Velychenko has written, one of the censors' priorities was to prevent any publications evoking actual disturbances.[50] This concern was not at all irrational: the last peasant disturbances in Ukraine that were connected with the memory of the Cossack past had taken place in 1855, when a false rumour had spread that those who volunteered as Cossacks for the Crimean War would be liberated from serfdom. In 1859, one year after the incident with Kostomarov's book, his new work *Stenka Razin's Rebellion* was permitted, again only after substantial revisions because of the detailed description of atrocities motivated by class hatred. This book dealt with the famous insurrection on the Volga in 1670–1, which was led by a Don Cossack Stepan Razin.[51]

In 1858 Kostomarov and Danylo Mordovets, a Ukrainian civil servant in Saratov, submitted to the St Petersburg censors the *Little Russian Collection*, a work that contained scholarly articles, folk songs, and new poetry. The censor Matskevich was as alert to the danger of Ukrainian political nationalism surreptitiously conveyed to the public through historiography as he had been while serving in Kyiv under Nicholas I. Matskevich found Kostomarov's description of the negotiations between Khmelnytsky and Polish delegates in 1649 to be problematic. It included the hetman's long anti-Polish monologue, which included statements against the nobility. The censor focused also on Mordovets's defence of the Little Russian language: he called upon readers to write in it, otherwise it might be completely absorbed by the Great Russian language. Despite this warning, Mordovets predicted a wonderful future for the Little Russian language if it were developed and refined. Mordovets's historical article on Cossacks and the Black Sea also elicited a comment from Matskevich: "The author regrets [the disappearance of] the previous way of life and manifestly prefers it to the present. He mentions the Cossacks' battles against Muscovy and the Poles. In short, the author depicts the ancient Cossacks and Ukraine as an independent country. He shows himself everywhere as a local Little Russian patriot."[52]

Matskevich described in detail Kostomarov's short story "The Riddle." According to the censor, Kostomarov portrayed a noble landowner "as a kind of an idiot and drunkard."[53] In the story, the landowner brings into his home a peasant woman who begins to rule the household. The nobleman decides to expel the woman, but before he can carry out his plan, he loses consciousness while drunk. The peasant woman carries her drunken master out of the house in full view of his peasants. When the landowner wakes up in the street, he realizes that he cannot get rid of his mistress and decides to marry her. In addition to manifestations of Ukrainian nationalism and irreverent attitude towards the existing social hierarchy, the censor disapproved of songs that depicted premarital sex, marital infidelity, and the sorrow expressed by recruits who face twenty years of army service.

The St Petersburg Censorship Committee referred the *Little Russian Collection* to the Main Administration of Censorship, which permitted the book but with substantial cuts that included the entire text of "The Riddle." The main administration agreed with the St Petersburg censors in that Uvarov's last circular on the Cyrillo-Methodians, dated 2 June 1847, was in force and applicable to the case.[54] Works presenting the Ukrainian past in an idealized light and regretting the loss of ancient liberty were still forbidden. However, now the censors implemented these guidelines more modestly than had been the practice under Nicholas I, and the *Little Russian Collection* was published after the offending pages were removed. That the decision about this book could be made only on the highest level of censorship indicates confusion, hesitation, and fear of personal responsibility among lower-ranking censors at a time when the scope of the permissible was expanding rapidly.

Another case that marked the limits of permitted national activism was the banning of the second edition of the *History of the Rus'*, which was submitted to the St Petersburg censors in 1858. There was still no awareness that this book was apocryphal and unreliable as a historical source. The *History of the Rus'* was banned because of its local patriotism. It was certainly bad luck for the publication project that the initial evaluation of the book was written by Matskevich. Nevertheless, the censor's negative opinion received full support from the Main Administration of Censorship. Matskevich grasped the essential message of the book and made his point explicit: "This history is written in the spirit of local patriotism. It tells about the originality (*samobytnost*) of the Little Russian nation and its constant, innate love of liberty and independence. The joining of Ukraine into the Russian realm and especially the loss of earlier rights and privileges are regretted. Many passages reveal the hostile feeling of Little Russians toward Great Russians, who are considered oppressors."[55]

Matskevich specified inappropriate passages on 37 of the book's 261 pages. At the Main Administration of Censorship the review of the *History of the Rus'* was entrusted to the censor Aleksandr Grigorevich Troinitskii. Although he found permissible some of the passages that Matskevich wanted to ban, in his general evaluation he agreed with Matskevich. However, Troinitskii argued that cutting all the undesirable passages would seriously harm the book, which he recognized as an important historical source. Out of this ostentatious respect for the *History*, Troinitskii proposed instead to ban the second edition altogether, without retrospectively banning the first edition published in 1846. He emphasized that the book should not be made accessible to the wider public (*obshchedostupnym*), as it would evoke the hopes and dreams that had not entirely disappeared from the national memory of the Little Russians. Furthermore, the publication of the book with the proposed cuts might, according to Troinitskii, evoke a harmful reaction in the press.[56] The Main Administration of Censorship accepted Troinitskii's proposal and banned the book.

However, the Main Administration of Censorship was not unanimous in its stance on the ban. The *History of the Rus'* found a defender in one of its members, Dmitrii Nikolaevich Bludov, president of the Academy of Sciences and head of the Second Department of His Imperial Majesty's Own Chancellery, which was responsible for drafting laws. As a Great Russian and elderly veteran of the civil service who had participated in the investigation of the Decembrists, Bludov could hardly be suspected of Ukrainian nationalism or excessive liberalism.

However, even after the decision had already been made, Bludov refused to sign the records of the Main Administration of Censorship, in which the decision was recorded. He argued that this work was one of the most remarkable histories of Little Russia, and claimed that even before the appearance of the first edition, it was known in all educated families living east of the Dnipro and in Kyiv Gubernia. Archbishop Heorhii Konysky, who was the author, as Bludov believed, had been faithful to Russia and Orthodoxy, and earned the trust of Empress Catherine II. According to Bludov, the book was popular because of its scholarly and artistic worth. To ban a book necessary for the study of history would hardly bring any benefit. He also pointed to the manifest inconsistency of banning an entire book while admitting that the book was good. In his view, it would definitely have been better to publish the second edition with some cuts, if it could not be published in its entirety. However, his own opinion was that the entire text of the *History of the Rus'* should have been permitted. Although Bludov did not deny the local patriotism in the chronicle, he found that it belonged to the past and had already lost all its potential harmfulness. However, his arguments failed to convince the minister of public enlightenment, Kovalevskii, who did not act on Bludov's letter.[57]

Although Bludov was not as successful in his defence of the *History of the Rus'* as Aleksandr Tolstoi had been in his recent lobbying for Kulish, both these men are noteworthy for their tolerant attitude to Ukrainian local patriotism. Despite his generally liberal reputation, Kovalevskii held stricter opinions on the Ukrainian question than these two imperial dignitaries. While Kovalevskii did not pay much active attention to Ukrainian activists, in the cases of *Hramatka* and the *History of the Rus'* he wanted to set definite limits to expressions of Ukrainian national ideas in the printed word. Kovalevskii, who was minister in the years 1858–61, held this opinion in a relatively peaceful time and before Ukrainian publishing reached its peak in the early 1860s. It is somewhat symptomatic that both Troinitskii and Bludov presumed that the ideas of the *History of the Rus'* had lost their relevance over time. Bludov perceived this process as one that was already completed, while Troinitskii thought that completion still lay ahead. In other words, these imperial bureaucrats were convinced that local Ukrainian patriotism belonged to the past and that the all-Russian identity was becoming increasingly stronger. Neither of them seemed to envision the intensification and expansion of Ukrainian national agitation which was already proceeding.

Another incident that defined the limits of the permissible was an attempt to publish a primer called *New Ukrainian Alphabet*, which introduced Latin letters. It was submitted to the Kyiv censors in 1859. The documents of the Main Administration of Censorship do not contain the names of either the authors or the publishers. However, it is likely that they were Polish students at St Vladimir's University in Kyiv.[58] Most of them were locals from Right-Bank Ukraine, and a rather strong Ukrainophile orientation was emerging among them. The superintendent of the Kyiv school district, Nikolai Ivanovich Pirogov, informed Minister Kovalevskii about the primer. Pirogov presumed that it was connected with similar attempts to introduce the Polish alphabet for the Rusin (Rusyn) population of Austrian Galicia "in order to suppress by literary influence the Rusin nationality (*russinskoi narodnosti*) and estrange it from the influence of Russian literature."[59] Pirogov proposed to refuse permission for the primer and to establish a rule whereby even in the future Little Russian publications that were aimed at the common people could be permitted only if they were written in what he called Russian letters. Kovalevskii agreed with Pirogov, and a little-known ban dating to 1853 on writing Russian with Latin-Polish letters was re-enforced by a circular that was distributed to all school districts.[60]

The censors were concerned about Ukrainian publications that were directed at the common people. This became evident in December 1859, when the Main Administration of Censorship rejected a petition to permit a journal for peasants. The petition came from the two publishers of the Russian journal *Narodnoe chtenie* (*Popular Reading*): civil servant Aleksandr Obolenskii and Colonel Grigorii Shcherbachev. They submitted a plan to launch a Ukrainian supplement entitled *Selo* (*Village*).[61] Since the publishers wanted a separate subscription for supplement, their plan was in fact to launch an additional, Ukrainian, journal. According to the Soviet Ukrainian historian M.D. Bernshtein, Kulish was the actual initiator of the Obolenskii-Shcherbachev plan.[62] The publishers were not known previously for any Ukrainian-related activities, and the documents of the Main Administration of Censorship do not reveal that their journal prior to their application had any problems with censorship. They explained that the journal circulated widely in the Great Russian provinces, but had no success in South Russia. They perceived that the cause of this discrepancy was that *Popular Reading* appeared only in the North Russian language. The planned supplement was to feature articles on local history and remarkable individuals who were originally descended from the Ukrainian common people, information about laws and other government decrees, poetry, medical advice, and data on agriculture, industry, and trade. The St Petersburg Censorship Committee backed the petition and submitted it to the Main Administration of Censorship, which, however, refused its permission in December 1859. The publishers were told that permission could not be granted because the St Petersburg Censorship Committee did not have "a censor for the Ukrainian dialect" and the contents of the *Narodnoe Chtenie* had already been confirmed.[63] Both arguments were unconvincing: many Ukrainian books were being published in St Petersburg, and approval of changes for previously established contents of journals was a regular practice in censorship. Furthermore, almost at the same time as permission for *Selo* was rejected, *Osnova* (*Foundation*), the organ of Ukrainian national activists, was permitted. It is likely that the Main Administration of Censorship was motivated both by a wish to restrict the access of common people to Ukrainian publications and negative information about *Narodnoe Chtenie*, which was received after the petition was submitted. In March 1860 *Narodnoe Chtenie* was admonished for publishing articles "incompatible with the aim of the journal."[64] While a Ukrainian journal was permitted, one directed specifically at the peasants was not.

From its modest beginnings, Ukrainian literature expanded substantially in the second half of the 1850s. The quantity of Ukrainian publications increased and the censors interfered much less in their contents than they had done in the reign of Nicholas I. This chapter contains the first systematic study of the censorship policies regarding Ukrainian publications in the second half of the 1850s. The new findings include the rejection of the authorization of the second edition of the *History of the Rus'*, the disagreements which that decision evoked among the authorities, the censorship case of Mordovets's *Little Russian* collection, Minister Kovalevskii's concern over Ukrainian nationalism in Kulish's *Hramatka*, and the fact that the censors considered Uvarov's circular of 2 June 1847 as being still in force. Together, these cases show that Main Administration of Censorship paid attention to the Ukrainian question, took it seriously, and strove to maintain limitations regarding Ukrainian national ideas which were permissible in print.

Chapter Four

Ukrainian Publishing, Russians, and the Empire at the Beginning of the 1860s

Ukrainian writers' most important achievements at the beginning of the 1860s were the tremendous increase in literature directed to common people and the launching of the first Ukrainian journals. In 1860 Danylo Kamenetsky, the director of Kulish's printing press, launched a series of popular books in Ukrainian at his own expense. Because of their small size, from ten to sixty pages, these publications were inexpensive and thus accessible to peasants. Although Kamenetsky remained the most active publisher of such books, other individuals contributed, too. Of the ninety-eight books published in Ukrainian in the Russian Empire in 1860–63, sixty-eight can arguably be included in this category.[1] They included fiction by Hanna Barvinok, Petro Kuzmenko, Matvii Nomys, Oleksa Storozhenko, Marko Vovchok, Hryhorii Kvitka-Osnovianenko, and Taras Shevchenko, examples of collected folklore, and Kulish's essays entitled *Lysty z khutora* (*Letters from a Country Homestead*). Some of the books, like Shevchenko's poems "Tarasova nich" (Taras's Night), Kulish's *Lysty* and his play *Kolii* (*The Haidamak Uprising*), or the above-mentioned folk tale "Trouble in Ochakov," contained a more or less explicit national message. In *Lysty*, Kulish contrasted the decadent Russian city with the virtuous Ukrainian countryside, thus contributing to the construction of Ukrainian stereotypes of Great Russians. A peasant mother in St Petersburg who prostituted her daughter and other unscrupulous attempts at gaining money represented the city, while the South Russian peasants supported themselves with honest work. By using the term "Judaizing" (*zhydovyty*) for the unscrupulous greed of town dwellers, Kulish conflated Great Russians with Jews in anti-Semitic overtones. He even claimed that it was better to remain uneducated than lose one's language in existing schools.

Kulish's disapproval of higher material well-being and upward social mobility probably prevented his message from being received by peasant readers.[2]

In 1861–3, fourteen instructional textbooks in Ukrainian were published. They included seven primers, two books on mathematics, two on religion, one on natural science, one on history, and one that explained the emancipation to the peasants. Ukrainian national activists wrote and published most of these books, and often they tried to transmit their own values to readers or listeners. For instance, all the primers mentioned the Cossacks and all except one mentioned Shevchenko. However, the silence of the textbooks regarding Russia and Russians was remarkable. Only two primers mentioned this country and its people, and only one mentioned Alexander II. Russia and Russians were mentioned in Kulish's historical work *Khmelnyshchyna* (*The Khmelnytsky Era*), which will be discussed below. The only additional Ukrainian textbook that did mention the emperor was published by the authorities of Kharkiv Gubernia and included explanations of the complicated manifesto on the abolition of serfdom and land reform. The relative silence on Russia was most likely caused by two considerations: first, it was better to keep silent than write something that could cause problems with the censorship, and second, the authors of the textbooks wanted their readers to identify with Ukraine rather than with Russia.

Those books in which Russia and Russians were mentioned did not diverge from the general pattern of emphasizing Ukraine rather than Russia: in his primer the Moscow student Leonid Iashchenko emphasized the democracy and freedom of the Cossack political system, claiming that in ancient times all Ukrainians were Cossacks. The Cossacks had fought in defence of Ukraine and the Orthodox faith. Iashchenko ended his description of Ukrainian history with the destruction of the Zaporozhian Sich on Catherine II's command, although he did not evaluate that event. Although Iashchenko mentioned Alexander II, it was evident that the most important thing to be learned was the existence of Ukraine: "Nowadays we, Ukrainians, or Little Russians, number about 15 million, and apart from a good two million under German rule, who are called Galicians, we all belong as subjects of the Muscovite realm, where the emperor is now Alexander II. We are all Orthodox."[3] It is noteworthy that at the time of the publication of his primer Iashchenko was being questioned for having distributed the works of Alexander Herzen and other forbidden publications. Iashchenko's activities in Muscovite revolutionary student circles will be examined in the next chapter.

Mykola Hatchuk's *Ukraïnska abetka* (*Ukrainian ABC*) was the other primer in which Russia or Russians were mentioned. It contained a humorous story that emphasized the difference between Ukrainians and Muscovites, as the author called them:

> Once from somewhere a Muscovite came to Ukraine. We have entirely enough of such people, probably they came from their swamps. So he came, and that would have been all right, since he felt bad there in his own place, or perhaps there was some misfortune. As it is said, a fish seeks deeper water, man seeks a better place. But, no: the Muscovite leaves his country, but does not give up his wicked character. It happened thus: because of his madness he did not remain honest and began to do all kinds of evil things. Despite all his cunning tricks, in which he was rather skilful, he was caught. So, under the interrogation that began, he pretended that he was a Ukrainian; he said that he had been on the road for a long time, had temporary jobs, and did not remember in which village he was born. But, it was instantly clear that he is a Muscovite. He was accustomed to speaking our language, but pronounced with a Muscovite accent, so one could see who he is.[4]

In Hatchuk's story, the interrogators posed linguistic questions to the Muscovite. Remembering the word *katsap* led him to make a mistake. "At once the interrogators caught him by his beard, and he confessed from where he was and what he had done."[5] Here, evildoing follows from national character, and nationality practically amounts to a crime. To be sure, this was a comic story. Apart from this story, Hatchuk's book also included an illustration of a bearded *katsap*.

The censors were initially concerned about launching inexpensive Ukrainian books. However, after some hesitation they permitted them. The question arose in connection with a new edition of Kvitka's works, his Ukrainian stories having been published in one volume in 1858. Despite this, in 1860 the St Petersburg Censorship Committee refused its permission for a new edition, basing its decision on the fact that the stories would be published each one separately. However, Kamenetsky appealed to the Main Administration of Censorship, which repealed the decision and permitted the publication in the form of individual booklets.[6] A similar incident happened in connection with three short stories by Kulish and Hanna Barvinok, which were originally published in a collection called *Khata* (Home) (more on this below). The three stories, "Grey Horse," "Something Good out of Adversity," and "Summer in Autumn," depicted peasant life without the slightest allusion to politics. However, the Moscow Censorship Committee refused its permission to publish them as separate printings. Kulish appealed to the Main Administration of Censorship, which permitted the publication of the brochures in January 1861.[7]

Neither the St Petersburg nor Moscow Censorship Committees offered any reasons why they permitted some texts as parts of a larger collection, but tried to prevent the publication of these same texts as small separate booklets. Most likely the answer lies in the general censorship policy: what was permitted for educated readers from the upper strata of society was often forbidden to readers from the lowest stratum – the common people.[8] Underlying this decision was the idea that Kvitka's and Kulish's works were suitable for the Ukrainian nobility and the intelligentsia, but not for the common people. To be sure, there were also some politically sensitive aspects to Kvitka's stories. His criticism regarding the inappropriate functioning of the government is most notable in "Kozyr-divka" (The Intrepid Woman), a story about the arrest and sentencing of an innocent man on charges of burglary. Although the man is finally saved from injustice, the difficulty of getting a fair hearing is not at all concealed. In "Marusia," conscription is described as a grave personal misfortune, and avoiding it by lawful means is considered praiseworthy. Furthermore, in some of Kvitka's stories the image of Great Russians is negative. In "Perekotypole" (Tumbleweed), one of the characteristics of a criminal society is its multiethnic composition: it includes local Little Russians, Gypsies, Jews, and "Muscovites" (*moskali*). This is part of a general contrast between the virtuous village and the morally suspect and dangerous town. In "Saldatskyi patret" (A Soldier's Portrait), the anonymous narrator from the common people emphasizes the difference between Ukrainians and Russians, portraying the latter as inclined to earn money by dishonest means and even questioning whether Russians have the same faith as Ukrainians: "There is the whole Muscovite nature, there are pure Muscovites, like in Turkey there are Turks. They are a cunning people: they do not eat or sleep properly, but all the time they think about earning money. That is their Muscovite habit! ... That is their Russian faith, to squeeze from everyone."[9] Thus, in Kvitka's works the peasants could encounter the idea that Great Russians were greedy and untrustworthy people, possibly prone to criminal activities. The popular editions of Kvitka's works, published in 1860–1, did not include his "Letters to My Dear Countrymen," which advised peasants to be obedient to the authorities and their landlords, and described Russians in a positive tone.

The fear of Ukrainian publications becoming accessible to peasants was made explicit in the processing of permission for Kulish's book *Khmelnyshchyna* (*The Khmelnytsky Era*), a popular history of the Khmelnytsky uprising. This case also reveals serious disagreements among the censors on the Ukrainian question. V. Beketov, for example, found inappropriate a few passages "that hint that Little Russia was oppressed when the Russians occupied it."[10] Furthermore, he doubted whether a history of Little Russia could be permitted at all, for such a book "seems to express [the idea of] the independence of that region."[11] The St Petersburg Censorship Committee shared Beketov's opinion and referred the matter to the Main Administration of Censorship, which referred the manuscript for evaluation to censor Aleksandr Vasilevich Nikitenko, professor of Russian Literature in St Petersburg, who was of Ukrainian peasant background. Nikitenko disagreed with Beketov, declaring that censorship could not prevent the publication of separate histories of those parts of the empire that had previously been independent. However, he stipulated that the authors of such histories must write them only with scholarly and literary aims, "without any idea of the possibility of separate existence, without any separatist doctrines and intentions."[12] Nikitenko doubted whether *The Khmelnytsky Era* was just such a book. Since he had only a sample of the text at his disposal, Nikitenko did not give his final verdict on the entire book. However, he agreed that the passages marked by Beketov, which "cast a shadow on the relationship between Little Russia to Russia in the past,"[13] must not be permitted. He added that censorship must be especially alert with regard to Kulish's publications because he was writing them with the aim of making them accessible to the common people.

Nikitenko's evaluation of *The Khmelnytsky Era* almost triggered a circular against Ukrainian "separatist" historiography. Remarks made on the margins of Nikitenko's evaluation indicate that at first a decision had been made to distribute a circular to all the censorship committees, to serve as a guideline. However, once the circular was prepared, the director of the Main Administration of Censorship, Nikolai Aleksandrovich Mukhanov, cancelled and destroyed it. Nevertheless, he included Nikitenko's main findings in his response to the St Petersburg Censorship Committee, and added that the case of Kulish's work must be decided according to those considerations. The book was permitted after the excision of the passages about Russian oppression of Little Russia, which Beketov had marked. It is noteworthy that the documents do not indicate that Minister Evgraf Kovalevskii was even informed about this matter. The most likely explanation is that Kovalevskii had already fallen into the emperor's disfavour and was about to ask for his own dismissal in April 1861. Kovalevskii's fall from grace was caused by criticism of his general laxity both in terms of censorship and the radical student movements in the universities.[14]

Why did Mukhanov cancel his own decision? He had decided to send the circular on 21 January 1861 and cancelled it a month later, on 22 February. The abolition of serfdom was enacted between these two dates, on 19 February. It is possible that Mukhanov was loath to cause unnecessary unrest at such a time. However, it is even more likely that he reacted to the events in Warsaw: on 15 February Russian troops fired on Polish nationalist demonstrators, leaving five persons dead. After this incident, the government remained passive when an ad hoc Polish administration practically took control of the city – without resorting to armed force. This situation lasted for several weeks, before the government restored order by force. The events in Warsaw brought home to the imperial bureaucrats the threat of another Polish uprising against the empire. In this situation, Mukhanov found it expedient to permit Kulish's book *The Khmelnytsky Era* and other, similar Ukrainian publications as a counterweight to Polish agitation. Thus, the Warsaw demonstrators and the negative image of Poles and Polish rule in Kulish's work helped make it accessible to the Ukrainian public. However, despite the cuts, the published book still contained some historical ideas unfavourable to Russia. To be sure, Kulish mentioned the Muscovites as allies of the Cossacks. Yet, he also depicted Muscovite duplicity and how the Cossacks' political principles were incomprehensible to them. Muscovy was successful in war only when the Cossacks helped it. Kulish's description of the events ended with the period when Khmelnytsky feared a possible Polish-Russian alliance against the Cossacks.[15]

Ukrainian national activists began to plan the launch of their own journal in 1858. Kulish applied for permission to publish *Khata* (*Peasant House*), a Ukrainian journal. He claimed that the journal's aim was to promote moral unity between the two Russian tribes. After some hesitation, the Main Administration of Censorship did not reject the petition outright, but asked for the opinion of the Third Section. Vasilii

Dolgorukov responded by stating that, because of Kulish's involvement in the Cyrillo-Methodian case, he was against granting permission. Furthermore, according to Dolgorukov, the incident with *Hramatka* indicated that Kulish "follows in his literary activities his previous orientation, which has been the cause of special government actions against him."[16] The Ministry of Public Enlightenment did not hazard to permit *Khata* now that the Third Section had rendered such an opinion. It is noteworthy that Dolgorukov (correctly) identified Kulish's political orientation as social egalitarianism rather than adherence to the old autonomy of nobility. From the whole process Kulish got the impression that Minister Kovalevskii was not against permitting a Ukrainian journal, if only an acceptable editor were found.[17]

Kulish now petitioned to publish the materials that he had wanted to include in the first issues of the journal as a book. This time permission was granted. *Khata* went through two printings in 1860, which indicates that the book was popular. It consisted of prose and poetry. In a lengthy foreword Kulish now expressed opinions that were opposite to those he had written in the epilogue to *The Black Council*: he perceived Ukrainian (not South Russian) literature as fully independent and separate from Russian literature. He found that books published in the two Russian capitals, St Petersburg and Moscow, could not replace Ukrainian literature. Here, Kulish seemed to have forgotten the fact that most Ukrainian books were published in St Petersburg. Nevertheless, he did not exhort his audience not to read Russian books: good Russian works, like those by Pushkin and Gogol, were as useful as the works of Byron, Schiller, Mickiewicz, and other similar foreign literature. Among Russian, and hence foreign, authors Kulish included even Gogol. He also placed Mickiewicz and Shevchenko, as "all-Slavic poets," on a higher level than Pushkin. Kulish praised Vovchok for having cleansed the Ukrainian language of polonisms and russianisms.[18]

Except for the foreword, the writings published in *Khata* did not broach Ukrainian–Russian relations. Politically, the most relevant was Kulish's play *The Haidamak Uprising*, which described the situation in Polish-ruled Ukraine on the eve of the *haidamak* uprising in 1772. In the play Jews and Poles were negatively portrayed, and once again Kulish wrote about atrocities committed against these groups in an approving tone. Three poems by Oleksandra Psol, published anonymously under the title "A Maiden's Three Tears," lamented the fate of the Cyrillo-Methodians, depicting them as martyrs and heroes. Although the members of the society were not mentioned by name, the year when the poems were written was given as 1847. Furthermore, a selection of Shevchenko's previously unpublished poems in *Khata* included those written during his army service, although Nicholas I had expressly forbidden him to write. Only one of them, "The Abandoned House," was politically somewhat sensitive because it described conscription as a misfortune.

After Kulish, Vasyl Bilozersky applied for permission to publish the South Russian journal *Osnova*. Bilozersky was well suited to the task since, after serving his sentence, he had advanced to the rank of court councillor in government service, the seventh rank as listed in the table of ranks. Ivan Davidovich Delianov, superintendent of the St Petersburg school district, backed Bilozersky's petition and submitted it to the Main Administration of Censorship in November 1859. According to Bilozersky, the goal of the journal was to study the South Russian region in all its aspects with a special emphasis on economy and industry. It would also devote attention to the commonweal and interests of all social ranks. Kovalevskii requested an opinion from the Third Section. On Christmas Eve 1859 Dolgorukov informed the minister about his opposition to granting permission, basing his opinion on Bilozersky's previous sentence. Normally, this would have precluded the granting of permission to the journal. However, in February 1860 the Ministry of Public Enlightenment permitted *Osnova* despite Dolgorukov's opposition. Such a decision was exceptional. Although the documents of the Main Administration of Censorship do not contain detailed information about the process, it is unlikely that Kovalevskii would have dared to bypass Dolgorukov's opinion without informing the emperor and receiving his support.[19]

Granting permission to *Osnova* was a controversial issue, and, soon afterwards, the government blocked the plan to establish another Ukrainian periodical. In May 1860 members of the Kyiv Ukrainian society Hromada, the students Kalenyk Sheikovsky and Pylyp Levytsky, submitted an application to the censors in Kyiv for permission to publish *Golos* (Ukr. *Holos; The Voice*), a weekly newspaper in Russian and South Russian.[20] *Golos* was planned as more than a local newspaper, since it was slated to have correspondents spread throughout Ukraine, in St Petersburg, Moscow, and Warsaw. Sheikovsky and Levytsky wanted *Golos* to review all Russian (probably including Ukrainian) and Polish books published in Right-Bank Ukraine. Books published outside of Right-Bank Ukraine would also be reviewed, inasmuch as they were relevant to the region by their contents or language. The newspaper was to include a feuilleton in which local public and private life would be discussed. The application was processed after permission was granted to *Osnova*, but before the journal published its first issue. The Kyiv Censorship Committee functioned under the liberal superintendent Nikolai Pirogov, who was in favour of granting permission. Most likely, to suppress any periodical would have been contrary to Pirogov's political ideals. Furthermore, the superintendent generally favoured Ukrainian activities as a counterweight to Polish clandestine nationalist organizations, which were rather strong at the local university. Pirogov followed the regular administrative procedure and forwarded the application to the governor-general, asking for his opinion. Vasilchikov responded with an ambiguous answer: he did not deny permission, but voiced his disapproval of a number of issues.[21] For example, he opposed the use of "the local dialect" in the prospective newspaper, as well as the inclusion of a feuilleton about Kyivan life. The governor-general doubted whether it was suitable for students to publish a newspaper, but ostensibly left that matter to Pirogov and Kovalevskii's discretion. However, simultaneously with his letter to Pirogov, Vasilchikov sent another one to Kovalevskii, rejecting the petition altogether. The governor-general found it impermissible that students would publish a newspaper with political and economic news. Furthermore, he expressed concern over the tensions at the university among students of different nationalities, and did not want to exacerbate national passions by having them channelled "either from life to the newspaper or from the newspaper to life."[22]

Vasilchikov's double dealing is striking: Why did he write two letters with such markedly different opinions? There are two likely explanations, which do not exclude each other: first, the governor-general wanted to deny permission without having to bear political responsibility for his decision before the educated public. Vasilchikov wanted the Main Administration of Censorship to reject the petition, but in such a manner as though he himself had had no part in the decision. Second, by giving a more positive answer to Pirogov, Vasilchikov encouraged him to submit the petition to the main censorship administration, so that the superintendent would thereby earn the disfavour of his superiors. Prior to the question of permitting *Golos*, Vasilchikov had disagreed with Pirogov on many vital questions, the most important of which was the question of granting permission for the founding of the first Sunday school in Kyiv.[23] If Vasilchikov wanted to discredit Pirogov, he succeeded: Pirogov forwarded the application to the Main

Administration of Censorship, adding a favourable evaluation of Sheikovsky's and Levytsky's behaviour. As might have been expected, the Main Administration of Censorship sided with Vasilchikov and denied permission. Furthermore, it admonished Pirogov by stating that the Kyiv Censorship Committee should not even have submitted the petition in the first place.[24] Although the Main Administration of Censorship had bypassed the opinion of Dolgorukov and the Third Section when permitting *Osnova*, it did not want to nullify the general practice whereby permission for new periodicals required the support of the local authorities. Furthermore, it would have been unusual indeed in the Russian Empire to permit students to publish periodicals aimed at the general public. Suspicion of Ukrainian nationalism, too, definitely played a role in the final decision, since the prospective use of South Russian was one reason why Vasilchikov was opposed to granting permission to *Golos*. Indeed, prior to the Valuev circular, this was the only case in which the Ukrainian language was found impermissible as such, regardless of what was written in it.

The Journal *Osnova*, Its Political Orientation, and the Stereotypes of Russians in Its Contents

The fate of *Golos* did not affect *Osnova*, which was launched in January 1861. According to Ukrainian historian Viktor Dudko's estimation, the journal had in 1861 about 1400 subscribers.[25] The journal wrote extensively on the relations between northern and southern Rus'. Politically, it followed the Cyrillo-Methodian line, supporting a federal solution to the Ukrainian question. Owing to official censorship and prudent self-censorship, the editors did not state this program explicitly, but it was not difficult to read between the lines. The prospective federation included at least Russia, Ukraine, and Poland, and it was based on popular representation. This program was broached in a number of articles and pieces of fiction.

The first issue included Kostomarov's article "O federativnom nachale v Drevnei Rusi" (On the Federative Principle in Ancient Rus'). The author's point of departure was that the main reason for the existence of both centripetal and centrifugal tendencies in Russian history was, on the one hand, the national differences among various parts of Rus' and, on the other, their similarity and relatedness to each other. The author was convinced that the federal tendency existed globally "everywhere where the moral strength of a human being has not been suppressed by violent unification, or where the parts have not become completely separate from each other as a result of circumstances unfavourable to the preservation of unity."[26] The historian identified six main nationalities in Rus' during the medieval period of small principalities: South Russians, Severian (Chernihiv region), Great Russians, Belarusians, Polesians, and Novgorodians. The South Russian nation stretched from the east bank of the Dnipro to Galicia: "The South Russian branches were always inseparable from each other, even to the final submission of Galicia to Poland, and Volyn, Podillia, and Rus' [Kyiv region] to Lithuania."[27] Kostomarov thought that the national unity of the South Russians had been preserved to his day. Common ancestry, customs, language, dynasty, and the Orthodox religion united all the various Russian nationalities. When writing about such customs, which had existed everywhere in Rus', Kostomarov emphasized that they were shared also by all of Slavdom. Most importantly, all the Slavs based their political system on freedom, and democratic decision making in the popular assembly, the *veche*.

In another article, "The Features of National South Russian History," which was also published in *Osnova*, the historian claimed that elected popular representation was a typical South Russian institution that had been established in medieval Rus'.[28] In his emphasis on freedom and democracy as Slavic character traits, Kostomarov may have been influenced by the Polish historian Joachim Lelewel and the poet Adam Mickiewicz. For Kostomarov, linguistic relatedness had strengthened the sense of unity of all Rus' more than that of all Slavs, for even the Galicians were linguistically closer to Great Russians than to Bulgarians or Poles. However, South Russians felt greater affiliation with each other than with Great Russians. Kostomarov thought that at one time the system of small principalities had been beneficial because it had prevented the complete dissolution of Rus', which would have been a possible result of a premature attempt at unification by force. In the end, he also wrote that the final unification of the country under Moscow had been desirable, for it represented a higher principle. Although this last statement did not fit well with his general scheme in the article "On the Federative Origins," Kostomarov reiterated his support for political union with Russia in other articles that he published in *Osnova*.[29]

The second issue included Kostomarov's messianic poem "For Good Night," possibly written in the 1840s, under the old pseudonym Ieremiia Halka.[30] The poet expected the fall of Babylon and the victory of liberty in the world. Even the fall of "the tyrant" was predicted. Kostomarov's article "Vyhovsky's Hetmanate," which was published in the fourth and seventh issues of the journal, was another example of political agitation through historiography.[31] The article dealt with Khmelnytsky's successor, who had sided with Poland against Muscovy. In 1658 Hetman Ivan Vyhovsky had concluded the Treaty of Hadiach with Poland-Lithuania, which granted the Russian Grand Principality (*Velikoe Kniazhestvo Russkoe*, not to be confused with Muscovy) the status of a third constituent state in the Polish-Lithuanian Commonwealth. Kostomarov perceived Great Russian disrespect of local customs, pressure on the local Orthodox Church to submit itself to Moscow, and the curtailment of Ukrainian autonomy as the causes leading to the Union of Hadiach. Although he criticized Vyhovsky, Kostomarov let his Vyhovsky deliver a number of speeches with heavy criticism of Muscovite policies. The article also included a speech by King Jan Kazimierz, in which he emphasized the attempted union as one between two Slavic nations.

Kostomarov described the atrocities committed by Russian troops, basing his information on Velychko's chronicle. The historian alluded to customary Russian crudeness in his description of Russian prince Pozharskii's execution. The Crimean Tatars had taken Pozharskii prisoner and he was escorted to the khan. Disregarding his plight, Pozharskii shouted crude words at the khan, and the Crimean ruler responded by ordering his beheading. According to Kostomarov, "Pozharskii revealed himself as a true Great Russian national warrior."[32] This statement was ambiguous, since the prince's behaviour was marked by foolishness and crudeness as well as bravery. Concerning the Hadiach treaty itself, Kostomarov's opinion was ambiguous. Although he described the treaty in more or less positive terms, he also stated that neither side was sincere while concluding it. Furthermore, the treaty had not been supported by the majority of rank-and-file Cossacks.

Commenting on new collections of sources published by the Kyiv Archeographic Commission, the editors of *Osnova* explicitly backed Kostomarov's pan-Slavic orientation:

> The best statesmen (*deiateli*) of their time wanted to establish, maintain, and expand the [new] political order. Their goal was not submission of one nation to another, not even submission of a part to the whole, but a federal, equal relationship among the parts. This order was based on a perpetual peace and strong alliance, to which … the Muscovite monarch and people would also join. The Polish nobility either was not able or did not want to understand this noble task, although … that solution followed

> from the nature of things, from the relatedness and geographic unity of the Slavic world. Egoism of social rank prevented the natural course of Polish and Russian, consequently, also of all Slavic history. That egoism was the source of bloodshed and misfortune ... Submitting themselves to cold and unfeeling Jesuit ideas, the Polish nobility was the first to sever the ties that united the neighbouring Slavic nations with each other. Only in the future ... perhaps, it will be possible to renew the natural principles that elevated them.[33]

Promoting a federation of Russia, Poland, and Ukraine was a bold act and incompatible with autocratic policies. The above-cited text was published in April 1861, at the time of serious unrest in the Kingdom of Poland. However, the editors' message was softened both by criticism of the Poles and by its context. It was included in the foreword of an article by the chairman and editor of the Kyiv Archeographic Commission, Mikhail Iuzefovich and Nikolai Dmitrievich Ivanishev, respectively. In that article, the authors defended the commission against Polish accusations of the tendentious selection of documents for publication. By praising Iuzefovich's article, the editors of *Osnova* managed to place their subversive pan-Slavic ideas in the context of a defence of the government's policies.

The discussion of serfdom in *Osnova* provides us with additional materials for defining the journal's political orientation. Although the journal duly praised Alexander II for the emancipation of serfs, it added in its commentary on the reform a historical discussion that placed responsibility for serfdom in Ukraine solely on Russian rule and claimed that this institution was completely alien to Little Russians: "In the sixteenth and seventeenth centuries, serfdom came to us from the west, and in the second half of the eighteenth century it came from the north."[34] The commentary ended with a long quote from Catherine II's decree introducing serfdom in the previous Hetmanate in 1783. While it is true that serfdom was introduced to that region by the imperial government, the editors of *Osnova* forgot to mention the local nobility's interest in and profit from serfdom. The perception of serfdom as a phenomenon imported from Russia was repeated in other articles and works of fiction.[35]

Osnova did not hesitate to criticize the Russian government on a number of lesser contemporary political questions. The journal disapproved of the regulations that limited the curriculum of Sunday schools to the elementary level of parish schools. The government was suspicious of Sunday schools, which functioned thanks to a volunteer workforce. According to *Osnova*, the decreed restrictions hampered the development of Sunday schools and were unnecessary.[36] After Pirogov was dismissed from his position as superintendent of the Kyiv school district for his failure to ban university students from wearing national Ukrainian and Polish costumes, *Osnova* praised Pirogov's activities and described in great detail how he was feted by the local intelligentsia before his departure from Kyiv.[37] Hryhorii Ge complained about the fact that the Emancipation Act was not translated into South Russian language,[38] and Oleksandr Konysky told the readers how Poltava authorities had prevented the establishment of a literature society and newspaper *Niva*.[39] On the whole, *Osnova* was clearly an organ of opposition to the Russian government, adhering to democratic pan-Slavic ideas and criticism of the existing social hierarchy. To be sure, this did not preclude an occasional positive evaluation of some government measures, especially the abolition of serfdom and the activities of the Kyiv Archeographic Commission.[40]

In fiction and non-fiction, *Osnova* promoted a rather negative perception of the historical role of Russia and Russians in Ukraine.[41] The journal published Shevchenko's poem "Nevilnyk" (The Captive, 1859), in which the destruction of the Zaporozhian Cossack host was strongly condemned, and the defection of many Cossacks to Turkish service was described with understanding.[42] A few verses disrespectful to Catherine II were excised from the poem, either as a result of censorship or self-censorship. The same topic was raised in five other texts by different authors.[43] Criticism of Russian policies in the past appeared in several other texts. These included Kulish's articles, some of which were written in Ukrainian. Although only *The Khmelnytsky Era* was ever published as a book, several other parts of his prospective history of Ukraine were published in *Osnova*. Kulish's perception of Vyhovsky's war against Muscovy was more explicitly anti-Russian than Kostomarov's. For instance, he wrote about a battle between the Muscovites and Vyhovsky's Cossacks: "Having burned and robbed Pyriatyn in a Tatar manner, [the Russian commander] Romodanovskii attacked Hulianytsky ... However, as his [Hulianytsky's] was a true, brave, and orderly Cossack host, Romodanovskii could do nothing to it."[44] In Kulish's description, the Russians lost the Battle of Konotop (1659) because they did not take their opponents seriously. The author was thus hinting at Russian arrogance. Kulish's description of Vyhovsky's war against Muscovy ends after the Battle of Konotop, when Vyhovsky's pro-Polish

Cossacks attained rule over most of Ukraine. In his overview of the history of Ukrainian literature, Kulish emphasized how the country had become poorer and many crafts had disappeared since the beginning of the eighteenth century, explaining this phenomenon as the result of incorrect administrative practices.[45] Another article, ostensibly a work of fiction by the little-known author "D. Khorechko," but actually Kulish's pseudonym, was a wholesale condemnation of Russian policies in Ukraine since Mazepa's time.[46] Although most Cossacks had fought against Mazepa, the country was treated as an occupied land. In violation of local laws, lands were distributed to Great Russian noblemen and peasants were turned into serfs. Concluding his article, the author held the Russian Empire responsible even for the troubles among the three nations that were closely related to each other. After his description of the abolition of autonomy, "Khorechko" wrote: "This was the horrible decay of the old order under the destructive impact of a wild force that shaped the moral character of the people for decades, perhaps even centuries, to come. It ruled that the three Slavic nations that were fruitlessly fighting against each other ceased to be what they had been; it covered the foundations of those nations with a rotten weight of the old forms of life."[47] By "wild force" was the author referring to the enmity among the three nations or to the Russian Empire? Kulish did not specify.

In his article "Two Russian Nationalities" Kostomarov painted a positive picture of Ukrainians by creating a negative "Other" in his description of the Great Russian national character. The historian claimed that various differences between North and South Russians in customs, dress, and appearance were secondary and resulted from the more fundamental difference in their national characters. The South Russian national character found its expression in disorganization, impracticality, incapacity for long-term undertakings, including conquests and the creation of a strong state power, inclination to democracy, tolerance towards various faiths and nationalities, and a strong sense of individual liberty and dignity: "Southern Rus' completely lacked the tendency to subjugate others, to assimilate foreigners ... Kyiv was in no way suited to being the capital of a centralized state; ... In the South Russian character there was nothing violent, levelling, there was no politics."[48] And: "The Greeks, Armenians, Jews, Germans, Poles, and Hungarians all found a free haven and got along with the local population ... That spirit of tolerance, lack of national arrogance, were later transferred to the character of the Cossacks and has remained within the people to this day ... The hostile acts against Catholic churches during the Cossack uprising did not issue from hatred of Catholicism but from resentment against the violation of freedom of conscience by force."[49]

The Great Russians, in their turn, aimed at establishing a powerful centralized state under one ruler. They wanted to subjugate all of Rus', regarded the community as more important than the individual, were extremely intolerant of other faiths and nationalities, and had an inflated opinion of themselves. "Already at that time [the twelfth century] there emerges the tendency to subjugate to their own land all the other lands of Rus'."[50] Kostomarov emphasized that the subjugating tendency followed from the Great Russian national character and popular will, not the princes' individual ambitions and ruthlessness. The tendency towards strong power and disregard of individual liberty facilitated the establishment of autocracy, which Kostomarov described in as dark colours as was possible in a censored publication. In his view, blind obedience to a ruler necessarily followed from the subjugation of the individual to the community. Kostomarov dealt with the problem of the Novgorodians and their archaic democracy by claiming that they were descended from settlers from South Rus' and were thus much more closely related to South Russians than to Great Russians.

The historian saw an essential difference between the religious life of Great Russians and South Russians. In Great Russia the accepted idea was that if any undertaking succeeded, it was in accordance with God's will. On this basis and because it was to its own benefit, the church hierarchy initially strongly supported the princes of Vladimir and then Muscovy, regardless of how sinful their actions were. The Muscovites also paid considerable attention to the external ritual forms of faith. A good example of this was the schism of the Old Believers. In Southern Rus' such a schism would have been impossible because the only heresies that occurred there stemmed from serious religious disagreements concerning the essence of faith. Indeed, Great Russians did not understand religion properly, for they were a nation with poorly developed spiritual capacities: "The Great Russian tribe has always shown and shows an inclination toward materialism. It loses to South Russians in the spiritual side of life, in poetry, which is incomparably fuller and livelier among the latter."[51] This was also evident in that Great Russians most often read either only practical literature related to one's profession or works of very light content. Among the Great Russian folk songs the best ones were those about robbers, which expressed the same spirit that was apparent in the forming of the government.

The Great Russians were also incapable of appreciating the beauty of nature. They were a practical and materialistic nation that appreciated only useful things. On the other hand, the Great Russians had persistence and organizational skills, which the South Russians lacked. Because the South Russians were incapable of forming their own state, they should be satisfied with the governmental union with Great Russians and try to influence the latter in a benevolent way.

Kostomarov's description of Great Russians is exceptional, for one does not often encounter the stereotype of them as a practical nation known for its organizing skills. Indeed, the historian may have been influenced by Russian Slavophile theories, for his description of Great Russian materialism and narrow utilitarianism is reminiscent of the Slavophiles' critique of the West.[52] Another possible influence is the lectures that Mickiewicz gave in Paris at the Collège de France in 1840–4. The Polish poet emphasized the Russians' artistic insensitivity, which he explained by their partly Finnish-Mongolian ancestry.[53] To be sure, Kostomarov rejected this argument. His analogy between Moscow and Rome may echo the Slavophiles' criticism of the latter, although the target of Kostomarov's criticism was multiculturalism rather than the tradition of Roman law: "Moscow, like ancient Rome, had an immigrant population, and for a long time it maintained itself by a stream of new inhabitants from various corners of the Russian land … That kind of mixed population always eventually shows an inclination to expanding its territory, to achievements at the expense of others, to annexation of neighbours, to cunning politics … Moscow, in relation to Russia, has many analogies with Rome. There is a striking similarity in the means used by both to promote the unification of Italy and Russia under one government: the forcible emigration of townspeople and even entire townships (*volosti*), and the settlement of military personnel on subjugated lands."[54]

Kostomarov probably did not notice his inconsistency between the desirability of national tolerance in Ukraine and the undesirability of mixing populations in Russia. He also disagreed with the Slavophiles in his evaluation of the Great Russian village community, finding that communal possession of land violated that individual liberty which the South Russians held dear.[55]

At the end of his essay, Kostomarov briefly discussed the Poles, whose character was, he thought, much closer than the Great Russians' to the South Russians'. This was a rather politically involved statement because of the situation in Poland at the time his essay appeared in print: Warsaw was practically in the hands of patriotic demonstrators. However, according to Kostomarov, an important difference was that the Poles were an aristocratic nation, while the South Russians were a democratic nation. When any upper class was formed, the popular masses of South Russia soon tried to level them. Meanwhile, whenever Poles tried to talk about fraternity and equality, their Polish aristocratism would come through in their lordly attitude. Even the most liberal of them wanted to turn the South Russians into Poles and rid them of their language and nationality. In Kostomarov's view, that was why the South Russians should opt to unite with Great Russians, to whom they had so much to offer. For a reader who has read Kostomarov's essay, this last statement comes as a surprise, since it contradicts everything that precedes it.[56]

The stereotypes of Russians in Kostomarov's writings were repeated in other writers' articles. For instance, the anonymous author who wrote about nationality in religious life found the Great Russians to be a ritualistic nation whose members considered the external forms of piety as very important, whereas South Russians did not perceive that their religion was jeopardized by some borrowing of rituals from the Roman Catholic Church. The author considered it crucial to publish the Gospels in Ukrainian.[57] In Shevchenko's diary, published posthumously, the poet claimed that Great Russians did not understand nature and had an innate dislike of everything green.[58] Shevchenko wrote his diary a few years before Kostomarov's article. Indeed, many of Kostomarov's stereotypes were not products of his imagination, but had circulated among the Ukrainian intelligentsia since *The History of the Rus'* and Bodiansky's comparisons between the North and South in the 1830s. The stereotype of crude Muscovite behaviour often appeared on the pages of *Osnova*.[59] According to Kulish, Russian pilgrims travelling to a monastery would steal everything they could from the houses en route, while Ukrainian pilgrims never did such a thing. Kulish also found that Little Russians never made good lackeys because that was contrary to their nature; Russians, however, had an innate proclivity for that profession.[60] The dichotomy between Ukrainian honesty and Russian greed and theft was repeated in several articles.[61] Anton Kotenko has written about how the Russian-Ukrainian dichotomy and differences were emphasized in the travel stories in *Osnova* when depicting moving from the perceived Great Russian to Ukrainian ethnic territory. In an article, Mykhailo Levchenko defined the territory inhabited by Rusyns: Poltava, Kharkiv, Kyiv, Volyn, and Podillia gubernias, land of

Black Sea Cossacks, and parts of Chernihiv, Taurian, Katerynoslav, Lublin, and Grodno gubernias, in part of Bessarabia, Kingdom of Poland, in the Azov area, Galicia, Hungary, and Bukovyna.[62]

Last but not least, many authors who contributed to *Osnova* were concerned about the Russian cultural impact on Ukrainians. Kulish may have been the most extreme in his disapproval: he wrote that the peasants should remain without education rather than be educated in Russian and cease speaking and thinking in Ukrainian.[63] In his Russian-language short story "Drugoi chelovek" (The Other Man) Kulish describes the fate of a Ukrainian conscript who is suddenly promoted to officer rank and the status of nobleman after having acquitted himself well in a battle against the Decembrists.[64] The soldier returns to his village, having lost his nationality and become stupider than he was before, but having learned the Russian contempt for Ukrainian peasant culture. Many other authors railed against the Russian impact, which was often perceived in the increase of crime, especially stealing, greed, sexual licence, and general crudeness of behaviour. Here, the national dichotomies were intertwined with the dichotomy between the virtuous village and the immoral town.[65] Somewhat more creative was Vasyl Kulyk's correspondence from Poltava. Kulyk was a pharmacist and an active member of Poltava Hromada. He found the economic role of Russian merchants detrimental to Ukraine, since they aimed to establish a monopoly and regulate prices in order to pay as little as possible for local products and sell their own products as expensively as possible.[66] Kulyk found the presence of Jewish merchants a beneficial counterweight to the Russians, for the Jews prevented the establishment of a total Russian monopoly in trade.[67]

The same stereotypes of Russians which are evident in *Osnova* permeate also the first realist novel in Ukrainian, Anatolyi Svydnytsky's *Liuboratski: Simeina Khronika* (*Liuboratskys: A Family Chronicle*), which was completed in 1862. *Liuboratski* depicts a clerical family in Podillia in the decades before the abolition of serfdom. The author sent the novel to *Osnova* and received in response a promise about publication. However, *Liuboratski* never appeared in *Osnova*, perhaps because the journal had to cease its existence. The novel was published posthumously in Lviv, Austria-Hungary, in 1886. As a priest's son, Svydnytsky knew his topic well. Central themes are denationalization under Polish and Russian cultural pressure, administrative arbitrariness and peer bullying at church schools, and the clergy's materially precarious existence. *Liuboratski* is remarkable also for its negative stereotypes of Russians.

Because of economic reasons, priests' daughters often have to accept a husband nominated by the church hierarchy. This is how Tymokha Petropavlovskii, a Russian priest candidate, enters the Liuboratskys' life: the local bishop nominates him as the bridegroom to one of the three Liuboratsky daughters. When entering the house, Tymokha makes ten signs of cross, but shows disrespect and arrogance in his communication with the Ukrainian host family. Tymokha examines the three daughters without speaking with them, but studying their appearance "like a horse on sale."[68] He disapproves of the habit of asking for a girl's own consent for marriage: "To take into account some girl! Oh, what those mazepas have invented!"[69] After settling in the village and becoming its priest, Tymokha seizes all the property of his mother-in-law and, finally, expels her. He frequently beats his wife, Orysia, who says to her relatives: "Is there a hell worse than to live with a *katsap*!"[70] Because of Tymokha's violent behaviour and embezzlement of parish funds, the parishioners write a petition requesting his removal from the parish and appointment of any other priest, "only not a *katsap*."[71] The parishioners ask that Tymokha be sent "to *katsap* land whence he came."[72] As a result, the church hierarchy disciplines Tymokha by a penitentiary period in a monastery. However, after returning to his parish, Tymokha kills his wife. Orysia's mother states: "That is how it is with a *katsap*!"[73] Tymokha personifies most of the negative traits of Russians in Ukrainian stereotypes: superficial religiosity, egoism, urge to dominate other people, arrogance, greed, a violent character, disrespect of Ukrainians and their culture, and male disrespect of women.

There were some exceptions to the bleak perception of Ukrainian–Russian relations that was often expressed on the pages of *Osnova*. Ethnic antipathy to the Russians did not preclude *Osnova* from praising some individuals, like Pirogov for his educational policies or Leo Tolstoy for his activities in the field of popular enlightenment. Some achievements of Russian culture, like the poetry of Alexander Pushkin and Mikhail Lermontov, were also mentioned in a positive fashion. Kulish praised the confiscation of church lands by Catherine II. In Shevchenko's diary, which was written in Russian and published in *Osnova*, the poet expressed his affiliation to Russian culture, for instance, by calling Mikhail Lermontov "our great writer."[74]

Vasyl Kulyk's positive evaluation of the role of Jewish merchants was an exception in *Osnova*, which contained a number of anti-Semitic stories and articles.[75] Indeed, the Russian-language Jewish journal *Sion* criticized *Osnova* for its hostility to Jews. *Sion* also found suspect *Osnova*'s tendency to separate one part of the Russian nation from the whole. The *Osnova-Sion* controversy cannot be discussed here in all of its aspects. Both Kulish and Kostomarov wrote rather aggressive responses to *Sion*'s criticism, evaluating the role of both historical and contemporary Jews as detrimental to the South Russians. Historically, they emphasized the Jews' siding with the Polish nobility and acting as nobles' agents in their relations with peasants. In the present, they disapproved of the economic role of Jews who, according to them, as leaseholders of noble estates, innkeepers, and money lenders oppressed South Russian peasants. Furthermore, Kostomarov and Kulish blamed Jews for not identifying with the interests of the Ukrainian common people, but remaining isolated from them. In his "To the Jews" Kostomarov combined the Jewish question with the [Great] Russian question, claiming that *Sion*'s accusations of distancing South Russians from Russia were a groundless and dishonest denunciation. This was a problematic claim, since *Sion* criticized texts which were already made public in *Osnova*. The authorities were able to notice the tendency of *Osnova* to distance Ukrainians from Russians without needing any additional information from *Sion*. In its discussion of Jews in Ukraine, *Osnova* demonstrated lack of understanding concerning the social structure of local Jewry, making sweeping generalizations on the economic role of all Jews. The aggressive tone in the discussion was a political blunder, since the Jewish intelligentsia was one group among which Ukrainian nationalism might have gained adherents. However, one argument of Kulish's and Kostomarov's responses to *Sion* was sound: there was no valid reason why South Russians would not have the right to develop their own language and culture, since other nationalities in the empire were permitted to do the same.[76]

Ukrainian–Russian relations developed in the context of the Russian-Polish-Ukrainian triangle. Poland was in political crisis, and Ukrainian–Polish relations had a profound impact on Ukrainian–Russian relations. *Osnova* wrote frequently about Ukrainian–Polish relations and past conflicts. Whether fiction or non-fiction, these texts consistently followed the established national mythology: Polish oppression had caused the Ukrainian uprising and liberation struggle. There was a greater variety of opinions on the contemporary Polish question. It was discussed in Kostomarov's articles "An Answer to the Claims of the Newspaper *Czas* and the Journal *Revue contemporaine*"[77] and "The Truth to the Poles about Rus'."[78] These were responses to Polish claims about the non-Slavic ancestry of Russians and their territorial claims to Right-Bank

Ukraine. Kostomarov admitted that the Russians had mixed with Finno-Ugrians. However, he claimed that the Slavic element in them was much stronger. Kostomarov emphasized how the majority of the population in the contested Right-Bank Ukraine were South Russians, not Poles. He found that historical arguments no longer had relevance for the present political situation. Calls for separation from Russia and union with Poland would only feed into the traditional enmity of South Russians towards Poles. The Poles should begin to treat the South Russians "as a nation equal to you, respect our striving for the independent development of our national forces (*narodnykh sil*)."[79] History was moving in the direction of the union of Slavic nations, not their separation from each other. Kostomarov thus renounced an alliance with the Poles against the Russian Empire, at the same time upholding the Cyrillo-Methodian idea of pan-Slavic unity. Kostomarov's rejection of Polish strivings for independence did not mean support for Russian imperial policies. Indeed, in March 1861 he attended a memorial mass in St Petersburg for the demonstrators who had been killed by Russian troops in Warsaw. Kostomarov attended in full knowledge of the fact that the event was a political demonstration. His presence was noted in the journal *Kolokol* (*The Bell*), which was published in London by the socialist Alexander Herzen.[80]

Kostomarov's "Answer to the Claims of the Newspaper *Czas* and the Journal *Revue contemporaine*" was one of the few articles to appear in *Osnova* that faced obstruction from the censors. During discussions of the article in February 1861, the St Petersburg Censorship Committee decided to suppress the article on the grounds that it might spark dissatisfaction among the Poles at a time when Poland was already in turmoil.[81] Furthermore, the committee noted that although Kostomarov was describing history, he was in fact writing about the contemporary situation in Poland. This was evident in a passage which he had at first written in the present tense, but then corrected it by changing into the past tense. It was also not the government's practice to respond to any foreign periodicals. Kostomarov appealed the decision to the Main Administration of Censorship, arguing that an article could only be banned if it violated the rules of censorship, but not on the basis of mere political expediency. Furthermore, he pointed to the fact that in the article he had emphasized his patriotic Russian stance. In his appeal, Kostomarov wrote: "There are no ethnographic or historical grounds for establishing a separate state on the territory between the Oder, Dvina, and Dnipro."[82] In his turn, the editor Bilozersky argued that although the government did not respond to foreign periodicals, this was not valid grounds for preventing private individuals from answering them. Taking into account the Polish impact on public opinion, especially in Austria and France, Bilozersky argued that it was necessary to refute their claims that the population of Right-Bank Ukraine was Polish.[83] The Main Administration of Censorship was convinced by these arguments and decided to permit the article, provided some minor cuts were made.

Kostomarov's disapproval of Polish strivings for independence did not mean that he was hostile to the Poles. As late as November 1861 Kostomarov criticized the Moscow Slavophiles for their antipathy to the Poles.[84] In February 1861 *Osnova* published a text that criticized imperial policies towards the Poles: this was a traveller's tale from Right-Bank Ukraine, written under the pseudonym P. Neobachny ("The Incautious One") and dated 28 February 1847, at the very time of the repressions against the Cyrillo-Methodians. The author describes the ruins of a Jesuit monastery, which were now being used as billets for Russian troops. The unpleasant impression that the scene left on the author was manifest.[85]

However, in the second half of 1861 *Osnova* began to publish articles evaluating the negative role of contemporary Poles in Ukraine. The young Kyiv-based Ukrainophiles Volodymyr Antonovych and Tadei Rylsky wrote on contemporary Ukrainian–Polish relations in an anti-Polish tone. These two authors were recent defectors from the Polish to the Ukrainian movement. Rylsky analysed all the intellectual camps among Poles in Right-Bank Ukraine, and disapproved of them all as being contrary to the interests of majority of the population – Ukrainians.[86] Rylsky found that those Poles who had retained their Polish identity placed themselves in a position of "colonists who act for the benefit of the metropolis."[87] At the beginning of 1862 Antonovych presented the same opinion much more aggressively in "*Moia ispoved*" (My Confession). He identified the current national antagonism between Ukrainians and Poles with the social antagonism between peasants and nobles. Antonovych did not mention those Polish nationalists who supported efforts to improve the peasants' lot and wanted to grant some cultural rights to Ukrainians. It is noteworthy that the Polish writer Tadeusz Padalica, to whom Antonovych responded with "My Confession," wrote his article in Ukrainian, but Antonovych responded in Russian, admitting that he knew it better than Ukrainian. Antonovych found no place for a Polish minority in Ukraine: "Polish nobles who live in the South Russian region have before their own conscience only two choices: either ... to return to the nationality once deserted by their ancestors, to compensate by constant work and charity ... for all the evil that they have caused to the people, who have fed many generations of colonists, who paid for their sweat and blood with contempt, curses, insults against their religion, habits, morals and personality. Or ... they can resettle in Poland."[88]

Thus, for Antonovych national and social liberation was tantamount to creating ethnic and cultural unity. His stance was tougher against local Poles than the Russian government's policies. Antonovych's article was inspired by an unwritten agreement concluded between the Kyiv Hromada and Governor-General Ilarion Vasilchikov. (This agreement will be explored in greater detail in the next chapter.) Its essence was that the Hromada would enjoy broad liberty of action in return for its anti-Polish position. Another indication pointing to the fact that both the Ukrainophiles and the government were adopting a more anti-Polish stand was Mikhail Iuzefovich and Nikolai Ivanishev's additional answer to criticisms that were being levied against the Kyiv Archeographic Commission. This time, the authors not only rejected accusations of tendentiously selecting documents, but attacked "Jesuitism" in contemporary Right-Bank Ukraine. The authors repeated the famous popular myth about Jesuits, claiming that they taught that the goal sanctifies the means. They found that some local nobles were still under Jesuit influence and expressed their bewildered frustration: "No civilization is able to uproot that pest in South-West Rus'."[89]

From the very outset *Osnova* was critical of the Polish national movement, especially its historical mythology and territorial irredentism. However, over time the journal adopted an even more antagonistic position regarding Polish nationalism. There were also essential differences among Ukrainian activists: for example, Antonovych's position was more anti-Polish than Kostomarov's. However, the journal's pan-Slavic and broadly liberal orientation meant that *Osnova* did not fully side with the Russian government either. In a prospective, ideal settlement of the relations among the three nations, the Poles would have democratic, elected institutions and the status of a federal state. Such reforms were impossible under the conditions of Russian autocracy.

In the spring of 1862, *Osnova* began to advocate the introduction of South Russian as the language of elementary instruction. This opinion was expressed for the first time in the rubric "Current South Russian News" (*Sovremennaia Južnorusskaia Letopis*) in the March issue which actually came out in April. The May issue, which appeared in June, contained Mykola Kostomarov's programmatic article about the language of introduction,[90] and thereafter *Osnova* frequently returned to this topic. Kostomarov wrote boldly on the topic, showing no political caution. His main argument was national: education in South Russian must be provided, for otherwise people will get educated in Russian and lose their nationality (*narodnost'*). Kostomarov demanded that the government permit the development of all nationalities and not consider any nationality the ruling one. This idea might well have gotten accepted at the beginning of the nineteenth century, but in the 1860s it ran counter to the nationalizing tendency which the government was developing, especially in the western provinces. Another author, St. Poharsky, wrote about the danger of clandestinely organized elementary education in Polish.[91] However, the journal also claimed that the use of South Russian produced much better results in literacy education than the use of literary Russian.[92]

The introduction of Ukrainian as the language of instruction in elementary education was a realistic proposal, for it was coherent with the opinions which were circulating in the imperial bureaucracy. In February 1862, the head of the State Council's chancellery, State Secretary Vladimir Butkov, submitted to Alexander II a memorandum which was written by Andrei Parfenovich Zablotskii-Desiatovskii, secretary of the legislative department of the State Council, who was from Ukraine. Butkov informed Alexander that Dmitrii Bludov, who now served as the chairman of the State Council, and Dmitrii Miliutin, minister of war, supported Zablotskii-Desiatovskii's ideas. Darius Staliūnas finds it likely that the prominent Slavophile and linguist Aleksandr Fedorovich Hilferding, who served under Zablotskii-Desiatovskii, was also involved in drafting the proposals which went under his superior's name.[93] Zablotskii-Desiatovskii perceived a danger of Polish influence over the local Russians (in today's language, Ukrainians and Belarusians) and Lithuanians. To counter the Polish influence, the languages or dialects of these groups were to be promoted through education and publishing activities. He proposed setting up elementary schools with the local dialects as the languages of instruction, publishing textbooks in them, and translating New Testament into them. Furthermore, according to Zablotskii-Desiatovskii, the local dialects should be taught as separate subjects at secondary schools and universities, sermons should be preached in them, and laws translated into them. By these means, he wished to gain the support of ethnic non-Poles of the western provinces. Alexander II's reaction was positive, but non-committed. Taking into account how connected especially Kulish was in the high imperial bureaucracy, it is likely that the editors knew about Zablotskii-Desiatovskii's proposals.

Judging from the documents of the Main Administration of Censorship, *Osnova* did not face any particular problems with censorship. None of its articles in 1861 were forbidden.[94] Apart from Kostomarov's article against Polish irredentism, the only case that reached it concerned the attempted publication of the charter of the Poltava Society for the Promotion of Literacy. Since the society had only petitioned for official permission to exist, not having been officially sanctioned yet by the authorities, the publication of its charter was suppressed.[95] The decision was based on the general rule whereby the charters of any societies were permitted for publication only after the society in question had been officially sanctioned. The cutting of the news about the society in *Osnova* was a routine decision. However, in 1862 *Osnova* received its share of the general toughening of censorship regarding all publications. In this year, the government turned to somewhat more conservative and repressive policies than previously. Most likely, the change in policies was motivated by the successful enactment of the emancipation reform and concern over the radical orientation among Russian intelligentsia. Radicals now were no more needed to counterbalance the adherents of serfdom. To be sure, the editors of *Osnova* were not considered radicals, and at the end of July the chairman of the St Petersburg Censorship Committee evaluated the journal favourably.[96] In 1862, at least four articles written for *Osnova* were forbidden, as Viktor Dudko has found out. The reason for banning them was that they contained criticism of government. Two of them discussed practical implementation of land reform and criticized the authorities' corruption and the unnecessary use of force against dissatisfied peasants. These articles contained also some discussion of the national question: in one, it was claimed that books in Ukrainian were confiscated and peasants who possessed them were prosecuted; in another, it was emphasized how Polish lords and Russian soldiers worked in unison against the peasants. Two banned articles were about schools: Pavlo Chubynsky found too cumbersome and complicated the procedure through which the village communes had to pass to establish a school, while Vasyl Shevych criticized in strong words the government ban on Sunday schools.[97]

Another Ukrainophile periodical, the bilingual *Chernigovskii listok*, was authorized for publication smoothly and without any disagreements in

May 1861. In principle, *Chernigovskii listok* was a weekly newspaper, but in practice it appeared more irregularly. It was published by a secondary school teacher, the Ukrainian writer and prominent member of the Chernihiv Hromada, Leonid Hlibov. The journal's Ukrainian orientation was expressed mainly in its occasional publications in the Ukrainian language and numerous reviews of Ukrainian books. In its last issues, which appeared in 1863, *Chernigovskii listok* became more outspoken, perhaps because *Osnova* no longer existed. Panteleimon Kulish proposed that elementary schools should first teach their pupils Ukrainian rather than Russian or Church Slavonic literacy,[98] and in another context, the newspaper complained about the fact that the emancipation law had not been translated into Little Russian.[99] In his story "The Maiden's Heart" Kulish portrayed Russia as a foreign land where "many of our countrymen live, like that Marko in hell," with their language "sweetening the treacherous, windy deserts."[100] Kulish also published the "Duma about Sava Kononenko," written in the style of epic folk poetry, about the Cossack leader of Muscovite origin who had cooperated with the Poles in their attempt to create a loyal Cossack elite clearly separate from the rank and file.[101] Kulish emphasized Kononenko's elitism and alien Muscovite background as his main faults. He thus repeated the stereotype of Russians as representatives of a hierarchical society as opposed to the purported democratic tendency of Ukrainians.

Chernigovskii listok also published Ivan Lashniukov's article about Galicia. The author perceived Poles as the enemies of Galician Russians, or Rusyns, who formed the majority of the population in that region.[102] He viewed as groundless the accusation against Galicians that they intentionally spoiled their literary language by borrowing from Great Russian. According to Lashniukov, Rusyns were not able to write in Great Russian for the simple reason that they did not know it. The literary Red Russian (*Chervono-Russkii*) language was closer to Little Russian than Great Russian and comprehensible to the common people. Hlibov added an editorial comment in which he claimed that the newspaper *Slovo* (*Word*) was unpopular. *Slovo* was the organ of the Galician Russophiles, who engaged in a dispute with local Ukrainophiles about the literary language. Finally, in May 1863, *Chernigovskii listok* published Kostomarov's report on the collection of funds for popular publications in South Russian,[103] in which Kostomarov urged readers to greater generosity to help further the cause. In its very last issues in August 1863, after the promulgation of the Valuev circular, *Chernigovskii listok* criticized imperial policies, which had led to the destruction in the eighteenth century of the Hetmanate's elective principle.[104]

Incidents of Suppression of Ukrainian Publications on the Eve of the Valuev Circular

The years 1861–2 were the most favourable period for Ukrainian publishing in the Russian Empire in the entire nineteenth century. To some extent, this may have been due to instability in the Ministry of Public Enlightenment: in July 1861 Evgraf Kovalevskii was forced to resign because of the unrest and rise of political radicalism among university students. He was succeeded by Admiral Efim Vasilevich Putiatin, who resigned in turn in January 1862. During his brief tenure as minister, Putiatin was preoccupied by the serious unrest at universities. He was replaced by Aleksandr Ivanovich Golovnin. For a minister of the Russian Empire, Golovnin was liberal. His idea was to establish the rule of law in censorship: the banning of any texts should be based on standard rules rather than arbitrary decisions, and those rules should be published. However, in 1862 Golovnin came to an arrangement giving a say in censorship to the Ministry of Internal Affairs. Since this meant that the new dual power in censorship limited his decision-making powers, Golovnin was happy to hand his control over censorship altogether to the Ministry of Internal Affairs in 1863. The minister of internal affairs was Petr Valuev, who finally put an end to the period favourable to Ukrainian publishing by dispatching his notorious circular in July 1863.

Some Ukrainian publications were banned or faced obstruction from censors even in the pre-Valuev period of 1861–2. The most important of these in 1861 was the bilingual newspaper *Niva* (Ukr. *Nyva; The Field*), with which Putiatin had dealt. Since the prominent members of the Poltava Hromada, like the secondary school teacher Aleksandr (Oleksandr) Stronin and director of the local telegraph Viktor Loboda, knew Governor Volkov's attitude to them, they chose as editor "the wife of a titular councillor," Nadezhda Zlygosteva. It was Zlygosteva who in the summer of 1861 applied to the Kyiv Censorship Committee for permission to publish *Niva*. Like *Chernigovskii listok*, *Niva* was supposed to include not only news but also a literary section, as well as articles on economics, the natural sciences, and medicine. The committee did not find anything objectionable and forwarded the petition to Governor Volkov, asking for his opinion. Volkov responded with an evaluation in which he portrayed Zlygosteva as too young, too inexperienced, and insufficiently educated to be launching a newspaper. Volkov suspected that behind the plan were other individuals who had reason not to publish their names. Furthermore, Volkov claimed that the work of censoring *Niva* in Kyiv would take such a long time that the newspaper would not be able to publish fresh news. The governor also suspected that the Kyiv censors might permit anti-government texts in *Niva* because of their lack of local expertise. Volkov was particularly concerned that *Niva*'s program included the publication of local administrative decisions, agricultural settlements between former serfs and their masters, and the details of court cases. Somewhat hypocritically, he stated that he would accept *Niva* if the chairman of the committee, Baron Aleksandr Nicolay, personally guaranteed that the newspaper would not adopt a subversive orientation. Nicolay forwarded the petition to the Main Administration of Censorship, stating that he would not provide such a guarantee, and permission was denied. Zlygosteva was not informed of the reasons for the final decision. This case demonstrates the importance of the role of local authorities: the only essential difference between the suppressed *Niva* and permitted *Chernigovskii listok* was the hostile attitude of the local governor to the former.[105]

In Kyiv at least three texts relating to Ukrainian activities were banned in 1862: Kalynyk Sheikovsky's Russian-language manuscript, *A Few Words about the South Russian Nation and Especially about Its Language*, M.A. Mandryk's *Hetman Petro Doroshenko: 1665–1676*, and Paulin Święcicki's poem *In Memory of Taras Shevchenko*, which was written in Ukrainian.[106] The censor Lazov, backed by the Kyiv Censorship Committee, banned Sheikovsky's work explicitly on the grounds that he found its Ukrainophile ideas and anti-Russian orientation unacceptable: "In the manuscript, only the last ten pages contain a discussion of the orthography of the South Russian language. All the rest consists of the author's opinions of the great importance and mission of the South Russian nation and of its oppressed situation between Rus' and Poland or, as the author expresses himself, between Scylla and Charybdis. The whole manuscript is full of antipathy to Russia, and it is written in the spirit of the exclusive Little Russian tendency. That is why I found that it must be forbidden."[107]

Lazov adjudged the manuscript on Doroshenko as one written by an adherent of Doroshenko's anti-Russian ideas: "The work may be seen as a protest against Russian rule in Little Russia."[108] The censor also found unacceptable the author's opinion that Russia, by signing the

Truce of Andrusovo with Poland in 1667, had nullified the previous Treaty of Pereiaslav and thus forfeited its legal right to rule over Little Russia. The author of *In Memory of Taras Shevchenko*, Paulin Święcicki, belonged to the group of Polish Ukrainophile students at the local university. Lazov disapproved of the complaints about Ukraine's present situation, which were expressed in Święcicki's poem, the expectation of improvements in that situation, and the excessive praise lavished on Shevchenko.

The minor writer Stepan Karpenko published his four-volume collected works in Russian, Polish, and Ukrainian. Although the manuscripts had all but been authorized for publication, the Kyiv censor O. Lebedev noticed, after the printing, several impermissible passages in a Ukrainian-language short story entitled "Devil Devylovych Asmodei and the Warsaw Student Ludwik Karpovicz Janicki." The story was suppressed because it contained light-hearted sarcasm directed against social hierarchy. For instance, the author disapproved of all hereditary privileges and described a service hierarchy that existed among the devils in hell, which resembled rather closely several imperial offices and positions.[109] The censors also prevented Viktor Loboda's attempt to respond to a statement published in *L'indépendence Belge* that there was a group in Poltava whose goal was the separation of Little Russia from Russia. This was a reference to the Poltava Hromada, a Ukrainian group. Loboda wanted to refute this information in a letter to *Moskovskie vedomosti* (*Moscow News*), but the Moscow Censorship Committee suppressed it.[110] Another member of the Poltava Hromada, Oleksandr Konysky, failed the censorship test with his article criticizing village schools, in which he protested against the introduction of the Russian language into Little Russia.[111]

That Petr Valuev's attitude to Ukrainian nationalism was more repressive than Golovnin's became evident even before the administrative transfer of censorship from the Ministry of Public Enlightenment to the Ministry of Internal Affairs. In 1862 a secondary school teacher named Fedir Petropavlovsky, who was a member of the Kharkiv Hromada, applied to the local superintendent Dmitrii Levshin for permission to publish *Ukrainskii vestnik* (*Ukrainian Messenger*).[112] The Ukrainian orientation of this newspaper was manifest in its title and bilingual character, as well as in the fact that it promised to publish ethnographic, historical, and economic articles dealing with South Russia. Like *Chernigovskii listok* and *Niva*, the newspaper also planned to publish prose (fiction) and poetry. Levshin supported the granting of permission and forwarded the paperwork to Golovnin. The minister requested opinions from both Valuev and Dolgorukov. The chief of gendarmes had nothing against *Ukrainskii vestnik*, but Valuev denied his permission. According to the minister of internal affairs, prior to the enactment of the new censorship rules it was undesirable to launch new periodicals "without special reasons, especially in the Little Russian and Western Provinces of the empire."[113] "The Western Provinces" was a term that was used in government circles for the territories that, prior to the partitions of the Polish-Lithuanian Commonwealth, had belonged to it. The western provinces included Right-Bank Ukraine. Valuev's conceptual association of all of Ukraine up to Kharkiv with the western provinces as a potentially unstable area was radical and ominous, especially considering the fact that Kharkiv had never belonged to Poland.

Valuev's critical attitude to Ukrainian nationalism was also apparent in the fact that he kept a close eye on *Osnova*. In August 1862 Golovnin received from Valuev's deputy a letter written on behalf of his superior.[114] The Minister of Internal Affairs had voiced his disapproval of two articles that appeared in *Osnova*: Kostomarov's "Christianity and Serfdom"[115] and G. Kokhovsky's "From the People's Words."[116] Valuev and his deputy declared that the censors should not have authorized these articles for publication. In their estimation, Kostomarov's religious opinions, which emphasized liberty rather than submission to God and acceptance of one's fate, were contrary to the doctrine of the Orthodox Church and impermissible in the press. Furthermore, the Ministry of Internal Affairs found some of the Little Russian proverbs published by Kokhovsky extremely contemptuous of Great Russians, and the popular opinions about the nobility quoted by the author were harmful enough to instigate enmity among social ranks. The text on the nobility was a reproduction of a discussion between two peasant women, one of whom wished that God would take all the lords to himself, but the other rejected the idea on the grounds that even the lords are part of God's creation and they want to live. Most of the proverbs and anecdotes about Ukrainian-Russian encounters were indeed without enmity, but three among them were somewhat negative: one emphasized the Russian's formal religious attitude – no matter how hard he prays and fasts, he will not comprehend God; another expressed the stereotype of Russians as quarrelsome people; and the third reported how lords disapproved when a peasant tried to discuss matters with them in Ukrainian.

In response to Valuev's accusations, the censor Stepan Lebedev, who had authorized all the issues of *Osnova*, explained that in fact he had submitted Kostomarov's article to the Holy Synod, which had authorized its publication. With regard to the proverbs and anecdotes about Great Russians, Lebedev found that these were normal jokes told by inhabitants of one region about the inhabitants of another. Golovnin did not take any measures and did not respond to the letter from the Ministry of Internal Affairs.[117]

The new findings in this chapter include analysis of Ukrainian stereotypes of Russians in *Osnova* and other Ukrainian publications in the years 1860–2. This chapter also contains the first systematic study of censorship policies regarding Ukrainian publications practised in those years. Several of the censorship cases discussed here, like those of the periodicals *Golos, Niva,* and *Ukrainskii Vestnik,* as well as the three books banned in Kyiv in 1862, are not mentioned in Miller's *The Ukrainian Question.* Although the censorship policies were lenient with regard to Ukrainian publications in the early 1860s, the Valuev circular of July 1863 did not appear out of the blue. Reluctance to permit expressions of Ukrainian nationalism as well as hostility to popular literature in the Ukrainian language were apparent in the censors' correspondence and decisions years before the Polish insurrection of 1863. Indeed, they cannot be explained merely as temporary measures triggered by that insurrection. Some Russian officials perceived the Ukrainian national movement as hostile to the empire. They were right: many legal and censored Ukrainian publications contained ideas that would have undermined the Russian Empire in the long run. Furthermore, there was a clandestine side to the Ukrainian movement.

Chapter Five

Ukrainian Clandestine Activities and Government Reaction, 1856–64

Many Ukrainian political activities took place in relatively small circles of the intelligentsia. Among the ideas expressed in them was the separation of Ukraine from the Russian Empire. Although these ideas were rarely disseminated among the wider public, they circulated widely within the national movement. The adherents of political radicalism formed an important part of the whole Ukrainian movement. However, the social radicalism of the Kyiv Hromada did not preclude tactical short-term cooperation with the imperial government.

In the latter half of the 1850s the Third Section received information about potential Ukrainian subversion through two intercepted letters. In October 1858 Kulish wrote to his Russian Slavophile friend Sergei Aksakov, predicting Ukraine's separation from Russia after his lifetime. The political police appreciated the importance of the letter, the contents of which were duly forwarded to Alexander II.[1] In December 1859 the Third Section intercepted another letter, this one from Silvestr Gogotskii to Priest Vasyl Hrechulevych in St Petersburg, the son of the religious writer Hrechulevych. The younger Hrechulevych had sent Gogotskii his Ukrainian primer in manuscript and asked for comments. In his answer, Gogotskii strongly disapproved of the primer because it promoted Ukraine's cultural separation from Russia. He argued against the idea of Ukrainian independence, since Ukraine could withstand Polish claims only with Russia's aid. The letter gives the impression of Gogotskii as an imperial loyalist and places doubt on Hrechulevych's loyalty. The Third Section tried to purchase the primer in order to compare its contents with Gogotskii's letter, but learned that it was unpublished.[2] Together, these two letters show that the political police were interested in and aware of Ukrainian nationalism at the end of the 1850s. However, they possessed little information about it and did not undertake much effort to gain more. This situation began to change in 1860–1.

Mykola Kostomarov published an important article on the Ukrainian question in Alexander Herzen's London newspaper *Kolokol*, which was banned in Russia. In January 1860 *Kolokol* published it anonymously under the title "Ukraine."[3] As he did later in *Osnova*, Kostomarov argued against Polish and Russian claims to Ukraine and for the existence of the Ukrainian nation. However, he did not demand independence, predicting instead the formation of a pan-Slavic federation. Such a federation was possible even under the leadership of the Russian emperor, "if only the emperor becomes the lord of free nations instead of Tatar-German Muscovy, which is swallowing everything."[4] Kostomarov presented Ukrainian history in accordance with the Cyrillo-Methodian perception of a nation inclined to liberty, democracy, and tolerance, but victimized by its neighbours. He called the partition of Ukraine between Poland and Russia in 1667–86 "a satanic act." Kostomarov denied that the Society of St Cyril and St Methodius had ever existed, claiming that it was invented in the Third Section. The historian also stated, incorrectly, that all Little Russian literature had been forbidden in 1847–55. Both of these erroneous statements have persisted to this day. However, according to Kostomarov, the beginning of Alexander II's reign marked a positive change. He thanked the emperor for his intention to abolish serfdom and then proceeded to present the Ukrainian demands in the present situation: (1) the abolition of estate privileges; (2) permission to work for the development of the Ukrainian language; and (3) the introduction of elementary education with Ukrainian as the language of instruction. Although Kostomarov found compromise with the government both possible and desirable, his construction of the Ukrainian national character undermined the possibility of such compromise. Indeed, he put forward some of the key values of the French revolution as being the essential traits of the Ukrainian national character. It was certainly a utopian idea that the empire at this time could have introduced the peasants' full legal equality with noblemen, to say nothing about the pan-Slavic union of free nations. Nevertheless, Kostomarov's article also made it clear that he abstained from revolutionary undertakings.

For some time after the arrest of the members of the socialist Petrashevskii group in 1849, Russia did not have any organized revolutionary groups. After this hiatus, the students of Kharkiv University formed the first Russian clandestine organization in 1856. The society aimed at revolution throughout the Russian Empire, the establishment of a democratic republic, and the abolition of all estate privileges. However, knowing their weakness, the members did not undertake any practical preparations for an uprising, but distributed handwritten proclamations and illegal literature. They corresponded with Herzen and provided local information for his publications. Although the conspiracy ostensibly disbanded in 1858, its members remained active, maintaining contact with each other even after the disbandment. In 1859 many of its former members moved to Kyiv and became active at St Vladimir's University. With superintendent Nikolai Pirogov's permission, they established literary circles and launched the first free Sunday school, where common people were offered an elementary education. A couple of Kyiv-based Sunday schools, including two started by the members of the clandestine society, used Ukrainian as the language of instruction. The Sunday school movement soon spread throughout the empire. Originally, the members of the Kharkiv-Kyiv group wanted to cooperate with Polish students, but the latter preferred to act on their own. The conspiracy was uncovered and its members were arrested in February 1860. In all, 22 people were involved, of whom 15 were found guilty. Five received the severest form of punishment: deportation to distant parts of European Russia. Although the strength of this group did not match its lofty task, the Kharkiv-Kyiv group should not be underestimated: the group's activities had a widespread impact on Russian society through the Sunday school movement, and later some of its members were active in the first Land and Liberty, an all-Russian revolutionary organization which was active in 1862–4.[5]

What was the Ukrainian aspect of the Kharkiv-Kyiv revolutionary group? Originally, some members supported an exclusively Ukrainian national orientation. One of the members, Petro Zavadsky, revealed under interrogation that it was from Shevchenko's works that he had gotten the idea that the Little Russian people suffered because of the Russians. At the time, Zavadsky perceived not only the government but Russians in general as enemies of Little Russia. However, during his studies in Kharkiv he had come across banned Russian literature and understood that there were also Russians who did not like their government. Instead of improving only the lot of Ukrainians, Zavadsky began to dream about the liberation of all Russia from the monarchy. However, the authorities also uncovered an incident that showed that the Ukrainian orientation persisted in the society: in December 1859 Petro Iefymenko had raised a toast to the independence of Little

Russia.[6] During the investigation Mytrofan Levchenko explained that the ambiguous references to political work in his papers referred to the opposition against Polonization of Little Russians in Right-Bank Ukraine. He also confessed that he had planned to travel to London and work with Herzen. Levchenko perceived the education of the common people as work that undermined the existing political order.[7] The information about Levchenko's and Zavadsky's testimonies was forwarded to Alexander II. During the investigation the authorities made note of the fact that Oleksandr Tyshchynsky owned a considerable number of Ukrainian books, although all of them were permitted by the censors.[8] Furthermore, the documents of the investigation reveal that the members used Ukrainian both in their private correspondence and their proclamations. Mytrofan Muravsky's proclamation *Ukrainskomu narodu* (*To the Ukrainians*) explained how the tsar was responsible for Russia's defeat in the Crimean War. Foreigners had a better leadership, while the present, weak Russian leaders had all been appointed by the tsar. It was necessary to dethrone the tsar and replace him with a parliament consisting of fifty members, one from each province, and the peasants should be liberated from serfdom.[9] Found among Tyshchynsky's papers was another proclamation, entitled *Golos iz sela* (*Voice from the Countryside*), which incited Little Russians against the emperor and the government. The literary use of Ukrainian in the private sphere, political agitation, and education far surpassed the conventional status of the language at that time. Furthermore, the disseminated proclamations included the idea of the Russian dynasty as alien, presumably to Ukrainians and Russians alike: the Romanovs were called the "successors of Batu" and the "Finnish dynasty, "the word for "Finnish" rendered by the derogatory word *chukhonskii*.[10] At least three members of this group participated in the Ukrainian movement in a later period: Petro Iefymenko, Oleksandr Tyshchynsky, and Veniamin Portugalov.[11]

In the latter half of the 1850s and early 1860s Ukrainian Hromada groups were formed in St Petersburg, Moscow, Kyiv, Poltava, Chernihiv, and Kharkiv. As unregistered societies, they were technically illegal but hardly genuinely secret. At least in St Petersburg, Kyiv, and Poltava these Ukrainian groups were not merely informal gatherings but more or less organized groups. No formal statutes of any of these groups are extant, and their members denied that any existed. This denial must be taken with a grain of salt, considering the severe penalties in criminal law that were meted out to members of secret societies. The Moscow-based Hromada had a leading body called the *rada* (council), which made decisions about the use of funds. The term *kurin*, borrowed from the Zaporozhian Cossack host, was used in Moscow and Chernihiv, and may have denoted an organizational unit.[12] Hromada groups became involved in Ukrainian publishing and Sunday school activities, and all of them sent correspondence to *Osnova*.

The St Petersburg Hromada emerged in 1858. Among its leading figures were the former Cyrillo-Methodians Kostomarov, Kulish, and Bilozersky. The group launched the journal *Osnova*, but held its meetings distinct from the journal's organization. In 1861 the Hromada organized Shevchenko's first funeral, in St Petersburg, and the later transfer of the poet's remains for a second funeral, which took place in Kaniv. The group also collected and administered funds for Ukrainian publications aimed at the common people. Since fundraising calls were published in journals and newspapers, this was not a clandestine action. The St Petersburg Hromada counted among its members a senator and member of the State Council, through whom it was able to lobby the government.[13]

The Kyiv Hromada and Its Tactical Alliance with Governor-General Vasilchikov

The Kyiv Hromada was the most important of the Ukrainian groups that existed in Ukraine. It was most likely established in 1860, but it had a prehistory that stretched back several years. In its early period the Kyiv Hromada was essentially a student organization, formed through the amalgamation of a group of Polish Ukrainophile students from the Right Bank with another student group, which included students from the Left Bank. The Polish Ukrainophile group began to take shape in 1857 in the context of the clandestine Polish student union at St Vladimir's University in Kyiv. Poles constituted roughly half of the university's student body. Within the Polish student union Ukrainophiles dominated the regional organization of Kyiv province. When questioned about its orientation, the Kyiv provincial organization of Polish students defined its policy in the following words: "[They] do not break with Polishness, but consider themselves citizens of the Rus' lands, and hold the defence of the interests of Rus' as the most important cause; the second is Poland, with which they join in a federation as freemen with freemen, equals with equals."[14]

The Polish Ukrainophile students promoted the interests of Ukraine within a prospected independent Poland restored to its pre-partition borders before 1772. Many of them were involved in the clandestine Polish independence movement. In 1857 a conspiracy called the "Triple Union" (*Związek Trójnicki*) emerged within the student union.[15] The actual meaning of the name is unclear; most probably it derived from the organizational structure, which was based on three-person cells, but it may have also denoted the three provinces of Right-Bank Ukraine. Antonovych belonged to the first triad. Soon the Triple Union oversaw all Polish student activities in Kyiv and established relations with other groups involved in the national conspiracy.

The combination of Ukrainian with Polish national identity runs counter to the tenets of present-day Ukrainian nationalism. In the 1850s, however, it was not a surprising choice for young, educated Right-Bank nobles with democratic and populist leanings. Within the Polish national movement, two different concepts of Polish nationality coexisted.[16] One of them was based on ethnicity and included the idea of either Roman Catholicism or the use of the Polish language as a necessary condition of Polish national identity. However, there also existed a Polish nationality concept based on the pre-partition, Polish-Lithuanian Commonwealth. According to this perception, all the inhabitants of Poland-Lithuania within its pre-partition borders were Poles. Yet, this state concept of nationality also meant that the Polish nation included Orthodox Ukrainian speakers. Indeed, the inhabitants of the Right Bank could choose from among three different national identities: Polish, Ukrainian, and all-Russian.

Although in the Ukrainian national movement the Polish insurgents of 1863 were seen as representatives of nobiliary interests, this view is biased. All Polish student activists opposed serfdom, and most of them supported land reform. Non-socialist, radical, social egalitarianism was quite widespread among Polish student activists, some of whom did not hesitate to express their antipathy to the nobility. However, for many students land reform was only a tactical consideration: the insurgents sought to proclaim a land reform in order to win peasant support for the national struggle.[17] Polish Ukrainophiles took their goals a step further in seeking to elevate the status of the Ukrainian language, gain federal status for Ukraine, and abolish all estate privileges. The group included both Roman Catholics and Orthodox. On their holidays they travelled around the countryside wearing peasant dress in order to get acquainted with the life of the people. They read Shevchenko's poetry to the peasants.[18] The uncontested leader of this group and of the Kyiv regional organization of the student union was Volodymyr Antonovych.

His ideological outlook was shaped mainly by the literature of the French enlightenment, such as that of Montesquieu, Rousseau, and Voltaire.[19] However, Antonovych's Polish influences included Michał Czajkowski's romantic works, which depicted the Cossack past in an idyllic way as part of Polish history, thereby bypassing Polish-Ukrainian conflicts. Volodymyr Miiakovsky disputed Antonovych's involvement in Polish insurgent organizations before his full conversion to an exclusively Ukrainian identity, pointing to the unreliable character of testimonies of Polish insurgents, who were pressured by the Russian authorities while they were interrogated.[20] However, several Polish memoirists confirm the fact that Antonovych indeed belonged to the leading triad of the Triple Union. There are two memoirs that confirm how Antonovych fulfilled his obligations as a Polish conspirator as late as 1860. Through Antonovych, students in Moscow and St Petersburg established contacts with Polish émigrés in Italy, who were organizing military training there.[21] Apart from Antonovych, many other Kyivan Ukrainophiles were spurred to an interest in Ukraine by the writings of the Polish-Ukrainian literary school. The Ukrainophile group had its roots in both the previous Ukrainian cultural movement in Left-Bank Ukraine and the Polish-Ukrainian romantics of the Right Bank. Some of its Polish adherents were even influenced by Herzen's pan-Slavic ideas.[22]

In 1860 the prevalence of the ethnic concept of Polishness among Polish patriots began making Polish Ukrainophiles uneasy. In 1860 the Polish student union proposed that a delegation be sent to St Petersburg to petition for the introduction of Polish as the language of instruction at the university. This provocative plan received wide support, but Antonovych suggested that the case be negotiated with the Ukrainians. It turned out that the Ukrainian students were ready to petition only for the establishment of chairs for the Polish and Ukrainian languages. Superintendent Pirogov may well have inspired this position, for it was in accord with his policy, at least concerning the Polish chair. The Poles deemed such a moderate action useless and decided to send their original delegation and petition regardless of the Ukrainians. At this point Antonovych threatened the Poles with a counter-delegation and counter-petition. As a result, the petition plans were dropped.[23]

In March 1861 Governor-General Vasilchikov sent a Polish student from Kyiv back to his parents for having behaved with disrespect while the imperial decree about the abolition of serfdom was being read out in public. However, after student meetings and protests, Vasilchikov cancelled his decision. During those meetings, the student body for the first time split into parties inspired by national differences: Poles, Russians, and Ukrainians. The Russians and Ukrainians demanded the organization of an all-university student union, in which Russians and Ukrainians would form three sub-unions and Poles two. Decisions would be made by the sub-unions, each of which would have one vote. Naturally, the Poles did not accept this proposal, which would have given the Russians and Ukrainians control of the student union, despite the fact that the Poles formed the majority of the students. Finally, the Russians (including the Ukrainians) and Poles handed two separate petitions to Pirogov, who forwarded them to Vasilchikov. The Russian petition represented ninety-two students. The Polish students asked the governor-general for protection from anti-Polish persecution that was being waged by the authorities. The Russian petition asked in much politer terms that investigation of student transgressions be conducted in accordance with existing regulations, with the participation of the university's representative. Vasilchikov gave a verbal response to both petitions, consented to the Russian demand, and refrained from punishing anyone. In the past, he had opposed recognition of any student societies, but now he sought to exploit the rift between the nationalities by using the Russians as a counterforce against the Poles.[24]

The rift between the Polish national movement and Antonovych took place most likely in the spring of 1861, and it was accelerated by the antipathy of the local Polish nobility, the events at the university, and the actions of the tsarist authorities. The nobility tended to disapprove of the Ukrainian tendencies of young Kyivans. In the winter of 1860 Antonovych had to explain his position to an informal meeting of Polish nobility. He argued for the compatibility of Ukrainian ideas with the all-Polish identity, but the antipathy did not disappear.[25] An indication of the mood among the nobility was the decision handed down by the Podillian provincial assembly of nobility in September 1862: it demanded from Alexander II the incorporation of all the western provinces of the Russian Empire into the Kingdom of Poland. Referring to the 1569 Union of Lublin, the nobles declared: "Throughout the centuries, the enlightenment and public life [of Rus'] have had an exclusively Polish character." To be sure, they did not fail to mention that the free development of the Ukrainian nationality was also one of their aims.[26]

In the first months of 1861 Antonovych faced a situation in which he had to make a definite choice between the Polish and Ukrainian nationalities. In January the continuous denunciations by the Polish nobility led to an investigation of Antonovych and Tadei Rylsky (Tadeusz Rylski). Rylsky was reported to have mixed socially with peasants with the aim of inciting them against the lords, and recounted stories about Cossack times and Shevchenko.[27] Although the denunciations against Antonovych were much less detailed, they indicated his leading role in the group. Antonovych and Rylsky were not arrested, but their lodgings were searched. Apart from a fragment of Rylsky's manuscript on Cossack history, some illegal literature, most notably excerpts from *Kolokol* and General Ludwik Mierosławski's military manual for Polish insurgents, were found.[28]

While Rylsky gave evasive answers when he was interrogated,[29] Antonovych laid out his principles in a frank manner. In order to prove his loyalty to the empire, he referred to widespread antipathy among the nobility. He explained that the slanderous denunciations stemmed from Polish nobles' resentment of his position that the Right Bank of the Dnipro was not Polish but South Russian territory, since the majority of the population was South Russian.[30] The final outcome of the investigation may be defined as a truce between the authorities and the Hromada.[31] Although the investigating commission did not fully trust Antonovych, it viewed his and his adherents' disagreement with the Polish nobility about the national character of Right-Bank Ukraine in a positive light, making practical proposals of cooperation between the government and Ukrainian activists:

> In Antonovych's answers, the disagreement that has emerged between some Polish students and local Polish lords concerning the South Russian character of this region deserves special attention and the necessity to recognize that fact without vain resistance against it … According to Antonovych, the students expected a press discussion as a result of the controversy. It is evident from his answers that he, together with Rylsky, is going to work on the [historical] materials that they have collected and to publish them … If the young scholars honestly have taken up objective research on the history of the South Russian region and, according to their own statement, need documentary materials, then it would be useful for them to join their work with that of the archeographic commission, since the commission has so many documents. They should seek reliable assistance in the commission's material resources, which are the best ones in the region. Their literary undertakings would be part of the commission's work. However, this would not in the least violate their right to send their articles to be printed in any publication of their own choice.[32]

It is likely that in return for such favourable treatment, Antonovych had to promise to abstain from subversive action and to follow an anti-Polish orientation. If Antonovych gave the investigators any information about the Polish student union and the Triple Union, it was not recorded in the official documents, and no action against their leading activists was taken. It is possible that the authorities did not demand such information from him, since that would have jeopardized the whole arrangement. For that same reason, no proper investigation of Antonovych's previous role in Polish organizations was undertaken, although the authorities could hardly have had any doubts about his involvement.

In the documents of the investigation there is no mention of the Hromada as an organization or any agreement with it, for such formal recognition would have run counter to the principles of the imperial administration. However, Antonovych soon wrote and published several anti-Polish texts, the most remarkable of which was *My Confession*, which was discussed in the previous chapter. In 1863 he entered the service of the Kyiv Archeographic Commission, as the investigators had proposed. Furthermore, the hypothesis of the existence of a truce between Ukrainian activists and the imperial authorities is corroborated by Governor-General Vasilchikov's actions. Immediately after receiving the final report of the investigating commission on Rylsky and Antonovych, Vasilchikov repealed the order to exile Rylsky to Kazan, even though it had already been confirmed by Alexander II. He wrote about this to Chief of Gendarmes Vasilii Dolgorukov on 31 March, the very day that Pirogov sent him the two student petitions. Vasilchikov changed his mind after receiving information from Pirogov to the effect that "Tadei is now approaching Russian students and by his behaviour he demonstrates sympathy toward them."[33] Alexander II accepted Vasilchikov's handling of the matter. In the following months Vasilchikov continued to show his benevolent attitude to Ukrainians. In May 1861 a certain Borys Poznansky was arrested in the village of Dudary in Kyiv province. He was deemed suspect mainly because he had abandoned his studies, taken up the position of village scribe, and adopted the peasant lifestyle. After the investigation revealed that Poznansky was a Ukrainian activist without uncovering any crimes, Vasilchikov instructed the local police to be more cautious and not arrest anyone without sufficient evidence of guilt.[34] He then offered Poznansky a position in the provincial administration, and was rather upset when his offer was declined. In October 1861 the chief of police in Radomyshl district was alarmed by the fact that some Ukrainian books, including Kulish's *Hramatka*, had been sent to the local priest. After the police confiscated the books, Vasilchikov ordered the local authorities to return them to the priest, since they were permitted by censorship.[35] In this instance, the governor-general ignored the local ban on *Hramatka*, which he himself had initiated in 1858. In February 1862 Kost Mykhalchuk came to the attention of the authorities because of his intensive distribution of Ukrainian books among the peasantry in the Volyn region. The local police and governor of Volyn considered his activities harmful, confiscated the books, and interrogated Mykhalchuk.[36] However, Vasilchikov ordered the local authorities to return the books, none of which were banned, to Mykhalchuk.[37]

Perhaps the most revealing is Vasilchikov's position on the publication of *Comment from Kyiv*, a collectively written article by twenty-one members of the Hromada, which was published in the newspaper *Sovremennaia letopis Russkogo vestnika* (*Contemporary Chronicle of the Russian Messenger*) in December 1862.[38] The article outlined the short-term policy of the Hromada, the focus on popular enlightenment, without mentioning the organization itself. The signatories claimed that they did not emphasize solidarity with any community larger than the village, thus defending themselves against accusations of Ukrainian national agitation. Aleksandr Golovnin queried Vasilchikov's opinion about whether permission should be granted for publication. Responding with a lengthy letter, Vasilchikov declared that there were no facts at hand proving the political unreliability of Antonovych and his group.[39] In Vasilchikov's view, the very existence of a society not sanctioned by the authorities spoke against permitting the article. However, permitting it would be useful because a public discussion would ensue, which would help the authorities to learn the exact opinions of the group. Furthermore, the opportunity to publicize their views would also prevent Ukrainians from becoming embroiled in subversive actions. Golovnin interpreted Vasilchikov's opinion as favourable enough to facilitate the permission of the publication. Vasilchikov's actions reveal that he had changed his earlier attitude and now considered the Ukrainian movement as a useful tactical ally in the struggle against the Polish independence movement.

At first, activists belonging to the Polish student union were among the members of the Hromada. The final break between the Hromada and the Poles took place in the fall of 1861, when the Ukrainian organization demanded that its members refrain from membership in any other national student union. According to Antonovych, fifteen members of the Polish student union opted to stay in the Hromada. Leon Syroczyński, who remained a Polish Ukrainophile, claimed that there were only six defectors. However, quite a few Polish Ukrainophiles showed their loyalty to the Polish movement and left the Hromada. The Polish Ukrainophile orientation remained fairly strong within the Triple Union even after its complete break with the Hromada.[40]

Pirogov promoted the establishment of the Hromada by pointing out to some Left-Bank students the necessity of a separate Ukrainian organization that would counter Polish dominance. By February and March 1861 the Hromada had begun to act as an independent group, siding with the Russians against the Poles. The most noteworthy activities of the early Hromada were in the spheres of student politics and popular enlightenment. Its members were active in the Sunday school movement and published elementary textbooks in Ukrainian. Ukrainian–Russian relations were not discussed in them.[41]

In the fall of 1861 massive student demonstrations shook most universities in Russia. The demonstrations were generally directed against the new repressive rules concerning students, like the ban on all meetings and the dramatic reduction in the number of students exempted from tuition fees. The demonstrations in Kyiv, however, had a Polish national character. Polish domination evoked opposition in other students. On 12 October a general meeting of all Russian and Ukrainian students was held. In violation of the new university rules and the emperor's explicit order sent by telegram, the new superintendent, Baron Aleksandr Nicolay (Nikolai), permitted the meeting to take place. A resolution was passed stating: "We, the signatories, delegated by 162 Little Russian and Russian students of Kyiv University, have the honour to inform Your Excellency [Nicolay] that we do not support the outbursts of the Polish students, which are occurring in the wrong place and are counter to the needs of the university and the South Russian region. We will not participate in them and categorically protest against them because all those outbursts express … a strong attempt to impose an alien nationality on a completely non-Polish region."[42] The decision was presented to the superintendent by five elected delegates. All the deputies were from Ukraine, three of them from the Right Bank. Antonovych was among the signatories, and on the whole the decision reflected the Hromada's position. Plans were afoot to publish it in a newspaper. Alexander II forbade this, but allowed it to be posted on a wall at the university.[43]

Despite the anti-Polish action of the Kyiv Hromada, its political orientation also contained aspects that were undesirable from the government's viewpoint. In October 1861 a student named Ievhen Mossakovsky was arrested at the Kyiv Military School. The son of a priest from Volyn and now an impoverished orphan, Mossakovsky financed his university studies by teaching at the school. He was accused of engaging his students in subversive discussions outside classes and giving them Herzen's works and other forbidden publications to read. These included some anonymous revolutionary poetry and Vissarion Belinsky's famous letter to Gogol, in which the Russian critic chastised Gogol for getting involved in otherworldly religion instead of seeking a remedy to Russia's social ills. However, there was also a Ukrainian angle to Mossakovsky's case. The materials that he had given to his students included Kostomarov's letter published in *Kolokol* and the (permitted) works of Kvitka-Osnovianenko. The forbidden literature found in Mossakovsky's possession included handwritten copies of Shevchenko's unpublished works, among them "The Dream," which was discussed in chapter 2. According to one of his students, Mossakovsky claimed that he had written an article on whether Little Russia could be independent. He had also criticized the Poles for their aim to unite Ukraine with an independent Poland. Mossakovsky was also a Sunday school volunteer. The authorities found an article that he had written about these schools. Although it did not contain any forbidden ideas, the author emphasized the difference between the pupils of different nationalities: Little Russians, Great Russians, and Poles. Indeed, in Mossakovsky's case, Russian egalitarian radicalism was one of the building blocks of the mental outlook of a Ukrainian activist. This did not shake Vasilchikov's commitment to his agreement with the Hromada: in the information that he sent to the Third Section, the governor-general omitted all the Ukrainian specifics of the case and even struck Shevchenko off the list of forbidden texts. Mossakovsky received a lenient punishment: deportation to Kharkiv, where he was permitted to complete his studies.[44]

The case of the lieutenant-colonel and landowning nobleman Andrii Krasovsky, who was sentenced for his clumsy attempt to conduct agitation among enlisted men, merits attention for three reasons: first, it indicates that some Hromada members sympathized with the Polish national movement; second, it provided the government with reliable information about the ideas that circulated among the members of the Kyiv Hromada, but were not disseminated publicly; and third, the case put in motion a process that led to the Valuev circular and other significant repressions against the Ukrainian movement. In September 1861 Krasovsky attended a memorial mass for the Polish historian and democratic émigré politician Joachim Lelewel, which was arranged by the Polish student union. During his subsequent interrogation Krasovsky answered a question about the Polish patriotic texts that had been found in his possession by stating that he had kept the papers as a memento of that great day.[45] In April 1862 the authorities issued a warning to Krasovsky and then placed him under secret police surveillance after he was seen wearing "Little Russian garb" and holding discussions with peasants in the small town of Korsun near Kyiv.[46] On 17 June 1862 Krasovsky was caught distributing copies of a handwritten proclamation among soldiers in Kyiv, urging them to refuse to suppress the peasant disturbances in nearby locales. According to the proclamation, the soldiers were being sent against "their own people, Russians,"[47] to shoot and beat the peasants to benefit the bureaucrats and landowners who were robbing the people. Any order to go against the peasants would be wicked, and Krasovsky compared such a task to that of the soldiers who had crucified Christ. When he was throwing the proclamation into the barracks, he was wearing a "Little Russian costume."[48]

After being severely wounded in the Crimean War, Krasovsky served in the army only nominally, without any real obligations, and the soldiers whom he tried to agitate were not under his command.[49] Although a brave and noble attempt, Krasovsky's agitation seems not to have been carefully thought out. When a sergeant-major questioned him on the spot, Krasovsky identified himself.[50] After his arrest he said he would explain his motives only to Alexander II in person.[51] He later expressed his satisfaction with the death sentence and sent the authorities a letter that, he claimed, he had received from the soldiers. The letter declared "honour and glory to the honourable and glorious sufferer, Little Russian lieutenant-colonel!"[52] Its purported authors claimed that Little Russian soldiers teased their Russian comrades in arms about the fact that among their ranks there were no people like Krasovsky. The latter's eccentric behaviour may be partly explained by the fact that his most severe wounds were to the head.[53]

The authorities found in Krasovsky's possession many handwritten, illegal texts: his own, Alexander Herzen's, Polish patriotic hymns and leaflets,[54] Taras Shevchenko's poems, and other materials. However, there was only one copy of each text, so Krasovsky was hardly in a position to distribute them. The authorities also found issues of *Samostaine slovo* (*Independent Word*) and *Hromadnytsia*, handwritten journals that were circulated among the members of the Kyiv Hromada.

Krasovsky's own texts included poems written in Ukrainian: one recounted a popular rebellion against the nobles and the emperor; another, entitled "Nahaika" (The Whip), described this instrument as an inescapable attribute of the Russian monarchy; and a third one described an ugly and immoral Russian innkeeper:

> In that bar a Russian (*katsap*) measures out portions of vodka ... The drink is disgusting and the Russian so ugly, like a beast, that it is unpleasant even to spit! ... Those eyes are like an owl's, they look askance, a most disgusting moustache, and snot under the nose. He never washes, never attends church. He came here barefoot and naked, but is now playing the boss ... He arrived poor and hungry, happy for a piece of bread, but now he is like a nobleman, claims everything, you must [give him]! He says he needs tea, vodka, and a snack, according to the *nobility's* habit [emphasis in the original] ...
>
> If he only sat humbly in the corner, but no, he pretends wisdom. If he were wise or even literate, but now it is sad to listen how that wretch lies: "We were sent from Russia," says the bearded man, "to tell you things, to enlighten the *khohols*!"
>
> ... To tell the truth, what is so great about that Russian? He is like a hairy bear.[55]

Krasovsky's poem contained attitudes corresponding to Ukrainian stereotypes of Russians, which were now firmly established: arrogance, an expansionist attitude, attachment to the values of nobility, and lack of religion. In this context, Krasovsky used the derogatory word *katsap*. An additional poem praised the emergence of *Osnova* and Krasovsky's financial contribution towards it.[56]

The issues of *Samostaine slovo* gave the authorities an opportunity to place Krasovsky's ideas within the wider context of the Kyiv Hromada. A writer using the pseudonym "Volodar," most likely Antonovych,[57] begins his article "The Relationship between Rusyns and Muscovites" with a negative description of the role of the Russian government in Ukraine. It had destroyed the ancient rights of the Ukrainians, suppressed all free thinking, and "chained [Ukrainians] in its autocratic chains."[58] Volodar also blames the government for oppressing the common people through taxes and army recruitments, and introducing landowning by nobles even in areas where it had never existed before.

The author admits that the government abolished serfdom, but it had decreed such high redemption fees that they were ruining the peasants. In short, the government is despotic. However, it is necessary to distinguish between the Russian government and Russian society. Volodar divides local Russian society into three groups: (1) officers and civil servants dispatched to Ukraine; (2) nobles of Ukrainian origin who had assimilated into the Russian culture; (3) the radical intelligentsia. The first group was interested only in its own material well-being. The second group could not admit the shame that their forefathers had sold their country out for the right to enserf their own brothers. It was a good thing that they called themselves Russians because the Ukrainian cause should be devoid of any nobility; the assimilated nobility was dirt that would be driven out of Ukraine. The third group consisted of radically-minded, educated Russians whose ideas were reflected in the underground revolutionary leaflet *Velikoruss* (*Great Russian*), Herzen's *Kolokol*, and the legal radical journals *Sovremennik* and *Russkii mir*. The members of the third group, who were more numerous in Russia than Ukraine, recognized the social and national rights of the Ukrainians; they understood that "our nation (*narod*) is not by right swept under their government; that it has the right to flourish in freedom now, and that in the future it has the right to independence."[59] With these good Russians, fraternal cooperation based on equality of both sides was possible and desirable. Volodar's view was an enlightened but overly optimistic take on Russian radicals. However, the authorities likely perceived in the article the danger of Ukrainian-Russian revolutionary cooperation. Furthermore, the same issue of *Samostaine slovo* contained a page of twenty-three folk proverbs about Russians, every one negative. Some of the proverbs were the same ones that Lazarevsky had published in 1853: "When you are with a Russian, keep a stone in your bosom"; "If a devil or a Russian have taken something, it will not be returned"; "A Russian is made of disaster, he dwells in it and causes disaster for everyone"; "A Russian is to dirt like a beetle is to shit"; "'Father! A devil is breaking into the house!' 'Don't worry! It is not a Russian!'"; "He is a good man, but a Russian."[60] The publication of this selection of proverbs showed that Krasovsky was not alone in his Russian-bashing: the habit was shared by other Hromada members.[61]

In another explicit political statement, an anonymous contributor to *Samostaine slovo* supported a pan-Slavic federation.[62] The author compares the government's policy in relation to the peasantry in Ukraine to the previous Polish rule before the Cossack wars and to the French order before the revolution.[63] To be sure, the author was not enthusiastic about the prospect of class war, preferring instead to avert it by improving the peasants' lot. His criticism of the Russian government did not mean that *Samostaine slovo* sided with the Poles: it criticized Polish claims to Ukraine and explicitly abstained from all sympathy to the imminent Polish insurrection. However, even criticism of the Poles contained statements that in government circles would be perceived as subversive: for example, the pseudonymous writer Hrytsko claimed that no Poles were equal to Russian radicals, like Herzen and the authors of *Velikoruss*, who did not grovel before the government and noble landowners.[64] The editors of both *Samostaine slovo* and *Hromadnytsia* specified that their anti-Polish position did not extend to Poles in the Kingdom of Poland, but concerned only attempts to establish Polish domination in Ukraine.[65] *Hromadnytsia* blamed the Great Russians (*moskali*) as well as Poles for their sense of superiority in relation to Ukrainians, and predicted that "our people" would in time renounce both and keep far away from them.[66] However, the journal's main thrust was against the demonstrations and disturbances that were organized by Polish students in St Vladimir's University. In addition to its strictly political ideas, *Samostaine slovo* focused attention on education and expressed disapproval of Russian-language instruction in Ukrainian Sunday schools.[67]

The authorities who interrogated Krasovsky and examined his confiscated papers probably perceived Ukrainians' lawful cultural activities and political subversion as closely connected with each other. Krasovsky had been in contact with Panteleimon Kulish, and during his court martial he spoke about his wish to introduce South Russian as the language of instruction in primary education. His correspondence reveals that he had received Ukrainian books for distribution among soldiers. Krasovsky received the death penalty, later commuted to twelve years of hard labour.[68]

Repressions against the Poltava Hromada and Pavlo Chubynsky

The mutual understanding between the Kyiv Hromada and Vasilchikov was a local arrangement that did not apply outside the Right Bank, which was under his administration. The Poltava Hromada, which was founded at the beginning of 1861 at the latest, was no more radical than its counterpart in Kyiv. However, while the Kyiv Hromada did not face many repressions, the authorities practically destroyed the Poltava

Hromada. The first information about the Poltava group reached the Third Section in February 1861. A local gendarme colonel named Belov wrote to Dolgorukov about revolutionary and Little Russian sympathies among the local high school students. Belov claimed to have received a denunciation from some students, who reported that their fellow students were discussing the possibility of an uprising in Little Russia and the destruction of the monarchy. Although the information was vague and unreliable, the colonel sent a report to the Third Section and Volkov, the local governor. He alerted them to the teachers Dmytro Pylchykov, Oleksandr Stronin, and Kovalsky. Dolgorukov immediately reported the matter to Alexander II, a rare occurrence in cases of unsubstantiated denunciations. The decision to apprise the tsar of this situation may have been sparked by a statement in the denunciation that some students were speaking disrespectfully about the emperor. Regardless of the context, the authorities considered all criticism of the emperor's person a serious crime.[69]

Colonel Belov was right: Pylchykov and Stronin were members of the Ukrainian Hromada in Poltava. Pylchykov had most likely been a member of the Cyrillo-Methodian Society in 1846–7, although he was never investigated.[70] Ukrainian activism in Poltava arose after the founding of local Sunday schools in April 1860 and Panteleimon Kulish's visit to the city, where a reception was organized for him that spring. Oleksandr Stronin was the director of the first Sunday school in Poltava. After three more schools were opened, a joint board controlled by the Hromada members was created, and the four Poltava schools introduced Ukrainian as the language of instruction. To support the schools, Pylchykov and Stronin organized public lectures and literary readings, charging a modest admission fee. The program of events included Pylchykov's lectures on Ukrainian history and readings of Shevchenko's works.[71] Apart from organizing the Sunday schools, the Poltava Hromada published and distributed permitted Ukrainian literature. A report on the inexpensive books in Ukrainian distributed by the Poltava activists was published in *Osnova*: 12,095 books were sold in twenty-five towns and villages between January and October 1861.[72] The exercises in Stronin's Ukrainian primer began with the word *volia* (liberty), and ended with a recommendation of works by Taras Shevchenko and Marko Vovchok.[73] Oleksandr Konysky's elementary arithmetic book introduced Ukrainian nationalism into the curriculum through assignments requiring pupils to count how many days Shevchenko lived and to compute the distance from Kyiv to the Zaporozhian Sich.[74] To be sure, these activities were well within the limits of the law. However, there was a subversive aspect to the group, as its members read illegal literature, discussed forbidden topics, and wrote seditious texts not slated for distribution. Oleksandr Stronin had met Herzen in London in 1858, before the existence of the Hromada.[75]

Two weeks after receiving the gendarme colonel's letter, the Third Section intercepted Konysky's letter to Kulish,[76] informing his colleague that "our society" had petitioned the governor to permit a society for the promotion of literacy. The society had celebrated the imperial manifesto decreeing the liberation of the serfs by holding a lunch. Toasts had been raised to the health of the serfs and Ukrainian writers, as well as to *Osnova*, but Konysky did not write a word about the emperor. "You brought our Ukrainian society great joy with the news that a political journal in our language will appear in Galicia ... Now the Russians will keep quiet! God willing, there will be a feast on our street too!!"[77] Konysky also wrote about plans to establish additional Sunday schools in Poltava. The letter made it clear to the gendarmes that an unregistered nationally-oriented society existed in Poltava, whose members were at least not actively loyal to the emperor, and that local Sunday schools were part of the society's activities. The Third Section asked Colonel Belov to keep an eye on Konysky and a couple of Hromada members who were mentioned in his letter.[78]

Over the next eighteen months Belov and the Third Section monitored the activities of the Hromada members in Poltava, in connection with whom they received denunciations.[79] In his reports Belov evaluated many members negatively as morally corrupt, suspect persons, but he failed to produce any hard evidence of subversion. At the same time, Hromada suffered from Governor Volkov's obstructionism with regard to many of its planned, lawful activities: he prevented the launching of an additional Sunday school, a newspaper, plays aimed at the common people, and a procession through the town in commemoration of Shevchenko. Volkov disapproved of the whole idea of staging plays for the benefit of the common people and especially of the fact that Kvitka-Osnov'ianenko's play *Shelmenko the Village Scribe* presented authorities in a comic light. Valuev shared Volkov's opinion and endorsed his decision to ban the staging of the play.[80] On 12 March1861some Hromada members had an argument with the local chief of police, to which Volkov and the Third Section's anonymous representative ascribed political motives.[81] In October 1861Volkov wrote a strongly worded denunciation of the Hromada to the chief of gendarmes, claiming that in Poltava a group of teachers and civil servants "who understood incorrectly the idea of progress and aimed at the revival of the Little Russian nationality"[82] opposed the local authorities. The lack of evidence did not prevent Volkov from naming nine individuals, four of whom he proposed to condemn to administrative exile without benefit of a trial: Oleksandr Stronin; Viktor Shchelkan, a teacher at the cadet school; Zlygostev, the local criminal prosecutor; and Viktor Loboda. Of these, the governor found Loboda's removal most urgent because, as the director of the Poltava telegraph agency, he endangered the confidentiality of official correspondence.

Ten days after Volkov's denunciation and most likely in agreement with him, Colonel Belov reported to his superiors the suspicion that Loboda had revealed to outsiders the contents of the emperor's telegram to the empress. In this denunciation, too, no evidence was produced. Dolgorukov contacted the minister of transport, Konstantin Vladimirovich Chevkin, who decided in December 1861 to transfer Loboda to Smolensk. However, Loboda managed to delay his move until May 1862.[83]

Additional repressions against the Poltava Hromada followed in the context of the government's general onslaught against radical intelligentsia circles in June 1862. At first, the great fires raging in St Petersburg sparked rumours that either Polish nationalists or Russian radicals had set the city on fire. No arsonists were ever found, but even some of the more astute people in government circles, like Valuev, believed these rumours. After a couple of populist propagandists were found to be teaching in two St Petersburg Sunday schools, all Sunday schools were closed. The most important intellectual leader of the Russian radicals, Nikolai Chernyshevskii, was arrested and sentenced on the basis of shaky evidence for having written a revolutionary proclamation addressed to the peasants. Ukrainian activists in Poltava received their share of these repressions because of their participation in the Sunday school movement, and because the frequent denunciations had prepared Dolgorukov to agree to administrative deportations based on unsubstantiated suspicions. On 11 June the chief of gendarmes decided that Stronin and Shchelkan should be exiled, but for some reason he did not undertake immediate action against Stronin, who was only dismissed from his position as a secondary school teacher. Valuev deported Shchelkan to Astrakhan.[84]

In August 1862 the authorities obtained additional evidence of the ideas that were circulating in the Hromada. It reached the authorities as a result of a strange incident: Vasyl Shevych, teacher and Sunday school activist in Lubni, had corresponded with Hromada members. Shevych's suitcase was stolen, and when the authorities located it, they discovered his correspondence in it.[85] On the basis of the contents of the correspondence and texts, the authorities arrested Shevych, Stronin, and a Kharkiv-based teacher, Andrii Shymanov. In connection with these arrests, more correspondence was found, which led to Loboda's arrest. In December 1862 Loboda, Shevych, and Stronin were condemned to administrative exile in far-flung areas of European Russia. Although Konysky was not indicted in connection with committing any illegal acts, except membership in the Hromada, he too was deported. The accused were charged with seeking the independence of Little Russia.[86]

The confiscated documents did not leave any doubt about the existence of Hromada, a secret society that was closely intertwined with public Sunday school activism and mentioned several times in members' correspondence.[87] The Poltava Hromada maintained contact with the Kyiv and Kharkiv Hromadas. In a letter to Shevych, Stronin mentioned that eighteen persons were involved in Hromada's activities.[88] Some illegal literature was found, most notably Herzen's works and issues of *Velikoruss*. The authors of *Velikoruss*, whose identity was never discovered, demanded land reform, a constitution, independence for Poland, and the right to self-determination for South Rus'.[89] Shymanov's correspondence revealed that he had ordered the (banned) works of Ludwig Büchner and Ludwig Feuerbach, which were critical of Christianity, that were being published at the time and distributed by radical Moscow students, who will be discussed later.[90] To be sure, the quantity of clandestine literature found in the Poltava activists' possession was so negligible that they hardly printed or distributed it. Nevertheless, the confiscated handwritten texts revealed that the arrestees were opposed to the existing order, and Loboda advocated the separation of Ukraine from the Russian Empire: "One or the other: state or liberty. There is no reason to be tempted by the status of a member of a large state. Such a country as Russia is unimaginable as free. Only despotism can keep together in the same conditions all those differences between a Finn and a Tatar, a Muscovite and a Ukrainian. In a free state the majority decides everything. That is again Muscovite domination."[91] Loboda's opinion was not necessarily representative of the whole Hromada, but other members also harboured subversive opinions. In a text entitled *Dogmatic and Historical Work*, Shevych gave a highly negative assessment of the Russian monarchy's historical role, and demanded a constitution.[92] Shymanov's manuscript about the aims and tasks of the Hromada movement mentioned the creation of a pan-Slavic federation after the overthrow of the Russian autocracy.[93] Shymanov stated explicitly that it was the task of the Hromada to struggle against the Russian government. In a letter to Shevych he wrote that the future political form of not only Russia but of all Slavs depended on the resolution of the South Russian question.[94] In a letter to Shevych, Stronin defined himself as a pan-Slav rather than a Ukrainophile.[95] Both Stronin and Shevych anticipated and welcomed an imminent revolution. After Loboda's departure to Smolensk, Stronin wrote to him regretting that they would not mark together the second anniversary of the emancipation of serfs on 19 February 1863, and discussed the prospect of forming a union of intelligentsia and common people in a rebellion against the nobility.[96] To be sure, the tone of his letter indicated that he was not expecting that rebellion to follow from his own actions. In another letter to Shevych he expressed his appreciation of the government's inconsistent policies because the arbitrariness angered some people, while the display of weakness emboldened others.[97] He added that Shevych should sow and not fall into apathy: perhaps there would be a harvest. Stronin argued with Loboda, who wanted to retain his faith in God, claiming that such a belief was incompatible with the establishment of equality, and mentioned socialism favourably.[98]

The members of the Poltava Hromada sympathized with revolution, but did not attempt to foment one. Nothing in the confiscated papers indicates that they had any plans to instigate any immediate disturbances. However, there are a few allusions to other kinds of agitation. Shymanov called Shevych to recruit landowners and asked him to burn the letter after reading it.[99] Shevych wrote to Shymanov about the need for agitation and to the physician Veniamin Portugalov, a former member of the Kharkiv-Kyiv revolutionary group. He boasted that in his Lubni circle there were already "negative and positive agitators," adding: "There are plenty of dissatisfied [people], there are [those] from among whom to select."[100] Loboda's manuscript of *A Tale of Two Brothers* contained his ideas on political strategy in a rather explicit form:

> Success will depend on the correct grasp of the circumstances and the relations between them, on the ability to drive the cause via a certain route, to strengthen this, avoid that, to gather the party of men strong in mind and will quietly and without noise. [It will depend on] the skilful preparation and inclining, not of the masses – that requires a century of

> work – but intelligent and influential people in various localities: in Kyiv, Kharkiv, Odesa, Kazan, Chernihiv; to force them to act not in isolation but together, to build and develop the certain cause not everywhere under one and the same appearance or the same goal, but according to the circumstances. Of course, in each locality there must be at least one person who would know the final goal, too. Young people, even rather intelligent ones, will not be told about the final aim unless everything is ready.[101]

Thus, the members of the Poltava Hromada aimed to expand their organization by recruiting additional like-minded individuals in order to engage in the political struggle with sufficient forces. Although Loboda did not want to recruit common people, he did seek to influence them. He wrote to Stronin: "In nos. 98 and 99 of *Severnaia Pochta* (*Northern Post*) there is an article, 'The History of the Soul Tax in Russia.' The article is subversive (*vozmutitel'naia*), very good for a public lecture."[102] *Severnaia Pochta* was an official newspaper that hardly published unequivocally subversive material, but this quotation reveals that the authorities' apprehensions that Hromada members were teaching in Sunday schools were not unwarranted.

Last but not least, the investigation uncovered a connection between the Poltava Hromada and the earlier Kharkiv-Kyiv revolutionary group. One of Shymanov's unsent letters, written in January 1860, reports the arrest of Petro Zavadsky.[103] Among his papers was an issue of the handwritten journal *Svobodnoe slovo* (*Free Word*) published by the Kharkiv-Kyiv group.[104] Shevych and Shymanov corresponded with a former member of the Kharkiv-Kyiv group, Veniamin Portugalov, and Shevych blamed him for inaction.[105] Loboda corresponded with Leon Zelensky, another member of the Kharkiv-Kyiv group who participated in the Sunday school organized by the Hromada.[106] While the decision to hand down an administrative sentence to those accused of Ukrainian separatism certainly was arbitrary, the authorities were not being paranoid in their perception of subversion.

However, there were also two cases in which the authorities punished Ukrainian activists for acts they had never committed. Volodymyr Miiakovsky has found out the pretext on the basis of which Pavlo Chubynsky was deported to Pinega in Arkhangelsk gubernia: he was accused of having authored the proclamation "To All Good People," which called peasants to armed insurrection.[107] Chubynsky was one of the signatories of the article "Comment from Kyiv" mentioned above. In 1862 he graduated from the Faculty of Law at the University of St Petersburg and moved to Boryspil, Poltava province, which was located near Kyiv. On 29 June 1862 Minister of War Dmitrii Miliutin forwarded to Dolgorukov a denunciation against the Kyiv Ukrainophiles.[108] Its author was Count Sivers, who had visited the city, where he noticed the high visibility of the Ukrainian orientation and national dress. Krasovsky had just been court-marshalled, under the jurisdiction of the Ministry of War. It is likely that Miliutin was concerned about the revelations in that case about the political ideas of Ukrainian activists in Kyiv. Sivers argued, correctly, that there was a connection between Krasovsky and the "Society of Khlopomans" (peasant-lovers) as he called the Kyiv Hromada. Dolgorukov forwarded the information to the emperor. In his letter Sivers included an additional anonymous denunciation, in which it was claimed that Kyiv Ukrainophiles were aiming at Ukraine's independence and acting in concert with the Polish underground, trying to incite the peasants against the existing order. The denunciation was clearly written by someone who was not satisfied with Vasilchikov's policy of cooperation between the authorities and the Hromada. Indeed, this unsubstantiated denunciation was the first one arguing the danger of Ukrainian-Polish revolutionary cooperation. The Krasovsky case indicates that such cooperation enjoyed some support in the Hromada. However, Antonovych and other important Hromada leaders opted instead for cooperation with Vasilchikov; hence that part of the denunciation was unsubstantiated. The same denunciation claimed that Chubynsky had carried out agitation among the peasants of Poltava province. A rumour was circulating that the peasants had reacted to Chubynsky's propaganda by beating him up.

In September Colonel Belov informed the Third Section that Chubynsky and a handful of other people had visited a village, where they recounted some legends of Ukraine's past liberty to the peasants.[109] The peasants had tried to arrest the men, but they escaped. Although Governor Volkov ordered a secret investigation, no evidence against Chubynsky was found, and the police discovered that at least some of the rumours were groundless.[110] The only reliable information was that Chubynsky and other young men mixed socially with peasants and drank vodka with them. Despite this, Belov suspected Chubynsky of subversive intentions against the existing order. He emphasized how "the local society" was concerned about Chubynsky's activities, which included visiting villages and reading Shevchenko's unpublished works to peasants, visiting Shevchenko's tomb, and singing Little Russian songs with subversive and immoral content. Finally, Belov produced the handwritten proclamation "To All Good People" and claimed that Chubynsky was suspected of being its author,[111] but he did not present any evidence to back his suspicion. The proclamation incited peasants to insurrection on the grounds that all the land was theirs, including the part that had remained in the possession of noble landowners after the emancipation. The fact that the author asked his readers to bide their time points to the document's possible Polish origin. Peasant disturbances on the Left Bank would have benefited the insurgents by diverting Russian troops. However, Fedir Savchenko was correct in noting the possibility that the gendarmes themselves had written the proclamation;[112] this is the most likely explanation. The author of the proclamation refers to the large fires that had caused extensive damage in the summer of 1862. He claims that among the arsonists were landlords who wanted to destroy the peasants economically, and the enemies of landlords who burned down only landlords' villages. The peasants were urged not to pay any heed to the latter because the action was directed only against landlords, who were their real enemies. It is extremely unlikely that the Polish insurgents would have found it advantageous to defend arson in a text aimed at a peasant audience. It was the Russian authorities, not the Polish insurgents, who connected the fires with the Polish and radical Russian underground.[113] Furthermore, the lack of any information about the proclamation's provenance in the files of the Third Section is striking. There is no information where, how, and when it was found, except for a statement that Chubynsky or his friends were suspected. Normally, gendarmes were interested in details when they wanted to find out the truth. Finally, Belov's letter, which contains the proclamation, seems to have been back-dated to 7 September 1862. In the Third Section file it is located after Valuev's information about the results of the police investigation, dated 6 October 1862. Furthermore, on orders from Belov, his superior, Gendarme Lieutenant Vasilev forwarded information about Chubynsky to the Third Section on 20 September. Vasilev's letter did not mention the proclamation, although Chubynsky's actions were found to be rather suspicious. If the Poltava gendarmes had the proclamation in their possession on 7 September, it is puzzling that they wrote to the Third Section on 20 September without making any reference to it. Furthermore, Chubynsky's case was investigated by the Commission for the Investigation of Political Crimes, headed by Aleksandr Golitsyn. Contrary to its usual practice, the commission recommended Chubynsky's deportation without questioning him or trying to gain any additional information.[114] All this indicates that the gendarmes were the authors of Chubynsky's proclamation. They committed this forgery because they were certain of his subversive tendency, but frustrated because of the lack of evidence. Chubynsky was released from deportation only in 1869.

Chubynsky's case demonstrates the importance of the local authorities. He was repressed because he happened to live and work in Poltava province, which was under Volkov's jurisdiction. It did not help matters that by the time of his arrest he had moved to Kyiv. Chubynsky's treatment by the authorities indicates that the Third Section, which in the past had adopted a wait-and-see attitude, had inched its policy closer to Volkov's position. Chubynsky's deportation on false charges was directed not only against the Ukrainophiles but also against Vasilchikov's policies toward them. Vasilchikov was informed about the whole process only in late September.[115] Because Chubynsky's place of residence was now in Kyiv, it was Vasilchikov who had to arrest him. However, someone from Vasilchikov's chancellery leaked the news to Chubynsky one day before his arrest,[116] and the warning allowed Chubynsky to get rid of any incriminating documents in his possession. For different reasons, it was in the interests of both Vasilchikov and Chubynsky that the authorities did not find any hard evidence: the governor-general did not want to foster criticism of his policies.

At this time Ukrainian activists could still place their hopes in Vasilchikov and Golovnin as prominent opponents of repression. The position of these two imperial politicians balanced the hostile attitude of the Third Section, Valuev, and Volkov. Unfortunately, Vasilchikov died suddenly in December 1862. After some hesitation, his successor Nikolai Nikolaevich Annenkov joined Dolgorukov and Valuev in their support of repressing Ukrainian national activists. Golovnin retained his benevolent attitude, but his importance shrank with the transfer of censorship from the jurisdiction of the Ministry of Public Enlightenment to the Ministry of Internal Affairs in March 1863.

Ukrainians, the Polish January Insurrection, and the First Land and Liberty

The Polish January insurrection began in the Kingdom of Poland on 10 (22) January 1863.[117] By April it had spread to Ukraine, and battles were fought as far east as Kyiv province. This was a local event. The Kyiv Hromada had to react to it in one way or another, especially since local insurgents included the Ukrainian cause in their agenda. In Kyiv the Polish insurrection had the character of a student action. At first, the students planned to attack government positions in Kyiv. The local military commander Edmund Różycki disapproved of such a foolhardy plan and demanded that insurgent units be formed instead in the countryside. The Polish students in Kyiv then decided to form their own unit, which fought near Kyiv. This happened on the night of 26–7 April, when about 550 insurgent troops departed from the town in a couple of units. On 1 May Russian troops attacked and completely routed them in the village of Verkholevsk.[118]

The Polish Ukrainophile students continued their advocacy of the need to improve the peasants' conditions. A propaganda unit consisting of twenty-one people led by Antoni Juriewicz departed from the city at the same time as the main Kyiv troops. They distributed among the peasants the so-called Golden Decree (*Złota Hramota*), written in Ukrainian. This document proclaimed the equality of all citizens regardless of social rank or religious confession, granted electoral rights to peasants on both the local and national levels, called for the transfer to the peasants of their fields and pastures without any redemption fees, and decreed complete freedom of religion and the right to use the local language in schools, courts, and local administration. Furthermore, each participant in the insurrection was to receive land from state domains.[119] In the village of Soloviovka, peasants armed by the government captured student agitators. According to Polish sources, twelve students were killed without putting up any resistance. This spelled the end of hopes to unite democracy and Polish national liberation in Right-Bank Ukraine.[120]

The authorities used the insurrection as a pretext to strike not only the Poles but also Ukrainian activists. The secret investigation of Chubynsky's case had exposed other Ukrainian national activists. Although no evidence was found against them either, they were placed under secret police surveillance. Among them was a secondary-school student named Volodymyr Syniehub, one of the signatories of the "Comment from Kyiv." On 28 January 1863, Dolgorukov wrote a strongly worded letter to Annenkov, in which he informed the newly appointed governor-general about the existence of the Hromada, a secret society that, according to Dolgorukov, was in contact with Polish regional organizations at the university.[121] Dolgorukov regarded the signatories of the "Comment from Kyiv" as the main activists of the society, and therefore ordered Annenkov to put an end to its activities. Thus, Vasilchikov's death had an impact on government policy: the governor-general and the Third Section had known about the Kyiv Hromada since 1861, but it became official news only now. Instead of being the government's allies against the Polish underground, Ukrainian activists in Kyiv were now suspected of siding with the Poles. Although a mere rank-and-file member of the Hromada, Volodymyr Syniehub was headed for trouble, being both Chubynsky's friend and a signatory of the "Comment from Kyiv." In early March Dolgorukov reinforced his position by sending Annenkov a copy of an anonymous denunciation, in which the planned translation of the Gospels was considered as a part of a campaign to separate Ukraine from Russia and join it in a federation with Poland.[122] The denunciation, which was ostensibly written by a group of concerned Little Russians, was not the cause of the government's attack on the Ukrainian national movement: Dolgorukov had adopted a hostile position to Ukrainians as early as October 1862, at the time of Chubynsky's deportation.[123]

Annenkov replied on 23 February, having placed all the signatories of the "Comment from Kyiv" under secret surveillance.[124] However, the governor-general wrote that by publishing their opinions in *Sovremennaia letopis*, the signatories had mitigated the danger of their activities. Since they had challenged the public to present evidence of any subversive acts they had committed, Annenkov hoped that polemics in the press would provide additional information about the group. The letter indicates that Annenkov still hesitated to use repression against the Ukrainian national activists, although he was urged by Third Section to do so. However, a month later the governor-general made up his mind and became an adherent of repression. On 17 March Annenkov sent another letter to Dolgorukov, in which he denied that the Ukrainian activists had acted in unison with the Poles: quite the contrary, they were opposed to "Latin-Polish propaganda."[125] Nevertheless, he agreed with the anonymous denunciator in that political rather than religious motives were behind the planned translation of the Bible. Annenkov claimed that Little Russian was such an undeveloped vernacular that it was impossible to express abstract concepts in it. In the event that the adherents of the Little Russian party had their translation of the Bible published, they would then demand autonomy on the grounds that they had their own language. Annenkov asked Dolgorukov to present this opinion to the emperor, which he did on 27 March. The way to the Valuev circular was paved by Dolgorukov's cooperation with Valuev and Annenkov.

Volodymyr Syniehub and his friend, the young nobleman Volodymyr Pylypenko, were arrested on 26 April in the village of Pylypchi in Poltava province. They were accused of recruiting members for a rebel unit to side with the Poles. Because of the Polish students' short-lived insurgent campaign, the timing was apposite for such an accusation. After their arrest Syniehub and Pylypenko soon revealed the identities of other people, including the local landowner Viktor Pototsky and his brother Leonid. At first, Syniehub and Pylypenko admitted their guilt. Syniehub confessed that Andrii Krasovsky had recruited him in the Little Russian Revolutionary Committee, which sided with the Poles. According to testimonies, Syniehub and his associates had mixed socially with young peasant men in order to recruit them to the secret insurrectionary society. However, the discrepancy between the various testimonies and uncovered evidence was striking: despite the lengthy confessions of the arrestees, the authorities found only one gun; owned by Pototsky, it was a typical possession of a noble landowner's household. Furthermore, the testimonies were far-fetched: according to Syniehub, he had planned to set fire to a village and murder all the local nobles in the event that the authorities discovered his plans. The peasants who were recruited to the insurrection had been urged to kill all the lords. Last but not least, Syniehub and Pylypenko's testimonies create the distinct impression that both men had frequently imbibed large quantities of vodka, to such an extent that they had no time or energy to devote to conspiracy.[126]

The testimonies were bizarre because much of them had been fabricated by the authorities. To be sure, they contain also some reliable information: Bohdan Klid has shown that the young men had indeed sung revolutionary songs, like Anatoly Svydnytsky's *U poli dolia stoiala* (In the Field Fate Awaited) and Chubynsky's *Shche ne vmerla Ukraina* (Ukraine Has Not Yet Died), which today is Ukraine's national anthem.[127] Both songs contain a call to revolutionary violence, the first one because of the peasants' social grievances, and the latter also because of the Russian rule in Ukraine. As Pylypenko recited the *Shche ne vmerla Ukraina* to interrogators who were not familiar with it, this is a rather convincing piece of evidence. However, it is not certain whether Syniehub and Pylypenko really sang these songs to peasants, since much of Pylypenko's testimony was dictated by the interrogators. Even if they did, this act of agitation does not equal raising an immediate insurrection, and all the information about planning such insurrection in the testimonies is rather fantastic. What really took place was that the young Ukrainophile noblemen mixed socially with the peasants, drank vodka with them, and sang at least folk songs, possibly also revolutionary songs. Even the local landowner was an eager participant in these activities. This was not an insurrection or conspiracy. No Little Russian Revolutionary Committee ever existed.

In June 1863 Syniehub and Pylypenko wrote to governor Volkov. Retracting their confessions, they claimed that the interrogators had threatened them, made false promises, and forced them to confess to things that had never taken place.[128] Volkov's reaction is not recorded in the files of the Kyiv governor-general, which I consulted. The authorities most likely ignored the two men's complaints, refusing to contemplate any retraction. The arrested were taken to St Peter and Paul Fortress in St Petersburg, and the investigation was continued by the Commission for the Investigation of Political Crimes. In early 1864, they were sent to Kyiv, because their original confessions, now rejected by the accused, involved so many locals. In January 1865 Aleksandr Pavlovich Bezak replaced Annenkov as governor-general. After familiarizing himself with the details of the case, Bezak found it essentially fabricated:

> The investigation has not revealed any information that would confirm that this party, known here as Ukrainophiles (*khokhlomanov ili khlopomanov*), tried to separate Little Russia [from the empire] and cooperated for that purpose with the Poles. Indeed, it could not have even revealed any such information. According to intelligence that has at different times been gathered in the local administration, Ukrainophile activities differed from Polish tendencies. The first group argued for the uniqueness (*samobytnost'*) of the South Russian region and strove to instruct common people in the countryside in South Russian national principles; Poles argued that this region is Polish, and tried to teach the common people in Polish in order to plant in them the idea of their purported Polish nationality …
>
> From a comparison of these testimonies and study of all the aspects of the case, it is impossible not to reach the [following] conclusion: if they now dishonestly deny all the acts of which they previously accused themselves, it is nonetheless manifest also that in their first testimonies they accused themselves of many things that did not happen (*mnogom nebyvalom*). This followed, if not from the instigation of the first investigators, then from the wish to present themselves as important and dangerous revolutionaries. Such a wish is quite understandable in inexperienced boys (*nedouchennykh malchikakh*) …

> It is evident from the facts learned during the investigation that Syniehub and Pylypenko were not agents of any secret society, which could be uncovered through further investigation.[129]

Bezak released the accused and proposed to punish only Syniehub for speaking about his political ideas to the peasants. Although that part of the accusation is plausible, it is questionable whether sufficient evidence existed to prove it. The Third Section and the Commission for the Investigation argued in favour of expanding the investigation to include most of the Hromada members who were mentioned in Syniehub's testimonies. The Third Section sent Bezak a list of 127 names, which included local inhabitants from all social classes and all the most prominent activists of the Kyiv Hromada. It took considerable perseverance on Bezak's part to get his proposal accepted and close the case without going to trial. Thanks to his resolve, Bezak saved dozens of Kyiv Ukrainophiles from arrests and, perhaps, arbitrary punishments. Syniehub was deported to Viatka.[130]

Why did the authorities at first want to punish Syniehub and others on trumped up charges? It was not essential to remove Syniehub: unlike Chubynsky, he was not a prominent Ukrainian activist and did not present any danger to the government. The most likely explanation is that Volkov and Dolgorukov needed an argument in defence of Valuev's circular, which was being prepared at the time. Certainly, the forthcoming repressions against Ukrainian publishing were still not defined in every detail. Nevertheless, the Third Section and the Ministry of Internal Affairs were pressuring the Holy Synod to prevent the publication of the New Testament in Ukrainian,[131] and it is likely that additional restrictions were already in the offing. One of the central arguments for the restriction of Ukrainian publications enacted in the Valuev circular was that the Ukrainian movement was siding with the Poles. The only evidence that the government had at its disposal to back this statement was from the Krasovsky case. Since the restrictions against Ukrainian literature were bound to evoke opposition in government circles, more evidence was needed, and it was produced through the use of unconventional methods.

In historiography, the Little Russian Revolutionary Committee, an ephemeral organization concocted by the authorities, had a remarkable afterlife. Soviet historiography was obliged to conform to Karl Marx's positive evaluation of the Polish insurrection of 1863–4. That a rather significant segment of the Russian public had disapproved of the insurrection and supported its suppression created a problem which Soviet ideologists and historians solved by emphasizing Russian-Polish revolutionary cooperation, which had indeed existed, although as a minority current.[132] The fact that Ukrainian Hromada groups had distanced themselves from the insurrection was somewhat problematic, too, since their stance did not correspond to the Soviet idea of revolutionary cooperation among nationalities. This thorny question was ultimately resolved by accepting the existence of the Little Russian Revolutionary Committee and ignoring Bezak's final analysis of the case. Accordingly, Syniehub, Pylypenko, and Krasovsky became good, revolutionary Ukrainians as opposed to the members of the Kyiv Hromada, which consisted of bourgeois Ukrainian nationalists.[133] More recently, the perception of Syniehub's case as one of revolutionary agitation has persisted only because historians have trusted their predecessors and have not referred to the sources.[134] Although the existence of the Little Russian Revolutionary Committee is rejected today, Syniehub is still considered a revolutionary agitator. His own explicit voice expressed in his complaint to Volkov has gotten lost several times for different reasons. I agree with Olga Andriewsky, who considers this case an example of arbitrary repression rather than an attempt at armed insurrection, although some political agitation of peasants may indeed have occurred, as discovered by Klid.[135]

If the authorities had waited for a few months, they would not have needed to fabricate evidence about Ukrainian revolutionaries siding with the Polish insurgents. The last and most serious case of Ukrainian involvement in revolutionary action came to the fore with the arrest of a young land surveyor named Ivan Andrushchenko in July 1863. This case affected the Ukrainians of Moscow and St Petersburg as well. Andrushchenko's case indicates that the activities of the Russian secret revolutionary society Land and Liberty overlapped with those of the Ukrainian Hromadas. Land and Liberty was formed in late 1861 or early 1862, and was more or less active until the spring of 1864, when it disbanded. Although little is known about Land and Liberty, its members demanded the establishment of republican rule, civil freedoms, land reform to benefit the peasantry, and the independence of Poland.

One of the most important geographic points of the overlapping Ukrainian nationalist and all-Russian revolutionary activities was Moscow, where the local branch of Land and Liberty was rooted in informal student groups at the university. These groups also included some young people from outside the university. One of the earliest groups was called the Library of Kazan Students, founded in the latter half of the 1850s. This study group, whose members promoted radical doctrines and held discussions, had a library that included illegal literature. Another group that overlapped with the Kazan students has come to be known as "Petr Zaichnevskii's group," perhaps because of the tendency of Soviet historiography to name groups after their real or supposed leaders.[136] Zaichnevskii's group emerged in 1860 around students' clandestine publishing activities. Their first publications were reprints of Herzen's works and Russian editions of the German materialist Ludwig Büchner's *Kraft und Stoff* (*Force and Matter*) and Ludwig Feuerbach's *Das Wesen der Religion* (*On the Essence of Religion*). The clandestine publishing house expanded its activities to other cities, including Kharkiv, Chernihiv, and Kyiv. It was these books that Andrii Shymanov obtained by subscription in Kharkiv and Mossakovsky distributed to his students in Kyiv. In Kharkiv, Büchner's work was a big seller.[137] Zaichnevskii's group tried to print Shevchenko's works, but as a result of a technical mistake in the printing process, the book was not published.[138] The students did not have time for a second attempt, as the first arrests took place in July 1861. The second wave of arrests, in August, included the Moscow student Leonid Iashchenko, originally from Ukraine's Pereiaslav region, who was the author of the Ukrainian primer discussed in chapter 3. In addition to the newly printed edition of Shevchenko's forbidden works, the works of Feuerbach, Herzen, and Nikolai Ogarev, Herzen's fellow exile, were found in Iashchenko's possession. The seized correspondence proved definitively that Iashchenko was an activist of the illegal publishing house.[139] Among his confiscated correspondence were letters to the Poltava bookseller Vasyl Trunov, a member of the local Hromada. They concerned the marketing of Iashchenko's primer and other permitted Ukrainian publications.[140] However, a letter to Iashchenko from Ilia Doroshenko, a secondary-school teacher and member of the Chernihiv Hromada, contained a request for a subscription for the works of Büchner, Feuerbach, and Herzen.[141] Doroshenko wrote his book request in Ukrainian. Although no other overt Ukrainophiles were arrested at the time, at least two more were involved: the brothers Ivan and Ievhen Andrushchenko, whom the authorities arrested later.[142] Thus, these clandestine publishing activities or circulation of specific publications involved at least four Ukrainophiles: Iashchenko, Doroshenko, and the Andrushchenko brothers. Of them, Iashchenko was the only one who was punished:

he was sentenced to six months in jail, and after the completion of his sentence, he was exiled for an indefinite time to Bugulm, in the province of Samara, now Tatarstan.[143] Although the authorities destroyed Zaichnevskii's group, during their detention the arrestees had time to write and publish *Young Russia*, perhaps the most radical of the Russian revolutionary proclamations issued in the 1860s. It demanded violent revolution, common ownership of the means of production, and the destruction of family and religion. However, the other informal group of radicals based at the University of Moscow, the Library of Kazan Students, was not uncovered at the time, and it soon became the nucleus of the Moscow branch of Land and Liberty.

Ivan Andrushchenko was involved in both of the above-mentioned radical groups in Moscow. However, he escaped arrest probably because he left Moscow in May 1861. After graduating from the Land Surveying Institute in Moscow, he worked in the Chernihiv province. There, he became acquainted with the physician Stepan Nis, the most prominent leader of the Chernihiv Hromada (with whom he lived for some time), and Leonid Hlibov, the writer and editor of *Chernigovskii listok*, which published Andrushchenko's correspondence from the district town of Kozelets.

The members of the Chernihiv Hromada gathered most often at the apartment of Dr Nis. The official harassment of the group began in the spring of 1862, when Governor Sergei Pavlovich Golitsyn summoned Nis and told him that any Ukrainian meetings at his home would not be tolerated.[144] In January 1863 the gendarme colonel in Chernihiv, Shulgovskii, reported to the Third Section that many young people from different class backgrounds were congregating in Nis's apartment, wearing national Little Russian costumes, singing folk songs, and reading aloud Shevchenko's poetry. Nis was also collecting money for some unknown purpose. Shulgovskii believed that these harmful activities were escalating. Although he did not mention the slightest suspicion of any illegal acts having been committed, he proposed that Nis be transferred to state service "to a Great Russian province, where his nationality will not find imitators."[145] However, Governor Golitsyn opposed the measure and Nis remained in Chernihiv.[146]

In June 1862 Andrushchenko obtained a land surveyor's position in Moscow, where his acquaintances from the Library of Kazan Students recruited him into the Moscow branch of Land and Liberty. Andrushchenko distributed revolutionary proclamations, helped organize the escape of a Polish political prisoner, and carried mail and money between the St Petersburg and Moscow branches of the society. He was told that the society numbered about 300 persons throughout the Russian Empire, a plausible number, and that there was a branch of the society in Poltava, but not in Kyiv. Land and Liberty had tried but failed to recruit Volodymyr Antonovych.[147]

Andrushchenko was soon offered another position, this time in Kyiv, and he left Moscow in early July 1863, bringing with him about 400 revolutionary leaflets to be distributed both en route and in Kyiv, where Land and Liberty hoped he could incline Antonovych to cooperation. Andrushchenko stopped in Chernihiv, where he stayed with Nis. Together with the landowner Oleksandr Tyshchynsky, a former member of the Kharkiv-Kyiv group, they visited Lieutenant Oleksandr Bilozersky, Vasyl Bilozersky's brother. Andrushchenko gave a small number of proclamations to Bilozersky. The next day Oleksandr Bilozersky read a proclamation that agitated against the suppression of the Polish insurrection to a fellow officer named Gerasimov, who was visiting. Bilozersky preached revolutionary ideas to Gerasimov, who later denounced him to the authorities. When questioned, Bilozersky admitted that he had received the proclamation from Andrushchenko, who was then arrested along with Nis. In addition to the revolutionary leaflets, a large number of letters were found in both men's possession, approximately 260 sheets of paper, most written in Ukrainian.[148] It gave the authorities plenty of information about the Chernihiv Hromada and its other affiliates. Among Andrushchenko's letters was correspondence from an exiled former member of the Kharkiv-Kyiv group, Petro Iefymenko, who called upon Moscow Ukrainians to form their own group in late 1860–early 1861.[149] The letters revealed a close friendship between Iefymenko and Andrushchenko, and indicated that the former exerted strong moral authority over the latter. A letter that Iefymenko tried to send through Andrushchenko to a group of Ukrainian students at the Pereiaslav Theological Seminary, which Andrushchenko failed to forward, reveals that he was mainly interested in cultivating the Little Russian language. He planned to implement this idea through an officially recognized society for the promotion of literacy in South Russia. However, in the event that the authorities would not permit the establishment of such a society, Ukrainians, he wrote, should act in secret. The letter also reveals that Iefymenko disapproved of Polish and Russian claims that the Little Russian language was a dialect of either one of these languages: "Such urge to prove to us that we are not Ukrainians but Poles or Russians – what for? Does this not display that greed, hunger for power, and despotism that are rooted in the flesh and blood of the Russian, and which are frequently manifested even in decent people?"[150] Iefymenko thus responded to Russian claims that Ukraine needed Russian protection:

> Times are different today; gone is the time of ruling over others by physical force. If such force is needed, it emerges only as a consequence of the homogeneity of the population. Nations now strive for decentralization, large states decay [and break] into their constituent parts. The same fate will befall Russia. This idea belongs to the best of the Russians: Radishchev, the Decembrists, and Aleksandr Ivanovich [Herzen]. Read the latter in *Kolokol* in 1859, "Answer to a Pole." There are good statements about Little Russia's future. It will be rather useful to disseminate it.

Iefymenko displayed remarkable foresight in his analysis of future developments. However, in the eyes of the authorities his letter was additional proof that Ukrainian national activists were not only cultivating their language and educating the common people, but also using these activities to promote broader political goals. Furthermore, Andrushchenko's correspondence revealed that he was a member of the local Ukrainian decision-making council (*rada*) in Moscow.[151] Andrushchenko also exchanged letters with Leonid Hlibov and his wife Paraska. Although those letters did not contain references to any illegal activities, they offered the authorities a pretext to close down *Chernigovskii listok* and dismiss Hlibov from his position as a secondary-school teacher.[152]

Nis's correspondence contained extensive information on Hromada groups in Chernihiv, Kyiv, and Poltava. However, apart from the existence of clandestine societies, no evidence of any actual political crimes was discovered. Nis corresponded with some repressed Ukrainians, like Iefymenko, Loboda, Chubynsky, and Konysky, but devoted his energy to the distribution of permitted Ukrainian books. Not surprisingly, his correspondence revealed resentment against the recent arrests of Ukrainian activists. Antipathy to the Russians and opposition to Russian cultural influence on Ukrainians were expressed in several letters that were sent to Nis, but not in any of his own texts. The idea of Ukrainian independence was mentioned in one letter to Nis.[153] He and Andrushchenko corresponded mainly in Ukrainian, and among Andrushchenko's possessions was Ukrainian national garb. During the search of his house Nis struck the local police chief three times with his fist, and tried to hit him with a violin as well, but that attack was prevented.[154]

While in detention in Chernihiv, Andrushchenko tried to send warning letters to his friends. He advised a fellow detainee to deliver his letters to Hlibov, who would then forward them to their destinations. Most of the letters were to Moscow, but one was to Vasyl Bilozersky in St Petersburg. However, the authorities intercepted the letters before they could be delivered to Hlibov. Thus, instead of helping people, the letters served to embroil them in the case. After spending a one month and a half in detention, Andrushchenko broke down and began telling the authorities what he knew about Land and Liberty. His testimonies were fairly reliable and they led to several additional arrests. Even today, Andrushchenko's testimonies are one of the most important sources on the history of Land and Liberty. However, it appears that he did not reveal everything that he knew.[155]

The most interesting information concerns the role of Vasyl Bilozersky. In addition to Andrushchenko's warning letter, the authorities found a letter that he wrote to his brother Oleksandr.[156] Most of the letter concerned *Osnova*. Vasyl advised Oleksandr to visit the teacher Ilia Doroshenko, who had been involved in Zaichnevskii's case through Iashchenko. He informed his brother that there were about ten Ukrainians in the Peter and Paul Fortress, who were imprisoned there following base denunciations. "Convinced, honest Ukrainians are our most precious treasure. So take care of yourself and the others. Careless words destroy more people than real action."[157] Because of the two letters, Andrushchenko's and Bilozersky's, the authorities searched the latter's apartment. The only important item found was a letter from a woman named Elizaveta Baranovskaia to the railway engineer Hieronym Kieniewicz, one of the leaders of the Polish insurrection.[158] Kieniewicz was the main initiator of the so-called Kazan conspiracy, an attempt to organize an armed insurrection in that city in the spring of 1863 with the aid of Russian revolutionaries.[159] He was acquainted with the activists of Land and Liberty, especially those based in St Petersburg, Moscow, and Kazan. The purpose of the Kazan uprising was to divert Russian forces from Poland, but the authorities uncovered the plan in April 1863. Kieniewicz only escaped arrest because he was absent from Kazan at the time. Later, he was a member of the underground national government, but was arrested in June 1863 and executed.[160]

The letter from Baranovskaia to Kieniewicz did not contain anything political. However, the author wrote that because she did not recall the number of his house, she was sending the letter to Bilozersky. This indicated at least that Bilozersky knew Kieniewicz. However, when questioned but not under arrest, Bilozersky claimed that he did not understand how the letter had appeared among his papers, and suggested that Kieniewicz was his wife's acquaintance.[161] He denied knowing anyone named Kieniewicz. Bilozersky later sent the authorities an additional explanation, claiming that his wife remembered the story of the letter, which she had received from Baranovskaia three or four years before the house search. She did not know any Kieniewicz either, and tried unsuccessfully to find him in order to deliver the letter. She then promptly forgot all about the letter, which she had kept in her home.[162] The explanation is utterly unconvincing because the wording of the letter indicates that it was sent through Bilozersky, who was supposed to be known to both the sender and the addressee, not through his wife. However, the authorities did not proceed further with this case.

Andrushchenko claimed that Nis did not know about the scope of his clandestine activities, even though he had shown Nis one proclamation, and another time Nis had brought him an issue of Herzen's *Kolokol*.[163] However, during the house search Nis tried to prevent Andrushchenko's suitcase from being opened by claiming that it was his,[164] which would indicate that he probably knew what was in it. Andrushchenko's testimonies and house searches revealed that several other Ukrainophiles were more or less involved in Land and Liberty. Of these, Ivan Rechytsky, a Moscow-based student from the province of Chernihiv, had stored Land and Liberty's proclamations for a time in his home. Rechytsky had met Andrushchenko at Nis's home, where they had discussed the Chernihiv Sunday schools and *Chernigovskii listok*.[165] Another Moscow student from Chernihiv, Kostiantyn Kozlovsky, distributed the proclamations in Moscow.[166] Kozlovsky's Ukrainian orientation is evident from the fact that during the search of his house the authorities discovered three lists of individuals who had contributed funds to the publishing of Ukrainian popular textbooks.[167] The Moscow student Ivan Driha had also corresponded with Andrushchenko about Herzen's publications, but he was a subscriber rather than a distributor.[168] Land surveyor Ivan Maslokovets corresponded in Ukrainian with Andrushchenko about the distribution of Land and Liberty's proclamations.[169] He was also acquainted with Nis, from whom he borrowed books from time to time. Under questioning Maslokovets admitted that he supported elementary education in Ukrainian, although this was not something in which the interrogators were primarily interested.[170]

Oleksandr Tyshchynsky had also received proclamations for distribution, although in smaller quantity than Andrushchenko.[171] Tyshchynsky corresponded with Iefymenko, a fellow member of Kharkiv-Kyiv group.[172] From the authorities' viewpoint, the contents of the letters were suspect because Iefymenko had recommended that all political and philosophical doctrines should be taught in Sunday schools, including socialism and communism, but in a non-committal way so that pupils could choose their own views. In his letter Iefymenko also mentioned the Central Committee of Land and Liberty. In all, nine people can be identified as Ukrainian activists who were involved in one way or another in Andrushchenko and Nis's case,[173] excluding Vasyl Bilozersky. Andrushchenko and Nis suffered most. Despite his cooperation with the interrogators, Andrushchenko was not released and died in the prison hospital of the Peter and Paul Fortress in October 1865. Although Nis was released from prison after interrogation, he was deported to Belozersk in the province of Novgorod, returning home only in 1871.[174]

After the suppression of the Sunday schools and Vasilchikov's death, Ukrainians suffered as a result of the government's policy to such a degree that the policy of cooperation with the government appeared rather unpromising. A cautious reorientation in the Hromada had taken place even before the promulgation of the Valuev circular. Borys Poznansky recounted this in his memoirs, having heard from Antonovych about an agreement that the latter had concluded with the Polish insurgents.[175] The Poles would leave Ukrainian activists in peace during their armed struggle, and in return the Ukrainians would observe neutrality. The probable date for these negotiations was late 1862–early 1863. Bohdan Klid has found interesting information indicating that Antonovych was one of those who helped Antoni Chamieć, a fellow Ukrainophile and former Kyiv student who had remained in the Polish movement, hide from the authorities and evade arrest.[176] Chamieć was the chairman of the Committee of Rus', the political leadership of the insurrection in Right-Bank Ukraine. The letters to Nis demonstrate that within the Kyiv Hromada there were different perceptions of the failed insurrection: while Oleksandr Stoianov described the Russian victory in a triumphant tone, Z. Hravovsky felt empathy for the insurgents, who were maltreated while under arrest.[177]

In the early months of 1864 an interesting correspondence took place between the Polish National Government, the underground Polish supreme authority during the January uprising, and an enigmatic group called the Progressive Rusyn Hromada. Only the former's response, dated 23 February (N.S.), has been preserved and published.[178] Most likely it was drafted by the Polish National Government's secretary for Rus' [Ukraine], the former Kyiv student Marian Dubiecki. The Hromada proposed that Poland officially renounce its historical rights to Rus' [Right-Bank Ukraine] and cease considering it an integral part of the Polish state. A liberated Rus' would then join a federation with Poland, and the Hromada would be ready to work for this goal. The Polish historian Stefan Kieniewicz presumed that the Progressive Rusyn Hromada was based in Lviv;[179] however, it is much more likely that it was headquartered in Kyiv. The Polish National Government sent its answer to Chamieć, who was responsible for Right-Bank Ukraine in the Russian Empire, not Galicia in Austria. From the answer it follows that the Hromada proposed that the Polish National Government would renounce its claim to Ukraine only in relation to Ukrainians, but not in relation to Russia. In other words, they wanted Poland's supreme authority to demand Ukrainian territory from Russia, but at the same time grant self-determination to Ukraine.[180] The territorial claim issue presented to Russia confirms the hypothesis that the discussion concerns Right-Bank Ukraine, not Galicia. Furthermore, there are references to the "Muscovite occupation" of the country and Russian slander that the Poles wanted to retain the peasants' work obligations, statements that were not applicable to Galicia in 1864.[181] At issue here is a discussion between the National Government and either the Kyiv Hromada or, perhaps, one part of it. The word "Progressive" in the title of the organization may imply the existence of another Hromada, which was deemed not progressive. Chamieć probably transmitted between the two parties not only the Polish National Government's answer but also the Hromada's original proposal.

To initiate negotiations with Polish insurgents after the demise of the insurrection in Right-Bank Ukraine is not as strange as it may seem. The renunciation of Polish claims to Ukraine would indeed have been an important political victory. Such renunciation would not have lost its relevance even after the end of the insurrection. The Polish National Government was facing its complete demise and could be expected to offer concessions. Furthermore, despite the initial success, the association of the Ukrainian cause with the Russian government's anti-Polish policies could now be deemed a failure. However, the initiative of the Hromada to seek cooperation between the Ukrainians and Poles did not produce the desired results. In its answer, the Polish National

Government indeed pointed to the Ukrainians' recent cooperation with the Russian authorities:

> In general, the Rusin[182] nationality did not enjoy the occupying power's recognition. Some minor concessions made for its benefit had a rather evident goal, although at first the Rusins [acted] as if they did not notice it: nationality was used as an instrument for the continuation of the occupation, as an obstacle for the Polish nationality, which strives for liberation. Today this fact has become so much more evident that we do not think that any Rusin can honestly deny it ... Rusins should comprehend without difficulty that the antipathy that their movement has recently confronted resulted from the evident association of Rusin activities with the occupier's ugly plans. From the minute this connection ceases to function, all Polish antipathy to Rusin national activities will certainly disappear.[183]

The Polish National Government recognized the right of the Rusin nationality to its independent (*samodzielnego*) development, but refused to renounce Poland's historical territorial rights. In its view, the insurrection was not something alien to Rus', inasmuch as it represented the interest of all three fraternal peoples (Poles, Lithuanians, and Rusins) that formed the ancient Polish Commonwealth. According to the Polish National Government, both Poles and Rusins were the original inhabitants of Rus'. It acknowledged that because of the ancient conflicts, historical enmity existed between Rusins and Poles, both sides having made mistakes. However, in the face of oppression suffered by both Poles and Rusins at present, there was no reason to remain bitter about the past: "The National Government considers ... the insurrection in Rus' equally a Rusin and Polish insurrection. The national authorities in Rus' are Rusin authorities who act in agreement and unity with the authorities of other lands that are united under the central leadership of the National Government equally for the good of the Rusin and common Fatherland."[184]

Although only one class of the Rus' population, the Polish nobility, participated in the insurrection, it still expressed internal-domestic needs. "This opinion is all the more well argued when that class is enlightened and concentrates in its possession the most important material interests of the land."[185] Since conditions were such that elections could not be held anywhere in Poland, the right to speak in the name of the country belonged to those who acted in its interests. "On this principle, the

National Government, not in the sense of forcing and usurpation, but with serious paternal and fraternal intention, considers itself the representative of the rightful interests and aims of Poland as well as Lithuania and Rus'."[186] The word "paternal" seems to be an unconsidered slip. Finally, the Polish National Government presented the argument for restoration: "The partitions of Poland violated public morals and justice in political relations. Poland cannot be raised except through the broadest execution of the principles of political and social justice."[187] The historical normative act concerning relations between Poland and Rus' was the Union of Lublin concluded in 1569, which the underground Polish government still considered binding. Although serfdom was a harmful phenomenon, it had emerged in Poland as a result of its union with Rus', first ruled by Norseman and later by Lithuanian conquerors. Poland had not experienced conquests in its history, and the harmful influence of the aristocratic magnates emerged only after the union with Rus'. However, Rus' had experienced much better times in union with Poland than later under Moscow's rule.

Poland's underground government backed its historical arguments with practical considerations. Lines of communication and strategic factors made the unity of Poland and Rus' a necessity. Without its Polish population, Rus' would lack significant intellectual and material forces which contributed to its development. Rusins themselves would notice this sooner or later and return to their native Polish element (*żywioł*). The 1772 borders were important for the Polish National Government not as such, but because they embodied a legal principle. If an anti-Polish movement resisting the union with Poland were to emerge within the pre-partition borders, the underground government would not attempt to use force to retain unity. Indeed, the government spoke about such a movement as hypothetical, as if deliberately ignoring the mainstream opinion of Ukrainian national activists. Furthermore, it declared that Rusins could not blame Poles for the fact that the 1772 borders had divided their nationality because the blame belonged to those who had submitted the territories lying east of the Dnipro to Moscow in the seventeenth century – a tacit reference to Bohdan Khmelnytsky. The reunification of the region beyond the Dnipro (Left-Bank Ukraine) with Poland or Rus' was possible in the future, but only if the population there voluntarily supported it. The restoration of the pre-partition borders could be a first step towards that goal. Finally, the Polish National Government rejected the Hromada's demand that Rus' be granted the status of a federal state. As a provisional body struggling solely for independence, the underground government did not consider itself entitled to make a decision about such a settlement, although it promised autonomy to Rus' and the other lands of the Polish Commonwealth. Federation was possible later, if the Rusins joined Poles in their struggle for liberation of the common fatherland.[188]

In the end, the Polish National Government was not capable of moving beyond the limits of Polish national mythology with respect to the prepartition commonwealth. This prevented the conclusion of a Ukrainian-Polish agreement even in the situation where the two prospective sides faced an overwhelming enemy: the Russian government. If the alliance with Vasilchikov had not produced the desired results, the Polish response to Progressive Rusyn Hromada's proposals showed that no better results could be expected from an alliance with the Poles.

The turn of the 1860s marked the sharpening of national dividing lines. In 1861 even many nationally indifferent members of the intelligentsia were pressured to choose a nationality. In this process, Ukrainian identity developed into an exclusive identity that was all the more difficult to combine with either Polish or all-Russian national identity. In retrospect, both the Ukrainian and Polish student movements had more in common than their eventual mutual conflict would suggest. Both aimed to strengthen their respective nationalities by elevating the status of peasants, and both represented a modern change of society in terms of national identity and the opposition to estate privileges based on birth. The initial role of the Russian government in the history of the Kyiv Hromada is somewhat surprising: instead of repressions, the local government's benevolence gave the Hromada a smooth start. At first, the Ukrainian movement sided with the government against the Polish insurrection. When this policy backfired as the government adapted a hostile attitude to the Ukrainian movement, at least some Kyiv Ukrainians were ready to switch to an alliance with the Poles, but with meagre results. Even the last Polish-Ukrainian contacts most likely took place between persons who knew each other from St Vladimir's University.

The authorities were not unfair or paranoid in their general perception that Ukrainian activists presented a danger to the Russian Empire. Even within a short span of time, the potential for the further development of Ukrainian nationalism was considerable. In April 1861 two thousand people attended Shevchenko's second funeral after his body was brought to Kaniv;[189] Ukrainian popular editions circulated in tens of thousands of copies. However, the authorities introduced arbitrary repressions and forged evidence to solve their problem. The repressions had two goals: to hinder the development of the Ukrainian movement, and to provide an argument against those government politicians who were opposed to repressive policies. Once a person was repressed without evidence, his guilt could be used as an argument for further repressions. Arbitrariness in the treatment of the Ukrainian question is evident also in the most notorious example of repressions at the beginning of the 1860s – the Valuev circular.

Chapter Six

Imperial Policies and the Ukrainian Movement, 1863–76

The policies of the Ministry of Internal Affairs, Third Section, and governor-general of Kyiv led to the notorious Valuev circular of 18 July 1863. By April 1863 these three government agencies had come to share a hostile attitude to the Ukrainian movement. The circular was an instruction that Petr Valuev sent to all censors with the emperor's permission. In a slightly ambiguous wording, he banned all literature aimed at readers among the common people, and even non-fiction that was meant for the educated: "The minister of internal affairs has deemed it necessary, until agreements with the minister of public education, the chief procurator of the Holy Synod, and the chief of the gendarmerie, in respect to book publishing in the Little Russian language, to issue a directive to the Censorship Administration to license for publication only such books in this language that belong to the realm of fine literature; at the same time, the authorization of books in Little Russian with either spiritual content or intended generally for primary mass reading should be ceased."[1]

The official procedure that gave rise to the circular is well known: formally, it was an initiative of the Kyivan censor Orest Markovich Novitskii, who sent an inquiry about the matter to the Main Administration of the Press on 27 June 1863. Novitskii argued that the separatist intention of a book was often manifest, even though its contents did not include anything ostensibly harmful. He directed attention to the fact that some individuals who had been punished as political criminals had participated in Ukrainian publishing activities, claiming – incorrectly – that the Kharkiv secret society had launched those activities. He suspected that Ukrainian separatism owed its origin to a Polish intrigue. Contrary to the facts, the Kyivan censor went so far as to claim that most Ukrainian-language manuscripts submitted to the censorship were authored by Poles. A mere six days earlier the influential Russian journalist Mikhail Nikiforovich Katkov had published a similar opinion in *Moskovvskie vedomosti* (*Moscow News*). With good reason Alexei Miller has opined that the similarity was hardly a coincidence.[2] Dolgorukov had already proposed the Polish-intrigue theory of the origins of Ukrainian nationalism the previous January.

The circular, which followed as a response to Novitskii's inquiry, was supported by Dolgorukov and endorsed by Alexander II. Valuev emphasized that some of the Ukrainian authors had committed political crimes. He also argued that the literary use of Little Russian evoked resentment among the majority of Little Russians, many of whom were of the opinion that no such language existed. He deemed it inappropriate to publish elementary textbooks in Little Russian before the government had decided whether that dialect could be used for pedagogical purposes. Finally, he repeated Dolgorukov's and Novitskii's Polish-intrigue theory of the origins of the Ukrainian national movement, including the false information about the majority of Ukrainian books being submitted to censorship by Poles.

Historians have offered several different motives for the Valuev circular. Fedir Savchenko thought that the authorities disapproved of the Ukrainian language and nationality as such, as well as Krasovsky's revolutionary radicalism. Savchenko emphasized the staged element in the accusations of Ukrainian separatism and the Ukrainian-Polish connection, pointing to the fact that in several cases no evidence was produced to back such accusations.[3] David Saunders argued that Valuev and many other imperial politicians perceived a difference between the Ukrainophiles and the Polish insurgents, and clearly understood that the aims of these two groups were not identical. Instead of short-term political circumstances, Saunders emphasized the long-term importance of Ukraine to the perceived ethnic Russian nation. To Valuev and other imperial functionaries who supported the restrictions on Ukrainian publications, it was inacceptable that the Ukrainian common people would adopt a national identity separate from the Russian identity. However, according to Saunders, Valuev and his adherents did not extend their hostility to Ukrainian publications that circulated among the educated public. Saunders views as especially important the question of the language of instruction in elementary schools, which was then being debated both among members of the general public and imperial politicians. While Ukrainian activists demanded instruction in Ukrainian, their request evoked opposition in government circles. According to Saunders, it is possible that Katkov and his journal *Russkii vestnik* (*Russian Messenger*) may have influenced Valuev.[4] Witold Rodkiewicz has emphasized how the Polish question was crucial to the government's approach to the Ukrainian question. Although the Ukrainian movement espoused different goals from the Polish one, imperial officials misperceived the first as a creation of the second. However, Rodkiewicz also noted the long-term inclination of some government circles towards ethnic Russian nationalism based on language.[5] According to Alexei Miller, government politicians feared both Ukrainian separatism as such and its possible alliance with the Polish insurgents. The views of Rodkiewicz and Miller are at variance with Savchenko and Saunders in that they perceive the authorities' fear of Ukrainian-Polish cooperation as sincere and not as a demagogical pretext. Miller agrees with Saunders in that the controversy over the use of Ukrainian in elementary education was also important.[6] In Ricarda Vulpius's view, the circular was essentially a reaction to the plans to publish a Ukrainian translation of the Gospels. The imperial politicians opposed the translation because it would have given to the Ukrainian language such dignity as was deemed incompatible with the project of the all-Russian nation. Although the secular authorities, like Dolgorukov and Valuev, were the most active, the Orthodox Church hierarchy shared their opposition to the translation, Vulpius observed.[7] Most recently, Andrii Danylenko has argued against Vulpius's interpretation of the genesis of the circular. He states that Pylyp Morachevsky's planned translation was by no means exceptional, since many religious works in Ukrainian had been permitted before. Furthermore, the translation was based on the vernacular language with no attempt to distance Ukrainian from Great Russian.[8]

I find Saunders's differentiation between the immediate and long-term causes of the circular to be a valid approach. As Miller, too, has emphasized, exclusive Ukrainian national identity and the idea of a large all-Russian nation were in conflict with each other. Since the government officially supported the latter idea, it was bound to have difficulties in accepting Ukrainians as a separate nationality. Ukrainian national activists made such acceptance even more problematic by emphasizing that Russia and Great Russians constituted the alien antithesis of Ukrainians, which defined Ukrainian nationality. Although it was possible to be a Ukrainian nationalist without sharing the negative stereotypes of Russians, those stereotypes were predominant in the national movement. This fact could not remain unnoticed by imperial politicians. In the long run, the government was bound to react to these tendencies.

However, the long-term factors do not suffice to explain the circular. The government applied the same repressive measures – exile, prison, and forced labour – against Ukrainian national activists as it did against other political opposition movements. Why were such measures deemed so inadequate that restrictions were enacted against a literary language? Novitskii's letter to Valuev, described above, contains one of the answers to this question: often the "separatist" intention of a text was obvious even if its contents did not include explicit violations of censorship rules. Indeed, as Russia's minister of internal affairs, Valuev repeated this observation, which was applied to Russian censorship in general, in one of his last memoranda to the emperor in 1868: where censorship was concerned, the authorities had to follow explicit rules, while writers could resort to allusions.[9] The tactics of the Ukrainian national movement were such that most activists could not be charged with political crimes. Although the government fabricated evidence against Chubynsky and Syniehub, it was not advantageous for it to practise such arbitrariness in a broader fashion. The enactment of restrictions against the Ukrainian language released the censors from the obligation to read hidden meanings between the lines, and the gendarmes – from concocting a multitude of cases on the same basis as those that were instituted against Chubynsky and Syniehub. Nevertheless, banning even texts that demonstrated the greatest loyalty to the empire merely on the basis of the language in which they were written was certainly an inept and counterproductive political measure.

The most important short-term reasons explaining the promulgation of the circular were the information the government received about the political orientation of Hromada groups and changes in the government personnel. Krasovsky's case produced reliable information about those radical egalitarian and anti-Russian tendencies, including the idea of independence for Ukraine, which existed in the Kyiv Hromada. The texts that were found in the homes of the members of the Poltava Hromada confirmed this information. Vasilchikov's death and the transfer of censorship from the jurisdiction of the Ministry of Public Enlightenment to the Ministry of Internal Affairs meant that by April 1863 all the key decision-making positions were held by advocates of severe measures against the Ukrainian national movement. However, imperial politicians' statements about Ukrainian-Polish cooperation or their opinion that the entire Ukrainian movement was a Polish invention should not be taken at face value. Like the Chubynsky and Syniehub cases, the Polish insurrection offered a useful argument against the numerous opponents of the Valuev circular within the government's own ranks. Both Dolgorukov and Valuev were perfectly aware that the Ukrainians' goals differed from those of the Polish independence movement. As the chairman of the Kyiv Censorship Committee, Novitskii knew that most Ukrainian manuscripts submitted to the committee were not authored by Poles. Nevertheless, he claimed they were because it was a politically expedient argument, which his superior Valuev repeated in his circular. Saunders is correct in emphasizing the staged element in official statements about the Polish danger.[10]

Among important political figures during the reign of Alexander II, Valuev was not a reactionary. His contribution was crucial to the enactment of the *zemstvo*, provincial, and district administration that was based on elected representatives from all social ranks. It was his intention to enlist elected representatives to the process of drafting new laws, and he submitted a relevant memorandum to Alexander II on 15 April 1863, proposing that representatives of the nobility, merchants, burghers, and Orthodox Church clergymen participate in the sessions of the State Council. To be sure, Valuev envisioned those representatives as possessing only advisory prerogatives without any limitation to the emperor's autocratic legislative power. Nevertheless, in the conditions of Russia in the 1860s such a reform would have been significant, and it might have facilitated a subsequent switch to constitutional rule. Valuev's proposal was discussed in the Council of Ministers, but rejected by most participants as well as the emperor.[11]

Valuev's adherence to such an important step towards a more democratic political order seems to be at odds with his circular. However, this apparent inconsistency maybe explained by his orientation to the interests of the nobility. Valuev's appointment in March 1861 as minister of internal affairs was a concession to the conservative nobility. The nobles resented his predecessor, Sergei Stepanovich Lanskoi, who had been very active in abolishing serfdom and enacting the land reform. Valuev thought that the nobility deserved compensation for the losses that they had suffered as a result of emancipation. Although the peasants gained representation in the *zemstvo* assemblies, Valuev took the nobility's interests into account above all. His "constitutional" proposal excluded peasants from participating in the State Council. Furthermore, his sympathy for the nobility had an impact on his policy regarding the different nationalities of the Russian Empire. In 1853–8 he served as the governor-general of Courland in the Baltic region, where the nobility consisted of Germans, while the peasants spoke Latvian. He got along well with the local nobles, who held dear their traditional autonomous institutions. With regard to the Polish question, Valuev was one of the most moderate imperial politicians; he disliked repressions and would have preferred to reach an agreement with the local aristocracy. He granted some legitimacy to the autonomous strivings of the Poles and Baltic Germans, since both these groups had their own nobility, high culture, and traditional institutions. On the basis of Valuev's policies regarding Poles, Darius Staliūnas has concluded that the minister did not perceive ethnic affiliation with Russians as a criterion of political loyalty.[12] Why was his attitude so different regarding Ukrainians? First, Ukrainians were a predominantly plebeian nationality. Furthermore, it was not the local nobility but the populist-leaning intelligentsia that was leading the project to create a high culture in Ukrainian. Valuev had little sympathy for any such plebeian national projects in general, and even less for the Ukrainian project in particular.

Restricting publications solely on the basis of the language in which they were written was not the traditional policy of the imperial government.[13] Even so, the Ukrainian case was not unique. Similar restrictions were applied or proposed in relation to at least two other languages and ethnic groups that were clearly separate from the perceived all-Russian nationality. The imperial decree enacted in March 1850 limited the scope of Finnish-language publications, allowing only religious and economic literature with a practical orientation.[14] That decree had been motivated by the desire to prevent the dissemination of political ideas among the Finnish common people rather than by any antipathy to the Finnish language per se, and it was repealed in February 1860. The Ukrainian case was similar to the Finnish one insofar as Valuev wanted to prevent the dissemination of subversive ideas, especially among the common people.[15] However, his explicit antipathy to the Ukrainian language was the major distinguishing feature of his circular as compared to the earlier ban on Finnish publications. Another analogy may be drawn to Valuev's attitude to the Yiddish language. In 1862 a Jewish civil servant named Markus Gurovich proposed a ban on publications in Yiddish and on the use of this language in education on the grounds that this "slang" (*zhargon*) prevented Jews from learning Russian and German. Valuev supported the proposal, arguing that "it [the ban] will prevent the further literary development of the slang and thus remove the possibility of it ever becoming the means of expression of those concepts that the Jews will, with the expansion of education among them, adopt from Russian and German books. [The ban] will thus promote a gradual replacement of the slang by Russian."[16]

Valuev did not attack Hebrew, the traditional language of Jewish religion and learning, or Yiddish in its capacity as a spoken language. Indeed, when a ban against popular enlightenment in Hebrew was proposed in 1867, he opposed it. However, he wanted to reserve for Russian the role of the modern language of high culture that Jews should use outside the religious sphere. He acknowledged the transformation of society and expansion of education that were taking place, believing that without restrictions Yiddish might develop into a language of high culture. However, Golovnin strongly opposed the proposed ban on Yiddish publications, which was never enacted.[17]

In the Ukrainian case, a year later Valuev could have his way because, in the meantime, control over censorship had been transferred to his ministry from Golovnin's Ministry of Public Enlightenment.[18] In Valuev's view, Ukrainian, like Yiddish, was not a fully-fledged language. In his circular on Ukrainian publications Valuev quoted opinions that denied the existence of the language, asserting that the local dialect was "nothing but Russian corrupted by Polish influence."[19] In both these cases, he wanted to prevent a vernacular from developing into a proper language of high culture. While in the Yiddish case Valuev also allowed German as an alternative literary language, for the Ukrainians he desired the exclusive use of Russian. In the Yiddish case, Valuev's antipathy to the vernacular and his desire to widen the use of Russian were not connected with the Polish question, which was not mentioned in his discussion with Golovnin. In light of his position regarding the literary use of Yiddish, Valuev's actions appear consistently hostile to the linguistic projects of traditionally non-dominant nationalities; hence the minister was not averse to using force against such projects.

By the time the circular was enacted, Valuev's situation had become somewhat precarious. His soft policy vis-à-vis the Polish question had evoked resentment in the upper ranks of the bureaucracy and among the members of the imperial family, and Alexander II disapproved of Valuev's proposed reform of the State Council, which he found incompatible with autocracy. Restricting Ukrainian publications gave Valuev an opportunity to show that he could be tough against a rebellious nationality. However, it was also certain that the restrictions against Ukrainian publications would evoke opposition. If the circular were a law, it should have been passed on to the emperor through the State Council, as the existing legislation and established procedure required.[20] As a ministerial circular, it was an administrative decree rather than a law, and consideration by the State Council was not obligatory. However, the enactment of such an important measure as an administrative decree was in itself rather questionable. Moreover, it was one of the main tasks of the Committee of Ministers to discuss such administrative decrees that impinged on the purview of several government agencies and for which the ministers needed the emperor's endorsement.[21] The circular clearly fit this category since, apart from the Ministry of Internal Affairs, it affected the purview of the Ministry of Public Enlightenment and the Holy Synod.

If the restrictions on Ukrainian publishing were discussed in either the State Council or Committee of Ministers, opposition to them was bound to arise. There were several influential imperial politicians who either resisted the circular or were likely to oppose it during a session of the State Council or Committee of Ministers. As mentioned in the previous chapter, the St Petersburg Hromada counted among its members a senator and member of the State Council. Furthermore, the chairman of both the State Council and the Committee of Ministers was Dmitrii Bludov, who had actively opposed the ban on the second edition of the *History of the Rus'*. As president of the Russian Academy of Sciences, Bludov was supporting Pylyp Morachevsky's translation of the New Testament.[22] Furthermore, at the end of April 1863, Bludov approached Alexander II with a request to permit a semi-official West Russia Association.[23] The prospected association was to establish primary schools where local languages, including Ukrainian but excluding Polish, were to be used in the beginning of instruction, in order to facilitate learning of Russian. The proposals to promote local languages were more modest than those which had been presented in 1862: now, the use of local languages on higher than an elementary level was not proposed. According to Staliūnas, the initiative to establish the society came from prominent Slavophiles and several enlightened bureaucrats. The Slavophiles included Mikhail Osipovich Koialovich and Aleksandr Hilferding, the enlightened bureaucrats Andrei Zablotskii-Desiatovskii and Nikolai Miliutin, senator and former deputy minister of the internal affairs under Valuev's predecessor, Sergei Stepanovich Lanskoi. Indeed, Slavophiles and enlightened bureaucrats overlapped, since Hilferding served as Zablotskii-Desiatovskii's assistant in the apparatus of the State Council. Several of the initiators had participated in drafting the abolition of serfdom. Valuev's nomination as the minister of internal affairs in 1861 had been directed exactly against this group of reformers, which many conservatives deemed too radical. The establishment of the society would have substantially reduced Valuev's influence on the policies practised in all the western provinces that had previously belonged to Poland-Lithuania. Golovnin, too, was a member of the State Council. In the context of the Yiddish discussion, Golovnin had clearly stated his opinion that no text should be banned merely because of the language in which it was written.[24] Clearly, Valuev had to act against Bludov's proposal, and to do it in the State Council entailed a considerable risk for him.

Alexei Miller has emphasized the temporary character of the circular, pointing to the fact that Valuev referred to recent political circumstances as one reason for the measure, meaning the Polish insurrection.[25] Examining Valuev's correspondence with Mikhail Katkov, Miller determined that Valuev "perceived the circular as a temporary measure for the time of the Polish uprising."[26] I cannot support his interpretation of Valuev's intentions and policy because Valuev indeed intended the restrictions to have force for an extended period. As will become evident below, the same file in which the circular is located offers evidence against the professed intention to enact a temporary measure. Furthermore, the fact that Valuev, against his better judgment, spread disinformation about the proportion of Poles among Ukrainian writers points to the insincere rhetoric of the circular. Paulin Święcicki, discussed in chapter 4, was the sole Polish author who in 1862 submitted to Kyiv Censorship Committee a manuscript in Ukrainian.[27]

The word "temporary," often attributed to Russian laws, should not be taken at face value. A number of laws were enacted as "temporary" without stipulation of any specific expiration date. This was the case with many laws that limited citizens' rights; their enactment as "temporary" simply reflected the uneasiness of high-level officials about such restrictions.[28] Perhaps the most famous is the security law decreed by Alexander III in 1881, which remained in force until 1905. The reform of censorship that Valuev introduced in 1865 was also decreed as "temporary regulations"; in this case, it increased citizens' rights by abolishing aspects of preliminary censorship. The provisional capacity of the law derived from its being a compromise that evoked much opposition in the high bureaucracy and the State Council. The enactment of the law only for "the present reform period in the judiciary and until further guidelines will be received from experience"[29] was a device that Valuev used to appease the opposition.[30] These "temporary" regulations, too, remained in force until 1905.

The temporary character of the circular on Ukrainian publications followed from the dubious manner in which it emerged, not from Valuev's supposed opinion that the restrictions were desirable only for a short time. As Miller has established, Valuev drafted the circular on the basis of a mutual understanding with Dolgorukov and Annenkov, but bypassed all other agencies and government politicians.[31] To be sure, his conduct was not altogether exceptional, for ministers did sometimes bypass the collegial decision-making bodies. Nevertheless, their colleagues often resented such actions.[32] The temporary character of the circular was Valuev's way to shield himself from criticism, which he knew his unilateral action would evoke. Clearly, he would be blamed less for temporary instructions than for permanent restrictions. Nevertheless, the circular was enacted for an indefinite period of time, setting the stage for further discussion and the prospect of a final decision in the matter.

Formally, the Valuev circular was a provisional measure that would remain in force until a final decision on Ukrainian publications was rendered. The circular defined the persons who would have a say in shaping the final submission to the emperor: Valuev, chief procurator of the Holy Synod Aleksei Petrovich Akhmatov, Dolgorukov, and Golovnin. However, it was Valuev who would seek out the opinions of others and then proceed with the matter further. No meeting of the four decision makers was stipulated, although such brief consultations were fairly common in the imperial administration. Thus, Valuev reserved the last word for himself. He did, however, request opinions from the others. Golovnin replied with an angry letter, arguing against the restrictions:

> The essential contents of a book, the ideas that are expressed in it, and the general idea that it disseminates all form the basis for banning or permitting it, not at all the language in which it is written. That authors strive to develop grammatically each language or dialect ... is rather useful for public enlightenment and deserves full respect. That is why the Ministry of Public Enlightenment has an obligation to encourage these attempts and contribute to them ...
>
> Concerning the opinion of the governor-general of Kyiv that it is dangerous and harmful to publish a Little Russian New Testament that is now under consideration by the ecclesiastical censorship, out of respect to General-Adjutant Annenkov I explain to myself such an opinion

> as a result of a writing error of some inexperienced clerk. The spiritual administration has the holy obligation to distribute the New Testament among all the different inhabitants of the empire in all languages … The Little Russian translation of the Gospels in the local dialect, corrected by the ecclesiastical censorship, is one of the most glorious deeds that mark the present reign.[33]

However, Golovnin was the only consulted functionary who defended Ukrainian-language publications. Dolgorukov sent a laconic letter supporting the restrictions because Ukrainian-language publications directed at the common people were, according to him, "useless" and "not necessary."[34] Akhmatov reacted to the circular by immediately arranging for the Holy Synod to stop the preparation of a Ukrainian translation of the Gospels and to instruct the ecclesiastical censors to prevent all Ukrainian publications in their field.[35] However, concerning the prospective final decision, he only replied to Valuev seventeen months later, on Christmas Eve 1864.[36] In the opinion of the chief procurator, some Little Russian patriots (*malorusskie patrioty*)[37] were definitely aiming at political separation of Little Russia from the empire. In addition, Poles might try to exploit the spurious, alleged differences between Russian tribes in order to divide Russia. Even the well-intentioned Little Russian cultural activists, who only wished to develop the language, were unconsciously helping the Polish cause.[38] Akhmatov's opinion of the Ukrainian language as a Polish tool in the struggle against the empire echoed the ideas that Valuev presented in his circular, even though by now the Polish insurrection had been crushed. Furthermore, Akhmatov claimed that popular education in Little Russian would restrict the local population within a rather narrow range of literature and thereby keep it ignorant: "My position concerning this question, like yours, is completely different from the view of the minister of public enlightenment, who finds … the attempts at separation of the Little Russian dialect fully respectable and who even states that the Ministry of Public Enlightenment has an obligation to encourage and support them."[39] Akhmatov found that in situations when a language developed into a vehicle of political ideas and harmful tendencies could be attributed to it, then the government had no alternative but to struggle against that language. If there were no other means to "prevent evil," an exceptional ban based on language should be enforced. In the present case, the ban was necessary because the harmful tendency had support in the government itself (a reference to Golovnin's position).

Valuev's closest subordinate in the affairs of censorship was Mikhail Turunov, the chairman of the St Petersburg Censorship Committee.[40] In March 1865, he wrote to Valuev reminding him about the impending final decision on the question of Little Russian publications.[41] The responses had now arrived from all persons from whom they were requested. Turunov wrote: "It turns out that the chief procurator of the Holy Synod and the chief of the gendarmerie fully share the opinion of your Excellency that there is no benefit and no necessity to print books in the Little Russian language for the common people. On the other hand, the minister of public enlightenment finds the printing of such books not only beneficent, but also absolutely necessary."[42] Turunov proposed solving the disputed question in "normal legislative order"[43] and to send the documents that contained the different opinions to the Second Section of the Imperial Chancellery that was in charge of drafting laws. This meant that the question would have passed through the State Council and been submitted to open discussion within the highest levels of the imperial bureaucracy before being submitted for imperial approval. Not only Valuev's own circular, but also Golovnin's letter would have circulated as materials for discussion. The chairman of the State Council was now Grand Duke Konstantin, who was well known for his (modestly) liberal ideas, and to whose circle Golovnin belonged. Furthermore, the "temporary regulations" of censorship that scaled down preliminary censorship in Russia were passing through the regular legislative procedure at this time, and were approved by the State Council on 24 March 1865. A number of imperial politicians criticized the regulations, finding them too restrictive. Valuev's opponents with regard to this question included Golovnin, Minister of Justice Dmitrii Nikolaevich Zamiatnin, Minister of War Dmitrii Alekseevich Miliutin, and chairman of the legislative department of the State Council, Modest Korf. Valuev won the decisive vote in the State Council: 28 for the regulations and 14 against.[44] In the face of such strong liberal opposition, it was certainly not in his interest to bring the restrictions on Ukrainian publishing to the State Council at the same time as the "temporary regulations": the incoherence between the two measures would have been manifest. On 3 April Turunov wrote on the upper margin of his submission: "Minister ordered to cease the further processing of the present file."[45] Thus, even after the demise of the Polish insurrection, Valuev wanted to keep the circular in force by avoiding discussion about it in government circles. In this he acted in violation of the imperial order contained in his own circular, which stipulated a second and final decision. This was the way the "temporary" circular remained in force until the Ems Decree of 1876.

Implementation of the Valuev Circular in Practice

The effects of the circular continued well after the Polish insurrection, as is evident from the number of Ukrainian editions that were published in the Russian Empire between 1860 and 1876:[46] 1860: 20; 1861: 28; 1862: 33; 1863: 15; 1864: 11; 1865: 2; 1866: 2; 1867: 2; 1868: 1; 1869: 4; 1870: 3;1871: 9; 1872: 8; 1873: 4; 1874: 32; 1875: 22; 1876: 17. Thus, even such publications that were permitted by the circular were reduced dramatically in number. A slight recovery of Ukrainian publishing began after Aleksandr Egorovich Timashev replaced Valuev as minister of internal affairs in 1868, but the circular appeared to have lost its relevance by 1874. However, we shall see that this was not entirely the case.

The Valuev circular was not easy to implement. As the quotation above indicates, the wording in the circular was not entirely clear as to exactly which Ukrainian publications were banned. It certainly forbade all publications directed at the common people and all books of religious content, but there was some ambiguity concerning works directed at the Ukrainian intelligentsia. Thus, the circular at first allowed only belles-lettres, but then proceeded to specifically ban publications aimed at readers from among the common people. Reading the circular just as it was written, a censor should have prevented publication of all books except belles-lettres for the educated public. However, one could arguably also read the circular in a manner that allowed the publication of secular non-fiction for the educated public because, strictly speaking, the circular said nothing about such works. This is how Saunders has interpreted the circular, remarking that it forbade "low-brow" literature, but allowed the "high-brow" variety.[47] However, Mykola Kostomarov interpreted the restriction in the broader sense: writing to Valuev in July 1863 he complained about the ban on "scholarly works" in Ukrainian.[48] Moreover, the term "Little Russian language" was ambiguous at the time. No literary standard as yet existed. The geographic limits of the language in the Belarusian provinces and Austrian Galicia were not established. Some Ukrainian authors, like Ivan Nechui-Levytsky and Fortunat Piskunov would, in the 1870s, still argue that Belarusian was a dialect of Ukrainian.[49] Among the Galician Rusyns there were several contesting language parties, of which the two most important were the Russophile and Ukrainophile orientations. The Russophiles wanted to develop the literary language closer to, although not identical with, Russian; the Ukrainophiles sided with Ukrainian national activists of the Russian Empire in their efforts to develop a fully separate literary language.[50]

The "temporary regulations" complicated the censors' tasks with additional ambiguities.[51] They exempted from preliminary censorship certain kinds of publications: individual works of over ten galley sheets; publications issued by the Academy of Sciences, universities, and learned societies; works in classical languages, and their translations. It was now formally legal to print these kinds of books in Ukrainian without preliminary censorship, although they were banned in Valuev's circular. The authorities did not at first pay attention to the Ukrainian aspect of the problem. However, since some Russian publications that were exempted from preliminary censorship were found to be politically and ideologically harmful from the government's point of view, the law was amended in 1872. Henceforth, the minister of internal affairs could temporarily prevent distribution of a book exempted from the preliminary censorship if he found it especially harmful.[52] In these cases, he had to make a submission to the Committee of Ministers, which had the power to ban such a book without an imperial endorsement. Publishers had to deliver for censorship several copies of the books they had printed without preliminary censorship. Distribution of such books was allowed only after the publishers received a positive response from the censors. In other words, the complete exemption from preliminary censorship was replaced by censorship after printing, but before distribution. However, the exemptions from preliminary censorship remained relevant, for the procedure of banning an exempted book was still rather complicated.

During the years 1864–8, while Valuev was still in office, his circular was consistently implemented. All Ukrainian publications issued during those years were either belles-lettres (eleven editions) or collections of folk literature (six editions).One exception was a brochure by Iason Blonsky explaining the judicial reform of 1864, which was published in 1866 in Katerynoslav.[53] As a Ukrainian non-fiction publication directed at readers from among the common people, it violated the circular. However, the brochure appeared as a result of a violation of the censorship procedure: bypassing normal bureaucratic channels, it was submitted to a benevolent censor, who was not entitled to review it. Following this incident, the director of the Main Administration of the Press, Mikhail Shcherbinin, wrote to the governor of Katerynoslav. He asked him to verbally tell the owner of the press that, in the future, he must turn to the nearest censorship committee, as the law stipulated.[54]

An incident in 1865 proves that it was indeed Valuev's policy to restrict Ukrainian publishing as such, to curb even publications that were formally permitted by his circular. Since 1860, the authorities were watching Mykola (Nikolai) Ballin and Elena Ballina, spouses and owners of a bookstore and a library in Kharkiv, for their activism in the Sunday school movement and their contacts with some adherents of the all-Russian revolutionary movement.[55] In 1865 Ballin advertised a forthcoming publication of the bilingual collection *Iuzhno-Russkoe literaturnoe delo* (*South Russian Literary Cause*),which had not been submitted to the censors.[56] As a result, Valuev ordered the closure of the library.[57] However, thanks to intervention of the local governor, Aleksandr Sivers, the minister soon changed his mind and allowed the library to continue its operations. Among the explicit reasons for the new decision was that Elena Ballina had accepted the governor's proposal not to sell any Ukrainian-language books at the bookstore.[58]

Although it was a difficult time for Ukrainian publishing in 1863–8, activities in this sphere were not entirely suppressed. In 1867 a new edition of Shevchenko's *Kobzar* was published in St Petersburg. The book contained over ten galley sheets, so it was legal to publish it without preliminary censorship. Furthermore, in order to be on the safe side, the editors Mykola Kostomarov and Hryhorii Vashkevych removed many politically sensitive passages before the book went to print. Nevertheless, at first the authorities prevented the distribution of the *Kobzar*, forbidding the printing press of the Academy of Sciences to deliver the printed book to the editors. The censor A. Smirnov evaluated the book, deeming it permissible, especially because its price made it inaccessible to the common people. However, Smirnov disapproved of passages "that seem to evoke separatism by comparing the later, miserable state of Little Russia to the situation before its incorporation into Russia."[59] He also proposed removing passages that depicted the nobles oppressing their serfs. After the publisher Dmitrii Kozhanchikov made some additional cuts on his own initiative, the book was authorized for publication.

The publication of sources on Ukrainian history continued under the auspices of the Kyiv Commission for the Publication of Ancient Documents. Volodymyr Antonovych worked in the commission from 1863, and in April 1864 he was appointed as editor. The appointment was due to the patronage of none other than Mikhail Iuzefovich, deputy curator of the Kyiv School District.[60] In the 1860s Antonovych edited collections of documents on the history of the Orthodox Church in Polish-ruled Right-Bank Ukraine, the Cossacks before the Khmelnytsky Uprising, the Cossacks of Right-Bank Ukraine in the period after the uprising until 1719, and the peasantry. By publishing these documents, the imperial government wanted to discredit the previous Polish rule in Ukraine. Antonovych's work served this purpose, but he was also able to present his Ukrainian viewpoint. His populist ideas were evident in his claim that since the medieval Kyivan period, the common people had inhabited Ukraine, whose tradition was democratic, while the boyars and nobility were foreign, at least prior to the Khmelnytsky uprising. When the Cossacks overthrew Polish rule, they "restored their ancient Russian communal (*obshchinnyi*) order."[61] He also portrayed the Zaporozhian Cossack host as the embodiment of the ideal to which the South Russian nation (*narod*) had always striven. Except for a handful of sketchy remarks, in which Antonovych favourably evaluated the union with Russians, who were "of one blood and faith" with Little Russia,[62] he did not discuss Ukrainian–Russian relations. For his opportunity to work in the commission, Antonovych had to pay with some loss of integrity. When he published a small book about the Orthodox Church under Polish rule, Iuzefovich added a few sentences, in which the imperial policies of repression against Greek Catholics were given a positive evaluation.[63]

The publication of studies on the Ukrainian language continued even after 1863. Oleksandr Potebnia's learned treatise *The Characteristic Sounds of Russian Dialects* did not encounter any obstruction from the censors, even though it discussed the sensitive issue of the relationship between the Great Russian and Little Russian dialects. A scholar ahead of his time, Potebnia called the whole Russian language an abstraction. Although he postulated a common Russian root language from which both Great Russian and Little Russian had developed, he claimed that their separation had begun long before the twelfth century, Great Russian having fully separated from the common Russian by the tenth century. In other words, the two dialects were, according to Potebnia, already separate by the late Kyivan Rus' period.[64]

Although suppression and repression were the order of the day, not all government functionaries agreed that this was the correct policy on the Ukrainian question. How Governor-General Aleksandr Bezak succeeded in mitigating the fate of Syniehub and those arrested with him was discussed in chapter 5. In that context, Bezak wrote to Dolgorukov in the Third Section, presenting his opinion on the Ukrainian question and intending it to reach the emperor. He fully rejected as false the idea that Ukrainian activists had shared their goals with the Poles or cooperated with them:

> The activities of this party … have recently much weakened. There is hope that, even if some of the extreme adherents of this party indeed hope that it will be possible for Little Russia to gain autonomy, this undertaking will collapse under the common sense of the people and judgement of public opinion. I am convinced that the government must paralyze Ukrainophile activities, not permitting the instruction in Little Russian at elementary schools or the publication of textbooks in it, and by other measures that now turn out to be necessary. However, suppression of all expressions of Ukrainophile tendencies will not bring relevant benefit. On the one hand, it may raise the self-esteem of Ukrainophiles, on the other, it may give to Poles and the foreign press a pretext to circulate rumours that not only Poles but even Little Russians are the internal enemies of the Russian government, and that the government implements harsh measures against them out of concern that they may assail the unity of the government.[65]

Bezak's statement indicates that he was opposed to the arrest, imprisonment, and deportation of Ukrainian activists. Furthermore, his formulation of the necessary censorship was milder than the policy which was being practised, for the governor-general mentioned only textbooks as impermissible publications. It is interesting that Bezak, one of the most anti-Polish functionaries of the empire, altogether dismissed the idea of the existence of Ukrainian-Polish cooperation, while Valuev, who was relatively soft on Poles, emphasized the danger of such cooperation. However, Bezak's dissenting opinion did not reach the emperor. In his submission to Alexander II, Dolgorukov abridged Bezak's statement so as to filter out his opposition to the prevailing policy. Nevertheless, his position had practical consequences: Syniehub's case was closed, and some Ukrainophiles were named as Arbitrators of the Peace, mediating between peasants and noble landowners in the local implementation of the land reform that accompanied the abolition of serfdom.[66]

Between 1869 and 1873, after Valuev's resignation, three works appeared that probed the limits of the circular. The first of them was Kalynyk Sheikovsky's historical brochure that was published in Kyiv in 1870 and expressed a clear Ukrainian tendency. Sheikovsky was a gymnasium teacher of classical languages in Bobruisk, in what is now

Belarus.[67] He argued that the people of Rus', as described by the tenth-century Arab traveller Abu Ali Ahmed Ben Omar ibn Dasta, were "our ancestors," not Great Russians or Norsemen.[68] Sheikovsky used the term *Rusyny* to denote his nation. The brochure also contained a Ukrainian translation from ibn Dasta's description of the Rus'. Sheikovsky's work was important in that it was the first scholarly publication in Ukrainian permitted since 1863. Because the brochure was directed at the intelligentsia it did not violate the narrow interpretation of the circular although as non-fiction it clearly violated the broader one. However, a year later an elementary textbook on natural science appeared, *De-shcho pro svit Bozhyi* (*Something about God's World*), which was exactly the kind of literature the Valuev circular banned.[69] This was the second edition of a book originally published in 1863 by activists of the Kyiv Hromada.[70] The book did not contain explicit references to Ukrainian nationality, although it did begin with Shevchenko's poem in which the poet exhorts his countrymen to study. A lengthy foreword argued for the usefulness of learning, introducing readers to the development of civilization, and, as a by-product, to the idea of progress. The book stated that literacy was a defence against malfeasance and made the payment of bribes superfluous. Furthermore, it explained that the earth was round, provided the fundamentals of astronomy, gave scientific descriptions of water and air, and explained the causes for a variety of weather conditions.

Fortunat Piskunov's *Slovnytsia ukrainskoï (abo Iugovoï-Ruskoï) movy* (*Dictionary of the Ukrainian (or South Russian) Language*), which was authorized for publication in Odesa in 1872, appeared the following year. The dictionary could be regarded as a work that fell squarely within the limits set by the circular, for it was clearly designed for an educated public and its foreword and explanations were in Russian. However, it contained an unequivocal nationalist message. The lengthy entries for historical terms denoting various aspects of Cossack administration contained criticism of the Russian monarchy's previous policies towards Ukraine. Piskunov emphasized the elected character of Cossack leaders. He developed the Ukrainian language, creating neologisms for such concepts as "citizen" (*hromadiannyk*), "government" (*keruiatstvo*), "democracy" (*myrosprava*), and "patriotism" (*odchyznist'*). He also attributed to the ancient word *rada*, a Cossack meeting, the modern meaning of "parliament." The dictionary contained a poem attributed to hetman Mazepa. The poem used allegory to portray the Hetmanate as situated between two menacing powers.[71]

The real turning point in the opportunities for Ukrainian publishing was the year 1874. Of the seventy-one Ukrainian editions published in the empire during the years 1874–6, eighteen definitely violated the circular and an additional dictionary contradicted its broader interpretation.[72] There were six books on natural science, five on history, three medical manuals, two that explained existing laws and regulations, one on economics, and one biblical history. The books on natural science introduced readers to the basics of physics, astronomy, geology, and some aspects of biology.[73] Khvedir Vovk's adaptation of a work on bears was perhaps the first piece of Ukrainian light non-fiction, for it introduced readers to its topic through dramatic hunting and bear stories.[74] Mykhailo Drahomanov's and Ivan Nechui-Levytsky's historical works presented Cossack history, Kyivan Rus', the period of Lithuanian rule, and the Brest church union of 1596 from a Ukrainian national viewpoint.[75] Nechui-Levytsky sided with the Orthodox Church against the Catholic Uniates, describing Orthodoxy as the proper Ukrainian national religion and Uniates as the "enemies of the Ukrainian people."[76] Since the government was officially abolishing the Greek Catholic Church in the Kingdom of Poland and converting all Greek Catholics to Orthodoxy,[77] the subject of Nechui-Levytsky's book was rather timely. A national interpretation of history was not limited to historical books only. Stepan Nis smuggled Cossack history into his medical handbook in a chapter on how to treat various wounds.[78] Vikhtur Shcherbaty's book on money presented populist ideas by emphasizing how only work, rather than money or financial transactions, produced value. The book encouraged peasants to form their own lending banks.[79] The limits of the Valuev circular were thus clearly transgressed. With these publishing successes, Ukrainian activists simultaneously made other important advances. In the two years between 1874 and 1876 they controlled a public organization, the South-Western Section of the Imperial Russian Geographic Society in Kyiv, and had editorial control over the Russian-language newspaper *Kievskii Telegraf* (*Kyiv Telegraph*) from January to August 1875.[80]

Given both the number and type of Ukrainian publications the censorship permitted, one may be inclined to assume that the Valuev circular had been secretly repealed. However, the documents of the Main Administration of the Press show that this was not the case. Up to 1876 and the Ems Decree, the circular was considered binding for censors. It was upheld in the Main Administration of the Press in 1872 in the context of the discussion on the policy regarding Ukrainian publications that were printed in Austria-Hungary. It was the government of Austria-Hungary that had raised the issue. The Minister of Foreign Affairs, Julius Andrássy, sent a note to the Russian ambassador in Vienna, asking Russia to permit the distribution on its territory of the publications of the *Prosvita* (Enlightenment) society based in Lemberg (Lviv).[81] Prosvita was the most important organization educating the peasant public in the Ukrainian spirit. In its field, *Prosvita* competed with Russophile organizations.

At the time, Austro-Russian relations were rather friendly; a year later both powers formed the League of Three Emperors with Germany. Both powers tried to preserve the status quo in Europe.[82] However, the nationality of Galician Rusyns was a question over which a conflict of interests between Russia and Austria-Hungary was possible. Although the Russian government did not actively play the Rusyn card in its foreign policy, Russophiles enjoyed wide support in Slavophile and some official circles. The Austrian government allowed the Poles to govern Galicia as an autonomous province, but, among Rusyns, preferred the Ukrainian orientation of *Prosvita* to the potentially dangerous Russophile orientation. Now the Russian Ministry of Foreign Affairs forwarded Austria-Hungary's note to Timashev, minister of internal affairs, without making any recommendations.[83]

The question belonged to the jurisdiction of the Committee of Foreign Censorship in St Petersburg. In order to define the language in which the books were written, the committee asked for an expert opinion of Hilferding, who in 1863 had been one of the initiators of the West Russia Association proposal and presumably, at that time, favourable to the limited use of Ukrainian in primary education. He concluded: "These books are in an artificial 'Rusin' language that is based on locally spoken Little Russian, but with a strong extract of Old Slavonic and Polish. Polish and Austrian parties in Galicia attempt to construct and establish this language in that country in order to prevent the adotion of a common Russian literary language there."[84] Hilferding disapproved of the books, but did not recommend forbidding them. He only insisted that the government not promote their distribution, especially in primary schools. The committee decided to permit the books, but nevertheless forwarded Hilferding's opinion to the Main Administration of the Press, probably expecting that measures would be taken to prevent the use of these books in schools.[85] However, the highest collegiate body of censorship, that is, the Council of the Main Administration of the Press, and Minister Timashev concluded that since Valuev's circular was in force, *Prosvita* publications could not be permitted in Russia. In his answer to the deputy minister of foreign affairs, Timashev wrote that the circular banned all publications in Little Russian, except belles-lettres.[86]

There are also other indications that the Valuev circular was in continuous use. The censor in Kyiv, Ilia Puzyrevskii, referred to it as a valid normative act in his letter to the Main Administration of the Press in April 1875.[87] David Saunders refers to a case in St Petersburg, two months before the Ems Decree was issued in 1876, in which the circular was still considered binding.[88]

Kalynyk Sheikovsky's *Budivlia svita* (*Creation of the World*) provides the clearest evidence that the circular was still in force. This was a Ukrainian translation of *Creatio mundi*, the section of Ovid's *Metamorphoses* that describes the beginning of the world.[89] Sheikovsky read the censorship law as strictly as it was written, and ignored the Valuev circular. Since the law exempted all translations from classical languages from preliminary censorship, this rule logically applied also to Ukrainian translations. Without preliminary censorship, Sheikovsky translated *Creatio mundi* and printed 420 copies on his own press in Bobruisk. This publication looks like it may have been a conscious provocation. A pagan text in Ukrainian without commentaries was not a publication likely to be well received by the authorities. In May 1875 Sheikovsky sent a few copies to the censor in Vilna (Vilnius), requesting the final permission to distribute the book. The censor reacted by asking the public prosecutor in Minsk to take legal action against Sheikovsky who, in the censor's opinion, had committed the crime of publishing a book without prior censorship.[90] The censor argued that the exemption from preliminary censorship did not apply to Sheikovsky's book given the publication's purpose, its cheap price, its content, and length. By these comments the censor probably meant to say that the book was not exempt from preliminary censorship because it was too brief and because price and language made it accessible to the common people, which by definition made it a violation of the Valuev circular. The censor did not explain what concerned him about the contents of the book. It was either the paganism or simply the censor's conviction that exemptions could not be granted to Ukrainian translations from classical languages. Sheikovsky, citing to the letter of the law, responded to the censor's charges by petitioning the Main Administration of the Press, asking it to repeal the indictment.[91] Perhaps somewhat confused, the public prosecutor in Minsk neither rejected the charge nor proceeded with the prosecution, but asked the Main Administration about its decision.[92] The Council of the Main Administration of the Press discussed the case in January 1876. A member of the council, Fedor Elenev, prepared a submission. He concluded that the printing of the book had actually not violated the censorship law; hence, all criminal charges against Sheikovsky had to be dropped. However, he continued, it was important to prevent the publication of the book for two reasons. First, the circulation of a pagan text among the ignorant common people could not be authorized. Second, there was the Valuev circular. Although Elenev admitted that the circular was normally binding only for preliminary and not punitive censorship, its restrictions should be followed in all cases pertaining to Ukrainian publications that clearly expressed Ukrainophile tendencies. According to Elenev, this applied to Sheikovsky's translation published in Bobruisk. It was written in a dialect spoken by inhabitants of Little Russian origin, people who now lived in the Belarusian and former Lithuanian provinces. In these regions, Ukrainophile tendencies could lead to even greater harm than in Little Russia proper. Because of these considerations, the council decided that the book should be banned exceptionally, as the amendment (decreed in 1872) to the censorship law allowed. Minister Timashev confirmed this decision.[93]

Timashev now had to submit the case to the Committee of Ministers for the final decision. The committee discussed the matter at its session on 4 May, a mere two weeks before the enactment of the Ems Decree and while the emperor was abroad. Timashev's memorandum repeated Elenev's arguments in all essentials. Concerning the language, Timashev wrote that the book was published "in that Little Russian dialect that is spoken by inhabitants of Little Russian origin in the South-Western and North-Western region."[94] The minister's statement can be interpreted to mean that he identified Belarusian as a dialect of Ukrainian, although it is hard to tell how aware of this he actually was. If he was conscious of what he was saying, then he may have been trying to extend the force of Valuev's circular to future Belarusian publications. Timashev found the Little Russian literature to be an "artificial construction" that was "directed at separation of the Little Russian tribe from the Great Russian."[95] He explicitly referred to the Valuev circular as a document that was still in effect: "Considerations that called this Imperial Decree into being retain their force even in the present day. From the documents of censorship it is evident that attempts to create a separate Little Russian literature for the people have not ceased even in the present day, and rather often the books in the Little Russian dialect come to us from abroad, from Poznań and Galicia, and fairly often consist of socialist and revolutionary propaganda."[96]

Like Valuev's similar claims made in 1863, Timashev's arguments hinting at a Polish peril were not based on solid facts. Although Ukrainian publishing was active in Galicia, no books in Ukrainian had appeared in the Poznań region of German Poland in 1870–6.[97] At least four populist revolutionary brochures were indeed published in Vienna in 1875–6, but they were never intended to pass Russian censorship.[98] Nevertheless, the Committee of Ministers banned *Budivlia svita*.[99] What Valuev had not dared to do in 1863–5 was now done: the circular passed through the Committee of Ministers and was fully accepted, although without the emperor's endorsement. Of course, the preparation of the Ems Decree, which by 4 May had reached the draft stage, influenced the decision of the Committee of Ministers.[100] On 31 May 1876, the Ukrainian Ovid was reduced to ashes as the whole edition was burned in Bobruisk.[101]

Censor Ilia Puzyrevskii's Window of Opportunity

Valuev's circular was still in force in the 1870s. How, then, was it possible that eighteen Ukrainian editions circumvented its limits in 1874–6? The answer can be found by focusing on their place of publication and examining local conditions. Of the eighteen editions, seventeen were published in Kyiv. Of the seventy-one Ukrainian publications that appeared during the years 1874–6, sixty-three appeared in Kyiv.[102] This was because two key posts in the city were held by persons who, each for his own reasons, were not disposed to be severe with regard to Ukrainian activities. In 1869–78, the governor-general of Kyiv was Aleksandr Mikhailovich Dondukov-Korsakov, who disliked arbitrariness and repressive police measures in general, seeking instead to negotiate with the local population. For certain local Poles, his attitude brought some opportunities in administration and exemptions from property confiscations despite their participation in the January insurrection of 1863. Under Dondukov-Korsakov's administration, Ukrainian activists were able to seize control over the newly established South-Western Section of the Imperial Russian Geographic Society and shape it into their own public organization. The governor-general was well apprised of the history and character of the Ukrainian movement. According to Valentyna Shandra, he favoured Ukrainian activists for two reasons: first, scholarly works by Ukrainophiles demonstrated the

Russian character of the region, understood in the broad sense of an all-Russian nation; second, Ukrainian activities could be controlled better when they were public.[103] Formally, the governor-general had no power over censorship, but the fact that he was not averse to easing it offered some leeway to local censors. In the 1870s there were two in Kyiv, the most important of whom was called the "individual censor (*otdelnyi tsenzor*) in Kyiv." From September 1872 to December 1875, the individual censor was Ilia Puzyrevskii, of Orthodox confession, born in Vilnius. The defensive tone of Puzyrevskii's report, describing his activities in 1874, which was written in early 1875, shows that his leniency towards Ukrainian publications had been noticed in the Main Administration of the Press.

> Since rather many Little Russian manuscripts are submitted to censorship and this points to the existence of a kind of national movement among the Little Russians, I have tried … to permit as few of them as possible. However, since those works, with very few exceptions, were not contrary to the rules of censorship, I did not use bans. Instead, under suitable pretexts, I tried to change the minds of the authors and to convince them that they should take their manuscripts back. The usual pretexts were the following: lack of literary merit and pointlessness of the work; finally, sometimes, lack of time to read too long, badly handwritten manuscripts. Thus without bans, I managed to prevent the publication of twelve manuscripts … of Little Russian poetry and prose.[104]

Puzyrevskii claimed that his method did not evoke dissatisfaction among Little Russians, as explicit bans would have. It is interesting that the censor found it necessary to explain and defend the actual number of Ukrainian publications, even though existing rules placed no limits on them. This indicates that, apart from the Valuev circular, there existed an unwritten convention in the censorship that limited the quantity of all Ukrainian publications. Such an approach was not exceptional, inasmuch as some repressive measures against Polish cultural activities were likewise never formalized in any written regulations.[105]

Puzyrevskii's policy was soon discontinued. Mikhail Iuzefovich and other adherents in Kyiv of the all-Russian national identity had already begun their denunciation campaign against the Ukrainian activists in Kyiv and against Dondukov-Korsakov, who was considered too sympathetic to them.[106] In February 1875 Mikhail Katkov's *Russkii vestnik* (*Russian Messenger*) published a highly polemical article against the Ukrainophiles in Kyiv, implicitly blaming the government for permitting a subversive movement.[107] In March, the director of the Main Administration of the Press Vasilii Vasilevich Grigorev turned to Puzyrevskii, calling on him to assume "an extremely careful attitude" in relation to Little Russian publications. "You must not let works through which carry ideas about the separation of the Little Russian tribe and its independent political or civic development," he wrote.[108]

However, Puzyrevskii was not discouraged. In late March 1875, he, in understanding with Dondukov-Korsakov, banned an article that Iuzefovich had written for the local conservative newspaper *Kievlianin* (*Kievan*), which severely criticized the South-Western Section of the Imperial Russian Geographical Society and the newspaper *Kievskii Telegraf*. Iuzefovich especially condemned the section for its Ukrainian publishing activities, in which the members were involved. He also hinted at an excessively permissive government policy regarding the South-Western Section and the Ukrainophiles who were active in it.[109] On 21 April, Puzyrevskii wrote an apologetic letter to the Main Administration, explaining his motives. The censor found that it was impermissible to criticize a government organization that was protected by the governor-general. Articles against Ukrainophilism evoked a negative response in Little Russians and led to tribal friction "between children of one and the same fatherland."[110] Puzyrevskii did not hesitate to defend *Kievskii Telegraf*, claiming that the articles therein did not contain Ukrainophile agitation. The censor then proceeded to explain his policy regarding Ukrainian publications and the Valuev circular:

> In allowing works in that dialect to be printed, I am constantly guided by the instructions that are presented in the secret letter of the Minister of Internal Affairs to the Minister of Public Enlightenment from 8 July 1863 [*sic*, should be: 18 July] … An exception has been made for merely two books that were aimed at a popular audience: a) *Church Union and Petro Mohyla*, which was published with a loyal goal, a contribution to the present movement of Uniates that aims to reunite them with the Orthodox Church. This book was permitted on the basis of the opinion of a member of the Ecclesiastical Censorship in Kyiv and [in view] of the benefit of distributing such a book among the Uniates; b) *How the Military Service Is Now Arranged*,[111] with the aim of bringing to an end the distorted rumours that have emerged among the people about the main foundations of universal military service. One may, of course, regret that these books appeared in the Little Russian dialect, and not in Russian. However, it

would be unfair to suspect the authors and distributors of such books of separatist tendencies, or of a lack of patriotism.[112]

Puzyrevskii was being evasive. By this time, he had permitted the publication of not two but about ten books that were in violation of Valuev's circular.

The enemies of the Ukrainian movement were also targeting Puzyrevskii. In June 1875, acting mayor of Kyiv, Nikolai Karlovich Rennenkampf, wrote a denunciation about *Kievskii Telegraf* to the Main Administration of the Press. He mentioned Puzyrevskii as the main protector of "agitation" as practised by the newspaper.[113] Rennenkampf offered an explanation to Puzyrevskii's actions: corruption. The censor had even sent written requests for bribes to different newspapers, and Rennenkampf ended up having some of them in his possession. Soon the Ministry of Internal Affairs was in possession of seven Puzyrevskii's letters, five to *Kievlianin*, one to *Drug naroda* (*Friend of the People*), and one to the publisher and printer Iosif Zavadskii.[114] Unfortunately, because of the indecipherable signature I have not been able to identify the person who forwarded the letters to the ministry. Nevertheless, the denunciation against Puzyrevskii evidently originated in the circle of *Kievlianin*. For his part, Puzyrevskii reacted by admitting that he had "borrowed some money, ... but had always tried to pay back in so far as possible."[115] On the Ukrainian side, Serhii Podolynsky's letter to the Russian revolutionary Valerian Nikolaevich Smirnov confirms Puzyrevskii's corruptibility: Podolynsky complained that an anonymous censor, "although he has been bought" (*podkuplennyi*),[116] still created sometimes problems for the Ukrainian publishing industry. The Main Administration of the Press reacted to the corruption charges by dismissing Puzyrevskii in December 1875.[117] However, no criminal charge was brought against him.

After Puzyrevskii's dismissal, in the early months of 1876, six additional publications appeared that clearly violated the Valuev circular. Either Puzyrevskii had already permitted them before his dismissal, or his aide and temporary replacement von Laiming preferred not to change the policy, anticipating a final decision concerning the Ukrainian publications. Finally, the Ems Decree of 18 May 1876 confirmed the restrictions against Ukrainian publications and removed the previous ambiguity in the wording of Valuev's circular: now there was no doubt that only belles-lettres and publications of historical documents were allowed.[118]

The Valuev circular was essentially not a reaction to the Polish insurrection, but reflected Valuev's fundamentally hostile, long-term stance towards Ukrainian as a literary language. Valuev's negative attitude towards publications in Yiddish indicates that the Ukrainian case was not completely unique. It was an example of the minister wanting to prevent another plebeian vernacular from developing into a full-fledged literary language and thereby force speakers to adopt Russian in that role. In the Yiddish case, Valuev did not oppose the adoption even of German. Here the minister potentially allowed another established literary language in the empire to take the place of a plebeian vernacular. His was an imperial rather than nationalistic attitude, but nevertheless, it amounted to the promotion of ethnic attributes of Russian nationality even among Jews who were never considered part of an ethnically defined Russian nation. The Ukrainian case was different from the Yiddish in that there was no alternative language they could really choose. Ukrainians, according to Valuev, could have only one acceptable established language: Russian. Polish was, of course, out of the question.

The unconventional way in which Valuev forced through his circular indicates that he anticipated some members of the State Council expressing their opposition to his policy. What we know about Dmitrii Bludov's opinions and the plan to launch the West Russia Association strengthens this conclusion. Despite the irregular way in which it emerged, the "temporary" circular retained its status throughout the whole period of 1863–76 as a document that bound censors in their decisions. However, there indeed were fluctuations in the strictness of the unwritten rules guiding the conduct of censors. Only after Valuev's departure did it become easier to publish works in Ukrainian, which, according to the letter of the circular, should have been permitted all along. The reason popular Ukrainian books were actually published in Kyiv between 1874 and 1876 can be explained by Dondukov-Korsakov's policies, Puzyrevskii's corruptibility, and the difficulties the imperial government had in implementing its policy there. How Ukrainians exploited the censorship situation in Kyiv is a prime example of the pattern that Stephen Velychenko has emphasized: the ineffectiveness of the imperial bureaucracy was often used to mitigate the centralization and integration that this same bureaucracy was supposed to promote.[119] The Ukrainian activists of the Kyiv Hromada were prepared to pay the price for their freedom.

Chapter Seven

The Ukrainian Movement and Russia in the 1870s

The period of quiescence that ensued in the Ukrainian movement after the enactment of the Valuev circular ended in the early 1870s, by which time the Imperial Russian Geographical Society began to offer a forum for lawful and public Ukrainian activities. After the Polish insurrection of 1863, Russian official circles deplored the fact that most of the information about the western provinces was produced by Polish scholars and writers.[1] Government circles sensed that after the military victory over the Poles, the empire needed an intellectual and ideological victory.[2] For that reason they supported scholarly studies of the region that advanced the Russian viewpoint. This combination of scholarly and political motives coloured the activities of the Geographical Society in the western provinces. It paid special attention to the ethnically non-Polish population of the region, striving to use their presence as an argument against Polish claims and in defence of Russian governmental policies. This tendency afforded the Ukrainophiles an opportunity to cooperate with the Geographical Society. This cooperation produced important scholarly results that provide much useful information about the Ukrainian position regarding Ukrainian–Russian relations in the first half of the 1870s.

In 1867 the Imperial Russian Geographical Society launched an expedition to the western provinces. Financed by the Ministry of Public Enlightenment, its most essential task was to define the geographic limits and populations of the local Christian Slavic ethnic groups. Ukrainian nationalism entered the project in the person of Pavlo Chubynsky, who was named a member of the expedition in May 1869 and assigned the task to study the south-west region, that is, the provinces situated on the Right Bank of the Dnipro River. Chubynsky had made an impression on the society through two studies he had written in his place of deportation, Arkhangelsk Province: one on the grain trade along the Dvina River, and the other on Little Russian customary law, the latter of which was published by the Geographical Society, whose intensive lobbying had played a decisive role in Chubynsky's release from deportation.[3]

Chubynsky set to work energetically. In 1869–71, he travelled extensively throughout the Right Bank gathering materials. He also successfully mobilized the local intelligentsia, including the Ukrainophiles, to contribute to the expedition.[4] The cooperation between Ukrainian activists and the Geographical Society was not without its problems. In late 1871 the Geographical Society asked Petr Andreevich Hildebrandt, a scholar with Slavophile leanings, to edit Chubynsky's text.[5] The society also objected to Chubynsky's use of Kulish's orthography, and specified the exact orthographic guidelines for this publication. Most importantly, one of the chapters discussing the Little Russian language was removed because it emphasized the specificity of the language in comparison with other Slavic languages. The deleted chapter had been written by Kost Mykhalchuk, the unofficial linguistic expert of the Kyiv Hromada, which was now resuming its activities.[6] Nevertheless, the Ukrainophiles' cooperation with the Imperial Russian Geographical Society was successful, borne out by the fact that the results of the expedition were published in seven volumes in 1872–8.[7] They contain legends, fairy tales, songs, and information about the popular calendar and customary law. The most interesting for us is the seventh volume, which appeared in two parts in 1872 and 1877. It includes chapters about Jews and Poles, statistics, and a study of the Little Russian language.

Chubynsky discovered Little Russians not only in the south-west region but also in the north-west (present-day Belarus), in the Kingdom of Poland, and the northern part of Bessarabia. According to Chubynsky, there were 380,000 Little Russians living in the north-west region in Grodno and Minsk provinces.[8] He argued for the Little Russian nationality of these people on linguistic grounds; their subjective identity was not taken into account in the statistics. Local inhabitants were not asked about which language they spoke. Chubynsky initially defined the linguistic territory of Little Russians on the basis of previously published studies, and only later studied local dialects on the spot. However, in the Kingdom of Poland, Chubynsky and other members of the expedition sought to conduct empirical research on the question of whether the local Greek Catholics spoke Polish or Little Russian. Religious and linguistic groups were not identical to each other: the expedition found Polish-speaking Greek Catholics and Little Russian–speaking Roman Catholics. Here, Chubynsky considered language as the defining factor of nationality: he included Little Russian–speaking Roman Catholics in the number of Little Russians, but excluded Polish-speaking Greek Catholics. However, he was not consistent in his use of language as the defining factor of ethnic identity, for he counted all Jews separately, regardless of their language.[9]

In addition to language, Chubynsky regarded customs, religious confession, and national character as relevant nationality traits. The published writings of the expedition include a brief description of Little Russians and their national character, including some comparisons with Great Russians. The description was surprisingly ambivalent. Chubynsky found Little Russians to be melancholy, and attributed this to their past sufferings and "unsuccessful attempts."[10] According to him, a Little Russian was slow in his (not her) movements, apathetic, not enterprising, and sometimes lazy: "The Little Russian especially likes to lie on the grass, on his back, fixing his eyes on distant space."[11] Although this observation did not apply to women, who, according to Chubynsky, worked hard, nevertheless Little Russians were old-fashioned and traditional in their economic activities. Trade was absolutely alien to them. Although a Little Russian had an excellent capacity for abstract and creative thought, this trait often led to scepticism and fruitless criticism of everything. This, in its turn, made it difficult for the Little Russian to make decisions. According to Chubynsky, Little Russians were very emotional, which trait was expressed in their warm family life and relationships with children. A wife's status in the family was superior to that of Great Russian women. However, although emotionality was a positive trait, it too tended to lead to negative results, such as fruitless sorrow and drunkenness. Chubynsky agreed with Kostomarov that Little Russians were individualists rather than collectivists, but this trait also had its negative aspects: it led to an inability to engage in collective action and neglect of social and political activities. In the past, individualism had even led to the Polonization of the Ukrainian nobility. In addition, individualism hindered economic development among the peasants, a view possibly reflecting Chubynsky's socialist sympathies. He found the general morals among Little Russians rather satisfactory: they did not like dishonesty, and even young, single men rarely despoiled young women, even though men and women spent much time together in search of a spouse.[12]

Chubynsky's comparison of Little Russians with Great Russians was not at all hostile to the latter. To be sure, he mentioned the stationing of soldiers or the proximity of factories as factors eroding the morals of Little Russians. His perception of Great Russians was clearly influenced by Kostomarov's *Two Russian Nationalities*. Nevertheless, Chubynsky's ideas about Great Russians were much more positive than Kostomarov's: "a Great Russian" was on a higher plane than "a Little Russian" in terms of his practical activities, especially economic ones. A Great Russian was also more industrious than a Little Russian. However, according to Chubynsky, a Little Russian was superior to a Great Russian in theoretical thought. Because of these differences, Little Russians and Great Russians were indispensable to each other, for they mutually complemented one another. Although this idea derived from *Two Russian Nationalities*, Chubynsky's perception of Great Russians was not negative. As for his description of Jews, Chubynsky viewed favourably their assimilation into Russian culture, without specifying into which one.[13]

Chubynsky's positive evaluation of the relations between Great Russians and Little Russians was consonant with the expedition's political background. The chapters on Poles, published in 1872, which he co-authored with Mykhalchuk, a former Pole of the Orthodox confession from the Right Bank, indicate that Chubynsky stood on the Russian side in the Russo-Polish political conflict. The two authors identified local Poles with the nobility's social and political conservatism and traditional Roman Catholicism. They criticized what they perceived as the imperial government's excessively soft policies towards the Poles in the period between the partitions and the 1830s. Indeed, Mykhalchuk later complained in his memoirs that Chubynsky had unilaterally exaggerated the negative characteristics of Right-Bank Poles, thereby placing Mykhalchuk, as co-author, in an awkward situation. The criticism of earlier government policies included a lengthy quotation from Mikhail Iuzefovich's article "On the Ancestry of Noble Families in South-West Russia." Chubynsky also included Iuzefovich's article on Bohdan Khmelnytsky in his own publication, *Kalendar Iugo-Zapadnogo kraia na 1873 g.* (*Calendar of the Southwestern Region for the Year 1873*). Relations between the Kyiv Hromada and Iuzefovich began to deteriorate only by the end of 1873, when Drahomanov criticized his political duplicity in an article published in *Vestnik Evropy*.[14]

Chubynsky and Mykhalchuk contrasted Russians favourably to Poles: while Poles represented reactionary adherence to a hierarchical society, Russians represented democracy: "Russian intellectual society (*intelligentskoe obshchestvo*) has always been democratic. In our literature, critical orientation, self-criticism, and the striving to get rid of all kinds of romanticism are rather well developed. Not incidentally, Russia is called a peasant state (*muzhitskim gosudarstvom*): its intelligentsia is closer to the people than in any other society."[15] In the view of the expedition members, the Russian Empire represented democracy, progress, and positivism in the south-west region, while Poles represented an outdated hierarchical society, reaction, and romanticism. It is hardly necessary to emphasize how biased the images of Poland and Russia were in this perception. Chubynsky's generalizations were coherent with the tone of official discourse of the western provinces in the 1860s, a topic that has been studied by Mikhail Dolbilov.[16]

Chubynsky subsequently reiterated his anti-Polish and pro-Russian position, most notably in his speech delivered at the founding meeting of the South-Western Section of the Imperial Russian Geographical Society in February 1873. Its creation was the result of Dondukov-Korsakov's cooperation with the Ukrainophiles and a number of local conservatives noted for their Slavophile leanings, Mikhail Iuzefovich being the most notable among them. However, the Ukrainophiles soon sidetracked the conservatives and turned the section into a legal Ukrainophile organization in all but name.[17] Unlike Shevchenko in his time, Chubynsky accepted wholesale European and Russian imperialist myths: "In subjugating Asian countries, the Russian element has gained them for science: thanks alone to the Russian intelligentsia, civilization is penetrating those countries."[18] Chubynsky perceived the period after 1863 in the south-western region as marking the liberation of the Russian peasantry from the yoke of centuries. He called the south-western region "the cradle of Russia,"[19] indicating that he accepted the myth of Moscow and the Russian Empire as the successors of Kyivan Rus'.

In 1873 Dondukov-Korsakov assigned the South-Western Section the task of conducting a one-day census of the Kyiv population; the local administration needed statistical information for its own practical purposes. The Hromada exploited this opportunity to emphasize the Little Russian character of the city and to express its ideas about the relationship among the three Russian tribes: Great Russians, Little Russians, and Belarusians. The governor-general let it happen. It is likely that Dondukov-Korsakov found it useful to assign this task to unpaid volunteer workers with an anti-Polish tendency. During the census, extensive information was gathered about the inhabitants' gender, age, family status, education, profession, etc., as well as detailed information about buildings and living conditions in them. In each residential building, the gathering of information was assigned to the proprietors. Volunteer participants then collected the information from the proprietors and checked its accuracy. Thus, in the majority of cases, the volunteers did not meet most of the inhabitants of a given building. The results of the census were published as a book that included eighty-two statistical tables.[20]

Shortly before the census date, 2 March 1874, Dondukov-Korsakov requested the removal from the questionnaire of the question about native language. He claimed that the answers to this question would lead to superfluous conclusions, since many inhabitants whose native language was not Russian would claim that they were Russian speakers.[21] However, the Organizing Committee of the Census, which was manned by Hromada members, insisted on including the language question in the questionnaire, arguing that statistics on native language "have been established in international congresses and were included in the census in St. Petersburg."[22] In this dispute, neither side mentioned the politically sensitive issue: the study of the number of Little Russian speakers in Kyiv. The questionnaire did not offer any specific choice of language, but proprietors were presented with a question about the native language of each resident.[23] If the answer was "Russian," the volunteer census takers had to ask the proprietor an additional question: which dialect, Great Russian, Little Russian, or Belarusian? However, this additional question was asked only about persons who belonged to the "common people" (*litsam iz prostonarodia*),[24] hardly a statistically exact concept. It was simply presumed that all other Russian speakers spoke the 'all-Russian language' (*Obshcherusskii iazyk*). As a result, Russian-speaking inhabitants of Kyiv were divided into four linguistic subcategories:[25]

All-Russian language	48,437
Great Russian dialect	9,736
Little Russian dialect	38,553
Belarusian dialect	1,479

Why did the Organizing Committee postulate an "all-Russian language"? The answer may be found in Mykhailo Drahomanov's sociolinguistic ideas. Drahomanov was a lecturer in classical antiquity at St Vladimir's University of Kyiv and one of the leading activists of the

Kyiv Hromada.[26] He notionally separated the all-Russian language from the Great Russian dialect,[27] the same idea that Amvrosii Metlynsky had advanced in 1854. Postulation of the differences between the all-Russian language and Great Russian dialect served as an argument for the existence of a separate literature in Little Russian: after all, Great Russians publish literature in their dialect, so why should Little Russians not do the same with theirs? Furthermore, the inclusion of the "all-Russian language" category changed the numerical relationship between Little Russians and Great Russians to the benefit of Little Russians. Only by using the category of "all-Russian language" could the Organizing Committee claim that there were more Little Russian than Great Russian speakers in Kyiv. Since most "all-Russian speakers" belonged to the middle and higher classes of society, it is likely that more than half of them were indeed (Great) Russian speakers. When the newspaper *Kievlianin* claimed that the census takers "forced the Little Russian language on the population,"[28] it had a point.

Although some Hromada members considered Chubynsky's abovementioned speech excessive in its imperial-mindedness,[29] he was not alone in the Ukrainian national movement: Drahomanov and Kulish, too, had advanced imperial and pro-Russian ideas. Kulish declared them in his Russian-language *Istoriia Vozsoedineniia Rusi* (*History of Reunification of Rus,* 1874–7). The Ukrainian public's negative reaction to the first three volumes may have been the reason why the book remained incomplete and ended with the events of the 1620s. Despite his pro-Russian position, Kulish emphasized the distinct character of Southern Rus' in comparison with Northern Rus'. In addition to these words, Kulish used several others for the two lands and their peoples: "Ukraine," "Muscovy," "Little Rus'," "Great Rus'," "Russia" (*Rossiia,* for the northern part only), "separated Rus'" (*otroznennaia Rus',* for the southern part under Polish rule). Kulish avoided using the adjective "Ukrainian," using instead "Russian" for the inhabitants of both the south and north, or "South Russian" (*iuzhnorusskii*) when he wished to emphasize that he was writing about the southerners only.

In his interpretation of sixteenth- and seventeenth-century events, Kulish now perceived the role of Russia in Ukraine in a much more favourable light than he had in the 1840s through the 1860s. Compared to Kostomarov's and his own earlier works, Kulish reduced Bohdan Khmelnytsky's importance to the union of Rus': the union was a logical outcome of a long development and the flaws that existed in the noble-dominated political and economic system of Poland-Lithuania. Without mentioning Nikolai Ustrialov's name, Kulish now supported his idea, according to which the two parts of Rus' had longed for reunification throughout the entire period of their political separation. According to Kulish, this dream was maintained by part of South Russian clergy, while in Northern Rus' it had never been forgotten in government circles. Furthermore, Polish rule over Southern Rus' had truly been incompatible with Russian culture. Perceiving Orthodoxy as a cardinal aspect of Russian identity, Kulish emphasized the imposition of the Uniate (Greek Catholic) Church as an attack on local Russian identity in Southern Rus'. For Kulish, the most important difference between the two confessions was not in their dogmas but in their inner structure and general role in society: the Roman Catholic Church represented an alien intrusion, the dictate of church hierarchy, and an alliance between the nobility and the clergy, while the Orthodox Church in Southern Rus' cultivated lay control over the clergy, and all social classes except the peasantry participated in its decision making. For Kulish, this difference between the two churches ran parallel to the fundamental difference between Poland and Rus': Poland represented estate privileges and a hierarchical society, while Rus' adhered to political and social equality and democracy (*narodopravstvo*). This applied to both Southern Rus' under Polish domination and Muscovite Northern Rus'. Russian autocracy's tendency towards social equality was evident in the fact that it had established the equality of all citizens in courts of law, which would have been unthinkable in the Polish republic of nobles. Since ancient times, Great Russians were inclined towards state building, and they were prepared to sacrifice themselves for their country. These positive traits had been necessary for all Rus' in order to defeat the rule of the Polish nobility. In the process of reunion/reunification, Great Russian practical political thought was on a higher level than the South Russians' theoretical musings. The South Russian common people had always perceived the Russian monarchy in a favourable light, as they appreciated strong power, which guaranteed personal safety and eliminated the factor of arbitrariness characteristic of oligarchical systems and restless times.[30]

Kulish's new ideas were closer to the mainstream Ukrainian movement than it seems at first glance. He upheld autocracy, but attempted to redefine it as a force incompatible with estate privileges. This idea was far-fetched: at the time when he wrote this, Russian citizens were not all equal in courts of law, to say nothing about the other remaining estate privileges. To be sure, the reform policies that had been practised for two decades had substantially reduced legal discrimination among citizens, but this was an attempt of government politicians to adapt to social change rather than anything inherent in autocracy throughout the centuries. In addition to his opposition to estate privileges, Kulish still shared common ground with other Ukrainian activists in his antipathy for the nobility. However, he included in his work crude personal attacks on Shevchenko, Kostomarov, and Maksymovych. Kulish emphasized that Shevchenko's ideas were contrary to the veneration of monarchs that was prevalent among the Ukrainian common people. If it were possible to publish all of Shevchenko's works, the public would realize that they contained little worth preserving, he wrote. Throwing out the rest would be a favour to the shadow of the poet, who was now "lamenting on the banks of Acheron of his past raving (*umoizstuplenii*)." Indeed, Shevchenko had often been "the most worthless" (*nichtozhnee vsekh*)."[31] Where Kostomarov is concerned, Kulish criticized a number of details and facts in his works on Cossack history. Some of the criticism was well founded, but it was conveyed in a very ironical tone. Kulish did not hesitate to characterize Maksymovych as "one of the most talentless persons who ever took to the writing profession."[32] Such impolitic and iconoclastic passages were bound to leave a painful impression on many readers. They harmed the dissemination of Kulish's pro-Russian message, which in any case had meagre chances of finding a wide Ukrainian audience after the Ems Decree of 1876.

Drahomanov's positive perception of Russia was not mere tactical rhetoric, inasmuch as he put forward pro-Russian ideas even in his Galician publications and private correspondence, which were not subject to Russian censorship. His world view was materialist, although the romanticism of the generation of the Society of St Cyril and Methodius still had some appeal to him. Even though Drahomanov was a socialist, his thought included reformist and moderate aspects. For a long time he wanted to avoid a complete break with the Russian government. At least until his emigration in 1876, Drahomanov was a Pan-Slav whose Pan-Slavism was centred not in Ukraine but in Russia. His pre-emigration texts reveal him as a representative of a dual Ukrainian and Russian identity. In his writings these identities were not mutually exclusive, and Ukrainians could identify with Russia as well as with their Ukrainian homeland. This was possible because Drahomanov's allegiance was not to ethnic Great Russia but to a larger Russia; one might even say, with some qualifications, to the Russian Empire. This allegiance was conditional, the prerequisite being that Russia would at least develop into a constitutional monarchy. Ukrainian national goals could, according to Drahomanov, be reached through an all-Russian reform, in which each nationality would be allowed to develop freely. His attitude to Great Russians and Russian culture was very positive. However, Russian culture was acceptable to him only if it delivered the political radicalism and philosophical materialism that he considered valuable for all humanity. His was the Russia of Alexander Herzen and Nikolai Chernyshevskii, not that of the Slavophiles or the imperial government.

In 1872 Drahomanov published in *Vestnik Evropy* an article entitled "German Eastern Policy and Russification."[33] In it, he presented his desire for a change in the nationality policies of the Russian Empire. Drahomanov began by postulating a German and Austrian threat to the country. From the Slavic viewpoint, Austria's expansion to Turkish territory was undesirable, for it would mean ipso facto the expansion of German hegemony. True, the Austrian empire too might break apart, but even then ethnic Germans would not voluntarily abandon Slavic territories. A German-Russian conflict was also possible in the Kingdom of Poland. However, Russia could defend itself from German aggression and possibly even expand if it prepared itself well for the future conflict. A necessary element of this preparation was making all the languages in the empire equal, to use Drahomanov's own term. This would create a supra-ethnic loyalty to Russia, similar to that which existed in Switzerland. In order to achieve this, the idea of a connection between the Orthodox religion and Russian national identity should be decisively rejected and all discrimination on religious basis abolished. Drahomanov also hinted rather clearly at the need for constitutional rule. His criterion of an ethnic group's acceptability was whether it had a stratum of common people. Thus, the liberal policy that he proposed would not apply to Baltic Germans or Poles outside the Kingdom of Poland, but would apply to Poles within the Kingdom of Poland, Ukrainians, Belarusians, Lithuanians, Letts, Estonians, and Finns. The German, Polish, and Swedish languages in those regions where they represented only the upper class of society would then be supplanted partly by the Russian language and partly by the languages spoken by local common people.

Thus, according to Drahomanov's proposal, the Russian language would still enjoy a privileged status. Drahomanov seems to have expected that in conditions of greater political freedom, the national minorities would willingly adapt the use of Russian in addition to their own languages, and he explicitly considered this kind of situation desirable for Ukrainians. This is not surprising, if we consider the fact that already at this time the intelligentsia in Ukraine had to use Russian in all official and educational spheres. Thus, the policy of bilingualism that he proposed was compatible with the expansion of the use of Ukrainian. According to Drahomanov, the domestic promotion of plebeian nationalities would have connotations outside Russia's borders, in view of the coinciding interests of Russia and of Slavs living in Germany and Austria-Hungary, which were in conflict with the interests of the Germans and Hungarians. On the other hand, Russians could not credibly resist national oppression in Germany and Austria-Hungary if they simultaneously supported similar policies within Russia. Germans could apply a double standard when evaluating the nationality policies of their own states and Russia because they were convinced of their own inherent superiority over the Slavs. For Russians, such a double standard presented difficulties, since they lacked a similar belief in their own superiority.

Like most St Petersburg and Moscow periodicals, *Vestnik Evropy* was exempt from preliminary censorship. Following its publication, Drahomanov's article "German Eastern Policy and Russification" was discussed in the Council of the Main Administration of the Press. The only aspect of the article to which the censors paid attention was its harsh criticism of the policy of Russification in the "Vistula region" (Kingdom of Poland). In the council's opinion, such criticism could have an effect harmful to the government if read by a Polish reader or a Russian reader who was implementing government's policies in Poland. Eventually, the censors decided only to flag the article as one that disapproved of Russian government policy in the Vistula region. This was the mildest degree of sanction, which became relevant only if a journal persisted in publishing articles approaching the impermissible. The editors of *Vestnik Evropy* were not informed of the censors' decision, and no inquiries were made about the identity of the pseudonymous author.[34]

While engaged in scholarly work in Italy, Drahomanov corresponded with the Galician Ukrainophile Volodymyr Navrotsky, who served as his link to *Pravda* (*Truth*), the most important Ukrainian journal in Galicia. In a letter written to Navrotsky in December 1872 Drahomanov criticized the antipathy to Russian culture that was prevalent among Galician Ukrainophiles. Inasmuch as Russian literature was progressive, oppositionist, and highlighted social problems, it was a natural ally of the Galician Ukrainophiles. Drahomanov proposed that

Pravda publish Ukrainian translations of the works of selected Russian authors: Ivan Turgenev, Aleksandr Ostrovskii, Alexander Herzen, Mikhail Saltykov-Shchedrin, and Nikolai Nekrasov. His reasoning was that the readers of *Pravda* should be informed about the history of radical literary criticism in Russia as embodied in the works of Vissarion Belinsky and Nikolai Dobroliubov. In July 1873 Drahomanov returned to this topic, finding even *Pravda*'s criticism of the Russian government inconvenient: "Leave the task of reforming Russia to us [Ukrainians in the Russian Empire] and Great Russians."[35] He insisted that through the South-Western Section of the Imperial Russian Geographical Society the Russian government was now supporting Ukrainian activities. However, he added another argument that contradicted the first one: criticism might prevent the circulation of *Pravda* in the Russian Empire.

What Drahomanov could not say in *Vestnik Evropy*, he managed to publish in *Pravda* in 1873–4 in the form of an article entitled "Russian, Great Russian, Ukrainian, and Galician literature."[36] This publication unquestionably reveals Drahomanov as both a Russian patriot and an adherent of federalism.[37] He argued for the widespread use of Russian in Ukraine on the grounds that it was impossible, at least quickly, to create a Ukrainian high culture comparable to the Russian culture. Galicians could use their language for the enlightenment of common people and the depiction of purely local subjects. Time would show the proper scope of literature in Ukrainian. When writing about other subjects, Galicians should adopt Russian. Drahomanov denied that the Russian literary language was the language of Great Russians only, for Ukrainians had participated in its development, and it was both written and spoken by Ukrainians in the Russian Empire. Galicians should prefer Russian to German, for Russian was closer to the Slavs and transmitted those elements of European culture that were not available in German.[38] Drahomanov thought that Galician Russophiles were correct in wanting to adhere to Russian culture. However, they chose the wrong Russia, that of the Slavophiles. He claimed that Ukrainian literature in both Russian and Austrian Ukraine had nothing comparable to progressive Russian literature to offer. Through translations, the Russian language transmitted the best achievements of Western culture. Indeed, according to Drahomanov, the Russian language had a chance of becoming one day the common language of all Slavs.[39] He condemned any literary separatism, by which he meant attempts to develop Ukrainian literature into a full-fledged literature encompassing both high and folk culture. However, he differed from Russian enemies of Ukrainian national movement on two important points: (1) He considered that Ukrainian should nevertheless be used as a literary language in certain limited functions; and (2) He was an adherent of introducing changes to the Russian political system.

Concerning the exact status of the Ukrainian language, Drahomanov was vague. Although in the foreseeable future he did not envisage the status of a language of high culture for Ukrainian, neither did he rule out such a prospect altogether. Since Drahomanov thought that Ukrainian could, and should, be used in scholarly texts that explored the life of the Ukrainian common people, he acknowledged that Ukrainian had a limited use in scholarship. Furthermore, he was in favour of expanding enlightening literature for the common people in Ukrainian. Drahomanov emphasized that literature should contain practical knowledge rather than Cossack romanticism, noting that it would take between twenty and thirty years to complete the tasks of Ukrainian literature in these two fields. If this project were successful, the scope of literary use of the Ukrainian language might expand further. He also advanced the notion that a substantial part of world literature was suitable for Ukrainian peasants. For example, translations from Homer, Shakespeare, Schiller, and Dickens were included within the limits he proposed for the use of Ukrainian.[40]

Drahomanov was quite optimistic about the political change that he anticipated in Russia, and he was convinced that the peasants' interests and democracy (*narodopravstvo*) were already gaining ground in Russian domestic policies. This would soon lead Russia to adopting progressive and even revolutionary ideas, and an alliance with the masses of the Slavic common people in neighbouring countries: "The political interests of Russia correspond with the interests of the struggle of the Slavic nations for their lives, and the government's interest corresponds with the interests of the common people in the great region from the Dnipro and Peipus to the Elbe and the Adriatic Sea,"[41] he wrote. Russia should reshape itself as an organized union of common people. Autonomy for regions and nationalities would inevitably ensue, since the interests of the common people did not reside in centralism and the loss of nationality. This prospect gave Russia force, although the Slavs might still live divided into three states, perhaps for a long time. Eventually one, two, or three Slavic unions might be established, but regardless of their number, Russia would remain strong.[42]

The Kyiv-based newspaper *Kievskii Telegraf* (*Kyiv Telegraph*) was politically the most important Ukrainophile publication of the 1870s.[43]

From January to July 1875 its publisher Avdotia Ivanovna Gogotskaia entrusted the newspaper to editors who belonged to the Hromada. From a denunciation submitted by the mayor, Rennenkampf, the Main Administration of the Press instantly learned about the newspaper's turn in the direction of Ukrainian nationalism. On 16 January 1875 the Main Administration sent the first instructions to the censor Puzyrevskii, ordering him not to permit any articles that expressed any Ukrainophile tendencies.[44] Furthermore, the Third Section informed the Main Administration of the Press that Gogotskaia herself had "a bad reputation."[45] The Main Administration did not endorse either of the two editors whom Gogotskaia submitted for its approval. Owing to the cooperation between Puzyrevskii and the Kyiv Hromada, the obstruction of the St Petersburg censors had a delayed impact on the newspaper. Pressured by Puzyrevskii, who feared for his own job, Gogotskaia dismissed the Ukrainian activists from *Kievskii Telegraf* in late July 1875. However, this measure was of no avail: the Ems Decree of May 1876 closed down *Kievskii Telegraf*, although by that time it was no longer a mouthpiece of the Ukrainian national movement.[46]

Kievskii Telegraf was modest in its emphasis on Little Russian identity. It did not identify Little Russians and Great Russians as separate nationalities, but rather as subgroups within the all-Russian nationality. The newspaper consistently wrote about "Little Russia," "Little Russians," or sometimes "South Russia" and "South Russians," and only rarely mentioned "Ukraine" or "Ukrainians." The arguments put forward in defence of Little Russian culture were most often practical: for instance, the newspaper argued that if not all the members of a jury understood Great Russian well, explanations in Little Russian should be permitted;[47] if the South-Western Section of the Imperial Russian Geographical Society would not study Little Russian ethnography, little would be left for it to study in its own region. Such moderate apologetics of Little Russian activities frequently appeared in the pages of *Kievskii Telegraf*. In a review of recent Little Russian literature, the editors abandoned all resentment with regard to the abolition of Cossack autonomy under Catherine II, noting, however, that the introduction of serfdom, enacted with the abolition of autonomy, had been a traumatic experience for the common people.[48] An editorial on the same topic emphasized the bilingual character of the Little Russian literary movement. The editors noted with satisfaction how contemporary Little Russian literature contained fewer centrifugal tendencies in comparison with the older literature: "That rising wave of the Little Russian literary movement which is visible now, differs ... from the previous one by the strength of self-criticism, very small dose of romanticism and veneration of ancient times, by the weakness of centrifugal tendency and superficial, exclusive nationalizing ... These qualities of the contemporary Little Russian trend have developed thanks to that human sympathy with which the best representatives of North Russian literature and journalism have encountered the Little Russian literary movement."[49]

The newspaper published official announcements concerning the politically sensitive issue of the abolition of the Greek Catholic Church in the Kingdom of Poland and the forced conversion of all Greek Catholics to Orthodoxy. It even claimed that the former Greek Catholics had made their new choice "completely freely and consciously."[50] *Kievskii Telegraf* criticized the decision of the Kyiv Slavic Charitable Committee to assist Venedykt Ploshchansky, the editor of the Galician Russophile journal *Slovo*. However, the alternative method that the newspaper proposed to assist Galicians was hardly anti-Russian: purchasing Russian literature for student libraries in Lviv.[51] Indeed, the newspaper did not perceive Russian literature as foreign. It called Pushkin "our writer"[52] and often published reviews of Russian books. If there was any kind of political message behind the reviews, it was a vague appeal for all-Russian democracy, or populism, not Ukrainian nationalism. Literary critics writing in *Kievskii Telegraf* disapproved of oligarchic ideas and hostile descriptions of political radicals, while in its foreign news the newspaper was sympathetic to expressions of pro-Russian opinions abroad.[53]

However, despite its generally moderate tone, *Kievskii Telegraf* published numerous texts in which imperial government policies were explicitly criticized either from a Ukrainian or a general populist viewpoint. The first editorial of 1875 railed against existing regulations, which mandated that only periodicals published in St Petersburg and Moscow were eligible to apply for an exemption from preliminary censorship. Furthermore, subscribing to foreign periodicals was possible only via St Petersburg. Even such foreign periodicals that technically could have reached Kyiv before St Petersburg arrived via St Petersburg several days late.[54] The newspaper also criticized the government's decision to limit the geographic scope of the activities of the local agricultural society in Kyiv Gubernia alone.[55] In a polemical article on the economic relations between North and South Russia, *Kievskii Telegraf* hinted at government measures as one cause of Little Russia's underdevelopment both in the past and present: roads had been built only in Great Russia, and even now Kyiv lacked a direct connection with Poltava and Kharkiv.[56] In the article "The Polish Question Here and in Poznan" the editors frankly proposed a softening of policies vis-à-vis Poles. They argued that in the Kyiv region the political question of belonging to Russia had been solved for good in 1863. Here, the Polish question existed only among Poles: would they work for the good of local Russian people, or would they maintain their old dreams? The editorialist added that Russians were able to help the reorientation of local Poles by developing all-estate institutions, religious tolerance, equal rights for Orthodox and Catholics in education, and tolerance for the Polish culture in the private sphere. This was indeed frank criticism of the policies that the government practised in relation to Poles, who were discriminated against on the basis of their religious confession. By the creation of all-estate institutions, the editors meant *zemstvo* reform, which had not been introduced in Right-Bank Ukraine. Furthermore, the editors also criticized Russian government policies in the Kingdom of Poland. According to them, "a centralist policy has been attempted which resembles that of [French revolutionary] Convent in Alsace and Prussian policies in the Poznan region."[57] They pointed to the awkward situation in which the Russian government found itself: concomitantly with these Polish policies, the imperial authorities advocated the liberation of fellow Slavs in the Ottoman Empire. The editorial concludes with a sympathetic description of the Poles' struggle against German pressure in the Poznan region of Prussia. German policies, the editorialists claimed, had led many Poles to seek a rapprochement with Russia. The editors then promised to discuss recent Polish proposals for this Polish-Russian rapprochement. The promise never materialized, probably because of censorship.

Kievskii Telegraf exceeded the limits set by censorship in its foreign news as well. According to the program confirmed by the Main Administration of the Press, it could only print foreign news based on reports published in St Petersburg and Moscow newspapers that had the right to report directly from abroad. However, *Kievskii Telegraf* often published its own foreign correspondence, especially from Galicia. It even published bibliographic information about recent foreign publications of Holy Scripture in Little Russian, preferring those that used Kulish's orthography and were close to the spoken vernacular.[58] The foreign news coverage indicates that the editors had their own "foreign policy": across Europe, they favoured democratic and republican movements, preferring France to Germany, the latter of which they deemed a force hostile to Slavs in general and to Russia in particular. This was a deviation from Russian foreign policy, which at this time was oriented towards cooperation with Germany and Austria-Hungary. In its Galician news, *Kievskii Telegraf* emphasized how the Polish landowning nobility oppressed local Russians/Rusyns (both terms were used interchangeably) and criticized Galician Rusyn politicians for excessive circumspection in their defence of national cultural rights.[59]

The Kyiv newspaper's orientation on the interests of the poorer social classes, especially peasants and workers, was manifest. This question was now presented in a much more practical tone than in the early 1860s. Peasants and workers were defended in articles discussing such contemporary questions as elections and sessions of the city council in Kyiv, peasant indebtedness and lack of access to cheap credit, and a published draft of labour legislation. The newspaper explicitly criticized the property census in municipal suffrage and the fact that it disadvantaged the poor. It proposed that *zemstvos* allocate funds for peasant agricultural credit, and criticized the labour law draft for its exclusive defence of employers' interests and creating an unequal legal relationship between employees, who had very few rights, and employers, who had many. The newspaper also published brief news items on strikes in various European countries, siding with workers rather than employers.

In several issues *Kievskii Telegraf* mentioned the campaign against the Ukrainophiles launched by Mikhail Iuzefovich and other conservative Russian nationalists in Kyiv. It engaged in vigorous polemics with *Kievlianin* (*Kievan*), the local conservative newspaper. This was in itself a somewhat risky undertaking, since *Kievlianin* received 6000 roubles a year in government subsidies.[60] When *Kievlianin* published a defence of Shevchenko, Kostomarov, and Maksymovych against attacks on them by Kulish, *Kievskii Telegraf* accused its rival of distorting the image of these Ukrainian writers: *Kievlianin* had contrasted them with contemporary Ukrainophiles and downplayed the older generation's national orientation as if that generation were not Ukrainophiles. *Kievskii Telegraf* emphasized that Shevchenko's activities included his membership in the Cyrillo-Methodian circle and many poems that still could not be published in Russia. Immediately after alluding to Shevchenko's political radicalism, the newspaper blamed *Kievlianin* for creating the bugbear of Ukrainian separatism. Such an image "weakened the cause of Russian rebirth in the Southwestern region," sowed dissension in (local) Russian society, and favoured "the clique of adherents of serfdom."[61]

In its response to the anti-Ukrainian article "Modern Ukrainophilia," which will be discussed below, *Kievskii Telegraf* wrote that "only adherents of serfdom can rise against 'modern Ukrainophilia.' Their ideals reside in the Polish republic of nobles, or Mazepa's Hetmanate, or suchlike social organizations."[62] Somewhat later, *Kievskii Telegraf* published a long quote from the article "Russian, Great Russian, Ukrainian, and Galician literature" in its original Russian. The newspaper claimed that the author's views on Ukrainian–Russian relations were similar to those of Mykhailo Maksymovych, who had been praised in *Kievlianin* as a Russian patriot.[63] While such a statement was tactically useful for Ukrainian national activists who were accused of Polish sympathies, it was not entirely insincere. For Drahomanov and his colleagues in *Kievskii Telegraf*, the conflict between local Russian nationalists and Ukrainian national activists was one between adherents of the old hierarchic society and greater democracy, reaction and progress. In April the newspaper even claimed that language was not the real issue in this controversy: "The author of the article 'Modern Ukrainophilia' is not at all an enemy of either Little Russian literature or art. He simply wishes that they should glorify the officers of Vyhovsky and Mazepa and entertain their descendants. He only hates the Little Russian rabble and that is why he hates the strivings of 'modern Ukrainophilia' to work for the enlightenment and well-being of that rabble."[64] The newspaper contrasted the ancient, Polish-oriented, Cossack upper class to the Little Russian common people, who "always, in 1654, 1662, 1709, and 1768, looked with trust and hope at the Russian realm of their relatives (*edinoplemennomu*)."[65]

While the conservatives' political apprehensions concerning *Kievskii Telegraf* were not groundless, one searches in vain for any Ukrainian separatism in its pages. Although the Kyiv Hromada was a secret society, its leaders took great pains to work lawfully within the existing political framework.[66] However, they knew that their newspaper was living on borrowed time. Serhii Podolynsky, who belonged to the circle around *Kievskii Telegraf*, wrote in May 1875 to the Russian revolutionary Valerian Smirnov:

> For the party cannot even have a [legal] newspaper; it does not have *one* member sufficiently acceptable [to the authorities] for [the authorities] to grant permission to put out a newspaper … Many of us repeatedly raised the question of abandoning the paper, for it was naïve to get involved in such a matter and it was not worth soiling one's hands. If we do not

abandon it, it is mainly because every day K.T. is, so to speak, on the verge of being closed down (by the administration), and we find it more convenient to have it suppressed, notwithstanding all its moderation, than to abandon it ourselves."[67]

Although Podolynsky was more radical and more sceptical of nonrevolutionary, legal political activities than the mainstream of Hromada, his words are a valuable indicator of the mood among the editors of *Kievskii Telegraf*: They realized that they had limited time at their disposal and thus tried to make the best of the situation.

Against Rapprochement: Ukrainian Revolutionary Activities, Persistence of Anti-Russian Stereotypes

However, the revolutionary option for Ukrainian work existed nonetheless, and Podolynsky chose it. The son of a wealthy landowner, he graduated from the Faculty of Science at St Vladimir's University in 1871. During his studies Podolynsky acquainted himself with the Hromada and became involved in local revolutionary-populist circles. He even participated as a representative of Kyiv in a meeting of the St Petersburg populist Chaikovtsy circle in 1871. After graduation he spent three years in Western Europe, studied medicine in Zurich, and travelled to Austria, Germany, France (Paris), and England (London). Podolynsky participated in the activities of Russian populist émigrés and was an observer at the Hague Congress of the First International in September 1872. Although he appreciated Karl Marx as a political theorist, Podolynsky felt more sympathy for Marx's anarchist opponents in the International. However, among Russian émigrés he preferred to work with Petr Lavrovich Lavrov rather than the anarchist Mikhail Aleksandrovich Bakunin. Lavrov was opposed to both Bakunin's anarchism and Petr Nikitich Tkachev's idea of the seizure of power by a small, disciplined group of conspirators. He emphasized how revolution had to be prepared for by gaining the support of a sufficient number of peasants. By working for the peasants' interests, the Russian intelligentsia could repay the debt that they owed to the peasants for living at their expense. Lavrov's orientation was often considered the most moderate current of Russian revolutionary populism. Although the conspiracies that recognized him as leader were never numerous, Lavrov's ethical ideas had a much wider resonance among the young, conscience-stricken gentry.[68]

For a few years Podolynsky was one of Lavrov's closest associates: he financed his journal *Vpered* (*Forward*), wrote for it, organized ways to smuggle it into the Russian Empire, and arranged contacts for its distribution there. He returned to Ukraine in 1874, and faced no persecution, since his revolutionary activities were not known to the authorities. He participated in the Hromada and practised medicine among the peasants, finding time to defend his doctoral dissertation in medicine at the University of Breslau (Germany) in 1876. By the time he returned to Ukraine, Podolynsky had become critical of *Vpered*. He considered Lavrov's approach to revolutionary agitation among the common people as being too cautious, and found that the *Vpered* group channelled an excessive part of its activities to the intelligentsia. He also resented Lavrov's negative attitude to nationalism in general and Ukrainian nationalism in particular. Furthermore, being an anti-Semite who believed in substantial biological differences between nationalities and races, Podolynsky also disapproved of Lavrov's opposition to discrimination against Jews in Russia.[69] Indeed, Podolynsky's aggressive and primitive anti-Semitism is in direct conflict with his advocacy of social egalitarianism. Yet, despite these disagreements, he was not hostile to Lavrov's organization and journal, and maintained contact with them for the rest of his active life.

After returning to Ukraine, Podolynsky began to organize Ukrainian revolutionary activities as separate from the Russian movement. His most important achievements in this sphere were the creation of the first revolutionary pamphlets in Ukrainian. He wrote *Parova Mashyna* (*The Steam Engine*) and *Pro Bahatstvo ta Bidnist'* (*On Wealth and Poverty*), which were printed in Vienna and Geneva, respectively; he translated and edited a Russian illegal pamphlet against unfair taxation, which appeared under the title *Pravda*; and published *Pravdyve Slovo do Selian ta Khutorian* (True Word to Peasants and Homesteaders) written by the Odesa populist Felyks Volkhovych.

Parova Mashyna is written as a tale in which a young Ukrainian peasant named Andrii is disabled while working for a Jewish entrepreneur, who leases a nobleman's estate: a steam-powered threshing machine injures Andrii, who is now facing a beggar's future. After the accident, the young man has a dream in which he visits his village several decades later, after the revolution: peasants no longer work for nobles or leaseholders but for themselves. They live in larger and better houses, are healthier, and life is more pleasant. The nobleman's house is now a school. The villagers tell Andrii that all lords, Jews, and civil servants have been expelled from Ukraine; village communes have taken over state and noblemen's lands, and workers' cooperatives now own all the factories. These changes took place after a long and persistent armed struggle against regular government troops, which finally went over to the insurgents. Land once held privately by peasants has not been confiscated, but most peasants have voluntarily handed it over to their communes. Elected representatives decide on the municipal and district levels matters that concern not just one commune. The outline of the political system remains somewhat ambiguous: Ukraine is discussed as one unit, but it is not clear whether it has any national government. No regular army exists, since all men are prepared to defend their liberty as Cossacks.[70]

Parova Mashyna is remarkable for its confusion of Jews with a social class instead of an ethnic group: as perceived oppressors, they have all been expelled from Ukraine. The pamphlet also contains the Ukrainian movement's first explicit approval of revolutionary violence since Mykola Hulak's discussions in the Cyrillo-Methodian Society. Russia is discussed as a political entity separate from Ukraine. Although *Parova Mashyna* uses the derogatory word *katsapy* for Great Russians, relations are not hostile, for the Russian common people, too, have taken power in their own country: "We expelled most of them [Jews and lords] to Germany, for in Russia the Russians (*katsapy*) rebelled soon after us, and they asked us not to take our lords there, since they have enough of their own ones. I heard that in Germany our lords and Jews had it rather bad, for they had to labour in sweat for their bread and learn from their own experience (*spiznaly na svoii shkiri*) how Ukrainian people had lived under their rule. As we finished with our enemies, we no longer had anyone to fear, for the Russians, too, had finished with their own enemies, and in Germany the lords and other authorities did not concern themselves with us, since there too the common people began to rebel."[71]

Podolynsky's pamphlet *Pro bahatstvo ta bidnist'* summarizes Marx's theory of surplus value, claiming that employers do not pay workers for all of their labour, but usurp part of it for free. Podolynsky draws an analogy between this industrial, capitalist exploitation and excessive rents for agricultural land in Ukraine. At this time, many peasants had to rent additional land either from noble landowners or middlemen leaseholders because after the emancipation the peasants had obtained insufficient land. This pamphlet reveals Podolynsky's negative attitude to *zemstvos*: he mentions *zemstvo* taxes as one form of burdensome taxation that brings no profit to the peasantry.[72] This radical view accords with his generally negative attitude to possible constitutional development in Russia, which he expressed in his letters.[73] In these opinions, he clearly differed from the mainstream of the Kyiv Hromada, whose members wanted *zemstvos* expanded to the Right Bank of the Dnipro.

Podolynsky's letters to Valerian Smirnov, written in 1875, discuss the relationship between Ukrainian and Russian socialist movements. Podolynsky claimed that an organization called the "Ukrainian Social-Democratic Party" existed. This led Smirnov to pose several explicit questions about that party and its relationship to Russian revolutionary organizations: what was the party's program, how did it relate to Russian radicals and Russian workers in Ukraine, to whom was Podolynsky referring with the words the "Ukrainian intelligentsia?" Podolynsky's answer reveals that his "Ukrainian Social-Democratic Party" was none other than the Kyiv Hromada and similar Ukrainophile groups in Poltava, Chernihiv, and elsewhere. Podolynsky presented the Hromada as a somewhat more radical organization than it actually was; he even claimed that the party accepted the decisions of the First International concerning the desirability of collective landownership. Indeed, Hromada members included people who espoused political radicalism in varying degrees, and it is highly unlikely that it ever decided to adopt such a radical position in the land question. According to Podolynsky, the party was close to the anarchists in that it wanted to establish a federation of small autonomous communities. He explained that there were "extreme separatists" in Poltava, whereas in Chernihiv and the Right Bank the members were "more inclined toward pan-Russian radicalism."[74] As long as different languages existed, nationalities would offer a convenient base for economic organization, although a global federation, too, was desirable. Podolynsky claimed that since Ukrainian women had never been as oppressed as women in Russia, the feminist movement was less energetic in Ukraine. Since most Ukrainians were peasants, the party relied on the peasantry. The members of the Ukrainian Social Democratic Party had a positive attitude to Russian radical groups that were active in Ukraine, and often assisted their activities. It was Ukrainophiles who distributed *Vpered* and other revolutionary literature in Ukraine, although in small quantities. Ukrainians had also hidden all-Russian radicals who were being sought by the authorities. If there was tension between Ukrainian and Russian radicals, it was because Russians did not recognize Ukrainians as a separate nation. Some of them even tried to agitate among Ukrainian peasants without knowing their language. According to Podolynsky, such attempts were absurd. The party membership had nothing against Russian workers who lived in Ukraine. Finally, Podolynsky forcefully defended Ukrainians' right to distinct cultural work, like ethnographic and linguistic studies and writing and publishing textbooks. In Russia, liberals engaged in such activities, and radicals were able to profit from their work. However, there were no Ukrainian liberals in Ukraine, where it was up to the radicals to work in these spheres.

Although Podolynsky's description of the Ukrainian Social Democratic Party was certainly marked by wishful thinking, his desire to perceive the Hromada as a revolutionary organization is in itself highly interesting. He was not alone in his Ukrainian revolutionary orientation: Russian populist conspiracies in Ukraine included persons with a strong Ukrainian national identity,[75] and radical sympathies even before 1876 and the promulgation of the Ems Decree are clearly visible in Drahomanov's writings and articles that were published in *Kievskii Telegraf*. However, it is less certain whether Ukrainian radicals formed any organization during this period. In his memoirs, written in 1880, Podolynsky claimed that the radically oriented Young Hromada had eighty members in 1871, but later joined forces with the "Old" Hromada.[76] However, Podolynsky's ephemeral "Ukrainian Social Democratic Party" points to his personal tendency of exaggerating the importance of revolutionary ideas and organizations within the Ukrainian national movement. Despite his stereotypical perception of dichotomy in the condition of women in Russia and Ukraine, Podolynsky was not hostile to Great Russians.

Volkhovych's *Pravdive Slovo* was printed in Vienna in 1876, but Austria-Hungary banned it and informed the Russian government about it. It is remarkable for its outspokenness: Volkhovych is against the tsar and criticizes him for fooling the people by his fake emancipation and land reform. He advises his readers to propagate revolution especially in the armed forces, which he deems ripe to rebel. The revolution will result in the division of land into equal plots and rule by elected representatives. Volkhovych discusses Ukrainian history, blaming hetmans and Cossack officers for "selling us to Poles and [a] Muscovite tsar."[77] However, he finds that in the Hetmanate the common people lived better than under Catherine II, who abolished autonomy and introduced serfdom. Volkhovych emphasizes social revolution and does not discuss how the relation between Ukraine and Russia will be arranged after the revolution.

Drahomanov, Chubynsky, Kulish, and *Kievskii Telegraf* clearly deviated from the negative stereotypes that had dominated Ukrainian texts about Great Russians in *Osnova* and many other publications in the early 1860s.It is remarkable how some of those stereotypes served as building blocks for the new, positive stereotypes of Great Russians: Kostomarov's ideas about Great Russian state-building capacities and inclination towards practical thinking are visible in Kulish's and Chubynsky's texts. However, the new pro-Russian ideas sparked criticism in the Kyiv Hromada: some members criticized Drahomanov for excessive Europeanism, concessions to all-Russian ideas, and insufficient attention to the Ukrainian nationality.[78] An example of this criticism is Oleksandr Lonachevsky-Petruniaka's letter to Drahomanov, written shortly after the Ems Decree and the latter's exile. Lonachevsky-Petruniaka was an inspector of a vocational school in Kyiv and active Hromada member. He criticized Drahomanov for using the term "Little Russia" (*Malorossiia*) instead of Ukraine. "Little" was an insult, and "Russia" brought Russian statehood to mind.[79] Lonachevsky then proceeded to criticize Drahomanov's Russophile ideas in general:

> You were once somewhat of an all-Russian, because you believed what the craftiest Muscovites wrote from time to time ... I was not an all-Russian, for I did not read their texts, but watched their acts. You told me that the best Muscovites ... agree with you and that they will help you and us ... In my lifetime, I have not met a Muscovite who is not an adherent of russification. Why should I fraternize with an all-Russian that is with the enemy? From the tsar to collegiate registrar, from Katkov to Lavrov, they are all adherents of russification ... My dear, search in your soul: on what grounds do you trust the Muscovite? Where are their actions to our benefit?[80]

Ivan Nechui-Levytsky and Panas Myrny's works of fiction provide remarkable evidence of how the old stereotypes persisted throughout the 1870s in their pure and simple form. Nechui-Levytsky graduated from the Kyiv Theological Academy in 1865, but chose to become a secondary-school teacher rather than a priest. He is best known as a prominent writer of Ukrainian realist prose. In the first half of the 1870s Nechui adopted a consistently anti-Russian position. Hostility against Great Russians as such was not apparent in his article "The Russian Party Press" (*Orhany rosiiskykh partii*), published in the Lviv-based Ukrainian-language newspaper *Osnova* in 1871. To be sure, Nechui forcefully attacked the Slavophiles for their undemocratic, reactionary orientation, hostility to minority languages and national cultures in the Russian Empire, and attempts to promote Great Russian as the common language for all Slavs. Nechui presumed that Mikhail Katkov's newspaper *Moskovskie Vedomosti* (*Moscow News*) had convinced government circles that the Ukrainian movement was the result of a Polish intrigue. He was mistaken, however, since those politicians who in 1863 began to disseminate the myth of Polish intrigue behind the Ukrainian movement did not themselves believe in it. Furthermore, Nechui criticized Russification measures in Ukraine and other western borderlands of the empire: "Straight and bravely, we advise the Russian government to give us liberty to develop our literature and language, if it wants us to support itself."[81] However, Nechui balanced his attack on the Slavophiles and the Russian government with a rather favourable view of the Russian Westernizing and liberal press. He emphasized how Russia had been under European cultural influence since Peter I, of whom he wrote favourably. Although polemical in nature, Nechui's article was an informative introduction to Russian intellectual currents and the Russian press for those Galician readers who were not directly acquainted with them.

However, three years later Nechui-Levytsky developed a fundamental antipathy against Great Russians. This is evident in his novel *Khmary* (*Clouds*), originally published in 1874. The novel contains scenes of student life at the Kyiv Theological Academy in the 1830s–40s. The students differ from each other according to their national background: "The students from Ukraine and Belarus were more civilized, refined. They were on a far higher level than the others, even in their mental development, and they looked like young lords and Europeans among the crude Great Russians."[82] For a Ukrainian peasant-loving populist like Nechui, this positive statement about lords is indeed noteworthy: Russians are not only non-Europeans, but their crudeness distances them from the educated strata of society. Of course, this idea may apply more to the Russian clergy than Russians in general. In the novel, it does not take long for the Russian student Vozdvizhenskii, who eventually becomes a professor, to reveal his national traits: "In the room everyone liked cleanliness, but Vozdvizhenskii and the Lapp seemed not to understand what it was. All of Vozdvizhenskii's things were not in their place ... He did not make his bed, and on it, all his things were in disarray."

Vozdvizhenskii's character was rather despotic. He used the informal *ty* (you) with everyone, even when a person was meeting him for the first time. Sometimes in the evenings, everyone would be sitting quietly reading or writing, and Vozdvizhenskii would begin to pace back and forth, stamping his feet. Everyone asked him to stop and yelled at him, but it did not help at all. He was walking as though he were the only person in the room."[83]

Soon everyone noticed that Vozdvizhenskii and the Lapp did not respect the right of ownership. If they had no tobacco, they boldly stretched out their hands and took it from the others. To be fair, they also readily gave their own tobacco to the others. Although all the students drank vodka, Vozdvizhenskii drank more than everyone else. Fortunately, "Dashkovych [a Ukrainian], Kalimeri [a Greek], Petrovych [a Bulgarian], and the other Slavs were more developed, more civilized: they exerted an influence on Vozdvizhenskii's crude and wild character."[84] Vozdvizhenskii prayed loudly at night, disturbing his colleagues who wanted to sleep. When he was reproached for this, he answered aggressively. Later, Vozdvizhenskii put an end to his praying sessions at home and began appearing frequently at church in order to make a good impression on his superiors. He was not a diligent student and had difficulties answering the exam question concerning Hegel's philosophy. However, in the view of the Russian metropolitan who graded the exam, it was enough that Vozdvizhenskii called Hegel a heretic and a fool, which comments netted him the top mark. He became a professor at the Kyiv Academy, despite the fact that "Vozdvizhenskii did not like learning, did not respect it, considering it only as a means to make his way in life and to gain as much money, food, drinks and all material good as possible!"[85] Nechui's Vozdvizhenskii is a narrow-minded, practical Russian devoid of high ideals and with an inclination to dominate other people. Even his religiosity is a clear-cut manifestation of the stereotype of Great Russian superficial and ritualistic religiosity, in which ethical aspects of Christianity are of secondary importance.

Panas Myrny and Ivan Bilyk (brothers Panas and Ivan Rudchenko) completed in 1875 the novel *Khiba revut voly, iak iasla povni?* (*Do the Oxens Bellow, When Their Mangers Are Full?*). Puzyrevskii authorized its publication but banned fourteen passages.[86] However, the brothers did not manage to publish the novel before the Ems Decree put paid to the prospect of it being published in the Russian Empire. That is why the novel appeared in Drahomanov's *Hromada* press in Geneva in 1880. It remained banned in Russia until 1903, when Panas Myrny managed to publish it under another title. *Do the Oxen Bellow* tells the story of the talented peasant Chipka, who has inclinations both towards honest work and crime. Frustrated by the class injustice he encounters in society, Chipka finally turns to professional and organized robbery. Stereotypes of Russians appear in the first chapters, which recount Chipka's family background and the history of his village in Left-Bank Ukraine since the eighteenth century. There the villagers had been free until the partitions of Poland. However, Catherine II then granted them and their land to a Polish general. Only those who had been defined officially as Cossacks remained free; the other villagers became serfs. Gradually, conditions under serfdom worsened, as the general's Russian widow settled in the village and brought Russian foremen with her. They were serfs, too, but did not resent their status and served the interests of their landowner as best as they could. The general's widow considered Ukrainian peasants more rebellious than Russians, and constantly expressed her hostility to those "Mazepas." Russian foremen laughed when the landowner's sons abused the Ukrainian peasant children by attacking them violently. In the 1840s the father of Maksym, a young man of Cossack status, let his son be conscripted because of his constant rowdy behaviour. Maksym thus has an opportunity to get to know Muscovy (*Moskovshchyna*) at first hand. Even Muscovite nature oppresses him:

> Before them stood frightening forests of pines, fir trees, and poplars. They walked for a day, another ... only forest!
>
> "Here, Muscovy begins," someone said.
>
> "This?! How gloomy it is! ... Wherever you look, only forest and woods ... only a glimpse of heaven is visible up there ..."
>
> Maksym became sad in the forest: he longed for his boundless steppes, his lofty sky. Here in the forest it was so narrow, fuggy, and the sky seemed so low and gloomy. It was indeed low and gloomy: it was already fall.[87]

Finally, Maksym's group of conscripts arrived at the first Russian village and was billeted in houses.

> Maksym wanted to spit ... Cockroaches and centipedes were running across the walls, and they were in the food and the *kvas* [non-alcoholic beer], too. The house had not been tidied; the rubbish heap reached to the knees and stank ... Maksym did not climb onto the oven, and he could not force himself to lie down in the swamp on the floor, either ... Smoke from the oven came straight into the house because there was no chimney. It pressed against the throat, stroked the eyes.[88]

After settling in a garrison town, at first Maksym finds it difficult to accept the begging and robbing trips in which the soldiers engage in order to supplement their meagre supplies. However, over time he gets used to it and to other Muscovite habits. He marries a prostitute, survives his twenty-five-year term of service, and returns to his Ukrainian village to become the leader of a gang of robbers, which Chipka joins. It is noteworthy that Maksym's grandfather was a freedom-loving Zaporozhian Cossack who warned his fellow villagers about serfdom. Because of the Russian impact, his Cossack family reaches utter decay in only two generations. Thus, in *Do the Oxen Bellow* both slavery and crime enter Ukraine from Muscovy, a land that is inherently alien and hostile. Myrny's and Nechui's works show that some Ukrainian nationalists maintained the established stereotypes of Russians and wished to distance Ukrainians from their northern neighbours.

Ems Decree Reinforces the Valuev Circular

In May 1876 the Ems Decree reinforced the restrictions of the Valuev circular on Ukrainian literature, led to the disbandment of the South-Western Section of the Imperial Russian Geographical Society, and banned *Kievskii Telegraf*. The enactment of the decree is not surprising, as no reorientation in the Ukrainian question had taken place on the level of the central imperial government. As Savchenko has emphasized, the Ems Decree cannot and should not be examined separately from the Valuev circular: the former was merely a reiteration of the latter, with some additional restrictions on Ukrainian publishing.[89] Indeed, the text of the decree, in a passage originally written by Iuzefovich and the director of the Main Administration of the Press, Vasilii Grigorev, expressed the same idea: "This measure is but an extension of His majesty's high order issued on 3 July 1863, whereby it was allowed to pass for publication in Little Russian dialect only works that belong to the realm of fine literature."[90]

The local conditions and the authorities in Kyiv had created improved opportunities for national activism. Even the founding of the South-Western Section had been made possible only because of support of Dondukov-Korsakov and a number of local conservatives, including Iuzefovich and Vitalii Iakovlevich Shulgin, editor of *Kievlianin*. The conservatives soon noticed that they constituted only a small minority within the section, which was dominated by the Kyiv Hromada. Personal insults and enmities, like Drahomanov's attack on Iuzefovich in *Vestnik Evropy*, contributed to the final outcome, since they increased the conservatives' motivation to denounce local Ukrainian activities to the central government. However, the political differences between the Hromada and the Kyivan conservatives were substantial enough. Because the central government had been hostile to Ukrainian activities all along, the Hromada, Dondukov-Korsakov, and their mutual cooperation were vulnerable to denunciations. The denunciations, too, followed the pattern that had been established in 1862–3: the Ukrainian movement was attributed to Polish nationalism and all-Russian revolutionary activities. The only new note was that Ukrainian activities in Russian Empire were now perceived in connection with the Austrian imperial and Galician provincial governments.[91] The allegation of a Polish intrigue was now even more spurious than it had been in the 1860s: now, no connections existed between the Polish underground and the Kyiv Hromada.

Kievlianin began to criticize the South-Western Section in 1874, after the census was completed. The first secret denunciation was made at the end of that year. It was submitted to the Third Section, from where the chief of gendarmes, Aleksandr Lvovich Potapov, forwarded it to the minister of public enlightenment, Dmitrii Andreevich Tolstoi, who sent it to Platon Antonovich, superintendent of the Kyiv school district. The identity of the author of the denunciation is not known, but Savchenko thought it might be Nikolai Rigelman, one of the leaders of the Kyiv Slavic Welfare Committee. This was the same man who in 1847 had recommended Kulish to a number of Western Slavic scholars. On the other hand, the end of the denunciation contains passages similar to Iuzefovich's banned article against the Kyiv Ukrainophiles, which will be discussed below. The author linked the Ukrainian movement in the Russian Empire with the similar movement in Galicia. He claimed that Poles had founded the journal *Pravda* in order to assimilate Galician Rusyns and turn them into Poles. He told the Third Section that *Pravda* had received subsidies both from the Galician provincial parliament and from Ukrainophiles in the Russian Empire. The information about the subsidies from Dnipro Ukraine was correct: In his memoirs Drahomanov mentions two instalments in the early 1870s, the first one in the amount of 700 roubles and the second, 6000.[92] Furthermore, the anonymous author claimed that *Kievskii Telegraf* shared pro-Polish aims with *Pravda*. He described the history of the Ukrainophile movement, claiming that it had split into two parts in relation to the Polish insurrection: some Ukrainophiles had aimed at union with Poland, while others dreamed of independence, with Galicia included in the Ukrainian state.[93]

Drahomanov became the first victim of the anti-Ukrainian campaign: His article "Russian, Great Russian, Ukrainian, and Galician Literature" was the direct cause of his dismissal from the university in August 1875. Until that article appeared, Platon Antonovich had refrained from instituting any sanctions against Drahomanov.[94] In February 1875 Katkov's *Russkii Vestnik* published the article "Modern Ukrainophilia," whose author hinted at Drahomanov's authorship of the article. Katkov's journal claimed that the article in *Pravda* expressed the tendency to the complete linguistic and political separation of Ukraine from Russia and sympathy for Polish nationalism.[95] *Russkii Vestnik* based its allusion to the Polish-Ukrainian union on Drahomanov's statement that, in the event of a resurgence of the Polish national movement on the Right Bank, some Polish youth would react by turning to the Ukrainian movement. This is clearly a tendentious interpretation. Among Ukrainians it was rumoured that Rigelman was the author of the article in *Russkii Vestnik*.[96] If this is correct, the attack against Drahomanov, a Pan-Slav, came from a representative of a competing, conservative current of Pan-Slavism.

The stakes were raised with Iuzefovich's article, which did not appear in *Kievlianin*, because Puzyrevskii, in agreement with Dondukov-Korsakov, banned it in March 1875. In substance, the article was an additional denunciation written with the goal of instituting repressions against the Ukrainophiles. Iuzefovich claimed that the Ukrainophiles had merely used him and a few other imperial loyalists as a cover in order to turn the South-Western Section of the Imperial Geographical Society into their own organization. This accusation was well founded, but the author added other, more questionable, allegations: he claimed, for example, that Galician Poles had invented the Ruthenian language (*rusinskii iazik*) in order to estrange Galician Little Russians from the Russian nationality, and that the Ukrainophiles in the South-Western Section were motivated by similar considerations in the Kyiv census. Iuzefovich attributed all emphasis on the Ukrainian nationality to political separatism and stated that Ukrainophile ideas were merely a cover for socialism. Like the author of "Modern Ukrainophilia," Iuzefovich aimed a personal attack at Drahomanov as the author of "Russian, Great Russian, Ukrainian and Galician Literature" without mentioning his name, but giving several hints. Iuzefovich continued the tendentious interpretation of Drahomanov's article, claiming that the author was opposed to Russification and implying that he was writing about preparations for an insurrection in cooperation with the Poles. While this was far-fetched, Iuzefovich was on stronger ground when he evaluated Drahomanov's democratic ideas as harmful to the Russian government.[97]

Drahomanov did not consider his case hopeless and expected that correct information about the contents of his article might clear his name before the authorities and the Russian Pan-Slavists. He showed the article to Bishop Porfirii, the chairman of the Slavic Welfare Committee in Kyiv. Prompted by *Russkii Vestnik*, Superintendent Antonovich reluctantly made inquiries of Drahomanov about the matter. The latter readily admitted his authorship and gave the superintendent a copy of the article. Drahomanov emphasized that the article did not contain any allusions to Ukrainian separatism. However, by this time Antonovich was under pressure from his superiors. In May 1875 the deputy minister of public enlightenment, Aleksandr Prokhorovich Shirinskii-Shikhmatov, wrote to him about the necessity to prevent Ukrainophile agitation, in which some ministry employees were engaged.[98] In this context, Shirinskii-Shikhmatov specifically mentioned Drahomanov and some other names. It was not surprising that Antonovich now found Drahomanov's article to be subversive. The superintendent wrote to Shirinskii-Shikhmatov asking for Drahomanov's dismissal from his university position. It is interesting that Antonovich emphasized mainly the nationally subversive aspect of the article, only vaguely hinting at its other, social and constitutional, connotations. The superintendent deemed the linguistic separation of Ukraine from Russia harmful as such. Among the evidence proving adherence to "false opinions," Antonovich mentioned that Drahomanov discussed the possibility that Ukrainian might be adopted someday as the language of instruction in elementary schools. Drahomanov moved to Geneva in spring 1876, just before his deportation was announced in the Ems Decree. Despite Drahomanov's dismissal, Antonovich continued to protect other Ukrainophiles, even claiming to his superiors that Volodymyr Antonovych was not one.[99]

In late August 1875 Alexander II nominated a special council "in view of the emergence of Ukrainophile activities and especially translations and publications of textbooks and prayer books in the Little Russian language."[100] The distortion of reality began in the act of nomination itself, for no prayer books in Ukrainian had been published in the Russian Empire since the Valuev circular. The commission consisted of Minister of Internal Affairs Aleksandr Timashev, Minister of Public

Enlightenment and Chief Procurator of the Holy Synod Dmitrii Tolstoi, Chief of Gendarmes Aleksandr Potapov, and Mikhail Iuzefovich.

Miller has remarked that the special council "did not try to discuss, analyse, and solve the problem ... Rather, it prepared the ideological ground for repressive measures."[101] Repression was taken as the point of departure rather than as one of several possible political alternatives. In early 1876 gendarmes quashed an attempt to distribute Ukrainian books to peasants in Volyn on the grounds that "the dissemination of the Little Russian nationality is incompatible with the government's goals."[102] All these books had passed censorship. It is a telling fact that they were confiscated at the beginning of 1876, *before* the council reached its conclusions and submitted them to Alexander II. The council based its activities on two memoranda: one was prepared by the Main Administration of the Press and dated 3 October, and the other was written by Iuzefovich later in the same month. The author of the Main Administration's memorandum was anonymous, but the text was approved by Timashev. His main point was that raising the Little Russian dialect to the status of a literary language could not be tolerated, since Little Russians were too numerous and formed too large a share of the empire's population. Furthermore, in the Russo-Polish contest Russia had gained the upper hand only after Little Russia joined it. The author understood Ukrainian separatism as a consequence of a Polish intrigue. The memorandum contained recommendations on limiting the publication of Ukrainian books and banning their importation, which were later adopted by the council.[103]

Iuzefovich's memorandum discussed the history of the Ukrainian movement to the present day. At first, he emphasized Little Russian loyalty to the empire. After the reunification in the seventeenth century, Little Russia constantly "strove to full assimilation into national unity."[104] Little Russians had used their own dialect for jokes, but had written all serious literature in literary Russian. Iuzefovich explained the emergence of an exclusive Little Russian identity (*malorusskoi izkliuchitelnosti*) through an Austrian-Polish intrigue. He portrayed the first generation of Ukrainian activists, especially Kulish and Kostomarov, as weak individuals who had been used by the Poles for their own ends. Iuzefovich claimed that the upsurge in the Ukrainian movement in the 1870s originated not in Kyiv but in St Petersburg, in the Geographical Society, which had given Chubynsky an influential position, at first in the expedition and later in the South-Western Section. Iuzefovich emphasized Chubynsky's earlier deportation for revolutionary agitation, and remarked that the South-Western Section had welcomed such members as Stepan Nis and Oleksandr Konysky, despite the fact that they, too, had previously been exiled for their revolutionary activities. Iuzefovich conveniently neglected to mention that none of the three men had been found guilty of revolutionary agitation in a formal trial. He even claimed that Nis had distributed the brochures of Land and Liberty, an accusation never confirmed by the authorities.[105] Finally, Iuzefovich speculated as to whether the upsurge in armed robberies was politically motivated and marked the beginning of a new *haidamak* movement, and went on to recommend unspecified energetic measures to combat Ukrainophiles.

The special council began its sessions only in April 1876. Defining all Ukrainian literary activity as an "infringement of state unity" and even "criminal activity,"[106] it claimed that "the aspiration of the Kyiv Ukrainophiles, so to speak, isolate themselves from Great Russian literature ... Sooner or later, such an opinion will throw Galician, and then our own, Ukrainophiles, into the arms of the Poles."[107] It is highly likely that the members of the council did not bother to study the views of Drahomanov and Chubynsky, for it was problematic to claim that these Kyiv Ukrainophiles aspired to isolate themselves from Great Russian literature. The special council passed its draft resolution on 24 April 1876, which repeated the restrictions on publishing in the Little Russian language stipulated in the Valuev circular and added new ones: the prohibition of the importation of literature, bans on public readings and staging of plays in Little Russian, prohibition of musical texts, and a ban on Kulish's orthography. It also removed the ambiguity of the Valuev circular concerning non-fiction intended for the educated public: now only fiction and historical documents could be published. All literature in Little Russian was to be removed from school libraries. It was decided to close down *Kievskii Telegraf* and subsidize *Slovo* (*Word*), the Russophile organ in Galicia. All school teachers with Ukrainophile sympathies were to be transferred to Great Russian provinces, and Great Russian teachers were to be invited to replace them. This last measure was an important deviation from the previously practised policy, according to which the Ukrainians were treated as Russians and thus had equal rights in civil service.[108]

Although the council's final draft of measures targeting Ukrainian activities was severe, it did not explicitly suppress the South-Western Section. It noted the necessity of instituting measures against Chubynsky and Drahomanov, but did not specify what those measures were.

Potapov submitted to Alexander II the issues of abolishing the South-Western Section and exiling Chubynsky and Drahomanov separately, as Iuzefovich's opinion, in addition to the council's less explicit conclusions. The cooperation of Potapov and Iuzefovich bore fruit: the emperor endorsed Iuzefovich's opinion in these two matters. Potapov and Iuzefovich relied on this intrigue, since Timashev had reservations concerning these measures and wanted to have the final word on them.[109] In this way, the two most Russophile Ukrainian activists in Kyiv were selected for repression, despite the fact that neither of them had been found guilty of any illegal acts.

Alexander II permitted Dondukov-Korsakov to issue a passport to Drahomanov for international travel. When the authorities sought him on the basis of the Ems decisions, he had already left the empire. Before his departure, Drahomanov agreed with the Kyiv Hromada that he would act as its representative abroad and publish an uncensored periodical. As a refugee, Drahomanov was more outspoken, and probably more dangerous to the empire than he had been in Kyiv.

Drahomanov's first publication after his escape from the Russian Empire was *Po voprosu o malorusskoi literature* (*On the Question of Little Russian Literature*),[110] a defence of literature in Ukrainian. The main text was dated 9 May, that is, shortly before the Ems Decree, but the author also included a foreword dated 14 July. The foreword included in full the circular which was sent to the censors about implementing the Ems Decree, and in the main text, Drahomanov told how he had lost his job at the university. Except for one short remark on the desirability of solving the agrarian question according to socialist principles, Drahomanov did not write about politics, but concentrated on a defence of literature in Ukrainian. One after another, he refuted arguments against Little Russian literature's right to exist: it was not a Polish invention or attributed to any single political tendency; the Little Russian language was not a mix of Russian and Polish; its history of literary use stretched back to the fifteenth century; and Little Russian was now used in many different settings, like courts of law and higher education in Galicia. If anything, Drahomanov was now a stauncher advocate of Ukrainian: he no more emphasized limiting its functions in order to leave a role for Russian. To be sure, he had not abandoned the idea that Russian might in the future become the language of international communication between Slavs. However, it would never replace other Slavic languages, of which Little Russian was one. Without literature in Little Russian, Galician Little Russians would become Poles or Hungarians.

Drahomanov's second post-emigration Russian-language brochure, *Turki vneshnie i turki vnutrennie* (*Foreign and Internal Turks*), was dated November 1876. He tied together Russia's foreign mission to liberate Balkan Slavs and its internal liberation, about which he now wrote fully explicitly: "It is a time for us to speak frankly ..., in straight words, as suits free people who are convinced in their ideas."[111] Drahomanov put into two words what he found necessary for Russia: "Political liberty!"[112] At the time, autonomous Serbia was at war with its suzerain Turkey, struggling to gain full independence and more territory. Among Russian society, there was wide interest in the situation in the Balkans, and Russian volunteers were fighting on the Serbian side. Drahomanov wanted Russia to declare war on Turkey, finish with Turkish rule in the Balkans, and let the Balkan nations form their own independent states. However, he emphasized how it was both inconsistent and practically impossible to implement this task without at first establishing civil liberties and constitutional rule in Russia, with elected representatives supervising the executive branch of administration.

The first issue of Drahomanov's Ukrainian-language periodical *Hromada* appeared in 1878. In it, Drahomanov described Ukraine as a fully distinct country and defined its geographic limits. They resemble the borders of present-day Ukraine with some differences: in the north, Drahomanov included some of the present-day Belarus, relying on Chubynsky's work; he included only the north-eastern slice of the Crimean peninsula in Ukraine, and in the east, the country stretched to Kuban. Drahomanov now explicitly stated his opinion that aliens – Russians, Poles, Hungarians, and Romanians – were ruling over Ukrainians and oppressing them. He found that Ukraine's development under Russia had stopped in the eighteenth century, while since 1866, the imperial government even in general had lost its reforming potential.

Drahomanov not only expressed his support for socialist movements, but he also emphasized how socialism and the Ukrainian national cause were inseparable: if one supported only one and not the other, one was either a bad socialist or a bad Ukrainian. Ukrainians should have their own socialist movement, separate from Russians or any other ruling nationality. Drahomanov supported an anarchist type of socialism, in which independent communities would live without the interference of a central government. He explicitly rejected the establishment of a national state as a political goal, since such a state would entail oppression characteristic of all centralized states. He found that socialists should settle in the countryside for long-term agitation work. Drahomanov explicitly accepted revolutionary violence, but disapproved of instigating it: only if the peasants themselves rose in rebellion could the agitators join it. Despite these explicitly revolutionary opinions, Drahomanov preferred evolution to revolution. Even to merely establish the rule of law, or constitutional monarchy in Russia, would be an important step forward. Except for his reformism, Drahomanov's radicalism indeed came close to Podolynsky's.[113]

In the 1870s pro-Russian and anti-Russian orientations alike existed in the Ukrainian movement. Indeed, the pro-Russian current within the movement emerged only in this period and challenged the traditional negative perception of Great Russians. Although Antonovych and the members of the Kyiv Hromada had sided with the empire against the Poles back in 1861–2, that had been a practical choice not based on a favourable evaluation of Great Russians or Ukrainian–Russian relations in general. Now, a decade later, Chubynsky, Drahomanov, and Kulish argued, each in his own way, for a principal reorientation of the Ukrainian movement with regard to the "Russian question." The statements against Mazepa that appeared in *Kievskii Telegraf* may have been motivated by a practical political strategy of the Kyiv *Hromada,* whose leaders wanted to retain their opportunity for lawful and public Ukrainian work in the empire. However, short-term practical considerations do not suffice to explain the existence of the pro-Russian current: Drahomanov's siding with Russia was based on deep personal conviction, which became less explicit only after his hard experience as a political refugee. There is no doubt that Drahomanov and Chubynsky's pro-Russian ideas were based on wishful thinking about the imminent democratization of the Russian Empire, or at least its tolerance for democratic ideas. Even Kulish's conservative political orientation was marked by an unrealistic perception of Russian autocracy as hostile to estate privileges. As Drahomanov noticed by the end of the year 1876, the imperial government was dominated by what he called "Turks," staunch supporters of autocracy, not moderate adherents of constitutional development or the legal equality of citizens. That is why, despite the fruitful cooperation between Dondukov-Korsakov and the Kyiv Hromada, a long-term alliance between Ukrainian nationalists and the imperial government was not a viable option: the government was simply not flexible enough for it to emerge. The Ems Decree endorsed the policy of repression that the government had chosen in 1863. In its perception of Great Russians, Ukrainian nationalism became dominated by the current represented by Kostomarov's *Two Russian Nationalities*, Svydnytsky, Nechui-Levytsky, and Myrny.

Government politicians failed to exploit the disagreement between the pro-Russian and anti-Russian currents within the Ukrainian movement, attempting instead to suppress the whole movement. This was an unrealistic strategy, for by the 1870s, the national movement was deeply rooted in the consciousness of part of the Ukrainian intelligentsia. Although its activists numbered a few hundred at most, they influenced many more people. Ukrainian nationalism could not be contained by the machinery of repression that the imperial government had at its disposal. However, it is unlikely that the anti-Russian current would have disappeared even under a more flexible and tolerant imperial policy, for it was a continuation of an established tradition.

Chapter Eight

Aftermath and Conclusions

The Ems Decree was revised in 1881, 1892, and 1895. In 1881, musical texts and dictionaries were permitted again.[1] However, a ban on all translations from Russian into Ukrainian was added in 1892,[2] and children's literature was forbidden three years later.[3] The official decisions are not the whole story, since the implementation of the restrictions on Ukrainian publishing fluctuated also in the period 1876–1904. Alexei Miller has emphasized the lax way in which he finds the Ems Decree was implemented in the initial period after its enactment. Shortly before its enactment, Drahomanov received a passport for foreign travel; Chubynsky was permitted to live in St Petersburg, and in 1879 was able to return to Ukraine; only six secondary-school teachers were forced to either leave their profession or accept positions in Russia proper; six Ukrainian books in all were removed from the school libraries. Miller admits the devastating impact of the Ems Decree on Ukrainian publishing, but emphasizes how only 30 per cent of the books submitted to the Main Administration of the Press from June 1876 to April 1880 were affected by censorship. He draws the conclusion that "all the authorities responsible for the implementation of the edict executed it without zeal."[4]

To some extent, Miller is right in his critique of Savchenko, whose *Zaborona ukraïnstva* can be translated as "prohibition of Ukrainism": even in its wording, the Ems Decree was not a prohibition of all Ukrainian activities, and it was not always strictly enforced. However, I find problematic Miller's thesis that the authorities always implemented the Ems Decree without zeal. Sometimes they indeed did, but it is also possible to find examples of repressions which surpassed the limits set in the

Ems Decree. In 1876, the editor of a St Petersburg journal, *Pchela* (Bee), Mikhail Osipovich Mikeshin, appealed to the Main Administration of the Press about the local censor's decision concerning his two Russian-language articles on Shevchenko. The censor had suppressed several passages. Mikeshin was especially upset about a passage in which "in his homeland, Ukraine" the word "Ukraine" was removed. Mikeshin found this decision arbitrary, since Shevchenko's Ukrainian origin was a widely known fact and it made no sense to suppress it. However, in response to Mikeshin's appeal, the Council of the Main Administration of the Press banned the articles altogether and instructed censors not to permit any texts about Shevchenko. The council referred to the Ems Decree, although the decree did not mention Shevchenko's name and applied only to publications written in Ukrainian.[5]

The statistics on books in Ukrainian published in the Russian Empire reveal a devastating initial impact of the Ems Decree: while in 1873–6 seventy-five titles appeared, in 1877–80 there were only twenty titles.[6] The worst year was 1879, with only one Ukrainian book appearing in the whole empire. Furthermore, none of the books published in 1877–80 violated the Ems Decree: they were all either fiction, or collections of historical documents. Non-fiction in Ukrainian remained off the limits of the permissible, and the slump in the number of all Ukrainian books indicates that it was now more difficult to get published even fiction, which was explicitly permitted in the decree. However, the 1880s saw a recovery of Ukrainian publishing: in 1881–4 seventy-one titles appeared, and in 1884–8 one hundred Ukrainian books were published – more than ever before. Thereafter, Ukrainian publishing continued to expand: 1889–92, 101 titles; 1893–6, 117; 1897–1900, 172; and 1901–4, 227.[7] There were fluctuations also regarding Ukrainian non-fiction: in 1882–3 fifteen titles were permitted, but thereafter the Main Administration of the Press returned to the strict implementation of the Ems Decree: in 1885–93, not a single book of non-fiction was permitted. Beginning from 1896, non-fiction and publications aimed at readers among the common people gradually became more frequent: from 1896–1904, censors permitted eighty-three such books that, according to the Ems Decree, should have been banned. However, the Ems Decree did not lose all its impact until the revolution in 1905. Although the implementation of the Ems Decree officially ceased only in 1906, in practice the revolutionary events in 1905 made it obsolete. As a whole, the Ems Decree did not fulfil its purpose of preventing the development of either Ukrainian literature, or Ukrainian nationalism. To be sure, it obstructed them, creating resentment and historical burden, which continues to impact on Ukrainian–Russian relations even today.

It is time to answer the questions presented at the beginning of this book. How did the national activists perceive the relationship between Ukrainians and Russians? Inclusive and exclusive nationality concepts coexisted in the national movement. The most prominent representative of the inclusive, all-Russian national identity was Mykhailo Drahomanov, who believed that Ukrainians would gain more rights in the future democratic Russia, and that they should not strive for full separation of their language from the Great Russian language. However, the exclusive concept of Ukrainian nationality enjoyed rather more support in the national movement than the inclusive concept. Most Ukrainian nationalists did not find it possible to combine Ukrainian and Russian nationalities: one had to be either one or the other. Even Mykhailo Maksymovych, who was a political conservative, ruled out the combination of these two nationalities, since for him, nationality depended on language, and he perceived the Ukrainian language as clearly separate from the Great Russian. However, perceiving these two nationalities as separate from each other did not preclude various ideas about the special and close relationship existing between Ukrainians and Russians. The adherents of such a close relationship included Maksymovych, Pavlo Chubynsky, and Panteleimon Kulish in the 1870s when he wrote *Istoriia Vozsoedineniia Rusi*. According to the special relationship idea, the two nations needed each other because they were closely related to each other, shared a long history with each other, had national characters that complemented each other, and politically needed each other. When the national characters were discussed, Great Russians were perceived as natural organizers of statehood, while the Ukrainians provided to Great Russians the principle of individual liberty and cultural creativity. It was perceived that the two nations politically needed each other, because only together could they overcome the Polish danger. Sometimes, Ukrainians were perceived as incapable of organizing a state of their own, which made the union with Russians necessary for them.

The idea of a special relationship between Ukrainians and Russians did not enjoy wide support in the national movement. Most national activists strove to distance themselves from Russians rather than emphasize proximity to them. The negative stereotypic perception of Russians recurs throughout the period being studied in this book, beginning from Shevchenko's "Dream" and ending with Ivan Nechui-Levytskyi's and Panas Myrny's fiction. Kostomarov's "Two Russian Nationalities" is the most prominent text in which these stereotypes are expressed. In their most extreme form, the stereotypes were presented in Anatoly Svydnytsky's *Liuboratskys*. In these stereotypes, Russians were perceived as undemocratic, prone to dominating other nations, collectivist rather than individualist, immoral in their violent behaviour, egoistic, lacking respect for others' property, and incapable of deep religiosity or high ideals in general. Furthermore, Russian males were deemed oppressive in their relation to women. According to the stereotypes, Russians were not inclined to cultural creativity, but rather the accumulation of material wealth. The stereotypes reflected the Ukrainian intelligentsia's own values as an image of what Ukrainians should not be. Many texts written by rank-and-file activists testify to the wide support these stereotypes enjoyed, but they were most certainly not shared by all national activists.

How was the relationship between Ukrainians and the Russian Empire perceived? In answering this question, it is necessary to discuss separately the intended long-term goals of the movement and immediate short-term political choices. For instance, the idea of Ukrainian independence enjoyed support in the Kyiv Hromada at the beginning of the 1860s, but this did not preclude cooperation with Governor-General Ilarion Vasilchikov in the short term. As the final long-term goal, Ukrainian independence was explicitly mentioned four times. In his letter to Aksakov, Kulish set independence as the distant final goal of the Ukrainian movement, presuming that it would be reached only after his own lifetime. Petro Iefymenko proposed a toast to Ukrainian independence in 1859. His letter to "Ivan Alekseevich" in 1861 provides additional information about his attitude to the Russian Empire. Iefymenko perceived an ongoing historical process in which all the empires were breaking into smaller nation states and the use of physical force for political purposes was losing its effectiveness. While he did not predict the exact time of the empire's demise, he clearly perceived that it was to happen rather soon. In his article in *Samostaine Slovo* in 1861 "Volodar," most likely a pseudonym for Volodymyr Antonovych, mentioned Ukraine's right to gain independence in an unspecified future. In the letter which Stepan Nis received in 1862, independence was mentioned as a goal which it would be good to reach, but which would likely not be reached. These are the four documented cases in which independence was discussed, but it is certain that our information about this topic is incomplete. Viktor Loboda wrote about the necessity to separate from Russia without clearly indicating the status he wanted Ukraine to reach after the separation. In his *Parova Mashyna* Serhii Podolynsky implied the separation of Ukraine from Russia, but was not specific concerning the establishment of a national state. Clearly, Ukrainian independence enjoyed support in the national movement, but it is not possible to measure its popularity.

Another prominent idea of the long-term political goal of the national movement was the status of a state in a federation of several nationalities. In its most radical form, this federal idea excluded Russia and thus entailed Ukraine's separation from Russia. The first case of this idea being proposed is in Iurii Andruzky's papers, which were confiscated in Petrozavodsk in 1850. It also was the aim of the Polish Ukrainophiles of the late 1850s and early 1860s. Before he abandoned the Polish national movement, Antonovych strove to gain for Ukraine the status of a federal state in the future independent Poland. Those Polish Ukrainophiles who remained in the Polish independence movement and participated in the January insurrection of 1863 shared this goal. Although the Polish underground state never accepted this idea, it influenced the policies of the insurgent administration in Right-Bank Ukraine in that it was proposed that Ukrainians have limited use of the Ukrainian language in local administration and education.

A federation in which Russia was to be included was mentioned more often than one without Russia. This was proposed as a goal by the Slavic Society of St Cyril and St Methodius, the journal *Osnova*, Andrii Shymanov, and Drahomanov. While the Cyrillo-Methodians envisioned a federation of all Slavs, *Osnova* rather advocated a triune federation consisting of Russia, Ukraine, and Poland. Shymanov was thinking in terms of a Pan-Slav federation. Drahomanov did not define the limits of the future federation, but it is clear that he thought it would be based on Russia, either by making the existing Russia a federation of nationalities, or combining such a reform with Russian expansion westward. However, he did not find it necessary to include all Slavs in a single federation. An autocratic state can hardly be federal, and that is why all federal ideas entailed a degree of democratization of Russia. For the Cyrillo-Methodians, the Slavic federation would consist of democratic republics, while *Osnova* was only able to vaguely imply a more democratic order in the future federation. Shymanov considered the overthrowing of Russian autocracy a precondition to the establishment of the federation. Drahomanov was more flexible and prepared even to live with the Russian monarchy, if it only would enact a constitution. However, he found it more desirable to establish a political system in which the lower classes of society would dominate politically.

Finally, some national activists were satisfied with a situation in which their cultural rights would be respected in the Russian Empire under autocracy. Examples of this orientation are Kulish in his *Vozsoedinenie* and Maksymovych. However, even Kulish found it necessary to revise the image of the empire by claiming that it was opposed to the estate privileges. It seems that this moderate orientation did not enjoy wide support in the national movement. Maksymovych's loyalist ideas notwithstanding, most Ukrainian national activists were politically to the left of the government and the existing order. Even when they did not discuss explicit political goals, they clearly aimed at improving the lot of the lower classes of society. Podolynsky was farthest to the left with his program of agrarian socialism based on local peasant communities, but even the most moderate Ukrainian activists identified with the interests of the peasants rather than those of the landowning gentry. A good example of their general democratic and plebeian orientation in social questions is *Kievskii Telegraf* in 1875.

The short-term political goals and means to reach them were not necessarily congruent with the long-term goals. The Slavic Society of St Cyril and St Methodius strove to establish a Pan-Slav federation of republics, but began its activities by political discussions in a small circle and with publications, which the authors submitted to censorship. Although Mykola Hulak spoke about violent means of gaining power, this was a theoretical discussion. In the reign of Alexander II, most Ukrainian activists used mainly lawful means in their political actions: they submitted their publications to censors and did not attempt to agitate the public against the government. However, the rigidity of Russian laws regarding oppositional activities made it impossible to remain fully within the limits of the law. Hromada societies could exist only in the underground or, at most, under the guise of a lawful organization, like the South-Western Section of the Imperial Russian Geographic Society. Also, it was illegal to even privately discuss any alternatives to the existing political order. Most Ukrainian activists acted in a precarious situation in which it was conceivable that they would be charged with political crimes. Most of them tried to remedy this situation by convincing the government about their loyalty rather than turning frankly against the government. A good example of this strategy is the letter of the members of the Kyiv Hromada published in *Sovremennaia Letopis* in December 1862. They claimed that they did not promote among peasants identification with any units larger than the village community. It is a small wonder that Petr Valuev and Vasilii Dolgorukov were not convinced, since they had access to *Samostaine Slovo,* in which independence was discussed. Usually, Ukrainians did not publicly demand anything more than the right to practise lawfully their cultural and educational activities. An additional public demand was introduction of Ukrainian as the language of instruction in elementary schools, which was discussed especially in 1862. In the Russo-Polish conflict, most Ukrainians sided with the Russian Empire rather than the Polish insurgents. Cooperation between Governor-General Ilarion Vasilchikov and the Kyiv Hromada lasted from spring 1861 to Vasilchikov's death in December 1862.

Not all Ukrainians supported the policy of short-term loyalism, however. Ukrainian members of the Kharkiv-Kyiv revolutionary group were convinced that the situation of Ukrainians could only be improved in an all-Russian revolution. Andrii Krasovsky sided with the Polish movement for independence and attempted direct agitation of rank-and-file soldiers to disobey their orders. Krasovsky was a brave and somewhat eccentric individual, but Ivan Andrushchenko's and Leonid Iashchenko's cases show that Land and Liberty had a wider potential base of support in the Ukrainian movement. It is likely that the overlap between Land and Liberty and Ukrainian Hromada groups was not limited to individuals who were involved in Andrushchenko's case. However, there is no trustworthy evidence that the Little Russian Revolutionary Committee postulated by the imperial authorities and Soviet historians ever existed. In the 1870s before the Ems Decree, Podolynsky was the most prominent representative of the revolutionary Ukrainian current. However, this was a minority current within the national movement.

In the imperial government, a number of different approaches to the Ukrainian question can be identified. Some of the most radical reformers within the government, like Superintendent of the Kyiv school district Nikolai Pirogov and Minister of Public Enlightenment Aleksandr Golovnin, did not perceive any danger in the Ukrainian movement.

Pirogov permitted the emergence of the Kyiv Hromada at St Vladimir's University, because he found it a useful balancing force against the Polish national movement. In his response to the Valuev circular, Golovnin draw an analogy between the repressions against the Finnish and Ukrainian languages. This shows that he did not perceive the status of Ukrainian as different from that of any other minority language in the empire. Golovnin's benevolent attitude to the Ukrainian activists is coherent with his general dislike of repressions and emphasis on the rule of law.

Often, governors-general of Kyiv were somewhat more sympathetic to the Ukrainian movement than the central imperial government was. Ilarion Vasilchikov, Aleksandr Bezak, and Aleksandr Dondukov-Korsakov, each in his own way, defended the Ukrainians from the repressions being urged by the central government. Vasilchikov's actions regarding Kulish's *Hramatka* and against the launching of a bilingual newspaper in Kyiv indicate that he was not a convinced friend of Ukrainian nationalists. The change in his policy and temporary alliance with Hromada in 1861–2 was a practical matter. He found it necessary because of the intensification of Polish clandestine activities in Kyiv in the years which preceded the January 1863 insurrection. After the original agreement, it was in Vasilchikov's own interest to protect the Ukrainian activists and either reject, or soften, political accusations against them. If he admitted that the central government was right and the Ukrainian activists were dangerous revolutionaries, his own policy would be discredited. Bezak's policies in 1864–5 were more cautious than Vasilchikov's, but he was instrumental in saving numerous Ukrainian activists from repressions. In this, Bezak acted out of concern over the public image of the government. He found extensive repressions unwise, since they would indicate that many Ukrainians were opposed to the government. Dondukov-Korsakov found public Ukrainian activities more desirable than clandestine ones, because they facilitated easier supervision over the movement. Dondukov-Korsakov's dispute with Hromada regarding the Kyiv census indicates that he was also guided by practical considerations rather than any genuine sympathy for the Ukrainian movement.

Another institutional pattern was that the officials in the Ministry of Public Enlightenment often advocated a softer policy regarding Ukrainian nationalism than did the Third Section and Ministry of Internal Affairs. Since rather many Ukrainian national activists worked at universities and secondary schools, large-scale repressions against them would have been destructive to education. Such repressions would also have compromised the reputation of educational authorities among the imperial bureaucracy and conservative public. The Third Section and Ministry of Internal Affairs were tasked with the struggle against subversion in the empire, and it is not surprising that they were less concerned over any potential damage to education. While condemning the Cyrillo-Methodian society, Sergei Uvarov belittled its importance and defended lawful Ukrainian activities, acting in the interests of his own ministry. Golovnin's opposition against the Valuev circular was based on his political convictions: he wished for predictability and the rule of law in censorship, and he was positively attuned to the development of all minority languages in the empire, including Ukrainian. While the conservative Dmitrii Tolstoi, who was minister of public enlightenment in 1866–80, never opposed himself to repression against Ukrainian activists, the superintendent of the Kyiv school district Platon Antonovich often defended them. Antonovich did not sympathize with the Ukrainian movement, but he understood the devastating effect any large-scale repressions against national activists would have on the functioning of his district.

The Russian government practised repressions against the Ukrainian movement throughout the period studied in this book. The imperial politicians had several motivations for these repressions. Here, too, it is fruitful to analyse separately the long-term and short-term considerations. As Alexei Miller has emphasized, the all-Russian and Ukrainian nationality concepts were in fundamental contradiction with each other. That is why it is not surprising that the government circles were opposed to dissemination of Ukrainian identity among the peasants. Furthermore, the general democratic orientation of the Ukrainian national movement was manifest. By its mere existence, the Ukrainian movement presented a challenge to the imperial government, which was generally inclined to deal with political opposition in a repressive manner. However, repression was not the only possible response to the challenge available to the imperial government, and the Valuev circular was an untraditional measure. The government might have responded to the challenge by merely rejecting the use of Ukrainian language in administration and education. The Valuev circular was enacted because of specific political events and circumstances: the government received reliable information about a revolutionary mood among the Ukrainian national activists; adherents of repression occupied the key government posts necessary to enact repressive measures; and they felt compelled to disseminate disinformation and bypass regular procedures, because they anticipated opposition in government circles against the repressions. By attempting altogether to prevent the expansion of the Ukrainian movement, Valuev and his colleagues set for themselves a too ambitious and unrealistic goal. Local history, language, and customs provided the conditions for the expansion of the Ukrainian national movement. With the means which the imperial authorities had at their disposal, it was not possible to prevent such expansion; at most, they could obstruct it. This does not mean that the all-Russian identity was not a viable option for many inhabitants of Ukraine, but merely that the competition between the two identities was unavoidable. The attempts to prevent the Ukrainian identity even from entering the contest were inept policy.

Since the Cyrillo-Methodian society was uncovered and its members punished in 1847, the existence of the revolutionary and anti-imperial current in the Ukrainian movement was not a secret to the government. The government of Nicholas I was extremely sensitive to any oppositional activities. The investigation of the Cyrillo-Methodian case revealed that Ukrainian revolutionaries were able to disseminate their message through legally published and censored publications. The government also gained information about the fact that many Ukrainian activists felt antipathy against Russians. Even in the most liberal period, in 1857–62, censors were alert to these tendencies and occasionally tried to prevent their dissemination. However, for the time being, the increasing unrest in Poland widened the opportunities for Ukrainian publishing. *Osnova,* with its federalist principles and peaceful means of action, was certainly a lesser evil to the government than the Polish underground movement for independence. In 1861, Pirogov and Vasilchikov in Kyiv and Nikolai Mukhanov in the Main Administration of Censorship clearly understood this fact. Through *Osnova* and intelligence gathered about Hromada groups, the government politicians knew well that the Ukrainian movement differed from the Polish movement.

However, reliable information about the revolutionary current in the Ukrainian movement surfaced in Krasovsky's case in 1862. It began the process that led to the Valuev circular. Valuev, who did not want to permit even the development of the Yiddish language, felt antipathy against plebeian linguistic projects in general. He understood well how the development of the Ukrainian language contradicted the idea of an all-Russian nation. Chief of Gendarmes Vasilii Dolgorukov supported Valuev's plan to enact restrictions against Ukrainian publishing. The gendarmes did not hesitate to forge a revolutionary proclamation in order to repress and exile Pavlo Chubynsky. In 1862–3, important changes took place in the government: censorship was transferred under Valuev's jurisdiction; Vasilchikov died and was succeeded by Nicolai Annenkov, who supported the restrictions on Ukrainian publishing. Even so, Dolgorukov and Valuev anticipated opposition against the restrictions. Suppression of publications on the bases of their language ran counter to the aims of many imperial politicians, who wanted to increase rather than restrict the freedom of the press. Furthermore, the idea of using the plebeian ethnic groups of the former Polish-Lithuanian Commonwealth as a counterweight to the Polish movement for independence was supported by several influential imperial bureaucrats, most notably Dmitrii Bludov, Andrei Zablotskii-Desiatovskii, and Aleksandr Hilferding, who all served on the State Council, Bludov as its chairman and the latter two in its administration. That is why Valuev had to enact the restrictions on Ukrainian publishing in an irregular way, bypassing the State Council and Committee of Ministers. The emphasis on the danger of Polish-Ukrainian cooperation in the circular should be taken with a grain of salt. This was an argument intended for those imperial politicians who remained unconvinced of the necessity of the circular. Conveniently, Poltava governor Volkov and the Third Section either staged or at least blew out of proportion Volodymyr Syniehub's case to back the myth of the Ukrainian-Polish threat.

From 1863 on, the Valuev circular guided government policy regarding Ukrainian literature. Petr Valuev intended it to have effect for a long period. This does not mean that it was always strictly adhered to. In 1874–6 local circumstances, Dondukov-Korsakov's policy, and Puzyrevskii's corruption favoured an upsurge in Ukrainian publishing in Kyiv. However, by this time, the balance of power between the Kyiv governor-general and central imperial administration had shifted to the benefit of the latter. The centre was now stronger than at the beginning of the 1860s, and that is why Dondukov-Korsakov had less opportunity than Vasilchikov to practise an independent Ukrainian policy. Furthermore, Vasilchikov had cooperated with Hromada before the central government chose repression as its policy in the Ukrainian question. By 1876, the repressive policy was firmly established and more difficult to challenge. There is no information about any opposition in the central administration to the Ems Decree, and the Committee of Ministers belatedly approved the Valuev circular in 1876. Although other opinions existed in government circles, the adherents of repression won. This was unfortunate for Ukrainians, Russians, and the Russian Empire.

Notes

1 Introduction

1 RGIA, f. 775, op. 1, 1863g., delo 188, l. 20–1.
2 GARF, f. 112, op. 1, ed. khr. 72, l. 162.
3 To the best of my knowledge, the perception of Russians as oppressors and Ukrainian stereotypes of Russians have not been an object of serious scholarly study. Myroslav Shkandrij offers some insights in his *Russia and Ukraine: Literature and the Discourse of Empire from Napoleonic to Postcolonial Times* (Montreal: McGill-Queen's University Press, 2001). However, Shkandrij limits his study to the image of the empire in Ukrainian literature and does not examine the image of Russians as a nationality or ethnic group.
4 Andreas Kappeler has identified four different meanings for the term *russkii* in the imperial period. It could mean all the inhabitants of the Russian Empire, those belonging to the privileged class only, the Russian Orthodox population, or all the East Slavic peoples. See Kappeler, "Einleitung," in Kappeler, ed., *Die Russen: Ihr Nationalbewustsein in Geschichte und Gegenwart* (Cologne: Markus, 1990), 9; Kappeler, *Russland und die Ukraine: Verflochtene Biographien und Geschichten* (Vienna: Böhlau, 2012) 17–20.
5 For an overview of the words referring to Ukrainians in this period, see Anton Kotenko, Ol'ga Martyniuk, and Aleksei Miller, "Maloross," in A. Miller, D. Svizhkov, and I. Schierle, eds., "Poniatiia o Rossii": *K istoricheskoi semantike imperskogo perioda*, 2 vols. (Moscow: Novoe literaturnoe obozrenie, 2012), 2: 392–426; Kappeler, *Russland und die Ukraine*, 20–3.
6 Fedir Savchenko, *Zaborona ukraïnstva 1876r.* (Kyïv: Derzhavne vydavnytstvo Ukraïny, 1930).

7 Alexei Miller, *The Ukrainian Question: The Russian Empire and Nationalism in the Nineteenth Century* (Budapest and New York: Central European University Press, 2003), trans. Olga Poato.
8 Serhiy Bilenky, *Romantic Nationalism in Eastern Europe: Russian, Polish, and Ukrainian Political Imaginations* (Stanford, CA: Stanford University Press, 2012).
9 Faith Hillis, *Children of Rus': Right-Bank Ukraine and the Invention of a Russian Nation* (Ithaca and London: Cornell University Press, 2014). My comments on this book concern only the part which overlaps with my book, up to 1870s.
10 The most important works in this field include Benedict Anderson, *Imagined Communities: Reflections on the Origins and Spread of Nationalism*, 2nd ed. (London: Verso, 1991); Ernest Gellner, *Nations and Nationalism* (Oxford: Blackwell, 1983) and *Encounters with Nationalism* (Oxford, UK; Cambridge, MA: Blackwell, 1994); Miroslav Hroch, *Social Preconditions of National Revival in Europe: A Comparative Analysis of the Social Composition of Patriotic Groups among the Smaller European Nations*, trans. Ben Fowkes (Cambridge: Cambridge University Press, 1985).
11 Anthony D. Smith, *The Ethnic Origins of Nations* (Oxford: Blackwell, 1986), *National Identity* (London: Penguin, 1991), and *Nationalism: Theory, Ideology, History* (Cambridge: Polity Press; Malden, MA: Blackwell, 2001); Miroslav Hroch, *In the National Interest: Demands and Goals of European National Movements of the Nineteenth Century: A Comparative Perspective*, trans. Robin Cassling (Prague: Faculty of Arts, Charles University, 2000), esp. 8–17.
12 Miller, *The Ukrainian Question*, 20–2, 31–2, 35–7.
13 Bilenky, *Romantic Nationalism*, esp. 255–64.
14 Nina Magometkhanovna Pashaeva, *Ocherki istorii russkogo dvizheniia v Galichine XIX–XX vv.* (Moscow: Gosudarstvennaia Publichnaia Istoricheskaia Biblioteka, 2001). However, Pashaeva, too, fails to analyse properly the local Russian identity that she takes as a self-evident point of departure.
15 Anna Weronika Wendland, *Die Russophilen in Galizien: Ukrainische Konservative zwischen Österreich und Russland, 1848–1915* (Vienna: Verlag der Österreichischen Akademie der Wissenschaften, 2001), Studien zum Geschichte der Österreichisch-Ungarischen Monarchie, vol. 21.
16 Andreas Kappeler, "The Ukrainians of the Russian Empire, 1860–1914," in Andreas Kappeler, ed., in collaboration with Fikret Adanir and Alan O'Day, *The Formation of National Elites*, Comparative Studies on Governments and Non-Dominant Ethnic Groups in Europe, 1850–1940, vol. 6 (New York: New York University Press; Aldershot, Hants, England: Dartmouth, 1992), 105–22.

17 Jaroslaw Pelenski, "The Contest for the 'Kievan Inheritance,'" in *Ukraine and Russia in Their Historical Encounter*, ed. Peter J. Potichnyj, Marc Raeff, Jaroslaw Pelenski, and Gleb N. Žekulin (Edmonton: Canadian Institute of Ukrainian Studies Press, 1992), 3–15; Serhii Plokhy, *The Origins of the Slavic Nations: Premodern Identities in Russia, Ukraine, and Belarus* (Cambridge, UK; New York: Cambridge University Press, 2006), 259–66; Stephen Velychenko, *National History as Cultural Process: A Survey of the Interpretations of Ukraine's Past in Polish, Russian, and Ukrainian Historical Writing from the Earliest Times to 1914* (Edmonton: Canadian Institute of Ukrainian Studies Press, 1992), 80–101; Aleksei [Oleksii] Tolochko, *Kievskaia Rus' i Malorossiia v XIX veke* (Kyiv: Laurus, 2012). The term "Kyivan Rus'" (*Kievskaia Rus'*) is a nineteenth-century invention and was unknown to the medieval inhabitants of Rus'. See Oleksii Tolochko and Petro Tolochko, *Kyïvs'ka Rus'* (Kyiv: Vydavnychyi dim Al'ternatyvy, 1998), 5–6.

18 To be sure, Sloboda Ukraine was populated in the seventeenth century by refugees from Poland-Lithuania, and in that sense the past of even these easternmost Ukrainians was connected with that country.

19 For a description of the Hetmanate, see Zenon Kohut, *Russian Centralism and Ukrainian Autonomy: Imperial Absorption of the Hetmanate 1760s–1830s* (Cambridge, MA: Harvard University Press and Harvard Ukrainian Research Institute, 1988), 24–64.

20 Zenon Kohut, "The Development of a Little Russian Identity and Ukrainian Nationbuilding," *Harvard Ukrainian Studies* 10, nos. 3–4 (December 1986): 565–76; on the emergence of this identity from the sixteenth to the eighteenth centuries, see Plokhy, *Origins*, 177–85, 187–93, 199–202, 236–41, 303–53.

21 Zenon Kohut, *Russian Centralism and Ukrainian Autonomy: Imperial Absorption of the Hetmanate, 1760s–1830s* (Cambridge, MA: Harvard University Press, 1988), 237–42, 248–73; George S.N. Luckyj, *Between Gogol and Shevchenko* (Munich: Wilhelm Fink Verlag, 1971), 20–3; Serhii Plokhy, *The Cossack Myth: History and Nationhood in the Age of Empires* (Cambridge: Cambridge University Press, 2012), 152–69.

22 Dmitrii Bantysh-Kamenskii, *Istoriia Maloi Rossii, so vremen prisoedineniia onoi k Rossiiskomu Gosudarstvu pri tsarie Aleksee Mikhailovichie*, vols. 1–4 (Moscow: Izhdiveniem sochinitelia, 1822).

23 Nikolai Markevich (Mykola Markevych), *Istoriia Malorossii*, 2 vols. (Moscow: V tipografii Avgusta Semena pri Imperatorskoi Mediko-Khirurgicheskoi Akademii, 1842), 1: 4.

24 Georgii Konisskii (Hryhorii Konys'kyi), "Istoriia rusov ili Maloi Rossii," *Chteniia v Imperatorskom Obshchestve Istorii i Drevnostei pri Moskovskom Universitete*, nos. 1–4 (1846); *Materialy oteschestvennyia*, 1–261. The chronicle

was also published as a separate book: *Istoriia rusov ili Maloi Rossii* (Moscow: V universitetskoi tipografii, 1846). On the emergence of the *History of the Rus'* and an analysis of its contents, see Plokhy, *The Cossack Myth*; Velychenko, *National History*, 156–68.

25 Mikhail Maksimovich (Mykhailo Maksymovych), *Ukrainskie narodnye pesni* (Moscow: V universitetskoi tipografii, 1827); for Maksymovych in general, see Serhii Bilenkyi and Viktor Korotkyi, *Mykhailo Maksymovych ta osvitni praktyki na Pravoberezhnii Ukraïni v pershiï polovyni XIX stolittia* (Kyiv: Vydavnychyi tsentr "Kyïvs'kyi universytet," 1999); Bilenkiy, *Romantic Nationalism* 65–6, 269–79, 285–6, 301–2.

26 Ibid., xii–xx. Maksymovych tended to use both words, "Ukrainian" and "Little Russian," the first one in reference to the language and the second to the ethnic group.

27 Izmail Sreznevskii, *Zaporozhskaia starina*, vols. 1–3 (Kharkiv: Izhdiveniem Izmaila Sreznevskago, 1833–8); Taras Koznarsky, "Izmail Sreznevsky's Zaporozhian Antiquity as a Memory Project," *Eighteenth-Century Studies* 35, no. 1 (2001): 92–100; Johannes Remy, "Government Promotion of Ukrainian Studies: The Careers of Izmail Sreznevskii, Osyp Bodians'kyi and Amvrosyi Metlyns'kyi, 1825–1855," in Michael Branch, ed., *Defining Self: Essays on Emergent Identities in Russia, Seventeenth to Nineteenth Centuries* (Helsinki: Finnish Literature Society, 2009) 254–7, 263–5.

28 Sreznevskii, *Zaporozhskaia starina*, vol. 1, book 2: 53.

29 Ibid., vol. 1, book 2: 106 –9.

30 For Bodiansky in general, see N.P. Vasilenko, *O. M. Bodianskii i ego zaslugi dlia izucheniia Malorossii* (Kyiv: N.P. Korchak-Novitskii, 1904).

31 Osip Bodianskii (Osyp Bodians'kyi), review of *Národnié zpievanky cili pisne swetské slowakuw w uhrah*, by Ján Kollár, *Moskovskii nabliudatel'* 1 (1835), pt. 4.

32 Osip Bodianskii, *O narodnoi poezii slavianskikh plemen: Razsuzhdenie na stepen' magistra filosofskago fakul'teta Pervogo Otdeleniia* (Moscow: V universitetskoi tipografii, 1837).

33 Bodianskii, review of *Národnié zpiewanky*, 584–5; Bodianskii, *O narodnoi poezii*, 122; also quoted in Bilenkiy, *Romantic Nationalism*, 281.

34 Bodianskii, review of *Národnié zpiewanky*, 583; in his dissertation, Bodians'kyi's North Russian no longer sings about "crude love" but about "family life": *O narodnoi poezii*, 117–18.

35 Bodianskii, review of *Národnié zpiewanky*, 583.

36 Ibid., 590; cf. Bodianskii, *O narodnoi poezii*, 131–3, where the same idea is expressed in somewhat softer wording.

37 The poems that deal with Cossacks and which are relevant to this argument are "Tarasova nich," "Ivan Pidkova," "Haidamaky," "Rozryta mohyla," "Chyhryne, Chyhryne," "Son" (Komediia), "Nevol'nyk,"

"Velykyi l'okh," "I mertvym, i zhyvym, i nenarodzhenym zemliakam moïm v Ukraïni i ne v Ukraïni moie druzhnieie poslaniie," "Kholodnyi iar," "Zashcho my liubymo Bohdana?," "Za bairakom bairak," "Irzhavets'," "Zastupyla chorna khmara," "Iakbyto ty, Bohdane p'ianyi," and "Buvaly voiny i viis'kovii svary."

38 Luckyj, *Between Gogol and Shevchenko*, 133–4.

39 According to Bilenky, Shevchenko considered it an advantage that the nation lacked the upper classes. See Bilenky, *Romantic Nationalism*, 298–300.

40 Kholodnyi iar," "Velykyil'okh," "Buvaly voiny i viis'kovii svary."

41 George G. Grabowicz, *The Poet as Mythmaker: A Study of Symbolic Meaning in Taras Shevchenko* (Cambridge, MA: Harvard Ukrainian Research Institute, 1982), 133–7.

42 On the confusion and multitude of terms used for the country and its regions, see Bilenky, *Romantic Nationalism*, 71–4, 76, 78–80; Kohut, "Development," 562–5.

43 *Polnoe sobranie zakonov rossiiskoi imperii, Sobranie vtoroe*, vol. 10 (1835), bk. 2, no. 8654, p. 1161. To be precise, Catherine II replaced this official name with "Gubernia of Kharkov" (*Khar'kovskaia guberniia*), but Paul I reintroduced it.

44 "Ot redaktora," *Ukrainskii zhurnal*, no. 1 (1824): 8–9.

45 Mikhail Maksimovich, "Pis'mo o galitsko-russkoi slovesnosti," *Galichanin, literaturnyi sbornik izdavaemyi Iakovom Fedorovichem Golovatskim i Bogdanom Andreevichem Deditskim*, bk. 1, vyp. 1 (Lviv, 1862), 109.

46 Bilenky, *Romantic Nationalism*, 73.

47 *Kyrylo-Mefodiïvs'ke tovarystvo: U tr'okh tomakh*, ed. P. Sokhan' et al. (Kyiv: Naukova dumka, 1990), 1: 150–72. The rules of the society, the manuscript "God's Law," and the proclamation "Ukrainian Brothers" (Braty ukraintsy) are found here.

48 E.g., Opanas Markovych to Mykola Hulak, 15 February 1846. Ibid., 1: 102.

49 GARF), f. 109, 1-ia eksp., op. 1859g., ed. khr. 230, l. 9, 14. Ilarion Vasil'chikov to Evgraf Kovalevskii, Minister of Public Enlightenment, 30 January 1860.

2 From the Cyrillo-Methodian Society to the Death of Nicholas I, 1845–55

1 This is the group's name in its documents. The name "Brotherhood" does not occur in them.

2 Bilenky, *Romantic Nationalism*, 286–300; George S.N. Luckyj, *Young Ukraine: The Brotherhood of Saints Cyril and Methodius in Kiev, 1845–1847* (Ottawa: University of Ottawa Press, 1991), 29–56, 85–110; Petr Andreevich Zaionchkovskii, *Kirillo-Mefodievskoe obshchestvo (1846–1847)* (Moscow: Izdatel'stvo Moskovskogo

universiteta, 1959), 79–110; *Kyrylo-Mefodiïvs'ke tovarystvo: U tr'okh tomakh*, ed. P. Sokhan' et al. (Kyiv: Naukova Dumka, 1990); Orest Pelech, "The Cyril and Methodius Brotherhood Revisited," in *Synopsis:A Collection of Essays in Honour of Zenon E. Kohut*, ed. Serhii Plokhy and Frank E. Sysyn (Edmonton: CIUS Press, 2005), 335–44; Pelech, "Toward a Historical Sociology of the Ukrainian Ideologues in the Russian Empire of the 1830s and 1840s," Ph.D. dissertation, Princeton University, 1976; Johannes Remy, "Panslavism in the Ukrainian National Movement from the 1840s to the 1870s," *Journal of Ukrainian Studies* 30, no. 2 (2005): 27–50; Mykhailo Vozniak, *Kyrylo-Metodiïvs'ke bratstvo* (Lviv: Fond "Uchitesia, Braty Moi," 1921).

3 The full text of the two versions of *God's Law* is in *Kyrylo-Mefodiïvs'ke tovarystvo*, 1: 152–69, 250–8. On p. 620 of vol. 2, we read that a third copy, found in Panteleimon Kulish and Vasyl Bilozersky's possession, has been lost. Dmitrii Bibikov, the governor-general of Kyiv, was the first to notice the similarity to Mickiewicz's text. See *Kyrylo-Mefodiïvs'ke tovarystvo*, 1: 44 (Bibikov to Aleksei Orlov, 3 May 1847); for an English translation of *God's Law* and discussion of this document, see Luckyj, *Young Ukraine*, 88–99 and 47–51, respectively; Vozniak, *Kyrylo-Metodiïvs'ke bratstvo*, 97–136; Zaionchkovskii, *Kirillo-Mefodievskoe obshchestvo*, 7–12, 79–82, 90–2.

4 Adam Mickiewicz, *Dzieła* (Warsaw: Czytelnik, 1955), vols. 8–12.

5 *Kyrylo-Mefodiïvs'ketovarystvo*, 1: 150– 2 (the charter of the society); 1: 170–72 (the proclamation "Braty ukraïntsi" (Ukrainian brothers).

6 Ibid., 1: 162–3, 167–8, 256, 258; the "German" character of the Russian government or Russian upper classes was a widespread claim in Polish and Russian thought. See Bilenky, *Romantic Nationalism* 162, 203, 237, 248.

7 Ibid.,1: 256.

8 Ibid., 1: 163.

9 Ibid., 1: 256.

10 Ibid., 1: 167.

11 Ibid., 1: 257.

12 Ibid., 1: 258; for a slightly different wording, see 1: 167.

13 Ibid., 1: 169, 258. The Decembrists were a group of officers with constitutional monarchist and republican views who conspired to foment a revolution during the interregnum following the death of Alexander I in December 1825. After the Decembrists were crushed by the government, their leaders were executed.

14 Ibid., 1: 172.

15 Luckyj, *Young Ukraine*, 46. Some sources on the society support this view. See Vasyl Bilozersky's explanations of the charter of the society in *Kyrylo-Mefodiïvs'ke tovarystvo*, 1: 393.

16 Ibid., 1: 24–6 (Aleksei Petrov's denunciation of 3 March 1847).
17 Ibid., 1: 177–8 (an arranged encounter between Petrov and Hulak, 15 May 1847).
18 Ibid., 2: 501 (Andruz'kyi's interrogation, 14 April 1847).
19 Ibid., 2: 507 (Andruz'kyi's interrogation, 14 April 1847).
20 Ibid., 1: 267 (Kulish to Kostomarov, 27 June 1846); Bilenky, *Romantic Nationalism*, 298.
21 P. Kulish, *Povest' ob ukrainskom narode; napisal dlia detei starshago vozrasta P. Kulish* (St Petersburg: V tipografii Imperatorskoi Akademii Nauk, 1846). References are to the reprinted work: Panteleimon Kulish, *Povist' pro ukraïns'kyi narod* (Lviv: Litopys, 2006), according to the pagination of the 1846 original edition; for an analysis of the contents, see Serhiy Bilenky, *Romantic Nationalism*, 296–8; Ievhen Nakhlik, *Panteleimon Kulish: Osobystist', pys'mennyk, myslytel': Naukova monohrafiia u dvokh tomakh* (Kyiv: Ukrains'kyi pys'mennyk, 2007) 1: 62–4.
22 Kulish, *Povest'*, 85.
23 Ibid., 61–2.
24 P. Kulish, *Ukraïna: Od pochatku Vkraïny do bat'ka Khmel'nyts'koho* (Kyiv: V universitetskoi tipografii, 1843), 32–4. Kulish's book is reprinted in *Kyrylo-Mefodiïvs'ketovarytstvo*, 2: 531–69. The passage was originally published by Izmail Sreznevskii, who claimed that it was a folk song that had been preserved in verbal tradition; in fact, it was a forgery, possibly Sreznevskii's own work. See Izmail Sreznevskii, *Zaporozhskaia starina*, 2 vols. (Kharkiv: V Universitetskoi tipografii, 1833–8), pt. 1, vyp. 2: 106–9; on the forgery of epic songs, see Volodymyr Antonovych and Mykhailo Drahomanov, eds., *Istoricheskie pesni malorusskago naroda s ob"iasneniami Vl. Antonovicha i M. Dragomanova*, 2 vols. (Kyiv: Tipografiia M.P. Fritsa, 1874–5), 2: ii–iii.
25 P. Kulish, *Mikhailo Charnyshenko, ili Malorossiia vosemdesiat let nazad*, 3 vols. (Kyiv: V universitetskoi tipografii, 1843) 2: 38–9, 79–80, 88–9, 103–5, 107, 109.
26 *Kyrylo-Mefodiïvs'ke tovarystvo*, 3: 90 (Kulish to Markovych, 14 March 1846); P. Kulish, *Povne zibrannia tvoriv*, ed. Hryhorii Hrabovych [George Grabowicz] et al. (Kyiv: Krytyka, 2005–),1: 95–6 (Kulish to Shevchenko, 25 July 1846).
27 Kulish, *Povne zibrannia tvoriv*, 1: 29–31 (Kulish to Mikhail Iuzefovich, 23 November 1843). To be sure, after waging a lengthy campaign for a position in St Petersburg, he missed his Little Russia. Ibid., 1: 81 (Kulish to Mikhail Pogodin, 13 April 1846); Nakhlik, *Panteleimon Kulish*, 1: 39–42, 46–7.
28 Taras Shevchenko, *Selections: Poetry, Prose*, trans. John Weir (Kyiv: Dnipro Publishers, 1988), 99 (the complete text of the poem is on pp. 88–105).

For the Ukrainian original, see Taras Shevchenko, *Povne zibrannia tvoriv u dvanadtsiaty tomakh* (Kyiv: Naukova Dumka, 2001), 1: 273 and 265–78.

29 Shevchenko, *Povne zibrannia tvoriv*, 1: 311–12 (the poem "Slipyi," 1845). A negative interpretation of the Russian-Ukrainian political union is evident also in 1: 252, 254–5, 315–24, 327–8, 372, "Rozryta mohyla" (1843), "Chyhryne, Chyhryne" (1844), "Velykyi l'okh" (1845), "Za shcho my liubymo Bohdana?" (1845–6).

30 Shevchenko, *Povne zibrannia tvoriv*, 1: 343–7 ("Kavkaz" [1845]); Myroslav Shkandrij, *Russia and Ukraine: Literature and the Discourse of Empire from Napoleonic to Postcolonial Times* (Montreal: McGill-Queen's University Press, 2001), 134–41.

31 Shevchenko, *Povne zibrannia tvoriv*, 1: 277, 284, 321, 324, 372. In "Dream" (p. 277), the poet observes his countrymen who speak Russian and blame their own parents for not teaching them German, which would have smoothed their path to a career; p. 324: "But even there a Russian and a German will find a piece of bread" (*A moskal' ta nimets', i tam naidut' khlibets'*). The place is the cellar where the Russians are digging in order to find Bohdan Khmelnytsky's treasure. My purpose here is not to interpret the symbolic meanings of the cellar, but to point to the presentation of Russians and Germans together.

32 Ibid., 1: 319 ("Velykyi l'okh").

33 Ibid., 5: 207; for the published translation, see *Towards an Intellectual History of Ukraine: An Anthology of Ukrainian Thought from 1710 to 1995*, ed. Ralph Lindheim and George S.N. Luckyj (Toronto, Buffalo: University of Toronto Press in association with Shevchenko Scientific Society, Inc., 1996), 102. Because of some essential alterations that were made to the meaning of the original text in that translation, I retranslated the text. To give just one example, the published translation contains the following: "After all, we do not write in German," which does not give a hint of the original negative statement about Germans.

34 Shevchenko, *Povne zibrannia tvoriv*, 5: 208.

35 Ibid., 6: 14–15, 19, 21, 27, 31 (letters written between 1842 and 1844).

36 George G. Grabowicz, *The Poet as Mythmaker: A Study of Symbolic Meaning in Taras Ševčenko* (Cambridge, MA: Harvard Ukrainian Research Institute, 1982), 6–11.

37 Shevchenko, *Povne zibrannia tvoriv*, 6: 21 (letter to Hryhorii Stepanovych Tarnovsky, 25 January 1843); Pavlo Zaitsev, *Taras Shevchenko: A Life*, ed. and trans. George S.N. Luckyj (Toronto: University of Toronto Press, 1988), 41–2, 47, 56 (originally published in Ukrainian in 1955).

38 *Kyrylo-Mefodiïvs'ketovarystvo*, 2: 428.
39 Ibid., 2: 429.
40 Ibid., 2: 428–30; Bilenky, *Romantic Nationalism*, 290–1.
41 Andruzky reiterated this idea in his plays and poems. See *Kyrylo-Mefodiïvs'ke tovarystvo*, 2: 442–7, 468–72. To be sure, some of Andruzky's poetry contained a more realistic presentation of Ukrainian lords as allies of the Muscovites.The identification of nations with social classes was not unique to Ukrainians. A somewhat similar idea of an "aristocratic Poland" circulated among the Russian intelligentsia. See Bilenky, *Romantic Nationalism*, 211;Andrzej Walicki, *Russia, Poland, and Universal Regeneration: Studies on Russian and Polish Thought of the Romantic Epoch* (Notre Dame: University of Notre Dame Press, 1991), 54–69.
42 *Kyrylo-Mefodiïvs'ke tovarystvo*, 2: 434–5, 452–3, 457–8, 480 (Andruzky's poems, pp. 469–72, his story "The Last Zaporozhian" in poetry and prose).
43 Ibid., 2: 504.
44 Ibid., 2: 468–72.
45 Ibid., 2: 455–6; the poem beginning with the words *Liashchenku, liashche*. The proposed armed struggle is described in old Cossack terms as one fought with swords on horseback. That it is a contemporary call to arms is not the only possible interpretation.
46 Ibid., 2: 570; Andruzky's plan for a constitution. Interestingly enough, his prospective Ukraine included Galicia as well as Cracow, the Black Sea coastal region, and the Crimea. Bilenky, *Romantic Nationalism* 69–70.
47 Ibid., 2: 580; Governor of Olonets Nikolai Evarestovich Pisarev to the chief of gendarmes, Aleksei Orlov, 28 March 1850 (quotations from Andruzky's diary in the letter).
48 Ibid., 1: 100 (Bilozersky to Hulak in September–October 1846); *Moskvitianin*, nos. 1–2, 4 (1846). For a general comparison between Pogodin's and the Cyrillo-Methodians' pan-Slavism, see Džong Khi-Sok, "M. P. Pogodin i Kirillo-Mefodievskoe obshchestvo 30–50-kh. gg. XIX v. o slavianskom edinstve (sravnitel'no- istoricheskii analiz)," *Voprosy istorii*, no. 7 (1996): 137–49.
49 *Kyrylo-Mefodiïvs'ke tovarystvo*, 1: 271.
50 Džong Khi-Sok, "M. P. Pogodin," 144.
51 *Kyrylo-Mefodiïvs'ke tovarystvo*, 3: 13–19.
52 Ibid., 1: 393. In Bilozersky's explications of the society's charter there is a statement that "ordinary people should not be given any reason to think that this is about speaking and acting against the present order (*govoritsia i*

deistvuetsia v protivnom nastoiashchemu poriadku)." Here, "ordinary people" are clearly the people outside the society. I disagree with Bilenky (*Romantic Nationalism*, 248–9), who claims that the Ukrainian movement was not political, until the imperial authorities politicized it in 1846–7.

53 Shevchenko, *Povne zibrannia tvoriv*, 6: 11–39 (letters, 1839–47).

54 *Kyrylo-Mefodiïvs'ke tovarystvo*, 1: 96 (Kulish to Hulak, 4 March 1846).

55 Kulish, *Povne zibrannia tvoriv*, 1: 75 (Kulish to Sreznevskii, 7 March 1846).

56 David Saunders, *The Ukrainian Impact on Russian Culture, 1750–1850* (Edmonton: Canadian Institute of Ukrainian Studies, 1985), 250–1.

57 "Istoriia rusov ili Maloi Rossii," *Chteniia v Imperatorskom Obshchestve Istorii i Drevnostei pri Moskovskom Universitete*, nos. 1–4 (1846); *Materialy oteschestvennya*, 1–261. Henceforward, the journal will be referred to as *Chteniia*; the chronicle was also published as a separate book, *Istoriia rusov ili Maloi Rossii* (Moscow: V universitetskoi tipografii, 1846). For the emergence of the *History of the Rus'* and its general contents, see chap. 1 and the literature referred to there.

58 Plokhy, *The Cossack Myth*, 198; I disagree with Faith Hillis (*Children of Rus'*, 34), who does not perceive this distancing of Little Russians from Great Russians in *History of the Rus'*, but rather emphasizes how the author "presented Little Russia as an integral part of the Orthodox, East Slavic world."

59 "Istoriia rusov," *Chteniia*, no. 4 (1846), *Materialy otechestvenniia*, 235 (purportedly in a paraphrase of a letter written by Varlaam Vanatovych, metropolitan of Kyiv).

60 Ibid., no. 3 (1846), *Materialy otechestvenniia*, 98.

61 Here, the author may have thought about the murder of Paul I and accession of Alexander I on the throne in 1801.

62 "Istoriia rusov," *Chteniia*, no. 4 (1846), *Materialy otechestvenniia*, 135.

63 Ibid., *Materialy otechestvenniia*, 230. Polubotok also talks about the mistreatment of political prisoners as a Muscovite habit.

64 Nikolai Ivanovich Kostomarov, *Istoricheskie proizvedeniia: Avtobiografiia* (Kyiv: Izdatel'stvo pri Kievskom gosudarstvennom universitete, 1989), 454; *Kyrylo-Mefodiïvs'ke tovarystvo*, 2: 503, 507 (Andruzky's interrogation, 14 April 1847); George Luckyj, *Panteleimon Kulish: A Sketch of His Life and Times* (Boulder, CO: East European Monographs, 1983), 12; Zaitsev, *Taras Shevchenko*, 52; Iu.A. Pinchuk, *Mykola Ivanovych Kostomarov, 1817–1885* (Kyiv: Naukova Dumka, 1992), 69; Plokhy, *The Cossack Myth*, 47–51; Thomas M. Prymak, *Mykola Kostomarov: A Biography* (Toronto, Buffalo: University of Toronto Press, 1996), 12–13.

65 "Letopis' samovidtsa o voinakh Bogdana Khmel'nitskago i o mezhdousobiiakh, byvshikh v Maloi Rossii po ego smerti; Dovedena

prodolzhateliami do 1734 goda," *Chteniia*, nos. 1–2 (1846–7), *Materialy otechestvennyia*, 1–152 (the chronicle has its own pagination). See a more recent edition, *Litopys Samovydtsia*, ed. Ia. I. Dzyra (Kyiv: Naukova Dumka, 1971); see also Frank E. Sysyn, "The Cossack Chronicles and the Development of Modern Ukrainian Culture and National Identity," *Harvard Ukrainian Studies* 14, nos. 3–4 (1990): 595–607; Velychenko, *National History*, 186–7.

66 *Chteniia*, nos. 1–2 (1846–7), *Materialy otechestvennyia*, i (Kulish's foreword).

67 According to the most well-substantiated hypothesis, Roman Rakushka wrote at least a substantial part of the *Samovydets' Chronicle*. See Ia. I. Dzyra, introduction to *Litopys Samovydtsia*, 14–15; Serhii Plokhy, *The Origins of Slavic Nations: Pre-Modern Identities in Russia, Ukraine, and Belarus* (Cambridge, UK, New York: Cambridge University Press, 2006), 324–6; Sysyn, "Cossack Chronicles," 595.

68 *Chteniia*, no. 1 (1846–7): 48–9, 51, 54, 59, 63–5; no. 2 (1846–7): 78, and 93–6, which were written by another author.

69 Ibid., no.1 (1846–7): 69, 71–2; no. 2 (1846–7).

70 Ibid., no. 2 (1846–7): 138; before the *Samovydets' Chronicle* was published, Bodiansky learned of Kulish's scepticism concerning the reliability of the *History of the Rus'*. See Nakhlik, *Panteleimon Kulish*, 1: 30–1.

71 Issues no. 5 (28 December 1846); 6 (25 January 1847); 8 (29 March 1847); 9 (26 April 1847). Perhaps the most important of the other Ukrainian publications was Aleksandr Rigel'man, "Letopisnoe povestvovanie o Maloi Rossii i eia narode i kozakakh voobshche, otkol' i iz kakogo naroda onye proizkhozhdenie svoe imeiut, i po kakim sluchaiam oni nyne pri svoikh mestakh obitaiut, kak to: cherkasskie ili malorossiiskie i zaporozhskie, a ot nikh uzhe donskie, a ot nikh iaitskie, chto nyne ural'skie, grebenskie, sibirskie, volgskie, terskie, nekrasovskie, i proch. kozaki, kak ravno i slobodskie polki," *Chteniia*, nos. 5–9 (1846–7). Rigel'man's Little Russian chronicle (1785–6) was written in an ultra-loyalist tone, but it expressed a distinct Little Russian identity.

72 *Kyrylo-Mefodiïvs'ketovarystvo*, 2: 30, 35– 37, 39, 45 (Kulish's notes and his statement to the Third Section of 30 April 1847 at the latest).

73 Ibid., 3:20 (Posiada to Borovykovsky, November 1846). It is hardly surprising that under interrogation Posiada denied knowing anything about Bodiansky's participation, and claimed that he had written about him based on a rumour. See *Kyrylo-Mefodiïvs'ke tovarystvo*, 3: 32 (Posiada's testimony, 30 April 1847).

74 Ibid., 1: 268 (Kulish to Kostomarov, 27 June 1846); 3: 206 (P. Chuikevych to Kostomarov, 18 April 1847); Nakhlik, *Panteleimon Kulish*, 1: 50–1, 55.

75 Filaret, episkop Rizhskii, "Kirill i Mefodii, slavianskie prosvetiteli (Chitano 30-go noiabria, 1846 g).," *Chteniia* 4 (1846–7), zasedanie 30-go noiabria,

1846 goda: 1–28; Filaret's interest in Cyril and Methodius probably derived from his interest in using vernacular in missionary work with national minorities. He spoke both Latvian and Estonian. See Darius Staliunas, *Making Russians: Meaning and Practice of Russification in Lithuania and Belarus after 1863* (Amsterdam: Rodopi, 2007), 135–6.

76 *Kyrylo-Mefodiïvs'ke tovarystvo*, 1: 24–6 (Petrov's denunciation, 3 March 1847).

77 Ibid., 1: 33–8 (Orlov to Nicholas I, 28 March 1847); 1: 62–70 (Orlov to Nicholas I, 26 May 1847; 1: 279–87 (Kostomarov's interrogation, 15 April 1847); 1: 295–301 (Kostomarov's interrogation, 7 May 1847); 2: 500–9 (Andruzky's interrogation, 14 April 1847, and his additional testimony, 17 May 1847); 3: 28–33 (Posiada's interrogation, 30 April 1847); 3: 34 (Posiada's additional testimony, 17 May 1847); Zaionchkovskii, *Kirillo-Mefodievskoe obshchestvo*, 116–18, 121–31; Luckyj, *Young Ukraine*, 59–62, 66–9. Of these two, Zaionchkovskii's analysis of the investigation and the sentences is more useful because he had access to all the relevant documents; Pelech (*Toward a Historical*, 206–13, 226) fails to take seriously Zaionchkovskii's thesis about the deliberate softening of the charges in the Third Section, which leads him to belittle the political activities of the society. Pelech is also mistaken in his claim that the activities of the society ceased after Hulak moved to St Petersburg. Andruzky's testimonies indicate that the meetings continued even after that.

78 Džong Khi-Sok, "M. P. Pogodin," 145–6, provides information on Russian subsidies to foreign Slavic scholars. In February 1840 Nicholas I accepted Sergei Uvarov's proposal to distribute 2000 silver rubles to them. Jan Kollar, a Slovak scholar and pan-Slavist, was one of those who received money from those funds.

79 Zaionchkovskii, *Kirillo-Mefodievskoe obshchestvo*, 128–30, 138. The same tactic of diminishing the guilt of members of an uncovered conspiracy was adopted at least in one Polish case in 1840. See Johannes Remy, *Higher Education and National Identity: Polish Student Activism in Russia 1832–1863*, Bibliotheca Historica, vol. 57 (Helsinki: Suomalaisen Kirjallisuuden Seura, 2000), 144–8.

80 *Kyrylo-Mefodiïvs'ke tovarystvo*, 3: 308; also quoted in Zaionchkovskii, *Kirillo-mefodievskoe obshchestvo*, 129–30, and, in a slightly different translation, in Miller, *The Ukrainian Question*, 53 (a draft memorandum prepared for Orlov in the Third Section for submission to Nicholas I in May 1847. It was never submitted because Orlov wanted a shorter version).

81 *Kyrylo-Mefodiïvs'ke tovarystvo*, 3: 307; also quoted in Zaionchkovskii, *Kirillo-Mefodievskoe obshchestvo*, 129–30.

82 This was noted by Olga Andriewsky, "The Russian–Ukrainian Discourse and the Failure of the 'Little Russian Solution,' 1782–1917," in *Culture, Nation, and Identity: The Ukrainian–Russian Encounter (1600–1945)*, ed. Andreas Kappeler, Zenon E. Kohut, Frank E. Sysyn, and Mark von Hagen (Edmonton, Toronto: CIUS Press, 2003), 210; cf. David Saunders, "Russia's Nationality Policy: The Case of Ukraine (1847–1941)," *Journal of Ukrainian Studies* 29, nos. 1–2 (2004): 405–6. Saunders dates the beginning of imperial suppression of Ukrainian activities to 1847.

83 *Kyrylo-Mefodiïvs'ke tovarystvo*, 1: 68–70 (Orlov to Nicholas I, 26 May 1847; the emperor's confirmation, 28 May); 1: 292 (Polikarp Vasylevych Tykhonovych to Kostomarov, no later than March 1847); 3: 116–17 (Orlov's report to Nicholas I, 30 May 1847); Alexei Miller, *The Ukrainian Question: The Russian Empire and Nationalism in the Nineteenth Century* (Budapest, New York: Central European University Press, 2003), 53–4.

84 *Ulozhenie o nakazaniiakh ugolovnykh i ispravitel'nykh* (St Petersburg: V tipografii Vtorago Otdeleniia Sobstvennoi Ego Imperatorskago Velichestva Kantseliarii, 1845), paragraphs 263–5.

85 *Kyrylo-Mefodiïvs'ke tovarystvo*, 1: 69 (Orlov to Nicholas I, 26 May 1847).

86 Ibid., 1: 67–8 (Orlov to Nicholas I, 26 May 26 1847). Orlov pointed to Shevchenko's strong physique, which made him suitable for military service, an evaluation that he would hardly have made of anyone who was born a nobleman.

87 Ibid., 2: 343–4 (Orlov's report to Nicholas I, 9 December 1849).

88 Ibid., 2: 309 (full text of the memorandum, dated 17 April 1847, 308–10).

89 Ibid.

90 Bilenky (*Romantic Nationalism*, 299) interprets Shevchenko's statement in the same way, and it may indeed have been Shevchenko's intention to give a general statement about Russia. However, what is a valid approach for a historian is inaccurate for an investigator in a criminal process where one should remain within the limits of uncontested facts.

91 In a case involving a single, unorganized, subversive discussion in July 1847. See Remy, *Higher Education*, 199.

92 *Kyrylo-mefodiïvs'ke tovarystvo*, 2: 97–8 (Orlov's report to Nicholas I, with the latter's decision handed down on 22 August 1847).

93 Ibid., 3: 146–7 (Orlov's report to Nicholas I, 18 April 1850).

94 Ibid., 2: 168 (the Third Section's information about Kulish's release, after 14 November 1850); 2: 409–10 (Orlov to Senator Fedor Durasov, 8 December 1850); 3: 48 (the Third Section's information on Posiada's release).

95 Ibid. 1: 461–2 (Orlov's report to Nicholas I, with the latter's decision handed down on 11 July 1853).

96 Ibid., 1: 233–4 (Orlov's report to Nicholas I, with the latter's decision handed down on 22 February 1855).
97 Ibid., 2: 584–6 (Orlov's report to Nicholas I, with the latter's decision handed down on 5 April 1850). Apart from his own texts described above, the confiscated texts included Kulish's *Ukraina*; ibid., 2: 531–76.
98 Ibid., 2: 597–8 (the Third Section's information on Andruzky, 10 September 1856).
99 Zaitsev, *Taras Shevchenko*, 131, 134. It seems that Shevchenko's appointment was based on Uvarov's recommendation.
100 Luckyj, *Panteleimon Kulish*, 39–42.
101 Nakhlik, *Panteleimon Kulish*, 1: 18–20, 22, 39–40, 48–50.
102 *Kyrylo-Mefodiïvs'ke tovarystvo*, 1: 68–70 (Orlov to Nicholas I, 26 May 1847); 1: 301–3 (Bibikov to Orlov, 13 May 1847); 2: 310–24 (the Third Section's summaries of Shevchenko's published and unpublished poems, 17 April 1847); 3: 293 (memorandum to Orlov written in the Third Section, 29 March 1847 at the latest).
103 Ibid., 1: 68 (Orlov's report to the emperor, 26 May 1847).
104 Ibid., 1: 301–3 (Bibikov to Orlov, 13 May 1847). These poems were published in Nikolai Kostomarov, *Ukrainskie ballady* (Kharkiv: V unyversitetskii drukarni, 1838), 3–4, 14–20, 31–2.
105 Ibid., 1: 302 (Bibikov to Orlov, 13 May 1847).
106 Kostomarov, *Ukrainskie ballady*, 20.
107 Eremiia Halka [Mykola Kostomarov], *Vitka* (Kharkiv: V unyversytetskii drukarni, 1840), 5–11.
108 *Kyrylo-Mefodiïvs'ke tovarystvo*, 1: 70 (the final sentence, confirmed by Nicholas I on 28 May 1847).
109 Cynthia Whittaker, *The Origins of Modern Russian Education: An Intellectual Biography of Count Sergei Uvarov, 1786–1855* (DeKalb: Northern Illinois University Press, 1984), 216–17.
110 Rossiiskii gosudarstvennyi istoricheskii arkhiv (Russian State Historical Archive, hereafter RGIA), f. 735, op. 10, delo 193, l. 22 (Uvarov's memorandum to Nicholas I, 8 May 1847). The entire memorandum is on l. 12–33; Whittaker, *Origins*, 217–19; for a slightly different interpretation, see T.N. Zhukovskaia, "S. S. Uvarov i kirillo-mefodievskoe obshchestvo ili krizis 'ofitsial'noi narodnosti,'" in R.Iv. Ganelin, ed., *Otechestvennaia istoriia i istoricheskaia mysl' v Rossii* (St Petersburg: Nestor, 2006), 196–207; Tatyana Zhukovskaia, "Count Sergei Uvarov and the Cyril and Methodius Society: The Crises of 'Official Nationality,' 1830–1850, in *Defining Self: Essays on Emergent Identities in Russia, Seventeenth to Nineteenth Centuries*, comp. and ed. Michael Branch (Helsinki: Finnish

Literature Society, 2009), 271–84. My view of Uvarov's position regarding this document differs from Zhukovskaia's, who finds that Uvarov distanced himself from all pan-Slavism.

111 RGIA, f. 735, op. 10, delo 193, l. 29.

112 Ibid., l. 30; Zhukovskaia, "Count Sergei Uvarov" (the same passage in a slightly different translation is quoted on p. 280); Pelech, *Toward a Historical*, 237, quotes the same passage in a slightly different translation.

113 *Sbornik postanovlenii i rasporiazhenii po tsenzure* (St Petersburg: V tipografii morskago ministerstva, 1862), 254.

114 *Kyrylo-Mefodiïvs'ke tovarystvo*, 3: 310–13.

115 Ibid., 3: 314

116 Ibid., 3: 315.

117 The original circular was not available to me. Its contents are presented in the context of a later case for the consideration of the Main Administration of Censorship in RGIA, f. 772, op. 1, delo 4413, l. 9–10 (an excerpt from the records of this institution, 17 May 1858).

118 "Perepiska i drugiia bumagi shvedskogo korolia Karla XII, pol'skogo Stanislava Leshchinskogo, tatarskago khana, turetskago sultana, general'nago pisaria F. Orlika i Kievskago voevody, Iosifa Pototskago, na latinskom i pol'skom iazykakh," *Chteniia*, no. 1 (31 May 1847), *Materialy otechestvennyia*, iii–iv, 1–68.

119 Cited in Lindheim and Luckyj, *Towards an Intellectual History*, 54–5 (an abridged translation of the document, pp. 53–64); "Perepiska i drugiia bumagi," cited in *Materialy otechestvennyia*, 2–3 (the complete document, in Latin, pp. 1–17). The complete text in modern Ukrainian translation is published in *Istoriia ukraïns'koï konstytutsiï*, comp. A. Sliusarenko and M. Tomenko (Kyiv: Pravo, 1997), 31–46.

120 "Perepiska i drugiia bumagi," 56.

121 "Protokol zasedaniia obshchestva 1847 goda, fevralia 29-go dnia," *Chteniia*, no. 8 (29 March 1847), ii.

122 *Kyrylo-Mefodiïvs'ke tovarystvo*, 3: 313.

123 Kostomarov, *Istoricheskie proizvedeniia. Avtobiografiia*, 438–51, 453–61.

124 Nikolai Barsukov, *Zhizn' i trudy M.P. Pogodina*, vols. 1–22 (Moscow: Tipografiia M.M. Stasiulevicha 1888–1910), 9:239.

125 Ibid., 9: 240–1(excerpts from Stroganov's letter to Uvarov, 11 July 1847). On this incident, see also Pelech, *Toward a Historical*, 241–3.

126 Cf. Miller, *Ukrainian Question*, 54.

127 RGIA, f. 735, op. 10, delo 182, l. 132b (Stroganov to Uvarov, July 8 1847).

128 Ibid., l. 140–1 (Orlov to Uvarov, 28 July 1847); P.I. Bartenev, "Ob ukraino-slavianskom obshchestve (Iz bumag D.P. Golokhvastova)," *Russkii Arkhiv*

1892, no. 7, 355–6 (Aleksei Orlov to Stroganov, 28 July 1847); *Kyrylo-Mefodiïvs'ke tovarystvo*, 3: 315 (the Third Section's information, May 1847). The censor of the *Ukrainian Ballads*, Ivan Mikhailovich Snegirev, was the only one thus pardoned: all the other censors who had permitted the works of the Cyrillo-Methodians mentioned above were officially reprimanded.

129 N.P. Vasilenko, *O.M. Bodianskii i ego zaslugi dlia izucheniia Malorossii* (Kyiv: N.P. Korchak-Novitskii, 1904), 161–3; Nikolai Barsukov, "Russkie paleologi sorokovykh godov," *Drevniaia i novaia Rossiia* 16, 1880: 544–5 (a quotation from Kubarev's letter to Ivan Petrovich Sakharov, 17 January 1849, in the former source; the letter in full in the latter).

130 Barsukov, *Zhizhn' i trudy*, 10:155.

131 Ibid., 9: 239–44, 10: 154–73, 552–7. Uvarov submitted Bodiansky's re-nomination to the emperor, who accepted it after Uvarov had left his ministry; Vasilenko, *O.M. Bodianskii*, 158–69. The journal's new title in Russian was *Vremennik Imperatorskago Obshchestva Istorii i Drevnostei pri Moskovskom universitete*.

132 Maksim Mikhailovich Shevchenko, *Konets odnogo velichiia:Vlast', obrazovanie i pechatnoe slovo v Imperatorskoi Rossii na poroge Osvoboditel'nykh reform* (Moscow: Tri kvadrata, 2003), 122–34; Whittaker, *Origins*, 220–7.

133 Shevchenko, *Konets odnogo velichiia*, 140–1; Whittaker, *Origins*, 235–7.

134 V.Iu. Omel'chuk, ed., et al., *Ukraïnomovna knyha, 1798–1916*, 4 vols. (Kyiv: Arbys, 1996), 1: 7–18. See also Vasilii Grechulevich, *Beseda po osviashchenii Podol'skoi eparkhii, Bratslavskogo uezda, sela Annopolia vozobnovlennoi i razshirennoi dvumia bokovymi pridelami Chudo-Mikhailovskoi tserkvi, proiznesennaia na malorossiiskom iazyke, toiazh tserkvi protoiereem Vasiliem Grechulevichem, 1852 goda, dekabria 6 dnia* (St Petersburg: Tipografiia K.Vingebera 1853). The book is not mentioned in *Ukraïnomovna knyha*, but it is listed in the catalogue of the National Library of Russia in St Petersburg.

135 Vasilii Grechulevich, *Propovedy, na Malorossiiskom iazyke, Protoiereja i Kavalera Vasiliia Grechulevicha* (St Petersburg: Tipografiia K. Kraiia, 1849); *Besedy katekhizicheskiia, na deviat' blazhenstv Evangel'skikh i desiat' zapovedei Bozhiikh, govorennyia, na Malorossiiskom iazyke, Protoiereem i kavalerom Vasiliem Grechulevichem* (St Petersburg: Tipografiia vtorogo otdeleniia sobstvennago Ego Imperatorskago Velichestva Kantseliarii, 1852); *Beseda po osviashchenii*. Michael Moser, "Clerics and Laymen in the History of the Modern Standard Ukrainian Language," *Journal of Ukrainian Studies* 37 (2012): 47–50.

136 On the inherent worth, or *dignitas*, of a language deemed worthy of communicating religious truths, see Ricarda Vulpius, *Nationalisierung der*

Religion:Russifizierungspolitik und ukrainische Nationsbildung 1860–1920, Forschungen zur osteuropäischen Geschichte, vol. 64 (Wiesbaden: Harrassowitz Verlag, 2005), 119–35.

137 Ibid., 141–2.

138 Grechulevich, *Propovedy, na Malorossiiskom iazyke*, ii–iii.

139 Ibid., iii.

140 Grechulevich, *Besedy katekhizicheskiia*, ii.

141 Mikhail Maksimovich, *Sbornik ukrainskikh piesen* (Kyiv: V tipografii Feofila Gliksberga, 1849).

142 Amvrosii Metlinskii, *Narodnyia iuzhnorusskiia piesni* (Kyiv: Izdanie Amvrosiia Metlinskago, 1854).

143 Amvrosii Metlinskii, ed., *Iuzhnyi russkii zbornyk* (Khark'kiv: V universitetskoi tipografii, 1848).

144 Levko Borovykovs'kyi, *Baiky i prybaiutky* (Kyiv: V universitetskoi tipografii, 1852).

145 *Kyrylo-Mefodiïvs'ke tovarystvo*, 1: 289 (Metlynsky to Kostomarov, 28 March 1847); I have quoted the same comment also in Remy, "Government Promotion," 266.

146 Amvrosyi Mohyla [Metlynsky's pseudonym], *Dumky i pesny ta shche de-shcho* (Kharkiv: V universitetskoi tipografii, 1839) 3, 15–17, 20–34.

147 Metlinskii, *Iuzhnyi russkii sbornik*, 10. Metlynsky used the term "South Russian" as the equivalent of the present-day "Ukrainian," whereas the terms "Little Russian" and "Ukrainian," as he used them, excluded Galician.

148 For discussion of this genre, see Jeffrey Brooks, *When Russia Learned to Read: Literacy and Popular Culture, 1861–1917* (Princeton, NJ: Princeton University Press, 1985), 269–76, 279–94.

149 Maksimovich, *Sbornik ukrainskikh piesen*, 3, 5, 13.The poem "O Palee i Mazepe" appears on pp. 88–91. This interesting *duma* blames Mazepa for the destruction of Baturyn, even though it was the imperial army that destroyed the city.

150 Mikhail Maksimovich, *Nachatki ruskoi filologii;Kniga pervaia: Ob otnoshenii ruskoi rechi k zapadnoslavianskoi* (Kyiv: V tipografii Feofila Gliksberga, 1848); Bilenky, *Romantic Nationalism*, 275–7.

151 Cf. Miller, *The Ukrainian Question*, 36–7. Miller emphasizes Maksymovych's linguistic classification of the East Slavs as a division into four parts.

152 Maksimovich, *Nachatki ruskoi filologii*, 43.

153 Ibid., 47.

154 Ibid., 52–4.

155 Ibid., 105–6, 109–11.
156 Borovykovs'kyi, *Baiky*, 97–8. In the poem "Teacher" (*Uchitel'*) a Russian hires a Frenchman as a tutor for his son, but he turns out to be an uneducated blacksmith. The main message is that parents have only themselves to blame if they fail to educate their sons properly.
157 Ibid., vi.
158 Izmail Sreznevskii, review of "Slowanskij Nàrodopis. Zestavil P.J. Šafarik," *Zhurnal Ministerstva Narodnago prosveshcheniia* 38 (1843): VI.21–2.
159 Borovykovs'kyi, *Baiky*, vi (in Metlynsky's foreword: "*iazyk vysshago, obrazovanneishago sosloviia*").
160 Mykhailo Drahomanov, *Literaturno-publitsystychni pratsi*, 2 vols. (Kyiv: Naukova Dumka, 1970), 1: 106–13; *Kiev i ego predmest'ia: Shuliavka, Solomenka s Protasovym Iarom, Baikova Gora i Demievka s Sapernoiu Slobodkoiu po perepisi 2 marta 1874, proizvedennoi i razrabotannoi Iugo-Zapadnym Otdelom Imperatorskago Russkago Geograficheskago Obschestva* (Kyiv: Po rasporiazheniiu g. Kievskago, Podol'skago i Volynskago General-Gubernatora, v tipografii Imperatorskago Universiteta Sv. Vladimira, 1875), 20–1. In this publication of the results of a one-day census in Kyiv, the Russian language was divided into four mutually exclusive alternatives, one being called language and the three others dialects: "General Russian language" (*Obshcherusskii iazyk*), "Great Russian dialect," "Little Russian dialect," and "Belorussian dialect." This question will be discussed in chapter 7.
161 Borovykovs'kyi, *Baiky*, vii–viii (Metlynsky's foreword).
162 *Istoricheskie pesni malorusskago naroda*, 1: xviii–xxiv; 2: iii.
163 *Narodnyia iuzhnorusskiia piesni*, v.
164 Ibid.
165 Ibid., ix.
166 Metlinskii, *Narodnyia iuzhnorusskiia piesni*, xvii. Metlynsky mentioned the Turks and Tatars as enemies, too.
167 Ibid., 428.
168 For general information on the commission, see Oleh Ivanovich Zhurba, *Kyïvs'ka arkheohrafichna komisiia 1843–1921:Narys istoriï i diial'nosti* (Kyiv: Naukova Dumka, 1993), 33–74.
169 Grigorii Grabianka [Hryhorii Hrabianka], *Deistviia prezel'noi i ot nachala poliakov krvavshoi nebyvaloi brani Bogdana Khmel'nitskogo, getmana Zaporozhskogo, s poliaki, za Naiiasneishikh Korolei Pol'skikh Vladislava, potom i Kazimira, v roku 1648,otpravovatisia nachatoi i za let desiat' po smerti Khmel'nitskogo neokonchennoi, z roznikh letopistsov i iz diariusha, na toi voine pisannoe, v grade Gadiachu, sobrannaia i samobytnykh starozhilov svidetel'stvi*

utverzhdennaia. Roku 1710 (Kyiv: Vremennaia Kommissiia dlia razbora drevnikh aktov, 1854); Samoil Velichko [Samiilo Velychko], *Letopis' sobytii v Iugo-Zapadnoi Rossii v XVII-m veke*, 4 volumes. (Kyiv: Vremennaia Komissiia dlia Razbora Drevnykh Aktov, 1848–64). The three first volumes were published in 1848–55. For a brief analysis of both works, see Sysyn, "Cossack Chronicles," 593–607 and Velychenko, *National History*, 149–52. Although Hrabianka's chronicle was published in 1793, the commission was not aware of this first edition.

170 Volodymyr Antonovych, *Tvory*, vol. 1 (Kyiv: Vseukrains'ka akademiia nauk, 1932), 60; Sysyn, "Cossack Chronicles," 605–6.

171 Pinchuk, *Mykola Ivanovych Kostomarov*, 66.

172 Velichko, *Letopis' sobytii*, 1: 172–3.

173 Zhurba, *Kyïvs'ka arkheohrafichna komisiia*, 70.

174 Grabianka, *Deistviia*, xxii, xxv, xxvii–xxviii (Ivan Samchevsky's foreword).

175 Ibid., vii–x, xiv–xv.

176 Ibid., 156–69, 186, 214–22, 235, 242, 257. However, Hrabianka described the Treaty of Hadiach between Vyhovsky and the representatives of Poland-Lithuania in a rather neutral tone.

177 Ibid., 179–82, 190–4; Hryhorij Hrabianka, *Hryhorij Hrabianka's The Great War of Bohdan Xmel'nyc'kyj*, with an introduction by Yuri Lutsenko, Harvard Library of Early Ukrainian Literature, vol. 9 (Cambridge, MA: Distributed by Harvard University Press for the Ukrainian Research Institute of Harvard University, 1990), 395–6, 554–6. The latter publication contains passages that were censored in the 1854 edition.

178 *Hryhorij Hrabianka's The Great War*, 395–6, 554–6; Miller, *The Ukrainian Question*, 54–5; "Tsenzura v tsarstvovanie imperatora Nikolaia I-go," *Russkaia starina* 35 (February 1904): 441–2; Stephen Velychenko, "Tsarist Censorship and Ukrainian Historiography, 1828–1906,"*Canadian-American Slavic Studies* 23, no. 4 (Winter 1989): 399.

179 Hroch, *In the National Interest*, 111–12.

180 A. Lazarevskii, "Malorossiiskiia istoricheskiia poslovitsy i pogovorki," *Chernigovskiia gubernskiia vedomosti*, no. 38, 1853 (*chast' neofitsial'naia*, 374).

181 *Chernigovskiia gubernskiia vedomosti*, no. 38, 1853 (*chast' neofitsial'naia*, 378); *Kyrylo-Mefodiïvs'ke tovarystvo*, 3: 179–81 (Tulub's interrogation on 30 March 1847, and the Third Section's finding of his non-involvement in the case, 13 April 1847, or after that date). Tulub admitted having discussed Little Russian history, serfdom, landowner oppression of peasants, Shevchenko's poetry, about returning to the use of Little Russian, the Little Russian national character, religion, philosophy, and the interrelationship between the latter two. The discussions took place at

Hulak's home and sometimes in Kulish's place, with the participation of Kostomarov, Markovych, Posiada, and Navrotsky.

182 "Tsenzura v tsarstvovanie," 441–2.

183 RGIA, f. 772, op. 1, delo 6069, l. 84 (Shirinskii-Shikhmatov's circular, 29 January 1854). The circular was included in a collection of relevant regulations compiled by the Main Administration of Censorship in 1862; "Tsenzura v tsarstvovanie," 441–2.

184 *Kyrylo-Mefodiïvs'ke tovarystvo*, 2: 109–10 (Panteleimon Kulish to Leontii Dubelt, 1 November 1847).

185 Ibid., 2: 111.

186 Ibid., 2: 31 (Kulish's undated note); 2: 137 (Dubelt to Kulish, 5 January 1849; this letter cites Orlov's words); 2: 501 (Andruzky's interrogation on 14 April 1847); Panteleimon Kulish, *Tvory v dvokh tomakh* (Kyiv: Naukova Dumka, 1998), 1: 251–4 (Kulish's autobiography); Luckyj, *Panteleimon Kulish*, 36–8, 45–6. Ievhen Nakhlik, the author of the most recent, excellent, and source-based biography of Kulish, takes Kulish's denial of his membership at face value (Nakhlik, *Panteleimon Kulish*, 1: 42–4, 56–7, 62).

187 *Kyrylo-Mefodiïvs'ke tovarystvo*, 2: 556 (Kulish's *Ukraina*).

188 Ibid., 2: 563.

189 Nakhlik, *Panteleimon Kulish*, 1: 73–4.

190 *Kyrylo-Mefodiïvs'ke tovarystvo*, 2: 123–4 (Kulish to Orlov, 28 August 1848).

191 Ibid., 2: 126–7 (Orlov to Uvarov, 25 September 1848).

192 Nikolai Ustrialov, *Izsledovanie voprosa kakoe mesto v Rossiiskoi istorii dolzhno zanimat' Velikoe Kniazhestvo Litovskoe* (St Petersburg: V tipografii ekspeditsii zagotovleniia gosudarstvennykh bumag, 1839); Alexei Miller, *The Romanov Empire and Nationalism: Essays in the Methodology of Historical Research* (Budapest: Central European University Press, 2008) 145–6; Velychenko, *National History*, 98–100.

193 *Kyrylo-Mefodiïvs'ke tovarystvo*, 2: 128 (Ustrialov's review submitted to the superintendent of the St Petersburg school district, Mikhail Nikolaevich Musin-Pushkin, on 6 October 1848; the complete review is on pp. 128–9).

194 Ibid., 2: 131. In October 1849 the local governor appointed Kulish assistant editor of the *Tul'skie gubernskie vedomosti* (Tula Provincinal News), but he was prevented from contributing to the newspaper. The appointment was arranged in order to solve his financial problems. See *Kyrylo-Mefodiïvs'ke tovarystvo*, 2: 156 and Nakhlik, *Panteleimon Kulish*, 1: 71–2.

195 *Kyrylo-Mefodiïvs'ke tovarystvo*, 2: 163–8 (correspondence between Kulish and Dubelt, the decision to end Kulish's deportation). Although there

was no response to Kulish's request for books, a remark on the margins of the letter notes that his book list was given to the treasurer. See 2: 168.

196 Ibid., 2: 170 (Kochubei to Dubelt, 4 January 1851). The full title of the book was *Petr Ivanovich Berezini ego semeistvo, ili liudi, vo shto by to ni stalo, reshivshiesia byt shchastlivymi* (Petr Ivanovich Berezin and His Family, or People Who Decided to Be Happy No Matter What).

197 Ibid., 2: 174 (an anonymous review of the Third Section, 20 January 1851; the full text of the review is on pp. 170–1, 174).

198 Ibid., 2: 175 (dated 24 January 1851; the full text of the letter is on pp. 175–6).

199 I disagree with Miller, *The Ukrainian Question*, 55, where the author claims that Russian authorities on all levels failed to appreciate the modern character of Ukrainian nationalism, perceiving in it only nostalgia to the past autonomy.

200 *Kyrylo-Mefodiïvs'ke tovarystvo*, 2: 177–9 (the Third Section's review of Kulish's translations, a summary of information on Kulish, and Dubelt's decision written on the margins, p. 179, after 4 April 1851).

201 Nakhlik, *Panteleimon Kulish*, 1: 79–82.

202 *Kyrylo-Mefodiïvs'ke tovarystvo*, 1: 332–4 (Kostomarov to the director of the Third Section, Leontii Dubelt, 1 July 1849; Dubelt to Bibikov, 12 July 1849; Bibikov to Dubelt, 10 August 1849); Prymak, *Mykola Kostomarov*, 64.

3 Ukrainian Literature and Censorship, 1855-9

1 *Kyrylo-Mefodiïvs'ke tovarystvo*, 1: 350–1 (Orlov's report to Alexander II, 27 June 1855); 2: 353 (the Third Section's information about Shevchenko's release from the army, after 1 May 1857); 2: 357–8 (the Third Section's memorandum on Shevchenko with a note from the chief of gendarmes Vasilii Dolgorukov about the imperial approval permitting him to live in St Petersburg, 4 February 1858); 2: 600–2 (Dolgorukov's report to Alexander II, 30 November 1856; Dolgorukov to governor of Poltava Aleksandr Volkov, 1 December 1856; and Volkov's answer, 8 December 1856).

2 *Ukraïnomovna knyha*, 1: 19–48. The actual number of titles may be higher, since this bibliography does not contain all of Vasyl Hrechulevych's books.

3 Nakhlik, *Panteleimon Kulish*, 1: 125–7.

4 Vasilii Grechulevich, *Besedy katikhizicheskiia na desiat' zapovedei Bozhiikh, govorennyia, na malorossiiskom iazike*, 2nd ed. (St Petersburg: V tipografii Eduarda Pratsa, 1859); *Besedy katekhizicheskiia, na simvol very,*

govorennyia na Malorossiiskom iazyke (St Petersburg: Tipografiia Ia. Ionsona, 1856); *Besedy katekhizicheskiia, pri ob"iasnenii molitvy Gospodnei, na Malorossiiskom iazyke* (St Petersburg: Tipografiia Ia. Ionsona, 1855); *Besedy na malorossiiskom iazyke o semi spasatel'nykh tainstvakh* (St Petersburg: V tipografii Aleksandra Iakobsona, 1858); *O dolzhnostiakh roditelei i detei: Dve besedy, govorennyia na Malorossiiskom iazyke* (St Petersburg: V tipografii Aleksandra Iakobsona, 1859); *Propovedy na Malorossiiskom iazyke,* 2nd rev. ed. (St Petersburg: Tipografiia A. Iakobsona, 1857).

5 Grechulevich, *Besedy katekhizicheskiia, na simvol very* (dedication before the beginning of pagination).

6 Grechulevich, *Propovedy, na Malorossiiskom iazyke* (2nd ed.), i.

7 Grechulevich, *Besedy katekhizicheskiia, pri ob"iasnenii,* 37–8.

8 Grechulevich, *Besedy katekhizicheskiia na deviat' blazhenstv,* 5; *Besedy katekhizicheskiia, na simvol very,* 28–9; *Propovedy na Malorossiiskom iazyke* (2nd ed.), 59.

9 Grechulevich, *Propovedy na Malorossiiskom iazyke* (2nd ed.), v–xii (foreword); Ukraine is mentioned on p. 129. The foreword was signed only by Hrechulevych. For Kulish's rewriting of Hrechulevych's sermons, see Nakhlik, *Panteleimon Kulish,* 1: 123–4.

10 Taras Shevchenko, *Psalmy Davydovi, perelozhyv po-nashomu Taras Shevchenko* (St Petersburg: [P. Kulish], 1860).

11 *Ukrainets, kniga 1* (Moscow: Mikhail Maksimovich, 1859).

12 Panteleimon Kulish, *Chorna Rada, khronika 1663 roku* (St Petersburg: Tipografiia A. Iakobsona, 1857); Kulish, *Chernaia Rada: Khronika 1663 goda* (Moscow: Tipografiia Aleksandra Semena, 1857).

13 Marko Vovchok [pseudonym of Maria Vilinska], *Narodni opovidannia* (St Petersburg: P. A. Kulish, 1858). Vovchok did not write about Ukrainian-Russian relations.

14 Taras Shevchenko, *Kobzar* (St Petersburg: P. Semerenko, 1860).

15 Kulish, *Tvory,* 1: 79.

16 Ibid., 1: 596. Ievhen Nakhlik in his commentary to *The Black Council.*

17 Kulish, *Chernaia Rada,* 231–53.

18 RGIA, f. 772, op. 1, delo 4027, l. 1– 6 (correspondence of Main Administration of Censorship concerning the epilogue, 5 January–24 May 1857). Originally, Kulish intended the article as a foreword rather than as an epilogue; Nakhlik, *Panteleimon Kulish,* 1: 120–2. My interpretation of this incident differs from Miller's (*The Ukrainian Question,* 61), who claimed that the Main Administration of Censorship ignored the case submitted by overzealous Lazhechnikov.

19 Panteleimon Kulish, *Zapiski o iuzhnoi Rusi*, 2 vols. (St Petersburg: P. Kulish, 1856–7), 1: 149. References to Muscovites as enemies also appear in 1: 135–6, 141, 165, 299–301; 2: 254, 256.
20 Ibid., 1: 291.
21 *Ochakovs'ka bida: Kozats'ke opovidannia* (St Petersburg: P.A. Kulish, 1861).
22 Johannes Remy, "The Ukrainian Alphabet as a Political Question in the Russian Empire before 1876," *Ab Imperio*, no. 2 (2005): 176–8.
23 Kulish, *Zapiski o iuzhnoi Rusi*, 2: 108.
24 GARF, f. 109, *sekretnyi arkhiv*, op. 1, ed. khr. 1762, l. 1–2; Miller, *Ukrainian Question*, 68–9.
25 RGIA, f. 772, op. 1, delo 4003, l. 1 (Evgraf Kovalevskii, chairman of Moscow Censorship Committee, to Main Administration of Censorship, undated, but received on 8 December 1856).
26 RGIA, f. 772, op. 1, delo 4003, l. 4–5 (extract from records of Main Administration of Censorship, 12 December 1856). Unfortunately, the documents of the Main Administration of Censorship do not contain more information about the changes that were made to the text.
27 [Panteleimon Kulish], *Hramatka* (St Petersburg: V tipografii P.A. Kulisha, 1857), 10–14, 27, 30, 33, 35, 37–9; on the forged songs, see *Istoricheskie pesni malorusskago naroda s ob"iasneniami Vl. Antonovicha i M. Dragomanova*, 2: ii –iii.
28 [Kulish], *Hramatka*, 28–9.
29 Nakhlik, *Panteleimon Kulish*, 1: 134–5; see also P. Gornitskii, "Iz-pod Kieva," *Osnova*, no. 1 (1861): 328–30. Six months after the censors' final approval of the book, the police found that about 80 copies had been sold in Kyiv alone. Tsentral'nyi Derzhavnyi Istorychnyi Arkhiv Ukrainy (Central State Historical Archive of Ukraine, hereafter: TsDIA Uk. f. 442, op. 808, delo 99, ark. 5 (Kyiv chief of police to Gesse, governor of Kyiv, 24 May 1858).
30 TsDIA Uk., f. 442, op. 808, delo 99, ark. 2 (Vasilchikov to Dolgorukov, 24 May 1858).
31 Ibid., ark. 1–2 (Vasilchikov to the governors in his jurisdiction and to Dolgorukov, 24 May 1858); Nakhlik, *Panteleimon Kulish*, 1: 134–5.
32 RGIA, f. 772, op. 1, delo 4503, l. 1–2 (Dolgorukov to Kovalevskii, June 1858).
33 Ibid., l. 5 (Kovalevskii to superintendent of Moscow school district, 17 June 1858; l. 9 (Kovalevskii to deputy superintendent of Moscow school district, 31 July 1858).
34 By implication, not beyond them, thus excluding Transcarpathia.
35 Kulish, *Hramatka*, 146–9.
36 Mikhail Pogodin, "O drevnem iazyke russkom (Pis'mo k I. Sreznevskomu)," *Moskvitianin* 1, no. 2 (1856): 113–39; for an analysis

of these polemics, see Miller, *The Ukrainian Question*, 66–7; Johannes Remy, "Otnosheniia Ukrainy s Rossiei v trudah Mihaila Maksimovicha 1850–1860-h godov," *Etnichna istoria narodiv Evropy:Zbirnyk naukovyh prats* 9 (Kyiv: Taras Shevchenko University, 2001), 60–4; Aleksei Tolochko, *Kievskaia Rus'*, 207–35; The same text in Ukrainian: Oleksyi Tolochko, "Kyievo-Rus'ka spadshchyna v istorychnyi dumtsi Ukrainy pochatku XIX st.," in V.F. Verstiuk, V.M. Horobets, and O.P. Tolochko, *Ukraïns'ki proiekty v rosiis'kii imperii* (Kyiv: Naukova Dumka, 2004), 331–45, 349–50.

37 M.A. Maksimovich, "Filologicheskie pis'ma M. P. Pogodinu," *Russkaia beseda*, no. 3 (1856), nauky 78–139.

38 Ibid., 84–6.

39 Tolochko, "Kyievo-Ruska spadshchyna," 331–45, 349–50; Tolochko, *Kievskaia Rus'* 207–35.

40 See chapter 1, endnote 23.

41 "Istoriia rusov," *Chteniia*, no. 4 (1846) (*Materialy otechestvenniia*, p. 135).

42 Mikhail Maksimovych, *Sobranie sochinenii*, 1–3 (Kyiv: Tipografiia M.P. Fritsa, 1876–80), book 3, 305.

43 Iu. A. Pinchuk, *Mykola Ivanovych Kostomarov 1817–1885* (Kyiv: Naukova dumka, 1992), 94.

44 Nikolai Kostomarov, *Bogdan Khmel'nitskii*, 2nd exp. ed. (St Petersburg: D.E. Kozanchikov, 1859), 149. This was the first book edition.

45 *Kyrylo-Mefodiïvs'ke tovarystvo*, 1: 353 (Kostomarov to Dubelt, 13 January 1856, with Dubelt's decision in the margins).

46 I. Butych, "M. I. Kostomarov i tsars'ka tsenzura," *Arkhivy Ukraïny*, no. 6 (1967): 62.

47 Ibid.

48 Ibid.

49 Ibid., 66 (extract from records of Main Administration of Censorship, 27 October 1856).

50 Stephen Velychenko, "Tsarist Censorship and Ukrainian Historiography, 1828–1906," *Canadian-American Slavic Studies* 23, no. 4 (1989).

51 RGIA, f. 772, op. 1, delo 4588, l. 3–4 (extract from records of Main Administration of Censorship, 27 September 1858.

52 RGIA, f. 772, op. 1, delo 4413, l. 3 (Shcherbatov, chairman of St Petersburg Censorship Committee, to Main Administration of Censorship, 4 March 1858; here Shcherbatov reveals Matskevich's opinions in detail).

53 RGIA, f. 772, op. 1, delo 4413, l. 4 (Shcherbatov to Main Administration of Censorship, 4 March 1858).

54 RGIA, f. 772, op. 1, delo 4413, l. 9–10 (extract from records of Main Administration of Censorship, 17 May 1858).

55 RGIA, f. 772, op. 1, delo 4565, l. 1 (Ivan Delianov, chairman of St Petersburg Censorship Committee, to Main Administration of Censorship, 18 August 1858; Delianov conveys Matskevich's arguments, repeating them in detail).
56 RGIA, f. 772, op. 1, delo 4565, l. 4–5 (Troinitskii's review of *History of the Rus'*, 24 October 1858).
57 RGIA, f. 772, op. 1, delo 4565, l. 9–10 (Bludov to Kovalevskii, 19 February 1859).
58 Remy, *Higher Education and National Identity*, 259–62.
59 RGIA, f. 772, op. 1, delo 4840, l. 1 (Pirogov to Kovalevskii, 5 April 1859).
60 Ibid., l. 2–7 (minutes of meeting of Main Administration of Censorship, 25 April 1859; circular signed by Nikolai Mukhanov on 30 May 1859).
61 RGIA, f. 772, op. 1, delo 4379, l. 56–7 (Delianov to Main Administration of Censorship, 17 December 1859).
62 M.D. Bernshtein, *Zhurnal "Osnova" i ukraïns'kyi literaturnyi protses kintsia 50–60-kh rokiv XIX st.* (Kyiv: Vydavnytstvo Akademiï Nauk Ukraïns'koï RSR, 1959), 19.
63 RGIA, f. 772, op. 1, delo 4379, l. 58 (Nicolai Mukhanov, director of Main Administration of Censorship, to Ivan Delianov, chairman of St Petersburg Censorship Committee, 12 February 1860).
64 Ibid., l. 60 (Baron Mikhail Nikolaevich Medem, chairman of St Petersburg Censorship Committee, to Main Administration of Censorship, 17 October 1860).

4 Ukrainian Publishing, Russians, and the Empire at the Beginning of the 1860s

1 *Ukraïnomovna knyha*, vol. 1, 26–48. Since no absolute criteria exist, the number of books in this category is only approximate. I have included in it publications of fiction with fewer than 60 pages and all textbooks regardless of their length.
2 Panteleimon Kulish, "Lysty z khutora. Lyst I," *Osnova*, no. 1 (1861): 310–18.
3 Leonid Iashchenko, *Hramatka za dlia ukrains'koho liudu* (Moscow: Drukarnia Katkova, 1862), 21–2.
4 Mykola Hatchuk, *Ukraïns'ka abetka* (Moscow: Universitets'ka drukarnia, 1861) 54.
5 Ibid., 55.
6 RGIA, f. 772, op. 1, delo 5488, l. 1–2 (undated and unsigned memorandum concerning the case, most likely written at the Ministry of Public Enlightenment and submitted to Deputy Minister Nicolai Mukhanov; the

decision, dated 12 November 1860, is marked in the margins; ibid., l. 4 (Kamenetsky to Mukhanov, 3 December 1860).

7 RGIA, f. 772, op. 1, delo 5512, l. 1 (Kulish to Main Administration of Censorship, 3 December 1860); l. 2 (Censor Nikitenko's evaluation of the stories as harmless, received 7 January 1861); l. 3 (Mukhanov to Moscow Censorship Committee, 20 January 1861).

8 To cite just one example: the Valuev circular of 1863 banned all publications intended for primary mass reading in Ukrainian, but allowed fiction written for the educated classes. For the complete text of the circular, see Miller, *Ukrainian Question*, 263–6; see also David Saunders, "Russia and Ukraine under Alexander II: The Valuev Edict of 1863," *International History Review* 17, no. 1 (1995): 23–50.

9 Kvitka-Osnov'ianenko, *Malorossiiskiia povesti*, 10.

10 RGIA, f. 772, op. 1, delo 5536, l. 1 (Medem, chairman of the St Petersburg Censorship Committee, to Main Administration of Censorship, 17 December 1860).

11 RGIA, f. 772, op. 1, delo 5536, l. 1.

12 Ibid., l. 2 (Nikitenko's evaluation of *Khmel'nyshchyna*, undated; received on 21 January 1861).

13 Ibid.

14 Ibid., l. 3–4 (decision about the circular, 21 January 1861; information about its rescindment, 22 February 1861; Nikolai Mukhanov to St Petersburg Censorship Committee, 22 February 1861); cf. Miller, *The Ukrainian Question*, 61–2, who finds that the Main Administration of Censorship naively failed to discover Ukrainian separatism in *Khmelnyshchyna*. Miller does not mention either the intended circular or that anything was removed from the text.

15 Panteleimon Kulish, *Khmel'nyshchyna* (St Petersburg: P.A. Kulish, 1861), 105–8, 110–12.

16 RGIA, f. 772, op. 1, delo 4619, l. 10 (Dolgorukov to Kovalevskii, 8 December 1858); quoted also in Viktor Dudko, "Zhurnal 'Osnova' u zhandarms'kykh materialakh," *Spadshchyna*, no. 2 (2006): 9.

17 RGIA, f. 772, op. 1, delo 4619, l. 1–2 (Kulish to Kovalevskii, 23 October 1858; in the upper margin an immediate refusal that was subsequently cancelled); l. 10 (Dolgorukov to Kovalevskii, 8 December 1858); l. 11 (A. Berte, head of the Chancellery of the Minister of Public Enlightenment, to Kulish, 24 December 1858); on Kulish's impression of the process, see Bernshtein, *Zhurnal "Osnova,"* 15.

18 Panteleimon Kulish, "Perednie slovo do hromady: Pohliad na ukraïns'ku slovesnost'," *Khata* (St Petersburg: P.A. Kulish, 1860), vii–xv; for general

discussion of *Khata*, including its reception, see Nakhlik, *Panteleimon Kulish*, 137–39.

19 RGIA, f. 772, op. 1, delo 5049, l. 1–3 (Delianov to Main Administration of Censorship, 30 November 1859); l. 17 (Dolgorukov to Kovalevskii, 24 December 1859; Mukhanov to St Petersburg Censorship Committee, 24 February 1860); l. 19 (approved program of *Osnova*); Dudko, "Zhurnal 'Osnova,'" 11–13; Volodymyr Menchyts', "Z spominiv," *Ukraïna*, no. 3 (1925): 67. Viktor Dudko presumes that Bilozersky successfully lobbied his cause through his superior Petr Fedorovich Brok. I doubt this, since Menchyts' mentions an anonymous dignitary who lobbied on behalf of Osnova and was a member of St Petersburg Hromada, and Brok's biography does not indicate that he had any connection to Ukraine. The anonymous dignitary with Ukrainian sympathies may rather have been Andrei Parfenovich Zablotskii-Desiatovskii, secretary of the state council's financial department, where Bilozers'ky served. As will be discussed in this chapter and chapter 6, Zablotskii-Desiatovskii lobbied for introduction of Ukrainian as a language of elementary instruction on two occasions. To be sure, he was not a senator as the person mentioned in Menchyts' memoirs was.

20 TsDIA Uk., f. 442, op. 810, spr. 187, ark. 2–3 (the application, which includes the prospective program of *Golos*; undated, but before 31 May 1860).

21 Ibid., ark. 4 (Vasilchikov to Pirogov, 11 June 1860).

22 RGIA, f. 772, op.1, delo 5350, l. 5–6 (Vasilchikov to Kovalevskii, 11 June 1860).

23 Liudmyla Heorhiivna Ivanova and Raisa Petrivna Ivanchenko, *Suspyl'no-politychnyi rukh 60-kh rr. XIX st. v Ukraïni: Do problem stanovlennia ideolohiï* (Kyiv: Mizhnarodnyi instytut linhvistyky i prava, 2000), 123–4, 135–41.

24 RGIA, f. 772, op. 1, delo 5350, l. 9 (Mukhanov to Kyiv Censorship Committee, 13 July 1860).

25 Viktor Dudko, "Auditoriia zhurnalu 'Osnova' (1861–1862): Kil'kisnyi vymir," *Kyivs'ka Starovyna*, no. 6 (2001): 73–85. In 1862, the circulation of *Osnova* was lower than in 1861. Since most of the journal's documents have not been preserved, Dudko had to make his estimation despite considerable difficulties with the sources.

26 Nikolai Kostomarov, "Mysli o federativnom nachale v drevnei Rusi," *Osnova*, no. 1 (1861): 121. In each issue of *Osnova* there were several paginations, and the pagination was not always consistent.

27 Ibid., 135.

28 N. Kostomarov, "Cherty narodnoi iuzhno-russkoi istorii," *Osnova*, no. 3 (1861): 140.

29 N. Kostomarov, "Otvet na vykhodki gazety (Krakovskoi) 'Czas' i zhurnala 'Revue contemporaine,'" *Osnova*, no. 2 (1861): 135; "Dve russkie narodnosti," *Osnova*, no. 3 (1861): 79–80; "Vospominanie o dvukh maliarakh," *Osnova*, no. 4 (1861): 53.

30 Ieremiia Halka, "Na dobra-nich," *Osnova*, no. 2 (1861): 44–8.

31 N. Kostomarov, "Getmanstvo Vygovskogo," *Osnova*, no. 4 (1861): 1–66; *Osnova*, no. 7 (1861): 67–114.

32 *Osnova*, no. 7 (1861): 93.

33 "Po povodu aktov, otnosiashchykhsia do iugo-zapadnoi Rusi," *Osnova*, no. 3 (1861): 1–2.

34 *Osnova*, no. 3 (1861). The editorial following the emancipation manifesto has no page number. With respect to this particular question, Kulish was an exception among the authors contributing to *Osnova*. In his view, the Ukrainian nobility and the Russian government shared equal responsibility for the establishment of serfdom. See Kulish, "Obzor ukrainskoi slovesnosti: V. Gogol', kak avtor povestei iz ukrainskoi zhizni," *Osnova*, no. 9 (1861): 59.

35 Oleksa Storozhenko, "Zakokhanyi chort," *Osnova*, no. 2 (1861): 19–20; "Lipovye pushchi: Nachalo romana, naidennago v bumagakh pokoinago D. P. Khorechko," *Osnova*, no. 5 (1861): 9, 23.

36 "Uchilishcha, obrazovavshiiasia na iuge v poslednee vremia," *Osnova*, no. 6 (1861): 93–6.

37 "Proshchanie N. Iv. Pirogova s uchebnym sosloviem i gorodom Kievom," *Osnova*, no. 6 (1861): 108–33. A considerable number of liberal and radical periodicals in Russia wrote about the event.

38 Grigorii Ge, "Vyderzhki iz zapisok mirovogo posrednika," *Osnova*, no. 2 (1862): 36.

39 Oleksandr Konysky [Oleksandr Perekhodovets', pseud.], "Z Poltavy (1 Ianvaria 1862)," *Osnova* no 2 (1862) 52.

40 The only instance of any other government measures being praised, P. Chubinskii, "Iz Borispolia," *Osnova*, no. 10 (1861): 134–5. Chubynsky wrote about insurance and credit unions that were established in *volosts*, local peasant administrative units.

41 Al. Lazarevskii, "Govoril li Polubotok Petru Velikomu rech', privodimuiu Konisskim?" *Osnova*, no. 8 (1861): 9–13.

42 Taras Shevchenko, "Nevol'nyk," *Osnova*, no. 4 (1861): 1–20.

43 Ia. H.Kukharenko, "Chornomors'kyi pobut na Kubani mizh 1794 i 1796 rokamy," *Osnova*, nos. 11–12 (1861): 10–11;[Panteleimon Kulish], "Lysty z khutora," *Osnova*, nos. 11–12 (1861): 126–7; N. Reviakin, "Semen Palii," *Osnova*, nos. 11 –12 (1861): 32; Oleksa Storozhenko, "Zakokhanyi chort,"

Osnova, no. 1 (1861): 19–20; Kuz'ma Shapoval, "Z podorozhnyka," *Osnova*, no. 1 (1862): 49–51.

44 Panteleimon Kulish, "Vyhovshchyna," *Osnova*, nos. 11–12 (1861): 9.

45 Kulish, "Obzor ukrainskoi slovesnosti," *Osnova*, no. 1 (1861): 231.

46 "Lipovye pushchi," *Osnova*, no. 5 (1861): 23–5; Oleksyi Ivanovych Dei, *Slovnik ukraïns'kykh psevdonimiv ta kriptonimiv (XVI–XX st.)* (Kyiv: Naukova Dumka, 1969), 383 (author's identity). I am indebted to Anton Kotenko for the information regarding Kulish's pseudonym.

47 Ibid., 24.

48 Kostomarov, "Dve russkie narodnosti," 47. The complete essay is on pp. 33–80.

49 Ibid., 61.

50 Ibid., 43–4.

51 Ibid., 64.

52 For the Slavophile perceptions of the West that are relevant to the present analogy, see Andrzej Walicki, *The Slavophile Controversy: History of a Conservative Utopia in Nineteenth-Century Russian Thought*, trans. Hilda Andrews-Rusiecka (Oxford: Clarendon Press, 1975), esp. 140–1, 151–2, 205–7, 210–14.

53 Adam Mickiewicz, *Dzieła*, 24 vols. (Warsaw: Czytelnik, 1955), vols. 8 – 11. Of course, this is not the whole story of Mickiewicz's evaluation of the Russians. Since he considered them a nation of mixed Slavic and Finnish-Mongolian ancestry, he also found good, "Slavic," traits in them. According to Mickiewicz, the Slavic aspect in the Russians' ancestry explained the fact that they had also produced some good literature. "Finnish" in Mickiewicz's scheme referred to all non-Slavic inhabitants of northern parts of Russia, not only to inhabitants of Finland.

54 Kostomarov, "Dve russkie narodnosti," 54–5.

55 Ibid., 73–4.

56 Ibid., 77–80.

57 G. T., "O narodnosti v religioznoi zhizni," *Osnova*, no. 4 (1861): 128–42.

58 Taras Shevchenko, "Dnevnik," *Osnova*, no. 8 (1861): 13.

59 For examples of Russian crudeness, see Shapoval, "Z podorozhnyka," 94; Kukharenko, "Chornomors'kyi pobut na Kubani," 33.

60 Panteleimon Kulish, "Ukrainskie nezabudki," *Osnova*, no. 9 (1861): 8–9, 46–7.

61 Velikorossianin O-ov, "Ukraintsy v Saratovskoi gubernii," *Osnova*, no. 9 (1861): 187–8; for another example of Muscovite dishonesty, see Oleksandr Perekhodovets' [Konys'kyi], "Lyst z dorohy," *Osnova*, no. 10 (1861): 146; for a comparison of Ukrainian and Russian pubs favouring the former, see

Pavel Iakushkin, "Putevyia zametki," *Osnova*, nos. 11–12 (1861): 111–12; for a thieving Muscovite among honest Ukrainians, see A. Iashchenko, "Z narodnikh ust, VI. Moskal' Kyrylo," *Osnova*, no. 1 (1862): 28–38.

62 Anton Leonidovych Kotenko, "Do pytannia pro tvorennia ukraïns'koho natsional'noho prostoru v zhurnali 'Osnova,'" *Ukraïns'kyi Istorychnyi zhurnal*, no. 2 (2012): 45–6, 49–50.

63 [Kulish,] "Lysty z khutora," *Osnova*, no. 1 (1861): 310–13. For another example of similar, although less extreme, concern over the denationalizing impact of education, see V. Kulyk, "De-shcho z Poltavy," *Osnova*, nos. 11–12 (1861): 103–5.

64 Panteleimon Kulish, "Drugoi chelovek," *Osnova*, no. 2 (1861): 56–104.

65 Panteleimon Kulish, "Obzor ukrainskoi slovesnosti, IV: Gogol', kak avtor povestei," *Osnova*, no. 4 (1861): 85–7; no. 5 (1861): 2–4, 10, 16–17, 30; Ia. Kukha, "Voronyi kin'," *Osnova*, no. 10 (1861): 21, 24; Anatolii Svydnyts'kyi, "Velykden' u podolian," *Osnova*, no. 10 (1861): 61–2; P. Chubyns'kyi, "Iz Boryspolia," *Osnova*, no. 10 (1861): 130–1; Ka-pa, "Moi vospominaniia," *Osnova*, nos. 11–12 (1861): 72; L. M., "Talant; Fiziologicheskii ocherk," *Osnova*, nos. 11–12 (1861): 77–8; Shapoval, "Z podorozhnyka," *Osnova*, nos. 11 –12 (1861): 112; no. 1 (1862): 53–4.

66 V. Kulyk, "De-shcho z Poltavy (do Redaktora.)," *Osnova*, no. 9 (1861): 180–2.

67 I disagree with Faith Hillis's perception of *Osnova* as a Little Russian organ which combined local identity with the broader all-Russian identity. See Faith Hillis, *Children of Rus': Right Bank Ukraine and the Invention of a Russian Nation* (Ithaca: Cornell University Press, 2013), 52–4. The exclusive Ukrainian (most often expressed as South Russian) identity not compatible with any other national identity dominates in *Osnova*, and the tendency to distance Ukrainians from Great Russians is manifest. To be sure, the journal did not support political separation of Ukraine from Russia.

68 Anatolyi Svydnytsk'kyi, *Tvory* (Kyiv: Derzhavne vydavnytstvo khudozhnoi literatury, 1958), 161.

69 Svydnytsk'kyi, *Tvory*, 161.

70 Ibid., 226.

71 Ibid., 218.

72 Ibid.

73 "Otake-to z katsapom!" Ibid., 232.

74 "Iasnaia-Poliana. Dva slova o novom iavlenii v dele narodnogo vospitaniia," *Osnova*, no. 8 (1861): 122–4; Kulish, "Obzor ukrainskoi slovesnosti," *Osnova*, no. 1 (1861): 183; N. Makarov, "Vospominaniia o N. A. Markeviche," *Osnova*, no. 1 (1861): 293; Taras Shevchenko, "Dnevnik," *Osnova*, nos. 11–12 (1861): 11–12 and no. 2 (1862): 9–10, 12.

75 For instance, Anna Barvinok, "S Volyni," *Osnova*, no. 1 (1861): 282–92; Panteleimon Kulish, "Drugoi chelovek," *Osnova*, no. 2 (1861): 64–7; "Nedorozumenie po povodu slova 'zhid,'" *Osnova*, no. 6 (1861): 134–42; Mytro Olelkovych, "Zhydivs'ka diaka," *Osnova*, no. 9 (1861): 73–8; for an analysis of Barvinok's text, see Myroslav Shkandrij, *Jews in Ukrainian Literature: Representation and Identity* (New Haven: Yale University Press, 2009) 39–40.

76 Nikolai Kostomarov, "Iudeiam," *Osnova*, no. 1 (1862): 38–58; Panteleimon Kulish, "Peredovye zhidy," *Osnova*, no. 9 (1861); for the Sion-Osnova controversy, see Roman Serbyn, "The Sion-Osnova Controversy of 1861–1862," in *Ukrainian–Jewish Relations in Historical Perspective*, ed. Peter J. Potichnyj and Howard Aster (Edmonton: Canadian Institute of Ukrainian Studies, 1988), 85–110; Miller, *The Ukrainian Question*, 83–5.

77 *Osnova*, no. 2 (1861): 121–35.

78 *Osnova*, no. 10 (1861): 100–12.

79 Nikolai Kostomarov, "Pravda poliakam o Rusi," *Osnova*, no. 10 (1861): 112.

80 "Peterburgskii universitet," *Kolokol*, 1 July 1861, 856–7. The invitations to the event were distributed at Shevchenko's (first) funeral in St Petersburg.

81 RGIA, f. 772, op. 1, delo 5603, l. 1 (unsigned and undated document written as background material for the session of the Main Administration of Censorship).

82 RGIA, f. 772, op. 1, delo 5607, l. 2 (unsigned and undated document written as background material to enable the Main Administration of Censorship to reach a decision; it includes the contents of Kostomarov's appeal; the quotation is not from Kostomarov but from this detailed recapitulation of his appeal).

83 RGIA, f. 772, op. 1, delo 5607, l. 2–4 (Bilozersky's arguments for the article to be permitted).

84 Nikolai Kostomarov, "Pravda moskvicham o Rusi," *Osnova*, no. 10 (1861): 11–12 (dated 29 November 1861).

85 P. Neobachnyi, "Znaidenyi na dorozi lyst," *Osnova*, no. 2 (1861): 233–8.

86 Faddei Rylskii [Tadei Ryl's'kyi], "Neskol'ko slov o dvorianakh pravogo berega Dnepra," *Osnova*, nos. 11–12 (1861): 90–9.

87 Ibid., 99.

88 Vladimir Antonovich [Volodymyr Antonovych], "Moia ispoved': Otvet g. Padalitse," *Osnova*, no. 1 (1861): 94.

89 M. Iuzefovich and P. Ivanishev, "Otvet Kievskoi kommissii dlia razbora drevnikh aktov na obvineniia nekotorykh gazet i zhurnalov," *Osnova*, no. 10 (1861): 91.

90 N.I. Kostomarov, "O prepodavanii na iuzhnorusskom iazike," *Osnova*, no. 5 (1862): 1–6.

91 St. Pogarskii, "O narodnom obrazovanii i o sredstvakh dlia izdaniia uchebnikov na ukrainskom iazyke," *Osnova*, no. 7 (1862): 13–18.
92 "Sovremennaia iuzhnorusskaia letopis'," *Osnova*, 3 (1862): 118.
93 Staliūnas, *Making Russians*, 48–50; for Hilferding, see Henryk Głębocki, *Kresy imperium: Szkice i materiały do dziejów polityki Rosji wobec jej peryferii (XVIII–XXI wiek)* (Cracow: Arcana, 2006), 186–244.
94 RGIA, f. 772, op. 1, delo 5979, l. 4 (list of journal articles banned in St Petersburg in 1861, 22 February 1862; none of the 14 articles is from *Osnova*; the list does not include those articles that were permitted in a modified form).
95 RGIA, f. 772, op. 1, delo 5785, l. 1–2 (Baron Medem, head of St Petersburg Censorship Committee, to Main Administration of Censorship, 3 August 1861; Ivan Delianov from Main Administration of Censorship to Baron Medem, 18 August 1861).
96 Dudko, "Zhurnal 'Osnova,'" 19.
97 Viktor Dudko, "Statti dlia zhurnalu 'Osnova'" (1861–1862) zaboroneni tsenzuroiu," *Kyivs'ka Starovyna* 1997, no 5 (317): 71–102. Dudko's publication includes both the banned articles and their analysis; Dudko, "Zhurnal 'Osnova,'" 7–45. Dudko finds that the authorities in general and the Third Section especially were not particularly hostile to *Osnova*.
98 Khutorianin [pseudonym of Panteleimon Kulish], "Kakiia rukovodstva udobnee upotrebliat' pri pervonachal'nom obuchenii krest'ianskikh detei?" *Chernigovskii listok*, no. 26 (1861): 202–4, no. 27 (1861): 210–12; for an another article on the same topic, see Al. Lazarevskii, "Zametka na pis'mo g. Dobrotvorskago," *Chernigovskii listok*, no. 9 (1863): 72. Lazarevsky rejected the accusations, according to which the Little Russian literary language introduced Polish influence to Russian education.
99 "Chernigov, 12 maia 1863," *Chernigovskii listok*, no. 2 (1863): 9.
100 Panteleimon Kulish, "Divoche sertse," *Chernigovskii listok*, no. 2 (1863): 14; a similar negative evaluation of St Petersburg as a "foul swamp" (*paskudnomu boloti*) appeared in M. Nomys, "Rasskaz o poezdke zaporozhtsev v Peterburg," *Chernigovskii listok*, no. 11 (1863): 83.
101 Panteleimon Kulish, "Duma pro Savu Kononenka," *Chernigovskii listok*, no. 3 (1863): 20–1.
102 Iv. Lashniukov, "Sostoianie istoricheskoi nauki u zapadnykh slavian," *Chernigovskii listok*, no. 1 (1861): 6–8; no. 2 (1863): 15–16.
103 N. Kostomarov, "O pozhertvovaniiakh v pol'zu izdaniia knig nauchnago soderzhaniia dlia iuzhnorusskago naroda," *Chernigovskii listok*, no. 3 (1863): 19–20.
104 Al. Lazarevskii, "Rasskazy iz istorii levoberezhnoi Ukrainy XVIII veka," *Chernigovskii listok*, no. 13 (1863): 101–4.

105 RGIA, f. 772, op. 1, delo 5844, l. 1–3 (Nikolai to Main Administration of Censorship, 17 October 1861).
106 RGIA, f. 772, op. 1, delo 5992, l. 19–21 (extracts from the records of Kyiv Censorship Committee, 9–23 February 1862).
107 Ibid., l. 19 (extract from the records of Kyiv Censorship Committee, 9 February 1862).
108 Ibid., l. 20 (extract from the records of Kyiv Censorship Committee, 10 February 1862).
109 RGIA, f. 772, op. 1, delo 5700, l. 1–6 (correspondence between St Petersburg Censorship Committee and Main Administration of Censorship regarding the Karpenko case, 10 April–9 June 1861).
110 RGIA, f. 773, op. 1, delo 43, l. 1–3 (chairman of Moscow Censorship Committee to Minister of Public Enlightenment Aleksandr Golovnin, 24 March 1862; includes Loboda's banned letter).
111 RGIA, f. 773, op. 1, delo 123, l. 1 (chairman of Moscow Censorship Committee to Golovnin, 16 May 1862).
112 RGIA, f. 773, op. 1, delo 258, l. 1–4 (Levshin to Golovnin, 11 September 1862; includes Petropavlovsky's petition and the proposed program of *Ukrainskii vestnik*).
113 RGIA, f. 773, op. 1, delo 258, l. 7 (Valuev to Golovnin, 11 October 1862); quoted also in Dudko, "Zhurnal 'Osnova,'" 31.
114 RGIA, f. 773, op. 1, delo 251, l. 2–3 (deputy minister of internal affairs to Golovnin, 13 August 1862).
115 M. Kostomarov, "Khrystyianstvo i krypatstvo," *Osnova*, no. 6 (1862): 9–12.
116 Vs. Kokhovs'kyi, "Z narodnykh ust," *Osnova*, no. 6 (1862): 29–53.
117 RGIA, f. 773, op. 1, delo 251, l. 5–6 (Lebedev's explanation, dated 11 September 1862, with Golovnin's decisions inscribed in the margins, 16 September 1862).

5 Ukrainian Clandestine Activities and Government Reaction, 1856–64

1 GARF, f. 109, secret archive, op.1, ed. khr. 1762, l. 1–2 (excerpt of a letter dated 28 October 1858). A notation in the margin states that it was presented to the emperor; Miller, *The Ukrainian Question*, 68 –71, contains the complete excerpt, but does not mention that Alexander II was informed.
2 Ibid., ed. khr. 1763, l. 1–6 (excerpt from the letter and Third Section's information about Gogotskii and Hrechulevych); Miller, *The Ukrainian Question*, 69–71.
3 [Nikolai Kostomarov], "Ukraina," *Kolokol*, no. 61 (15 January 1860): 499–503; below, some of the text repeats Johannes Remy, "The Ukrainophile

Intelligentsia and Its Relation to the Russian Empire in the Beginning of the Reign of Alexander II (1856–1863)," in *Imperial and National Identities in Pre-Revolutionary, Soviet, and Post-Soviet Russia*, ed. Chris J. Chulos and Johannes Remy (Helsinki: SKS, 2002), 185–8; see also Miller, *The Ukrainian Question*, 81.

4 [Kostomarov], "Ukraina," 503.

5 A.S. Baraboi, "Kharkovsko-Kievskoe revoliutsionnoe tainoe obshchestvo 1856–1860gg,"*Istoricheskie zapiski* 52 (1955): 239–52; L.H. Ivanova and R.P. Ivanchenko, *Suspil'no-politychnyi rukh 60-kh rr. XIX st. v Ukraïni: Do problemy stanovlennia ideolohiï* (Kyiv: Mizhnarodnyi instytut linhvistyky i prava, 2000), 79–81, 100–3, 140–1, 143–4, 148–9; Boris Koz'min, *Khar'kovskie zagovorshchiki 1856–1858 godov* (Kharkiv: Proletarii, 1930); *Obshchestvenno-politicheskoe dvizhenie na Ukraine 1856–1862* (Kyiv: Vydavnytstvo Akademiï Nauk Ukraïns'koï RSR,1963), 2–5, 19–22, 31–4, 49–53, 68–75. Henceforward, this collection of documents will be referred to as OPDU; Roman Serbyn, "La 'Société politique secrète' de Kharkiv (Ukraine), 1856–1860," *Canadian Historical Association: Historical Papers*, 1973: 159–77.

6 TsDIA Uk., f. 442, op. 810, spr. 185, ch. 1, ark. 170 (Vasilchikov to Dolgorukov, 18 February 1860); for Iefymenko in general, see Andreas Kappeler, *Russland und die Ukraine.* The book is, in addition to everything else, a biography of Iefymenko and his spouse Aleksandra, who both were later prominent ethnographers. Kappeler does not know about this toast, which went unreported in Soviet historiography.

7 TsDIA Uk., f. 442, op. 810, spr. 185, ch. 1, ark. 162–4 (governor of Kharkiv Ivan Dmitrievich Luzhin to Vasilchikov, 14 February 1860).

8 Ibid., ark. 141 (Vasilchikov to Luzhin, 13 February 1860).

9 Koz'min, *Khar'kovskie zagovorshchiki*, 55–6 (gendarmes' description of the proclamation in Russian translation; since neither Koz'min nor I found the original in the archive, it is probably lost).

10 GARF, f. 109, 1 eksp., 1860g, op. 35, ed. khr. 26, ch. 1, Lit. A l. 177 (description of documents found in Mytrofan Levchenko's possession located in the journal of the Investigating Commission, 30 May 1860).

11 These three former conspirators sent their texts to *Osnova*. Portugalov's letter about anti-Semitism in the Ukrainian movement was not published, but evoked an angry response from the journal's editors. See P. Iefymenko, "O malorossiianakh v Orenburgskoi gubernii," *Osnova*, no. 9 (1861): 189–93; "Nedorozumenie po povodu slova 'zhid,'" *Osnova*, no. 6 (1861): 134–42; A. Tishchinskii, "Zashchitniku golubichskoi shkoly," *Osnova*, no. 10 (1862): 78–81; O. Tyshchyns'kyi [Lesia-ii, prseudonym], "Z Horodnyts'koho povitu Chernih. Hub. (15 hrudnia 1861)," *Osnova*, no. 1 (1862): 59–62;

Tyshchyns'kyi [Lesia-ii], "Z Horodnians'koho povitu," *Osnova*, no. 2 (1862): 57–8; Tyshchyns'kyi [Lesia-ii], "Iz Gorodnetskogo uezda Chernig. gubernii (25 iiulia 1862g.)," *Osnova*, no. 8 (1862): 46–51; Viktor Dudko, "'Rannii'" Oleksandr Tyshchyns'kyi: Storinky zhyttia i tvorchosti," *Siverians'kyi Litopys: Vseukraïnsk'kyi naukovyi zhurnal* 10, no. 6 (2006): 76–83.

12 The Moscow Rada is mentioned in the letters of Ilia Derkach to Ivan Andrushchenko: GARF, f. 112, op. 1, 1863g., delo 72, l. 184–5, 188–9, 191. The three letters were written in 1860–1; in some of the letters received by Stepan Nis in Chernihiv, he was called "father of the *kurin*." See GARF, f. 112, op. 1, 1863g., delo 72, l. 271.

13 Marko Antonovych, "Z istoriï hromad na rubezhi 1850–1860-kh rokiv," *Kyïvs'ka starovyna*, no. 2 (1998): 32–45; Dudko, "Zhurnal 'Osnova,'" 11–12; A.M. Katrenko, *Ukraïns'kyi natsional'nyi rukh XIX st.*, pt. 2, *60–90-ti roky XIX st.* (Kyiv: Kyïvs'kyi natsional'nyi universytet imeni Tarasa Shevchenka, 1999), 8–22; Volodymyr Menchyts', "Z spomyniv," *Ukraïna*, no. 3 (1925): 66–7. See chapter 4, note 19 for a discussion of the identity of the mysterious state council member, who I suppose was Andrei Parfenovich Zablotskii-Desiatovskii.

14 [Paulin Święcicki], "Na gruzach: Powieść w dwóch tomach przez Teofila Szumskiego," *Sioło*, no. 2 (1866): 162. Also quoted in Remy, *Higher Education*, 259.

15 On the Triple Union, see Otton Beiersdorf, "Kijów w powstaniu styczniowym," in *Kraków-Kijów: Szkice z dziejów polsko-ukraińskich*, ed. Antoni Podraza (Cracow: Wydawnictwo Literackie, 1969), 77–9; Stefan Kieniewicz, *Powstanie styczniowe* (Warsaw: Państwowe Wydawnictwo Naukowe, 1983), 40, 50–3, 68; Remy, *Higher Education*, 253–5, 259–60, 326–8, 354–5; Leon Syroczyński, *O życiu młodzieży kijowskiej przed r. 1863 przez czlonka ostatniego zarządu Trojnickiego* (Lviv: I Związkowa Drukarnia, 1884), 10–14; Jan Tabiś, *Polacy na uniwersytecie Kijowskim 1834–1863* (Cracow: Wydawnictwo Literackie, 1974), 90–1.

16 Johannes Remy, "The Past of Poland-Lithuania in the Polish National Movement, 1830–1864," in *Statehood Beyond and Before Ethnicity: Transnational Perspectives onto Smaller States of Europe, 1600–2000*, ed. Linas Eriksonas and Leos Müller, 219–42. Multiple Europes 33 (Brussels: P.I.E. Peter Lang, 2005).

17 Wacław Lasocki, *Wspomnienie z mojego życia*, 2 vols., (Cracow: Nakładem gminy miasta Krakowa, 1933), 1: 203, 244–5;Remy, *Higher Education*, 255, 258.

18 [E. U.], "Paryż w m. czerwcu 1866," *Sioło*, no. 1 (1866): 148–9.

19 Volodymyr Antonovych, *Tvory*, vol. 1 (Kyiv: Vseukraïns'ka Akademiia Nauk, 1932), 40; for general discussion of Antonovych, see Bohdan Klid,

"Volodymyr Antonovych: The Making of a Ukrainian Populist Activist and Historian," PhD diss. (University of Alberta, 1992); Vasyl' Ul'ianovs'kyi and Viktor Korotkyi, *Volodymyr Antonovych: Obraz na tli epokhy* (Kyiv: Tov. "Mizhnarodna finansova ahentsiia," 1997).

20 Volodymyr Mijakovs'ky, *Nedrukovane i zabute: Hromads'ki rukhy dev'iatnadtsiatoho storichchia* (New York: Ukraïns'ka vil'na Akademiia Nauk, 1984), 323–34.

21 Leon Syroczyński, *Z przed 50 lat: Wspomnienie bylego studenta Kijowskiego uniwersytetu Leona Syroczyńskiego* (Lviv: Nakładem autora, 1914), 21; Gustaw Reutt, "Do legionów (Z notatek rodzinnych)," in *W czterdziestą rocznicę powstania styczniowego 1863–1903*, ed. Bronisław Szwarce et al. (Lviv: Nakładem Komitetu Wydawniczego, 1903), 357.

22 Antonovych, *Tvory*, 1: 8–10, 30–4, 40–6, 60–1; K. Mikhal'chuk, "Iz ukrainskogo bylogo: K vospominaniiam B. S. Poznanskogo," *Ukrainskaia zhizn'*, nos. 8–10 (1914); Boris Poznanskii, "Vospominaniia, *Ukrainskaia zhizn'*, no.1 (1913): 35–6; no. 2 (1913): 22–6; no. 3 (1913): 20–3; no. 4 (1913): 24; Syroczyński, *Z przed 50 lat*, 22, 25, 27, 33.

23 Tomasz Burzyński, "Wspomnienia," in *Wydawnictwo materyałów do historyi powstania 1863–1864*, 5 vols. (Lviv: Drukarnia Ludowa, 1894), 4: 134–6.

24 TsDIA Uk., f. 442, op. 811, spr. 59, ark. 1, 4–10 (Vasilchikov's correspondence with the Kyiv police chief, Superintendent Nikolai Pirogov, and the civilian governor); ibid., spr. 72, ark. 1–4 (Pirogov's letter to Vasilchikov, dated 31 March 1861, contains the two student petitions); Burzyński, "Wspomnienia," 132–3; V.M. Iuzefovich, "Tridtsat' let tomu nazad," *Russkaia starina*, nos. 10–11 (1895), here, 10: 168–76, 180–91; S.S. Simonov, "Studencheskoe dvizhenie v Kievskom universitete v XIX veke," Candidate of Historical Sciences diss. (Kyiv Taras Shevchenko University, 1963), 139–40, 157.

25 TsDIA Uk., f. 810, op. 810, sprava 132, ark. 272–3.This Polish handwritten text attacking Antonovych, who delivered it to the authorities, clearly indicates that Antonovych presented himself at the meeting as a Pole despite his Ukrainian sympathies. See Antonovych, *Tvory*, 1: 46–50. According to Antonovych, the accusations consisted of atheistic propaganda, agitation in favour of violence against the nobility, and calls to destroy the Polish nationality in the region.

26 The petition is published in Agaton Giller, *Historja powstania narodu polskiego w 1861–1864 r.* (Paris: Księgarnia Luxemburska, 1868), 2: 396–8.

27 TsDIA Uk., f. 442, op. 810, ark. 30–7, 91–2 (reports of the acting chief of the Kyiv police to Vasilchikov, 13 December 1860 and 9 January 1861).

28 TsDIA Uk., F. 442, op. 810, ark. 201–4 (description of Rylski's papers and books in the final report of the investigating commission, 18 January 1861);

f. 442, op. 810, ark. 235 (description of Antonovych's papers and books in the undated final report on him, received by Vasilchikov on 3 March).

29 TsDIA Uk., f. 442, op. 810, sprava 132, ark. 86–90 (Rylsky's testimony of 16 January 1861).

30 Ibid., ark. 259–63 (Antonovych's answers to the investigating commission, 11 February 1861).

31 I have mentioned this hypothesis briefly in an earlier publication: Johannes Remy, "National Aspect of Student Movements in St. Vladimir's University of Kiev 1855–1863," *Skhid/Zakhid, Istoryko-kul'turolohichnyi* zbirnyk, no. 7 (2005): 261–2; see also Hillis, *Children of Rus'*, 63–4.

32 TsDIA Uk., f. 442, op. 810, sprava 132, ark. 242 (final report of the investigating commission).

33 GARF, f. 109, 1 eksp., 1861g., ed. hr. 29, l. 1–3, 11–13, 18–19 (gendarme officer Gribovskii to Dolgorukov, 21 January 1861; Dolgorukov to Alexander II, 16 February 1861; Vasilchikov to Dolgorukov, OPDU, 86–7).

34 TsDIA Uk., f. 442, op. 811, sprava 91, ark. 23–4 (Vasilchikov to civilian governor of Kyiv province, 18 May 1861).

35 Ibid., sprava 186, ark. 1–3 (Radomyshl police chief to Vasilchikov, 2 October 1861); ark. 16–17 (Vasilchikov to Kyiv governor Pavel Ivanovich Gesse, 16 January 1862).

36 TsDIA Uk. f. 442, op. 812, sprava 56, ark. 1–4 (police officer Kharchenko to Vasilchikov, 19 February 1862); ark. 5–6 (governor of Volyn to Vasilchikov, 23 February 1862).

37 Ibid., op. 812, sprava 56, ark. 12 (Vasilchikov to the governor, 1 May 1862).

38 "Otzyv iz Kieva," *Sovremennaia letopis Russkogo Vestnika*, no. 46 (1862).

39 TsDIA Uk., f. 442, op. 812, sprava 85, ark. 25–30 (Vasilchikov to Golovnin, 23 October 1862).

40 Antonovych, Tvory, 1: 53–4; Syroczyński, *O życiu*, 19–20; Syroczyński, *Z przed 50 lat*, 29–30; Święcicki, "Na gruzach," 161–2; OPDU, 132–3; Tabiś, *Polacy na uniwersytecie Kijowskim*, 132.

41 Antonovych, *Tvory*, 1: 54–5, 59; K.P. Mikhalchuk, "Iz ukrainskogo bylogo," *Ukrainskaia zhizn'*, nos. 8–10 (1914): 70–1; Poznanskii, "Vospominaniia," *Ukrainskaia zhizn'*, no. 5 (1913): 41–2; Święcicki, "Na gruzach," 160, 162; Syroczyński, *Wspomnienie*, 19; Syroczyński, *Z pred 50 lat*, 21–2; Iuzefovich, "Tridtsat' let tomu nazad," no. 10, 171, 177–80, 186–90; Pavlo Zhytets'kyi, "Z istorii Kyïvs'koï ukraïns'koï hromady: Promova na Shevchenkovyh rokovynakh," *Zapysky naukovoho tovarystva imeni Shevchenka* 116, no. 5 (1913): 178–9.

42 K.N. Rennenkampf, "Kievskaia universitetskaia starina (Sobytiia v universitete Sv. Vladimira v 1860–1862gg.)," *Russkaia starina*, no. 7 (1899): 41.

43 GARF, f. 109, 1 eksp., 1861g., ed. khr. 359, l. 15–16 (Vasilchikov's telegram to Alexander, 10 October 1861 and Dolgorukov's answer, 11 October); RGIA, f. 733, op. 147, delo 41, l. 150 (Efim Putiatin to Nikolay, 23 October 1861); l. 197 (Rector Bunge to Nicolay, 19 October 1861); "Imennaia vedomost' o studentakh imperatorskogo universiteta Sv. Vladimira na 1861–1862 uchebnyi god," *Kievskiia Universitetskiia Izvestiia*, no. 2 (1861): 2–5, 8–9, 36–7, 50–1; Iuzefovich, "Tridtsat' let," no. 11, 98–104; OPDU, 199; Poznanskii, "Vospominaniia," no. 5, 42; Rennenkampf, "Kievskaia universitetskaia," 42–5.

44 OPDU, 160–7, 170–1, 187–95, 199–202 (testimonies of Mossakovsky's students, a revolutionary poem, and his article on Sunday schools); 442, op. 811, spr. 222, ark. 11–35 (final report of the investigating commission, 12 April 1862); ark. 40–8 (Vasilchikov to Dolgorukov, 28 April 1862); ark. 55 (Dolgorukov to Vasilchikov, 6 June 1862); spr. 222a, ark. 6–11 (testimony of student Ignatii Zamochnikov, no later than 30 November 1861). Unlike his colleagues, Zamochnikov mentioned Mossakovsky's criticism of the Poles and the story of the article concerning independence. Perhaps that is why his testimony is not in OPDU, which was published in Soviet Ukraine.

45 OPDU, 279. The Polish materials found in Krasovsky's possession consisted of songs, Lelewel's short biography, and his portrait.

46 Ibid., 270 (Krasovsky's interrogation, 20 June 1862).

47 Ibid., 265–7 (complete text of Krasovsky's proclamation).

48 Ibid., 269–70 (Krasovsky's interrogation, 20 June 1862); Krasovsky was not exceptional in wearing a national dress which carried a political message. For the significance of clothes in the national movement at this time, see Serhy Yekelchyk, "The Body and National Myth: Motifs from the Ukrainian National Revival in the Nineteenth Century," *Australian Slavonic and East European Studies* 7, no. 2 (1993): 31–59.

49 OPDU, 290 (verdict of the court martial, 11 August 1862).

50 RGVIA, f. 801, op. 80/21, 3-e otd., 2-oi stol, 1862, delo 48, sv. 667, l. 200–1 (Sergeant-Major Evstigneev's testimony, 22 June 1862). At first Krasovsky gave his real name, but later offered a false one.

51 OPDU, 270.

52 Ibid., 277 (purported soldiers' letter to Krasovsky, June–July 1862).

53 RGVIA, f. 801, op. 80/21, 3-e otd., 2-oi stol, 1862, delo 48, sv. 667, l. 529–30 (medical statement by Dr Meissner, Kyiv, 13 December, 1857; French translation from the Russian original).

54 Ibid., l. 275–7, 371–5. Apart from hymns, which were used by all orientations of the Polish movement, there was a short biography of Joachim Lelewel, in which it was emphasized how he was opposed to all

estate privileges and defended the legal equality of peasants and Jews. Also found in Krasovsky's possession were the banned poems of Aleksei Khomiakov, Nikolai Nekrasov, Petr Viazemskii, Alexander Pushkin, and Pierre-Jean de Béranger.

55 RGVIA, f. 801, op. 80/21, 3-e otd. 2-oi stol, delo 48, 1862, sv. 667, l. 470–2 ("Boroda i chupryna").

56 Ibid., l. 439, 457–8, 460–1, 470–2. There was an additional text, in which the emperor and nobles were described as oppressors of the common people and soldiers.

57 Antonovych was known under this name in the 1870s. See *Arkhiv Myhaila Drahomanova* (Warsaw: Ukraïns'kyi naukovyi instytut, 1937) 428.

58 RGVIA, f. 801, op. 80/21, 3-e otd. 2-oi stol, delo 48, 1862, sv. 667, l. 502.

59 Ibid., l. 503 (*shcho narod nash ne po pravdi pid ikhnyi uriad pidharbnen shcho prava ioho teper' na svobodne rozkvichan'e, a kolys' na samostainist' zovsim spravedlyvyi*). The demand that the other Slavic nations should respect Ukraine's *samostainist'* is also expressed in l. 526 (*Samostaine slovo*, no. 1), although there it may be read not only in the sense of political independence.

60 Ibid., l. 505 (*Pryslovky i prymovky*).

61 On the basis of these facts, among others, I disagree with Faith Hillis's perception of Hromada as a Little Russian organization which advocated all-Russian identity. See Hillis, *Children of Rus'*, 61–2, 269. She claims that the editor of the newspaper *Vestnik iugozapadnoi i zapadnoi Rossii*, Ksenofont Govorskii, was a Hromada member. However, the local Russian nationalists lobbied for a government subsidy to the newspaper on the grounds that it was opposed to a Little Russian (or South Russian or Ukrainian, all three terms were used) "separate party." Valuev agreed to the subsidy. See RGIA, f. 775, op. 1, 1863g., delo 322, l. 4 (Ivan Kulzhinskii to Valuev, 3 December 1863; ibid. l. 12–13 Valuev's memorandum to Alexander II, 30 January 1864, endorsed by the latter a day later).

62 RGVIA, f. 801, op. 80/21, 3-e otd. 2-oi stol, delo 48, 1862, sv. 667, l. 526 ("Pro pohliad pol's'koho hromadnyts'koho tovarystva na Ukraïnu," *Samostaine slovo*, no. 1).

63 Ibid., l. 513–14 (*Samostaine slovo*, no. 4).

64 Ibid., l. 508 (*Samostaine slovo*, no. 4).

65 Ibid., l. 512 ("Poliakam-Rusynam," *Samostaine slovo*, no. 4); l. 520 (Aleksandr Stoianov, "Poliaki i russyny v Kievskom universitete," *Hromadnytsia*, no. 2). In this context, Stoianov expressed explicit sympathy for the Poles' struggle for liberty in the Kingdom of Poland.

66 Ibid., l. 517–18 ("Polytychnyi Ohliad," *Hromadnytsia*, no. 2).

67 Ibid., l. 526 ("Deshchytsia pro nedil'ni shkoly," *Samostaine slovo*, no. 1).
68 OPDU, 289 (verdict of the court martial, 11 August 1862); RGVIA, f. 801, op. 80/21, 3-e otd., 2-oi stol, 1862, delo 48, sv. 667, l. 126, 358–9, 448 (records of the court martial, Danylo Kamenetsky to Krasovsky, 22 January 1862). It is also possible to read the phrase *dlia moskaly* meaning that Krasovsky took the books for distribution among Russians. However, it is more likely that it refers to the soldiers.
69 GARF, f. 109, 1 eksp., op. 36, 1861, delo 69, l. 1–3 (the colonel to Dolgorukov, 9 February 1861). The only existing monograph on the Poltava Hromada is Hnip, *Hromads'kyi rukh*; see also Ivanova and Ivanchenko, *Suspil'no-politychnyi rukh*, 219–34; Pobirchenko, *Pedahohichna i prosvitnyts'ka diial'nist'*, 2: 24–63.
70 *Kyrylo-Mefodiïvs'ke tovarystvo*, 2: 501 (Andruzky's interrogation, 14 April 1847); 3: 84 (Opanas Markovych's interrogation, 3 April 1847); 3: 92, 95 (Bilozersky to Markovych, 30 August 1846 and December 1846); 3: 113–14 (Markovych's interrogation took place no later than 20 May 1847); 3: 179 (Oleksandr Tulub's interrogation, 30 March 1847). Pylchykov had lodged for some time in Mykola Kostomarov's apartment. Andruzky named him as one of the members; Pylchykov corresponded with Markovych, and Vasyl Bilozersky mentioned him favourably in his letters that were subsequently confiscated.
71 GARF, f. 109, 1 eksp., op. 36, ed. khr, 69, l. 79 (schedule of public readings sent to the Third Section with a denunciation; the general title of Pylchykov's lectures was "Russian History," but all the specifics were Ukrainian-related).
72 "Svedenie o chisle prodannykh deshevykh izdanii na ukrainskom iazyke," *Osnova*, no. 10 (1861): 155–6.
73 [Oleksandr Stronin], *Azbuka po metode Zolotova dlia Iuzhno-russkago kraia* (Poltava: V gubernskoi tipografii, 1861), 8, 15, 21.
74 Oleksandr Konyss'kyi, *Arykhmetyka abo shchotnytsia: Dlia ukrains'kykh shkil* (St Petersburg: V tipografii P.A. Kulisha, 1863), 23–4.
75 Hnip, *Hromads'kyi rukh*, 9–13, 28; D. Hrakhovets'kyi, "Pershi nedil'ni shkoly na Poltavshchyni ta ikh diiachi (1860–1862 r.r.)," *Ukraina* 29, no. 4 (1928): 52–3, 58–61, 64–9; Pobirchenko, *Pedahohichna i prosvitnyts'ka diial'nist'*, 2: 27–48, 51–2.
76 GARF, f. 109, sekr. arkh., op. 1, ed. khr. 1764, l. 1–2 (excerpt from the letter, 24 February 1861); Dudko, "Zhurnal 'Osnova,'" 14–15.
77 GARF, f. 109, sekr. arkh., op. 1, ed. khr. 1764, l. 1.
78 Ibid., l. 1, 5 (unsigned and undated remarks, possibly made by Dolgorukov); ibid., op. 36, 1861, ed. khr. 69, l. 4–5 (Dolgorukov to Belov, 5 March and 20 March 1861).

79 The two files in GARF f. 109, 1 eksp., op. 36, 1861g., ed. khr. 69, and op. 37, 1862g., ed. khr. 73, are full of reports and denunciations on the Poltava Hromada.
80 GARF, f. 109, 1 eksp., op. 36, ed. khr. 69, l. 20–4 (Volkov to the minister of internal affairs, 28 April 1861); ed. khr. 69, l. 26 (Valuev to Petr Andreevich Shuvalov, 25 May 1861). In addition to *Shel'menko,* the staging of Ostrovskii's play *Poverty Is Not a Vice* was planned.
81 Ibid., l. 55–71 (copy of Volkov's letter to the police department of the Ministry of Internal Affairs; the date is illegible, but it was written in 1861; undated anonymous gendarme report).
82 Hnip, *Hromads'kyi rukh,* 195 (full text of Volkov's letter to Dolgorukov, 10 October 1861, pp. 194–9).
83 Ibid., 50; GARF, f. 109, 1 eksp., op. 36, 1861, delo 69, l. 43 (Belov to Dolgorukov, 20 October 1861); l. 97 (Belov's telegram to Aleksandr Potapov, head of the Third Section, 15 August 1862).
84 GARF, f. 109, 1 eksp., op. 36, 1861, ed. khr. 69, l. 83–4 (the *Zapiska dlia pamiati* prepared for Dolgorukov in the Third Section, 11 June 1862); l. 89 (Valuev to Potapov, 17 July 1862); Hnip, *Hromads'kyi rukh,* 150 (records of Stronin's interrogation, 1 November 1862).
85 Hnip, *Hromads'kyi rukh,* 171 (Shevych's interrogation, 1 November 1862).
86 GARF, f. 109, 1 eksp., op. 37, 1862, ed. khr. 230, ch. 128; l. 14 (Colonel Belov to the Third Section, 4 September 1862); l. 17 (sent from Ministry of Internal Affairs, signature illegible, to Dolgorukov on 9 September 1862); l. 19 (gendarme lieutenant Serov to Dolgorukov, 11 September 1862); l. 71 (the Third Section's information about the deportations; some time in December 1862).
87 Hnip, *Hromads'kyi rukh,* 122 (Shymanov's interrogation, 1–10 December 1862); 183 (Shevych's interrogation, 27–29 November 1862; the gendarmes cited information from the letters in their questions to the arrestees).
88 Ibid., 159.
89 *Russko-pol'skie revoliutsionnye sviazi,* 2 vols. (Moscow: Izdatel'stvo Akademii Nauk SSSR, 1963), 1: 75–84; *Velikoruss,* nos. 1–3 [1861].
90 Hnip, *Hromads'kyi rukh,* 148 (Shymanov's interrogation, 1–10 December 1862).
91 Quoted in Hnip, *Hromads'kyi rukh,* 36–7.
92 Ibid., 192–3. A document entitled "Sochinenie Dogmatiko-Istoricheskoe" was discovered among Shevych's papers.
93 Mykhailo Hnip, "Do istorii hromads'koho rukhu 1860 rr. (Zapyska A. L.Shymanova)," *Za sto lit* 5 (1930): 170–82.The article includes the full text of Shymanov's presentation. Shymanov participated in the activities of the Poltava and Kharkiv Hromadas, and the presentation was written for the Kharkiv Hromada.

94 GARF, f. 109, 1 eksp., f. 109, ed. khr. 230, ch. 128, Lit. A, l. 152 (Shevych's interrogation). The gendarmes cited the contents of Shymanov's letter during their questioning of Shevych.
95 Hnip, *Hromads'kyi rukh*, 228 (Stronin to Shevych, 18 September 1861; full text of letter on pp. 228–9).
96 Ibid., 218 (Stronin to Loboda, 4 July 1862; full text of the letter on pp. 216–19); 186 (Shevych's letter to Veniamin Portugalov, 12 August 1861; at the time, Shevych expected the outbreak of a revolution in 1862).
97 Ibid., 231 (Stronin to Shevych, undated letter).
98 Ibid., 221–4 (Stronin to Loboda, undated letter).
99 Ibid., 183 (quotation); 187 (Shevych's interrogation reports, 27–29 November 1862; the gendarmes quoted from his letters during his questioning).
100 Ibid., 187.
101 Ibid., 191. The whole manuscript *Tale of Two Brothers* is on pp. 190–1.
102 Ibid., 226 (Loboda to Stronin, undated letter, but written between May and September 1862).
103 Ibid., 147 (Shymanov's interrogation).
104 Ibid., 148.
105 Ibid., 100–2 (Shymanov's interrogation, 1–6 November 1862); 170–1,186–8 (Shevych's interrogations, 1 November and 27–9 November 1862).
106 Ibid., 70–1 (Loboda's interrogation, 1 November 1862). Stronin, too, counted Zelensky among his acquaintances: ibid., 151 (his interrogation, 1 November 1862).
107 Mijakovs'kyi, *Nedrukovane i zabute*, 228, 233–4, 244–5, 335–42.
108 GARF, f. 109, 1-ia eksp., op. 37, 1862, ed. khr. 230, ch. 38, ll. 2–5 (Sivers's denunciation, 21 June 1862, and another, undated and anonymous, one; both texts are published in full in Savchenko, *Zaborona ukraïnstva*, 183–5; Savchenko finds that the anonymous denunciation was also written by Sivers); see also Miller, *The Ukrainian Question*, 97. Both Savchenko and Miller emphasize the importance of this correspondence to the enactment of the Valuev circular.
109 GARF, f. 109, 1-ia eksp., op. 37, 1862, ed. khr. 230, ch. 38, l. 13–16 (Colonel Belov to Dolgorukov, 28 July 1862, and Lieutenant Vasilev to Dolgorukov, 20 September 1862); Savchenko, *Zaborona ukraïnstva*, 186–8.
110 GARF, f. 109, 1-ia eksp., op. 37, 1862, ed. khr. 230, ch. 38, l. 17–23 (Valuev to Dolgorukov, 6 October 1862; the letter includes a copy of the records of the secret police investigation).
111 Ibid., l. 24–6 (Belov to Dolgorukov, 7 September 1862); the proclamation is published in full in Mijakovs'kyi, *Nedrukovane i zabute*, 244–5 and Savchenko, *Zaborona ukrainstva*, 350–1. Hillis, *Children of Rus'*, 64 is

mistaken when stating that Chubynsky instigated peasants on the Right Bank to rise against Polish nobles. He was active on the Left Bank.

112 Savchenko, *Zaborona ukraïnstva*, 190. Savchenko did not pass definite judgment on the question, leaving the resolution up to future researchers.

113 Franco Venturi, *Roots of Revolution: A History of the Populist and Socialist Movements in Nineteenth Century Russia*, trans. Francis Haskell (London: Weidenfeld and Nicolson, 1960), 300–1.

114 GARF, f. 109, 1-ia eksp., op. 37, ed. khr. 230, ch. 38, l. 29 (Golitsyn to Dolgorukov, 29 October 1862).

115 TsDIA Uk., f. 442, op. 812, od. zb. 166, ark. 1–7 (Volkov's letter to Vasilchikov, dated 22 September 1862, arrived on 26 September).

116 GARF, f. 112, op. 1, 1863, delo 72, l. 283–4 (letter from a member of the Kyiv Hromada to Stepan Nis, illegible signature, dated 3 December 1862; it is also possible that the anonymous civil servant who brought the news acted on his own initiative).

117 The Kingdom of Poland used the Gregorian calendar, unlike Russia proper, which followed the Julian calendar.

118 Beiersdorf, "Kijów w powstaniu," 106–7.

119 Mijakovs'kyj, *Nedrukovane i zabute*, 246–7 (complete text of the Golden Decree).

120 Beiersdorf, "Kijów w powstaniu," 105–6.

121 GARF, f. 109, 1-ia eksp., op. 37, 1862, ed. khr. 230, ch. 38, l. 41 (Dolgorukov to Annenkov, 28 January 1863).

122 Ibid., l. 42–4 (denunciation, 2 March 1863, and Dolgorukov to Annenkov, 4 March 1863).

123 Cf. Miller, *The Ukrainian Question*, 98–9. According to Miller, Dolgorukov was more concerned about the social rather than the national aspect of Hromada activities. "Dolgorukov provided Annenkov with no tangible compromising evidence, thus excluding the menace of police persecution." Considering Chubynsky's recent deportation and the arrest of Volodymyr Syniehub shortly afterwards, Miller's statement runs counter to the facts.

124 GARF, f. 109, 1-ia eksp., op. 37, 1862, ed. khr. 230, ch. 38, l. 45–7.

125 Ibid., l. 55–7.

126 TsDIA Uk., f. 442, op. 813, od. zb. 541, ark. 156–86 (report of the Kyiv investigating commission, 22 March 1865; it includes Pylypenko and Syniehub's confessions following their arrest in 1863; the whole report is on ark. 156–309).

127 Bohdan Klid, "Songwriting and Singing: Ukrainian Revolutionary and Not So Revolutionary Activities in the 1860s," *Journal of Ukrainian Studies* 33/34 (Summer 2008–Winter 2009): 263–77.

128 TsDIA Uk., f. 442, op. 813, od. zb. 541, ark. 215–17 (report of the investigating commission, including extensive quotations from Syniehub and Pylypenko's letters to Volkov).

129 Ibid., ark. 127, 129–30 (the complete text of Bezak's letter to Dolgorukov, dated 6 August 1865, is on ark. 126–31).

130 Ibid., ark. 135–46 (the Third Section's Nikolai Mezentsov to Bezak, 4 September 1865; the letter contains a list of names); ark. 327–30 (Bezak to Petr Aleksandrovich Shuvalov, head of the Third Section, 25 May 1866); ark. 332 (Shuvalov to Bezak, 5 June 1866); ark. 337 (Valuev to Bezak, 16 June 1866). The presence of 127 names in the list does not mean that the authorities intended to repress so many people. Such lists were often compiled during the investigations and trials of individuals accused of political crimes. They included anyone who might be questioned. Not every person on such a list was actually interrogated, and the number of people who were in any way repressed was usually less than half of the number of names on the list.

131 Miller, *The Ukrainian Question*, 100–2.

132 There is a wealth of literature on the subject of Russian-Polish revolutionary cooperation. See, e.g., V.A. D'iakov, ed., *Vosstanie 1863g. i russko-pol'skie revoliutsionnye sviazi 60-kh godov: Sbornik statei i materialov* (Moscow: Izdatel'stvo Akademii Nauk SSSR, 1962); I.D. Koroliuk and I.S. Miller, eds., *Vosstanie 1863g. i russko-pol'skie revoliutsionnye sviazi 60-kh godov* (Moscow: Izdatel'stvo Akademii Nauk SSSR, 1960); *Vosstanie 1863 goda: materialy i dokumenty: Russko-pol'skie revoliutsionye sviazi*, 2 vols. (Moscow: Izdatel'stvo Akademii Nauk SSSR, 1963). Although biased, the emphasis on Russian-Polish revolutionary cooperation produced impressive, positive results in the series of documentary publications on the insurrection: *Vosstanie 1863 goda: Materialy i dokumenty*, the fruit of Soviet-Polish scholarly collaboration.

133 See, e.g., G.I. Marakhov, *Sotsial'no-politicheskaia bor'ba na Ukraine v 50–60-e gody XIX veka* (Kyiv: Vyshcha shkola, 1981).

134 Miller, *The Ukrainian Question*, 106, 160; A.M. Katrenko, *Ukraïns'kyi natsional'nyi rukh XIX st.*, pt. 2, *60–90-ti roky XIX st.* (Kyiv: Kyïvs'kyi natsional'nyi universytet im. Tarasa Shevchenka, 1999), 43; Ivanova and Ivanchenko, *Suspil'no politychnyi rukh*, 182, 196–9. Ivanova and Ivanchenko explicitly mention that Syniehub later retracted his testimonies. Nevertheless, they still consider that the testimonies show him to be a revolutionary, and they accept at face value the information on the political contacts between Krasovsky and Syniehub. Miller accepts as fact Syniehub's revolutionary contacts with Krasovsky, noting,

however, that the authorities later deemed Syniehub's first testimonies not entirely trustworthy.

135 Olga Andriewsky, "The Russian-Ukrainian Discourse and the Failure of the 'Little Russian Solution,' 1782–1917," in *Culture, Nation and Identity: The Ukrainian-Russian Encounter (1600–1945)*, ed. Andreas Kappeler, Zenon E. Kohut, Frank E. Sysyn, and Mark von Hagen (Edmonton: CIUS Press, 2003), 212.

136 For general information on this group, see Mikhail Lemke, *Politicheskie protsessy v Rossii 1860-kh gg. (po arkhivnym dokumentam)*, 2d ed. (Moscow; Petrograd: Gosudarstvennoe izdatel'stvo, 1923), 3–54. *Politicheskie protsessy 60-kh g.g.*, ed. B. P. Koz'min (Moscow; Petrograd: Gosudarstvennoe izdatel'stvo, 1922), 138–269.

137 *Politicheskie protsessy 60-kh*, 206–8 (Aleksandr Novikov to Pericles Argiropoulos, 28 April [probably 1861], Kharkiv).

138 Lemke, *Politicheskie protsessy*, 5; *Politicheskie protsessy 60-kh*, 206, 208. The authorities found parts of the following poems: "Kavkaz," "I mertvym, i zhyvym," "Ieretyk," "Kholodnyi iar," "Dumka," and "Markevychu."

139 Lemke, *Politicheskie protsessy*, 6, 23–4, 35, 46–7; *Politicheskie protsessy 60-kh*, 206–8.

140 *Politicheskie protsessy 60-kh*, 216–18.

141 Lemke, *Politicheskie protsessy*, 28, 49; *Politicheskie protsessy 60-kh*, 219–22.

142 GARF, f. 112. op. 1, ed. khr. 72, l. 490 (Ivan Andrushchenko's interrogation, 27 August 1863); f. 112, op. 1, ed. khr. 73, l. 364 (Ievhen Andrushchenko's interrogation, 6–7 October 1863).

143 Lemke, *Politicheskie protsessy*, 46–7, 50, 52–3.

144 GARF, f. 112, op. 1. ed. khr. 72, l. 571–2 (copy from Chernihiv governor Golitsyn's report to the Ministry of Internal Affairs, 6 February 1863).

145 Ibid., l. 569–70 (quotation on p. 570; copy from Shulgovskii's report to the Third Section, 12 January 1863).

146 Ibid., l. 571–2 (copy from Golitsyn's report to the Ministry of Internal Affairs, 6 February 1863).

147 *Vosstanie 1863 goda: Materialy i dokumenty: Russko-pol'skie revoliutsionnye sviazi*, 2: 130–44 (Andrushchenko's interrogation, 7–12 September 1863); GARF, f. 112, op. 1, ed.khr. 72, l. 477–91(Andrushchenko's interrogation, 27 August 1863); B. Bazilevskii, *Materialy dlia istorii revoliutsionnago dvizheniia v Rossii v 60-kh gg.* Zhurnal Russkaia Istoricheskaia Biblioteka, no. 2 (St Petersburg: Izd. B. Bazilevskago, 1906), 81–9 (the Senate's summary of Andrushchenko's involvement).

148 GARF, f. 112, op. 1, ed. khr. 72, l. 139–401.

149 Ibid., l. 139–42 (Iefymenko to Andrushchenko, 6 February (*Studnia)* 1860 and 5 January 1861).
150 This quotation and the next one, ibid., l. 162 (Iefymenko to "Ivan Alekseevich" in Pereiaslav, undated, but most likely 1861; the full text of the letter is on l. 159–62).
151 Ibid., l. 184–5 (Il'ia Derkach to Andrushchenko, 21 July 1860).
152 Borys Sheveliv, "L.I. Hlibov i tyzhnevyk 'Chernigovskii listok' u protsesi S. Nosa, I. Andrushchenka ta insh. 1863–1868 rr.," in *Za sto lit* 4 (Kyiv: Istorychna sektsiia Vseukraïns'koï Akademiï Nauk, 1929), 25–40.
153 GARF, f. 112, op. 1, ed. khr. 72, l. 368. It has not been possible to identify the author of the letter sent to Nis on 13 October 1862. Judging by the contents of the letter, he was a member of the Kyiv Hromada. He mentions independence as a desirable goal whose achievement, however, is unlikely.
154 Ibid., l. 12–15 (Vorzer, commander of the Chernihiv Battalion, to Alexander II, 13 July 1863); *Materialy dlia istorii*, 81–2, 121–9 (the Senate's summaries concerning Andrushchenko, Oleksandr Bilozersky, Oleksandr Tyshchynsky, and Nis).
155 Ibid., l. 447–64 (documents concerning Andrushchenko's intercepted letters, including the original letters; the civilian governor of Chernihiv sent them to the St Petersburg investigating commission on 5 August 1863); *Materialy dlia istorii*, 82–3.
156 GARF, f. 112, op. 1, ed. khr. 72, l. 83 (Vasyl Bilozersky to Oleksandr Bilozersky, 12 November 1862); Dudko, "Zhurnal 'Osnova,'" 36–40.
157 GARF, f. 112, op. 1, ed. Khr. 72, l. 83.
158 Stefan Kieniewicz, *Powstanie styczniowe* (Warsaw: Państwowe Wydawnictwo Naukowe, 1972), 336–7, 403.
159 Venturi, *Roots of Revolution*, 303–15.
160 Kieniewicz, *Powstanie*, 463.
161 GARF, f. 112, op. 1, ed. khr. 73, l. 159 (Vasyl Bilozersky's interrogation, 25 September 1863). The grammatical form of the fragment of the letter that was quoted during the interrogation indicates that it was sent to Vasyl Bilozersky, not to his wife, to be forwarded to Kieniewicz; Dudko, "Zhurnal 'Osnova,'" 40 mentions shortly this letter.
162 Ibid., l. 177 (Vasyl Bilozersky's addendum to his testimony, 27 September 1863).
163 *Materialy dlia istorii*, 124–5.
164 Ibid., 125–6.
165 GARF, f. 112, op. 1, ed. khr. 73, l. 279–86 (Rechytsky's interrogation, 10 October 1863); *Materialy dlia istorii*, 118.

166 *Materialy dlia istorii*, 120.

167 GARF, f. 112, op. 1, ed. khr. 73, l. 237–8 (record of the house search in Kozlovs'ky's apartment, 26 September 1863); 239–42 (the lists of names, which contain 139 names, though many occur twice or several times).

168 *Materialy dlia istorii*, 129–30; Driha may be identified as a Ukrainophile since he appears on Kozlovetsky's list of donors to the Ukrainian publishing cause. See GARF, f. 112, op. 1, ed. khr. 73, l. 239–42.

169 *Materialy dlia istorii*, 120–1.

170 GARF, f. 112, op. 1, ed. khr. 73, l. 16–23 (Maslokovets's interrogation, 16–17 September 1863).

171 *Materialy dlia istorii*, 123–4.

172 Ibid., l. 203–5 (Iefymenko's two letters to Tyshchynsky, one undated and the other bearing the date of 10 July 1863).

173 Ivan Andrushchenko, Ievhen Andrushchenko, Ivan Maslokovets, Kostiantyn Kozlovsky, Ivan Rechytsky, Ivan Driha, Oleksandr Tyshchynsky, Stepan Nis, and Petro Iefymenko.

174 GARF, f. 109, 1 eksp., op. 38, 1863, ed. khr. 97, ch. 70, prodolzhenie, l. 124 (decision to release Nis from exile handed down by the head of the Third Section, 8 May 1871).

175 Poznanskii, "Vospominaniia," no. 5, 46.

176 Klid, "Volodymyr Antonovych," 114–15.

177 GARF, f. 112, op. 1, ed. khr. 72, l. 292–3 (Stoianov to Nis, 29 May 1863); l. 294–5 (Hravovsky to Nis, 4 May 1863).

178 *Dokumenty komitetu centralnego narodowego i rządu narodowego 1862–1864* (Wrocław: Wydawnictwo Zakładu im. Ossolińskich, 1968), 327–38.

179 Kieniewicz, *Powstanie styczniowe*, 702.

180 *Dokumenty komitetu centralnego*, 327.

181 Ibid., 328, 330.

182 Orthography of the original retained: the National Government wrote about Rusins, not Rusyns.

183 *Dokumenty komitetu centralnego*, 328–9.

184 Ibid., 329.

185 Ibid.

186 Ibid.

187 Ibid., 330.

188 Ibid., 336.

189 TsDIA Uk, f. 442, op. 811, od. zb. 91, ark. 156 (Hesse, governor of Kyiv, to Vasilchikov, 16 May 1861).

6 Imperial Policies and the Ukrainian Movement, 1863–76

1 Miller, *Ukrainian Question*, 264 (complete text of the circular in Olga Poato's English translation is on pp. 263–4, the Russian original, on pp. 265–6).
2 Ibid., 107–9.
3 Savchenko, *Zaborona ukraïnstva*, 183–93.
4 Saunders, "Russia and Ukraine under Alexander II," 23–50; David Saunders, "Russia's Ukrainian Policy (1847–1905): A Demographic Approach," *European History Quarterly* 25, no. 2 (April 1995): 181–208; Saunders, "Mikhail Katkov and Mykola Kostomarov: A Note on Petr A. Valuev's Anti-Ukrainian Edict of 1863," *Harvard Ukrainian Studies* 17, nos. 3–4 (December 1993): 365–83.
5 Witold Rodkiewicz, *Russian Nationality Policy in the Western Provinces of the Empire (1863–1905)* (Lublin: Scientific Society of Lublin, 1998), 192, 197–202.
6 Miller, *Ukrainian Question*, 109.
7 Vulpius, *Nationalisierung der Religion*, 127–35.
8 Andrii Danylenko, "The Ukrainian Bible and the Valuev Circular of July 18, 1863," *Acta Slavica Iaponica* 28 (2010): 1–21.
9 Iurii Zel'dich, *Petr Aleksandrovich Valuev i ego vremia:Istoricheskoe povestvovanie* (Moscow: Agraf, 2006), 333. Zel'dich writes about Valuev's political career, including the censorship reform, without mentioning the Valuev circular; Charles Ruud, *Fighting Words: Imperial Censorship and the Russian Press, 1804–1906* (Toronto: University of Toronto Press, 1982), 137, also mentions Valuev's wish to "secure effective means to limit periodicals that obeyed the letter but not the spirit of the law."
10 Saunders, "Russia's Ukrainian Policy," 184–5.
11 Zel'dich, *Petr Aleksandrovich Valuev*, 245–50.
12 Darius Staliūnas, *Making Russians: Meaning and Practice of Russification in Lithuania and Belarus after 1863* (Amsterdam: Rodopi, 2007), 72, 93, 103, 111, 119, 139–42, 150–1, 192, 278, 299.
13 Saunders, "Russia and Ukraine," 24.
14 Kristiina Kalleinen, *Suomen kenraalikuvernementti: Kenraalikuvernöörien asema ja merkitys Suomen asioiden esittelyssä* (Helsinki: Painatuskeskus, 1994), 205–6; *Sbornik postanovlenii i razporiazhenii po tsenzure s 1720 po 1862 god.* (St Petersburg: V tipografii morskago ministerstva, 1862), 264.
15 Stephen Velychenko has emphasized how censors were generally inclined to allow Ukrainian intellectuals to discuss among themselves ideas that were forbidden in publications aimed at a broader audience. See his article "'Tsarist Censorship' and Ukrainian Historiography, 1828–1906,' *Canadian-American Slavic Studies* 23, no. 4 (Winter 1989): 393–5, 401–3.

16 RGIA, f. 773, op. 1, delo 40, l. 17 (Valuev to Aleksandr Golovnin, 18 July 1862). Valuev wanted to permit religious literature in Yiddish. The background of the discussion was the launching of the Yiddish newspaper *Kol Mevaser* in Odesa. See David E. Fishman, "The Politics of Yiddish in Tsarist Russia," in *From Ancient Israel to Modern Judaism: Intellect in Quest for Understanding: Essays in Honor of Marvin Fox*, ed. Jacob Neusner, Ernest S. Frerichs, and Nahum M. Sarna, 4 vols. (Atlanta, GA: Scholars Press, 1989), 4: 159–60. The plan to ban Yiddish publications, but not Valuev's position on this issue, is discussed in Theodore R. Weeks, "Jidiš il lietuvių kalbos Rusijos imperijoje: Politia dviejų 'uždraustų kalbų' atžvilgiu 1863–1913 m.," in *Raidzių draudimo metai: Straipsnių rinkinys*, ed. Darius Staliunas (Vilnius: LII Leidykla, 2004), 175–90. I am familiar with the article in the English manuscript version.

17 RGIA, f. 773, op. 1, delo 40, l. 20–1 (Golovnin to Valuev, 25 July 1862); Valuev was not alone in his hostility to Yiddish. In 1866, Governor-General of Vilna (Vilnius) Kaufman proposed the banning of Yiddish publications. However, Kaufman wanted to prevent Jews from adopting German through Yiddish, a prospect which Valuev found desirable. After 1868, that is, after Valuev's tenure as the minister of internal affairs, very few books in Yiddish were authorized to publication. See Staliūnas, *Making Russians*, 211–14.

18 For discussion of the relations between the two ministries and the background to the transfer of censorship to the Ministry of Internal Affairs, see Aleksandr Mikhailovich Skabichevskii, *Ocherki istorii russkoi tsenzury (1700–1863 g.)* (St Petersburg: F. Pavlenkov, 1892), 462–4, 471–495. The Ministry of Public Enlightenment was deemed too close to literature and too positively attuned to it to retain its responsibility over censorship. Skabichevskii ends his work at this milestone in the history of Russian censorship. See also Ruud, *Fighting Words*, 118–36.

19 Miller, *Ukrainian Question*, 264 (English translation of the circular).

20 *Svod zakonov Rossiiskoi imperii, izdanie 1857 goda*, 15 vols. (St Petersburg: Tipografiia Vtorogo Otdeleniia Sobstvennoi Ego Imperatorskogo Velichestva Kantseliarii, 1857), bk. 1, pt. 1, no. 50, p. 12. Hereafter referred to as *SZ*. See also Nikolai Eroshkin, *Istoriia gosudarstvennykh uchrezhdenii Rossii*, 3rd rev. exp. ed.(Moscow: Vysshaia shkola, 1983), 144–5, 197–8; George L. Yaney, *The Systematization of Russian Government: Social Evolution in the Domestic Administration of Imperial Russia, 1711–1905* (Urbana: University of Illinois Press, 1973), 250–6.

21 *SZ*, bk. 1, pt. 2, Uchrezhdenie komiteta ministrov, no. 12, p. 3; Eroshkin, *Istoria gosudarstvennykh uchrezhdenii*, 145–6.

22 Vulpius, *Nationalisierung* 128.
23 Staliūnas, *Making Russians*, 52–4.
24 RGIA, f. 773, op. 1, delo 40, l. 20–1 (Golovnin to Valuev, 25 July 1862).
25 Miller, *Ukrainian Question*, 109–10.
26 Ibid., 109–12 (the quotation appears on p. 111).
27 RGIA, f. 775, op. 1, 1863, delo 188 (*O tsenzirovanii knig izdavaemykh dlia naroda na Malorossiiskom narechii*); ibid., f. 772, op. 1, delo 5992 (records of Kyiv Censorship Committee for the year 1862, including the lists of all submitted manuscripts for January–May and all permitted books for the whole year; since the file includes records of the sessions even for the period from June to December, it is unlikely that they omit any rejected manuscripts.
28 Jonathan W. Daly, "On the Significance of Emergency Legislation in Late Imperial Russia," *Slavic Review* 54, no. 3 (1995): 602–8.
29 *Polnoe sobranie zakonov Rossiiskoi Imperii, sobranie vtoroe*, 55 vols. (St Petersburg: V tipografii II otdelenia Sobstvennoi E. I. V. kantseliarii, 1830–84), bk. 40, pt. 1, 1865, no. 41988, p. 396. Hereafter referred to as II *PSZ*.
30 Valentina Grigor'evna Chernukha, *Pravitel'stvennaia politika v otnoshenii pechati: 60–70-e gody XIX veka* (Leningrad: Nauka, Leningradskoe otdelenie, 1989), 66–7.
31 Miller, *Ukrainian Question*, 98–109.
32 Yaney, *Systematization of Russian Government*, 261–4, 267–9, 292–4.
33 Mikhail Lemke, *Epokha tsenzurnykh reform 1859–1865 godov* (St Petersburg: Knigoizdatel'stvo M.V. Pirozhkova, 1904), 268–9; Miller, *Ukrainian Question*, 117, mentions Golovnin's position.
34 RGIA, f. 775, op. 1, 1863, delo 188, l. 18 (Dolgorukov to Valuev, 24 July 1863); Miller, *Ukrainian Question*, 118.
35 GARF, f. 109, 1-ia eksp., op. 37, 1862, ed. khr. 230, l. 74 (Valuev to Dolgorukov, 21 July 1863); Vulpius, *Nationalisierung der Religion*, 133–34.
36 RGIA, f. 775, op. 1, 1863, delo 188, l. 19–26 (Akhmatov to Valuev, 24 December 1864).
37 Ibid., l. 20.
38 Serhy Yekelchyk, "The Nation's Clothes: Constructing a Ukrainian High Culture in the Russian Empire, 1860–1900," in *Jahrbücher für Geschichte Osteuropas*, neue folge, vol. 49, no. 2 (2001): 230–9 emphasizes how the restrictions on Ukrainian cultural work made all such work political. Akhmetov's opinion is a good illustration of this point.
39 RGIA, f. 775, op. 1, 1863g., delo 188, l. 23. Cf. Miller, *Ukrainian Question*, 110: "In all probability both Akhmatov and the censors thought that the suppression of the Polish uprising had abolished the 'political circumstances' that Valuev had mentioned in his letter to the tsar." To back his interpretation of Akhmatov's position, Miller refers to this same document.

40 Lemke, *Epokha tsenzurnykh reform*, 268.
41 RGIA, f. 775, op. 1, 1863, delo 188, l. 27–31 (Turunov's submission to Valuev with two drafts of the letter to Sergei Urusov, head of the second section of the imperial chancellery; one of the drafts is dated March, the other April 1865, with no specific date mentioned).
42 Ibid., l. 27.
43 Ibid.
44 On the controversy concerning "temporary regulations," see Ruud, *Fighting Words*, 140–7.
45 RGIA, f. 775, op. 1, 1863, delo 188, l. 27 (*G. Ministr izvolil prikazat' prekratit' dal'neishee proizvodstvo nastoiashchago dela*); Miller, *Ukrainian Question*, 110 mentions Turunov's proposal and interprets it as an attempt to soften policies regarding Ukrainian publications. However, he does not mention the final outcome of the proposal.
46 *Ukraïnomovna knyha*, 1: 36–97. This number also includes bilingual books in both Ukrainian and Russian; cf. Miller, *Ukrainian Question*, 135–6. Miller, too, mentions the devastating effect of the government policy on Ukrainian publishing.
47 Saunders, "Russia and Ukraine," 24; Rodkiewicz, *Russian Nationality Policy*, 199, agrees with Saunders, claiming that the authorities were indifferent to such literature in Ukrainian, which was aimed at the educated classes of society.
48 RGIA, f. 775, op. 1, 1863, delo 205, l. 1–2 (Kostomarov to Valuev, 23 July 1863).
49 I[van] Levyts'kyi, *Tatary i Lytva na Ukraïni* (Kyiv: Tipografia S.T. Eremeeva, 1876), 24; Fortunat Piskunov, *Slovnytsia ukraïns'koï (abo Iuhovoï-Rus'koï) movy* (Odesa: E.P. Raspopov, 1873), iv.
50 Ostap Sereda, "'Whom Shall We Be?': Public Debates over the National Identity of Galician Ruthenians in the 1860s," *Jahrbücher für Geschichte Osteuropas* 49 (2001): H 2, 200–11.
51 II *PSZ*, XL/1, 1865, no. 41988 and 41990, 396–406.
52 II *PSZ*, XLVII/1, 1872, no. 50958, 815–17.
53 Iason Blons'kyi, *Korotkyi vyklad iz ustava 20 noiabria 1864 hoda ob uholovnim sudi dlia iuzhno-rus'kykh krestian* (Katerynoslav: Druk. Ia. Chausskoho, 1866).
54 RGIA, f. 775, op. 3, delo 284, l. 24 (Shcherbinin's letter, 8 August 1866).
55 GARF, f. 109, 1-ia eksp., op. 37, 1862, ed. khr. 230, ch. 24, l. 4–8, 11–12, 18, 29, 47–50 (correspondence of Third Section concerning the Ballins, July–September 1862).
56 GARF, f. 109, 1-ia eksp., op. 37, 1862, ed. khr. 230, ch. 24, l. 110–11 (Mezentsov from the Third Section to von Mesenkampf, the gendarme officer in Kharkiv, 7 May 1865).

57 Ibid., l. 115 (Valuev to Mezentsov, 20 June 1865).

58 Ibid., l. 119–20 (Valuev to Mezentsov, 22 July 1865). The other arguments were: nothing was found during the house search; the Ballins had not been found guilty of subversive activities; and the books were not read in the library, but were loaned out. Valuev mentioned only the sale of Ukrainian books, and his letter does not indicate whether lending them was banned as well.

59 Quoted in Olena Nadtochii, *Rosiis'ka tsenzura i vydannia tvoriv Tarasa Shevchenka (1861–1916 rr.)* (Cherkasy: Brama, 2006), 30.The case pertaining to this book is discussed on pp. 29–32.

60 Vasyl' Ulianovs'kyi and Viktor Korotkyi, *Volodymyr Antonovych: Obraz na tli epokhy* (Kyiv: TOV "Mizhnarodna finansova ahentsiia,"1997), 55, 88–9.

61 Vladimir Antonovich [Volodymyr Antonovych], "Soderzhanie aktov o kozakakh 1500–1648 god," in *Arkhiv Iugo-Zapadnoi Rossii, izdavaemyi vremennoiu komissieiu dlia razbora drevnikh aktov, vysochaishe utverzhdennoiu pri Kievskom Voennom, Podol'skom i Volynskom general-gubernatore* 3, book 1 (1863), 116. As was customary in the commission's publications, Antonovych's introduction to the documents was long enough to form an entire monograph. For his general perception of the Cossack wars, see also 22–4, 45–6, 119; Klid, *Volodymyr Antonovych*, 203–26.

62 Antonovich,"Soderzhanie aktov," 46.

63 Ulianovs'kyi and Korotkyi, *Volodymyr Antonovych*, 55.

64 Aleksandr [Oleksandr] Potebnia, *Dva issledovaniia o zvukakh russkogo iazyka: O polnoglasii i o zvukovykh osobennostiakh russkikh narechii* (Voronezh: Tipografiia V. Gol'dshteina, 1866), 138–40.

65 TsDIA Uk., f. 442, op. 813, od. zb. 541, ark. 132 (Bezak to Dolgorukov, 6 August 1865).

66 Ibid., ark. 144–5 (undated and unsigned copy of the submission to Alexander II. Since it outlines Bezak's ideas, expressed in his letter to Dolgorukov, the latter is most likely the author. For Bezak's anti-Polish policy and nomination of Ukrainophiles as Arbitrators of Peace, see Valentyna Shandra, *Heneral-Hubernatorstva v Ukraïni: XIX–pochatok XX st.* (Kyiv: Institut istoriï Ukraïny NAN Ukraïny, 2005), 299–304.

67 Isai Zaslavs'kyi, "Kalenyk Sheikovs'kyi – etnohraf, folkloryst, movoznavets', vydavets'," *Kyïvs'ka starovyna*, nos. 1– 2 (January–April 1997) (315): 86–100.

68 K.V. Sheikovs'kyi, *Shcho take Ibn-Dastova "Rus'"* (Kyiv: K.V. Sheikovs'kyi, drukarnia E. Ia. Fedorova, 1870).

69 *De-shcho pro svit Bozhyi*, 2nd ed. (Kyiv: Drukarnia Fedorova, 1871).

70 *De-shcho pro svit Bozhyi*, Koshtom K. Hurta (Kyiv: V drukarni Miniatova i Fedorova, 1863).

71 Piskunov, *Slovnytsia*, 14–16, 30, 34, 51, 53–5, 64, 78, 96–7, 101, 106–7, 141.

72 *Ukraïnomovna knyha*, 1: 74–97.
73 *De-shcho pro svit Bozhyi*, 3rd ed. (Ades: Drukarnia A. Byrukova, 1874); N. Horbunov, *Shcho robytsia u vozdusi i shcho z toho treba znaty zemlerobu. Pereklad na ukraïns'ku movu Y. M.R.* (Kyiv: V tipografii gazety "Kievskii Telegraf," 1875); A. Ivanov, *Rozmova pro nebo ta zemliu. Zde-iakymy odminamy i dodatkamy. Pereklav na ukraïns'ku movu M. Komarov* (Kyiv: Tipografia M. P. Fritsa, 1874); Ivanov, *Rozmova pro zemni syly. Z de-iakymy dodatkamy ta odminamy pereklav na ukraïns'kumovu M. Komarov, knyzhka druha. (z maliunkamy)* (Kyiv: Tipografia M.P. Fritsa, 1875).
74 [Khvedir Vovk], *Pro zviriv: (Po Bremu). Zlozhyv Iastrubets'. Mniasoïdy abo khyzhi zviri 1. Vedmedi* (Kyiv: Tipografia M.P. Fritsa, 1876).
75 M. Drahomanov, *Pro ukraïns'kykh kozakiv, tatar ta turkiv* (Kyiv: Tyskarnia V.I. Davydenko, 1876); I. Levyts'kyi, *Pershi kyïvs'ki kniazi Oleh, Yhor, Sviatoslav i sviatyi Volodymyr i eho potomky* (Kyiv: Tipografia M.P. Fritsa, 1876); Levyts'kyi, *Tatary*; Levyts'kyi, *Unia i Petro Mohyla Kyïvs'kyi Mytropolit* (Kyiv: Tipografia M.P. Fritsa, 1875).
76 Levyts'kyi, *Unia* 26. For discussion of the Union in nineteenth-century Ukrainian historiography, see Velychenko, *National History*, 198–204.
77 See Theodore R. Weeks, "Between Rome and Tsargrad: The Uniate Church in Imperial Russia," in Robert P. Geraci and Michael Khodarkovsky, eds., *Of Religion and Empire: Missions, Conversion, and Tolerance in Tsarist Russia* (Ithaca, London: Cornell University Press, 2001), 77–87.
78 [Stepan Nis], *Pro khvoroby: Iak ïm zapomohty* (Kyiv: Tipografia M.P. Fritsa, 1874), 27–32.
79 Vikhtur Shcherbatyi [pseudonym], *Pro hroshi* (Kyiv: Tipografia M. P. Fritsa, 1874). This work purports to be a translation from the Russian, but the original work is not identified.
80 Miller, *Ukrainian Question*, 155–62; Savchenko, *Zaborona ukraïnstva*, 5–6, 13–64, 75–89, 140–54.
81 RGIA, f. 776, op. 11, 1872, delo 70, l. 2 (Andrássy to the Russian ambassador in Vienna, 14 April 1872).
82 See David MacKenzie, "Russia's Balkan Policies under Alexander II, 1855–1881," in *Imperial Russian Foreign Policy*, ed. and trans. Hugh Ragsdale, asst. ed. Valerii Nikolaevich Ponomarev ([Washington, DC]: Woodrow Wilson Center Press; Cambridge, New York: Cambridge University Press, 1993), 219–46.
83 RGIA, f. 776, op. 11, 1872, delo 70, l. 1 (Deputy Minister of Foreign Affairs Vladimir Vestman to Timashev).
84 Ibid., l. 4–5. Quoted in the report of the Committee of Foreign Censorship to the Main Administration of the Press, 19 May 1872.
85 Ibid., l. 5 (Committee of Foreign Censorship to the Main Administration of the Press, 19 May 1872).

86 Ibid., l. 7 (Timashev to Vestman, 11 July 1872).
87 RGIA, f. 776, op. 11, 1872, delo 80, l. 93.
88 Saunders, "Russia's Ukrainian Policy," 182.
89 RGIA, f. 776, op. 11, 1875, delo 65 (*O broshiure na Malorossiiskom iazike Sheikovskogo "Budivlia Svita"*; Zaslavs'kyi, "Kalynyk Sheikovs'kyi," 94, mentions this case briefly).
90 Ibid., l. 1–2 (censor of Vilnius to the Main Administration of the Press, 27 May 1875).
91 Ibid., l. 11–12 (Sheikovs'kyi to the Main Administration of the Press, 3 June 1875).
92 Ibid., l. 8–9 (Shuiskii, interim public prosecutor in Minsk, to the Main Administration of the Press, 21 October and 8 December 1875).
93 Ibid., op. 2, delo 16, l. 21–4 (minutes of the council meeting on 13 January 1876; ministerial endorsement dated 30 January).
94 Ibid., op. 11, 1875, delo 65, l. 26. The complete text of the memorandum is on l. 25–8.
95 Ibid., l. 26–7.
96 Ibid., l. 27.
97 *Ukraïnomovna knyha*, 1: 61–97.
98 Nataliia Pobirchenko, *Korotkyi biohraficheskyi slovnyk chleniv Kyïvs'koï staroï hromady (druha polovyna XIX–pochatok XX stolittia)* (Kyiv: Intelekt, 1999), 54–5; *Pro parovu mashynu* (1875), *Pro bidnist'* (1875), *Pro khliborobstvo* (1875), *Pro bahatstvo ta bidnist'* (1876).
99 RGIA, f. 776, op. 11, 1875, delo 65, l. 29 (excerpt from the minutes of meeting of Committee of Ministers, 4 May 1876).
100 On the events that preceded the Ems Decree, see Miller, *Ukrainian Question*, 179–86 and chapter 7 of this book.
101 RGIA, f. 776, op. 11, 1875, delo 65, l. 31–2 (governor of Minsk to Main Administration of the Press, 5 June 1876).
102 *Ukraïnomovna knyha*, 1: 74–97.
103 Shandra, *Heneral-Hubernatorstva*, 304–15. Although Dondukov-Korsakov was comparatively soft on Poles and Ukrainians, his policies included anti-Semitist aspects, e.g., the continuation and expansion of discrimination against Jews.
104 RGIA, f. 776, op. 11, 1872, delo 80, l. 97 (excerpt from Puzyrevskii's report on his activities in 1874).
105 For the unwritten rules regarding the Polish question, see Rodkiewicz, *Russian Nationality Policy*, 166–7.
106 Miller, *Ukrainian Question*, 158–9, 161–9; Savchenko, *Zaborona ukraïnstva*, 57, 62–8.
107 "Sovremennoe ukrainofil'stvo," *Russkii vestnik* 115, no. 2 (1875): 838–41.

108 RGIA,f. 776, op. 11, 1875, delo 44, l. 4 (Grigor'ev to Puzyrevskii, 7 March 1875).

109 Miller, *Ukrainian Question*, 166; Savchenko, *Zaborona ukraïnstva*, 62–3, 368–72. The latter contains Iuzefovich's article.

110 RGIA, f. 776, op. 11, 1872, delo 80, l. 93 (Puzyrevskii to the Main Administration of the Press, 21 April 1875; the complete text of the letter is on l. 92–3).

111 Mykola Trots'kyi, *Iak teper odbuvatymet'sia voienna sluzhba* (Kyiv: Tipografia M.P. Fritsa, 1874).

112 RGIA, f. 776, op. 11, 1872, delo 80, l. 93.

113 Ibid., op. 3, 1866, delo 414, l. 158 (Rennenkampf to Mikhail Shidlovskii, 21 June 1875).

114 Ibid., op. 11, 1872, delo 80, l. 101 (Timashev to Dondukov-Korsakov, 4 October 1875); l. 102 (unidentified individual to the director of the General Department of the Ministry of Internal Affairs, 24 September 1875).

115 Ibid., l. 41a–1b (Puzyrevskii to the Main Administration of the Press, 17 October 1875).

116 Serhii Podolyns'kyi, *Lysty ta dokumenty*, ed. Roman Serbyn and Tetiana Sliudikova (Kyiv: Tsentral'nyi derzhavnyi istorichnyi arkhiv Ukraïny, 2002), 244 (Podolyns'kyi to Smirnov, 17 May [1875]). For this source, I am indebted to Roman Serbyn.

117 RGIA, f. 776, op. 11, 1872, delo 80, l. 43 (Puzyrevskii's dismissal signed by Timashev).

118 Miller, *Ukrainian Question*, 270–2 (full text of the Ems Decree).

119 Stephen Velychenko, "Local Officialdom and National Movements in Imperial Russia: Administrative Shortcomings and Under-Government," in *Ethnic and National Issues in Russian and East European History*, ed. John Morison (Houndsmills: Macmillan Press Ltd.; New York: St Martin's Press, 2000), 74–86; see also Velychenko, "Tsarist Censorship," 401–3.

7 The Ukrainian Movement and Russia in the 1870s

1 Vytautas Petronis, *Constructing Lithuania: Ethnic Mapping in Tsarist Russia, ca. 1800–1914* (Stockholm: University of Stockholm, 2007), 125–8.

2 Savchenko, *Zaborona ukraïnstva*, 28–9.

3 "Zasedanie komissii po snariazheniiu etnograficheskо-statisticheskoi ekspeditsii v Zapadno-Russkii krai, 6go maia 1869g.," *Izvestiia IRGO* 5, no. 5 (1869): 241–2; "Zhurnal zasedaniia Otdeleniia Etnografii. 21go fevralia 1869 goda," *Izvestiia IRGO* 5, no. 3 (1869): 179; "Zhurnal obshchego sobraniia IRGO. 12go marta 1869 goda," *Izvestiia IRGO* 5, no. 2 (1869): 104–7; "Zhurnal zasedaniia Soveta IRGO, 30 ianvaria 1869 g.,"

Izvestiia IRGO 5, no. 1 (1869): 13; Pavel Platonovich Chubinskii, "Ocherk narodnykh iuridicheskikh obychaev i poniatii v Malorussii," *Zapiski IRGO. Po otdeleniiu etnografii* 2 (1869), 677–715; Petronis, *Constructing Lithuania*, 134–8, 140–1, 153–9; P.P. Semenov pri sodeistvii A.A. Dostoevskogo, *Istoriia poluvekovoi deiatel'nosti Imperatorskogo russkogo geograficheskogo obshchestva 1845–1895* (St Petersburg: V tipografii V. Bezobrazova i Komp., 1896), 375–6, 382–8.

4 Savchenko, *Zaborona ukrainstva*, 10–13.

5 "Zhurnal komissii po snariazheniiu ekspeditsii v Zapadno-Russkiikrai. 27go noiabria 1871g," *Izvestiia IRGO* 8, no. 1 (1872): 4.

6 Kost' Mykhalchuk, "Avtobiohrafichna Zapyska," *Kyïvs'ka Starovyna*, no. 6 (1994): 31.

7 *Trudy etnografichesko-statisticheskoi ekspeditsii v zapadno-Russkii krai, snariazhennoi Imperatorskim Russkim Geograficheskim Obshchestvom. Iugo-Zapadnyi otdel. Materialy i issledovaniia, sobrannyia d. chl. P.P. Chubinskim*, 7 vols. (St Petersburg: Imperatorskoe Russkoe Geograficheskoe Obshchestvo, 1872–8).

8 Ibid., 7: 361. This part of the volume was published in 1877.

9 Ibid., 175–82 (Jews), 362, 364–74, 453–5 . The statistics on Jews was published in 1872, the statistics on the Orthodox and Catholic inhabitants of the Kingdom of Poland in 1877.

10 Ibid., 346. The author did not specify the "attempts." Most likely, he referred to the various Cossack rebellions which had either independence, or defence of the Cossack autonomy, as their goal.

11 Ibid., 346.

12 Ibid., 342–59.

13 Ibid., 346, 350, 357. Jewish assimilation, which Chubynsky supported, did not include conversion to Christianity. His perception of Jews was rather stereotypical, and he was opposed to the immediate abolition of legal discrimination against Jews. To be sure, he believed that their eventual emancipation was necessary.

14 "Nevidomyi avtobiohrafichnyi Lyst K. Mykhal'chuka. (Z arkhivu Iv. Steshenka)," *Ukraina* 24, no. 5 (1927): 64; *Trudy etnografichesko-statisticheskoi*, vol. 7, 215, 220–2; Savchenko, *Zaborona ukraïnstva*, 29–32, 106–8.

15 *Trudy etnografichesko-statisticheskoi* 7: 271; published in 1872. The authors also criticized government policies towards that issue before 1863, convinced that the interests of the peasantry had not been reckoned with sufficiently.

16 Mikhail Dolbilov, "The Stereotype of the Pole in Imperial Policy: The 'Depolonization' of the Northwestern Region in the 1860s," *Russian Studies in History* 44, no. 2 (Fall 2005): 44–88.

17 Savchenko, *Zaborona ukraïnstva*. The first 119 pages are a detailed study of the section; on the bypassing of local conservatives, see also Miller, *Ukrainian Question*, 158–9.

18 "Prilozhenie k zhurnalu zasedaniia Iugo-Zapadnago Otdela Imperatorskago Russkago Geograficheskago Obshchestva 13 fevralia 1873 goda (st. 6). Rech' P.P. Chubinskago," in *Zapiski Iugo-Zapadnago Otdela Imperatorskago Russkago Geograficheskago obschestava*, vol. 1 (1873) (Kyiv: Tipografiia Universiteta Sv. Vladimira, 1874), 5.

19 Ibid., 4.

20 *Kiev i ego predmest'ia: Shuliavka, Solomenka s Protasovym Iarom, Baikova Gora i Demievka s Sapernoiu slobodkoiu po perepisi 2 marta 1874 goda, proizvedennoi i razrabotannoi Iugo-zapadnym Otdelom Imperatorskago Russkago Geograficheskago Obshchestva* (Kyiv: Po rasporiazheniiu g. Kievskago, Podol'skago i Volynskago General-Gubernatora, 1875). On the practical implementation of the census, see viii–ix, xvii–xix.

21 Ibid., xxi.

22 Ibid.

23 Ibid., xxvii–xxviii.

24 Ibid., li.

25 "Tablitsa VIII. Raspredelenie naseleniia po iazyku," *Kiev i ego predmest'ia*, 20–3.

26 For a general discussion of Drahomanov, see Taras Andrusiak, *Shliakh do svobody (Mykhailo Drahomanov pro prava liudyny)* (Lviv: Svit, 1998); Anatolii Kruhlashov, *Drama intelektuala: Politychni ideï Mykhaila Drahomanova* (Chernivtsi: Prut, 2000).

27 Mykhailo Petrovych Drahomanov, *Literaturno-publitsystychni pratsi*, 2 vols. (Kyiv: Naukova dumka, 1970), 1: 106–8, 111–13, 116–18, 127–32.

28 Quoted in Savchenko, *Zaborona ukrainstva*, 57.

29 Ibid., 23.

30 Panteleimon Kulish, *Istoriia vozsoedineniia Rusi*, 3 vols. (Moscow: Obshchestvo "Obshchestvennaia pol'za," 1874–7). The first two volumes appeared in 1874, the third in 1877.

31 Both quotations are cited in Kulish, *Istoriia vozsoedineniia*, 2: 25.

32 Ibid., 2: 273.

33 M.P. Dragomanov, "Vostochnaia politika Germanii i obrusenie," in *Politicheskie sochinenia* (Moscow: Tipografia I.D. Sytina, 1908), 1–219; Miller, *Ukrainian Question*, 155–7; David Saunders, "Russia, the Balkans, and Ukraine in the 1870s," in *Russia and the Wider World in Historical Perspective*, ed. Cathryn Brennan and Murray Frame (Houndsmills: Macmillan, 2000), 99–100.

34 RGIA, f. 776, op. 2, delo 10, l. 169, 174–9 (records of the Council of the Main Administration of the Press, 15 February 1872).

35 "Perepyska M. Drahomanova z V. Navrots'kym: Z pochatkiv sotsialistychnoho rukhu Halychyny," in *Za Sto lit: Materialy z hromads'koho i literaturnoho zhyttia Ukraïny XIX i pochatku XX stolittia*, vol. 1 (Kyiv: Derzhavne vydavnytstvo Ukraïny, 1927), 135; also quoted in Miller, *Ukrainian Question*, 159, in a slightly different translation.
36 Myhailo Petrovych Drahomanov, "Literatura rosiis'ka, velykorus'ka, ukrains'ka i halyts'ka," in Drahomanov, *Literaturno-publitsystychni pratsi*, 1: 80–220.
37 Miller (*Ukrainian Question*, 169) mentions Drahomanov's pro-imperial statements in this article.
38 Drahomanov, *Literaturno-publitsystychni pratsi*, 1: 201–2.
39 Ibid., 133.
40 Ibid., 175–7.
41 Ibid., 206.
42 Ibid., 206–10, 212, 217–20.
43 For the Ukrainian period of this newspaper, see Savchenko, *Zaborona ukraïinstva*, 127–60 and Saunders, "Russia, the Balkans," 87–8, 90–1, 100.
44 RGIA, f. 776, op. 3, 1866, delo 414, l. 130 (acting director of the Main Administration V. Grigorev to Puzyrevskii, 16 January 1875); f. 776, op. 3, 1866, delo 414, l. 126–9 (Rennenkampf's denunciation, 2 January 1875). Rennenkampf complained that *Kievskii Telegraf* had criticized those of his acts as mayor that were dictated by law. He did not mention the Ukrainophiles, but attached the announcement about the newspaper's new orientation and staff; Savchenko, *Zaborona ukraïnstva*, 142.
45 RGIA, f. 776, op. 3, 1866, delo 414, l. 124 (acting head of the Third Section Mezentsov to the Main Administration, 17 October 1874; the information came from Kyiv Gendarme General Pavlov). See Savchenko, *Zaborona ukraïnstva*, 141–2.
46 For the refusal to endorse the editors, see RGIA, f. 776, op. 3, 1866, delo 414, l. 108 (State Secretary Longinov to Gogotskaia, September 1874); l. 150 (acting director of the Main Administration V. Grigorev to Gogotskaia, 26 June 1875); Savchenko, *Zaborona ukraïnstva*, 141–5, 147–51, 156–7. After the Hromada members left *Kievskii Telegraf*, it was edited by individuals noted for their all-Russian populist sympathies. Although the closure of *Kievskii Telegraph* was decreed in the context of measures instituted only against Ukrainophiles, it may have been motivated by the newspaper's orientation during its post-Ukrainophile period, too. Gogotskaia did not get an editor endorsed even after the Ukrainophiles had left the newspaper.
47 "Nezhin. (Korres. Kievskago Telegrafa)," *Kievskii Telegraf*, 10 January 1875, 3.
48 "Kiev, 6 fevralia 1875 g. Malorusskoe literaturnoe dvizhenie v 1874 g.," *Kievskii Telegraf*, 7 February 1875, 1–2.

49 A.B., "Kiev, 8 marta 1875 g.," *Kievskii Telegraf*, 9 March 1875, 2.
50 "Vnutrenniia izvestiia," *Kievskii Telegraf*, 27 January 1875, 3.
51 "Spravka dlia kievskago otdela slavianskogo blagotvoritel'nago komiteta," *Kievskii Telegraf*, 7 February 1875, 2.
52 "Italianskii zhurnal 'Rivista Europea,'" *Kievskii Telegraf*, 7 March 1875, 2.
53 "Kiev, 21-go fevralia 1875 g.," *Kievskii Telegraf*, 22 January 1875, 1–2.
54 "Stolichnaia i provintsial'naia periodicheskaia pechat' na Iuge Rossii," *Kievskii Telegraf*, 2 January 1875, 1–2.
55 "V poslednei (dekabrskoi) knizhke 'Trudov' I. V. ekonomicheskago obshchestva," *Kievskii Telegraf*, 15 January 1875, 2–3.
56 "Ekonomicheskie otnosheniia severa i iuga Rossii," *Kievskii Telegraf*, 3 January 1875, 1–2; Savchenko (*Zaborona ukraïnstva*, 128–34) calls this article a response to the article in *Otechestvennye zapiski*, without mentioning the idea of the negative impact of Russian centralism on the Ukrainian economy in *Kievskii Telegraf*.
57 "Pol'skii vopros u nas i v Poznani," *Kievskii Telegraf*, 10 February 1875, 1–2.
58 "Bibliografiia," *Kievskii Telegraf*, 5 March 1875, 3.
59 "Pis'mo iz Galitsii," *Kievskii Telegraf*, 6 March 1875, 1. To be sure, the anti-Austrian opinions also circulated within the government circles. See Saunders, "Russia, the Balkans," 96–8.
60 Savchenko (*Zaborona ukraïnstva*, 144) quotes from Kyiv Gendarme General Pavlov's letter to the Third Section, 7 June 1875; on the polemics between *Kievlianin* and *Kievskii Telegraf*, see Miller, *Ukrainian Question*, 163–6. His description is more informative on *Kievlianin* than on *Kievskii Telegraf*.
61 "Kievlianin za Shevchenko," *Kievskii Telegraf*, 14 March 1875, 2.
62 "Nevol'naia propaganda ukrainofilov," *Kievskii Telegraf*, 23 March 1875, 2.
63 "Nekhitraia beztseremonnost' 'Kievlianina,'" *Kievskii Telegraf*, 28 March 1875, 3.
64 "Pis'mo g. Lysenka v 'Golose,'" *Kievskii Telegraf*, 11 April 1875, 1; also cited in Savchenko, *Zaborona ukraïnstva*, 139.
65 "Pominki Shevchenka v L'vove i V'ene," *Kievskii Telegraf*, 16 April 1875, 1. Khmelnytsky submitted himself and his realm to Muscovite suzerainty in 1654; in 1662 Vyhovsky unsuccessfully tried to reunite the Cossack polity with Poland-Lithuania; Mazepa sided with Sweden against Russia in 1709, but many Cossacks remained faithful to Russia; in 1768 the *haidamak* rebels rose up against the Polish nobility in Right-Bank Ukraine, hoping for assistance from the Russian Empire; I disagree with Faith Hillis, *Children of Rus'*, 87–8, 90–6, who perceives "a coherent Little Russian lobby" consisting of the adherents of *Kievlianin* and Drahomanov in the beginning of the 1870s. According to Hillis, the two groups only finally separated after the Ems Decree. Since the ideological orientations of the two groups substantially

differed from each other, I do not find that postulating their unity in a Little Russian lobby adds to our understanding of the debates in Kyiv in the 1870s. To be sure, Hillis is right in that at this time, Drahomanov and his followers did not advocate a fully separate Ukrainian national identity.

66 Miller, *Ukrainian Question*, 160–1.

67 Roman Serbyn, "In Defense of an Independent Ukrainian Socialist Movement: Three Letters from Serhii Podolynskyi to Valerian Smirnov," *Journal of Ukrainian Studies* 7, no. 2 (Fall 1982): 29 (Podolynsky to Smirnov, 12 May 1875).

68 Roman Serbyn, "Zhyttia i diial'nist' Serhiia Podolyns'koho: Biohraficnyi narys," in Serhii Podolyns'kyi, *Lysty ta dokumenty* (Kyiv: Tsentral'nyi derzhavnyi istorychnyi arkhiv Ukraïny, M. Kyiv, 2002), 43–100); Serhii Buda, "Do biohrafiï S.A. Podolyns'koho," in *Za Sto Lit: Materialy z hromads'koho i literaturnoho zhyttia Ukraïny XIX i pochatku XX stolittia* 5 (Kyiv: Derzhavne vydavnytstvo Ukraïny, 1930), 192–200; L. Ia. Korniichuk, "Zhyttia i diial'nist' S.A. Podolyns'koho," in S.A. Podolyns'kyi, *Vybrani tvory* (Kyiv: Kyivs'kyi natsional'nyi ekonomichnyi universytet, 2000), 17–47.

69 See, esp., his letters, written in 1873 and 1876, to Valerian Smirnov, in Podolyns'kyi, *Lysty ta dokumenty*, 188–9, 262–4, 269, 270–2.

70 Serhii Podolyns'kyi, *Vybrani tvory*, comp. and bibl. Roman Serbyn (Montreal: Ukraïns'ke Istorychne Tovarystvo, 1990), 11–28; Podolyns'kyi, *Vybrani tvory* (Kyiv ed.), 69–80; the original work was published as *Parova Mashyna* (Viden': Koshtom i zakhodom V. Kistky, 1875).

71 Podolyns'kyi, *Vybrani tvory* (Kyiv ed.), 77.

72 Ibid., 84. The original edition of *Pro Bahatstvo ta bidnist': Rozmova Perva* appeared in Geneva in 1876.

73 Podolyns'kyi, *Lysty ta dokumenty*, 257–8 (letter to Valerian Smirnov, 18 March 1876).

74 Serbyn, "In Defense," 20–1 (Podolynsky's letter to Smirnov, 17 May 1875).

75 Serhii Buda, "Ukraïns'ki pereklady revoliutsiinoï literatury 1870-kh rokiv," in *Za Sto Lit* 3 (Kyiv: Derzhavne vydavnytstvo Ukraïny, 1928), 50–65.

76 Podolyns'kyi, *Vybrani tvory* (Montreal ed.), 81.

77 RGIA, f. 776, op. 11, 1876g., delo 59, l. 4 (cited by Chairman of St Petersburg Committee of Censorship A. Petrov in his letter to Main Administration of the Press, 11 June 1876; the letter contains a description of Volkhovych's work with extensive quotations).

78 Savchenko, *Zaborona ukraïnstva*, 153–4.

79 Kotenko, Martyniuk, and Miller, "Maloross," 421–2.

80 Arkhiv Mykhaila Drahomanova, vol. 1 (Warsaw: Ukraïns'kyi naukovyi instytut, 1937), 167. The complete letter is on pp. 163–8.

81 Ivan Nechui-Levyts'kyi, *Ukraïnstvo na literaturnykh pozvakh z Moskovshchynoiu: Kul'turolohichni traktaty* (Lviv: Kameniar, 1998), 48. The article first appeared in the Lviv periodical *Osnova*, nos. 28–44 (1871).

82 Ivan Nechui-Levyts'kyi, *Zibrannia tvoriv*, vols. 1–10 (Kyiv: Naukova Dumka, 1965), 2: 8–9.
83 Ibid., 2: 10.
84 Ibid., 2: 13.
85 Ibid., 2: 50.
86 Panas Myrny, *Tvory*, vols. 1–5 (Kyiv: Derzhavne vydavnytstvo khudozhn'oï literatury, 1960) 2: 401–2. The background information was written by the editor, A.T. Synhaïvs'ka.
87 Ibid., 2: 147.
88 Ibid., 2: 148.
89 Savchenko, *Zaborona ukraïnstva*, 200.
90 Miller, *The Ukrainian Question*, 267; quote from English translation of the Ems Decree.
91 Saunders, "Russia, the Balkans," 96–9.
92 Drahomanov, *Literaturno-publitsystychni pratsi*, 2: 177, 200.
93 Savchenko, *Zaborona ukraïnstva*, 64–9; Platon Antonovich presumed that the local gendarme, Major-General Pavlov was either the author of the denunciation or, at least, had forwarded it to the Third Section. See GARF, f. 109, 3 eksp., op. 160, 1875 g., ed. khr. 245, l. 5 (Antonovich to Shirinskii-Shikhmatov, 5 July 1875).
94 Miller, *Ukrainian Question*, 167, 171–2. According to Miller, Antonovich did all he could to protect the Ukrainophiles. Although he was a native of Ukraine, he was not related to Volodymyr Antonovych.
95 "Sovremennoe ukrainofil'stvo," *Russkii Vestnik* 115, no. 2 (1875): 850–65 (statements on separation on 859–60 and 863–4; on the union with Poles, 854–5 and 864–5). The article was signed under the pseudonym "Z."
96 Savchenko, *Zaborona ukraïnstva*, 134–7.
97 Ibid., 366–72 (complete text of Iuzefovich's article).
98 Ibid., 323–4 (complete text of Shirinskii-Shikhmatov's letter).
99 GARF, f. 109, 3 eksp., op. 160, 1875 g., ed. khr. 245, l. 2–7 (Antonovich to Shirinskii-Shihmatov, 5 July 1875); Miller, *Ukrainian Question*, 267–9 (complete text of the Ems Decree, background of this document, and Drahomanov's departure, 162–72); Savchenko, *Zaborona ukraïnstva*, 324–34 (Antonovich to Shirinskii-Shikhmatov, 19 July 1875).
100 Savchenko, *Zaborona ukraïnstva*, 204.
101 Miller, *Ukrainian Question*, 183.
102 See GARF, f. 109, 1-ia eksp., op. 50, 1875g., l. 25 (Gendarme Lieutenant-Colonel Belov to Potapov, 3 April 1876); Miller (*Ukrainian Question*, 181–2) mentions this case.
103 Miller, *Ukrainian Question*, 179–80.
104 Savchenko, *Zaborona ukraïnstva*, 373 (complete text of Iuzefovich's memorandum, 372–81; summarized in Miller, *Ukrainian Question*, 180–1).

105 Cf. Miller, *Ukrainian Question*, 188. He writes that Nis and Konysky had been members of Land and Liberty. This is possible, but the authorities never claimed so.
106 The council's journal quoted in Miller, *Ukrainian Question*, 182.
107 Ibid.
108 Ibid., 183–5.
109 Ibid., 184–7 (complete text of the Ems Decree, 267–9).
110 Mikhail Dragomanov, *Po voprosu o malorusskoi literature* (Vienna: Carl Helf, 1876).
111 Mikhail Dragomanov, *Turki vnutrennie vneshnie: Pismo k izdateliu "Novogo Vremeni"* (Geneva: H. Georg, 1876), 7.
112 Ibid., 8.
113 Myhailo Drahomanov, "Perednie slovo do Hromady," *Hromada*, no. 1 (1878): 5–101.

8 Aftermath and Conclusions

1 *Ukrains'ka identychnist' i movne pytannia v Rosiis'kii imperii: sproba derzhavnoho rehuliuvannia (1847–1914). Zbirnyk dokumentiv i materialiv* (Kyiv: Instytut istorii Ukrainy NAN Ukrainy, 2013), 188–91. Nikolai Pavlovich Ignatev's memorandum endorsed by Alexander III, 3 October 1881.
2 Ibid., 247 (Main Administration of the Press to Kyiv censor, 10 January 1892).
3 I have not been able to locate the circular which banned children's literature. However, this circular, dated 2 December 1895, is referred to in the context of several later decisions made by censors. See *Ukrains'ka identychnist'*, 294–5, 301–2, 310–11.
4 Miller, *The Ukrainian Question*, 195; his analysis of the execution of the Ems Decree on 191–7. Concerning the repressions against Ukrainophile teachers, Miller refers to Savchenko, *Zaborona ukraïnstva*, 214–20, 222–3. However, according to Savchenko (212–13, 223), there were not six, but nine teachers repressed.
5 *Ukrains'ka identychnist'*, 144 (director of Main Administration of the Press Grigoriev to St Petersburg Censorship Committee, 13 August 1876); RGIA, f. 776, op. 2, delo 16, l. 201–7 (minutes of Council of Main Administration of the Press, 22 June 1876).
6 *Ukraïnomovna knyha*, 1: 97–114.
7 Statistics compiled on the basis of *Ukraïnomovna knyha*, vols. 1–3.

Bibliography

ARCHIVAL SOURCES

Gosudarstvennyi arkhiv Rossiiskoi federatsii (GARF)

f. 109. *Tret'e otdelenie sobstvennoi ego imperatorskogo velichestva kantseliarii.* Third Section of His Imperial Majesty's Own Chancellery. 1856–76.

f. 112. *Osoboe prisutstvie pravitel'stvuiushchego senata dlia suzhdeniia del o gosudarstvennykh prestupleniiakh i protivozakonnykh soobshchestvakh.* Special Court of the Governing Senate for Political Crimes and Illegal Organizations. 1863–5.

Rossiiskii gosudarstvennyi istoricheskii arkhiv (RGIA)

f. 735. *Kantseliariia ministra narodnogo prosveshcheniia.* Chancellery of the Minister of Public Enlightenment. 1847.

f. 772. *Glavnoe upravlenie tsenzury MNP.* Main Administration of Censorship at the Ministry of Public Enlightenment. 1856–62.

f. 773. *Osobennaia kantseliariia ministra narodnogo prosveshcheniia.* Special Chancellery of the Minister of Public Enlightenment. 1862–3.

f. 774. *Sovet ministra vnutrennykh del po delam knigopechataniia.* Council of the Minister of Internal Affairs concerning book printing. 1863.

f. 775. *Tsentral'noe upravlenie po tsenzurnomu vedomstvu MVD.* Main Administration of Censorship at the Ministry of Internal Affairs. 1863–5.

f. 776. *Glavnoe upravlenie po delam pechati MVD.* Main Administration of the Press at the Ministry of Internal Affairs. 1865–76.

Rossiiskii gosudarstvennyi voenno-istoricheskii arkhiv (RGVIA)

f. 801. *Glavnoe voenno-sudebnoe upravlenie.* Main Administration of Military Justice. 1862.

Tsentral'nyi Derzhavnyi Istorychnyi Arkhiv Ukrainy (TsDIA Uk.)

f. 442. *Kievskii, Podolskii i Volynskyi General-Gubernator.* 1856–65.

PUBLISHED SOURCES

A.B. [pseud.]. "Kiev, 8 marta 1875 g." *Kievskii Telegraf,* 9 March 1875.

Antonovich, Vladimir [Antonovych, Volodymyr]. "Moia ispoved': Otvet g. Padalitse." *Osnova,* no. 1 (1861): 83–96.

Antonovich, Vladimir [Antonovych, Volodymyr]. "Soderzhanie aktov o kozakakh 1500–1648 god." *Arkhiv Iugo-Zapadnoi Rossii, izdavaemyi vremennoiu komissieiu dlia razbora drevnikh aktov, vysochaishe utverzhdennoiu pri Kievskom Voennom, Podol'skom i Volynskom general-gubernatore.* Vol. 3, book 1, iv–cxx. Kyiv: V tipografii Fedorova, 1863.

Antonovych, Volodymyr. *Tvory.* Vol. 1. Kyiv: Vseukrains'ka akademiia nauk, 1932.

Antonovych, Volodymyr, and Mykhailo Drahomanov, eds. *Istoricheskie pesni malorusskago naroda s ob"iasneniami Vl. Antonovicha i M. Dragomanova.* 2 vols. Kyiv: Tipografiia M.P. Fritsa, 1874–5.

Arkhiv Mykhaila Drahomanova. Vol. 1. Warsaw: Ukraïns'kyi naukovyi instytut, 1937.

Bantysh-Kamenskii, Dmitrii. *Istoriia Maloi Rossii, so vremen prisoedineniia onoi k Rossiiskomu Gosudarstvu pri tsarie Aleksee Mikhailovichie.* Vols. 1–4. Moscow: Izhdiveniem sochinitelia, 1822.

Bartenev, P.I. "Ob ukraino-slavianskom obshchestve. (Iz bumag D.P. Golokhvastova)." *Russkii Arkhiv,* no. 7 (1892): 334–59.

Barvinok, Hanna. "S Volyni." *Osnova,* no. 1 (1861): 282–92.

Bazilevskii, B. *Materialy dlia istorii revoliutsionnago dvizheniia v Rossii v 60-kh gg.* Zhurnal Russkaia Istoricheskaia Biblioteka, no. 2. St Petersburg: Izd. B. Bazilevskago, 1906.

"Bibliografiia." *Kievskii Telegraf,* 5 March 1875.

Blons'kyi, Iason. *Korotkyi vyklad iz ustava 20 noiabria 1864 hoda ob uholovnim sudi dlia iuzhno-rus'kykh krestian.* Katerynoslav: Druk. Ia. Chausskoho, 1866.

Bodianskii, Osip [Osyp Bodians'kyi]. Review of "Narodnié zpievanki cili pisne swetské slowakuw w uhrah" by Ján Kollár. *Moskovskii nabliudatel'* 1, no. 4 (1835): 579–607.

Bodianskii, Osip. *O narodnoi poezii slavianskikh plemen: Razsuzhdenie na stepen' magistra filosofskago fakul'teta Pervogo Otdeleniia.* Moscow: V universitetskoi tipografii, 1837.

Boriak, Hennadii, Vasyl' Baran, Liubov Histsova, Liudmyla Demchenko, Ol'ha Muzychuk, Petro Naidenko, and Valentyna Shandra, eds. *Ukrains'ka identychnist' i movne pytannia v Rosiis'kii imperii: Sproba derzhavnoho rehuliuvannia (1847–1914). Zbirnyk dokumentiv i materialiv.* Kyiv: Instytut istorii Ukraïny NAN Ukrainy, 2013.

Borovykovs'kyi, Levko. *Baiky i prybaiutky.* Kyiv: V universitetskoi tipografii, 1852.

[Burzyński, Tomasz.] "Wspomnienia z czasów młodości." In *Wydawnictwo materyałów do historyi powstania 1863–1864.* 5 vols. Vol. 4: 93–234. Lviv: Drukarnia Ludowa, 1888–94.

"Chernigov, 12 maia 1863." *Chernigovskii listok,* no. 2 (1863): 9.

Chernigovskii listok. 1861–3.

Chteniia v imperatorskom obshchestve istorii i drevnostei pri moskovskom universitete. 1846–8.

Chubinskii, Pavel Platonovich [Chubyns'kyi, Pavlo]. "Iz Borispolia." *Osnova,* no. 10 (1861): 128–36.

Chubinskii, Pavel Platonovich [Chubyns'kyi, Pavlo]. "Ocherk narodnykh iuridicheskikh obychaev i poniatii v Malorussii." *Zapiski imperatorskogo Rossiiskogo geograficheskogo obshchestva. Po otdeleniiu etnografii,* vol. 2 (1869): 677–715.

Chubinskii, Pavel Platonovich [Chubyns'kyi, Pavlo]. "Prilozhenie k zhurnalu zasedaniia Iugo-Zapadnago Otdela Imperatorskago Russkago Geograficheskago Obshchestva 13 fevralia 1873 goda (st. 6). Rech' P.P. Chubinskago." *Zapiski Iugo-Zapadnago Otdela Imperatorskago Russkago Geograficheskago obschestva,* vol. 1 (1873), 5–8. Kyiv: Tipografiia Universiteta Sv. Vladimira, 1874.

De-shcho pro svit Bozhyi. Koshtom K. Hurta. Kyiv: V drukarni Miniatova i Fedorova, 1863.

D'iakov, Vladimir, ed. *Russko-pol'skie revoliutsionnye sviazi.* 2 vols. Moscow: Izdatel'stvo Akademii Nauk SSSR, 1963.

Drahomanov, Mykhailo. *Literaturno-publitsystychni pratsi.* 2 vols. Kyiv: Naukova Dumka, 1970.

Drahomanov, Mykhailo. "Perednie slovo do Hromady." *Hromada. Ukraïns'ka zbirka,* no. 1 (1878), 5–101. Zheneva: Pechatnia "Hromady."

Drahomanov, Mikhail Petrovich. *Politicheskie sochinenia.* Moscow: Tipografia I.D. Sytina, 1908.

Drahomanov, Myhailo [Dragomanov, Mikhail]. *Po voprosu o malorusskoi literature.* Vienna: Carl Helf, 1876.

Drahomanov, Mykhailo. *Pro ukraïns'kykh kozakiv, tatar ta turkiv.* Kyiv: Tyskarnia V.I. Davydenko, 1876.

Drahomanov, Mykhailo [Dragomanov, Mikhail]. *Turki vnutrennie i turki vneshnie. Pismo k izdateliu "Novogo Vremeni."* Geneva: H. Georg, 1876.

Drahomanov, Mykhailo, and Volodymyr Navrots'kyi. "Perepyska M. Drahomanova z V. Navrots'kym: Z pochatkiv sotsialistychnoho rukhu Halychyny." Edited by Kyrylo Studyns'kyi. In *Za Sto lit: Materialy z hromads'koho i literaturnoho zhyttia Ukraïny XIX i pochatku XX stolittia*, vol. 1, 83–153. Kyiv: Derzhavne vydavnytstvo Ukraïny, 1927.

"Ekonomicheskie otnosheniia severa i iuga Rossii." *Kievskii Telegraf*, 3 January 1875.

[E. U.]. "Paryż w m. czerwcu 1866." *Sioło* 1, no. 1 (1866): 148–9.

Filaret, episkop Rizhskii. "Kirill i Mefodii, slavianskie prosvetiteli (Chitano 30-go noiabria, 1846 g.)." *Chteniia* 4 (1846–7): *issledovaniia* 1–28.

Ge, Grigorii. "Vyderzhki iz zapisok mirovogo posrednika." *Osnova*, no. 1 (1862): 44–8; no. 2 (1862): 34–51.

Giller, Agaton. *Historja powstania narodu polskiego w 1861–1864 r.* Paris: Księgarnia Luxemburska, 1868.

Gornitskii, P. "Iz-pod Kieva." *Osnova*, no. 1 (1861): 328–30.

Grabianka, Grigorii [Hrabianka, Hryhorii]. *Deistviia prezel'noi i ot nachala poliakov krvavshoi nebyvaloi brani Bogdana Khmel'nitskogo, getmana Zaporozhskogo, s poliaki, za Naiiasneishikh Korolei Pol'skikh Vladislava, potom i Kazimira, v roku 1648,otpravovatisia nachatoi i za let desiat' po smerti Khmel'nitskogo neokonchennoi, z roznikh letopistsov i iz diariusha, na toi voine pisannoe, v grade Gadiachu, sobrannaia i samobytnykh starozhilov svidetel'stvi utverzhdennaia. Roku 1710.* Kyiv: Vremennaia Kommissiia dlia razbora drevnikh aktov, 1854. (See also Hrabianka, below.)

Grechulevich, Vasilii. *Beseda po osviashchenii Podol'skoi eparkhii, Bratslavskogo uezda, sela Annopolia vozobnovlennoi i razshirennoi dvumia bokovymi pridelami Chudo-Mikhailovskoi tserkvi, proiznesennaia na malorossiiskom iazyke, toiazh tserkvi protoiereem Vasiliem Grechulevichem, 1852 goda, dekabria 6 dnia.* St Petersburg: Tipografiia K.Vingebera, 1853.

Grechulevich, Vasilii. *Besedy katikhizicheskiia na desiat' zapovedei Bozhiikh, govorennyia, na malorossiiskom iazike.* 2nd edition. St Petersburg: V tipografii Eduarda Pratsa, 1859.

Grechulevich, Vasilii. *Besedy katekhizicheskiia, na deviat' blazhenstv Evangel'skikh i desiat' zapovedei Bozhiikh, govorennyia, na Malorossiiskom iazyke, Protoiereem i kavalerom Vasiliem Grechulevichem.* St Petersburg: Tipografiia vtorogo otdeleniia sobstvennago Ego Imperatorskago Velichestva Kantseliarii, 1852.

Grechulevich, Vasilii. *Besedy katekhizicheskiia, na simvol very, govorennyia na Malorossiiskom iazyke.* St Petersburg: Tipografiia Ia. Ionsona, 1856.

Grechulevich, Vasilii. *Besedy katekhizicheskiia, pri ob"iasnenii molitvy Gospodnei, na Malorossiiskom iazyke.* St Petersburg: Tipografiia Ia. Ionsona, 1855.

Grechulevich, Vasilii. *Besedy na malorossiiskom iazyke o semi spasatel'nykh tainstvakh.* St Petersburg: V tipografii Aleksandra Iakobsona, 1858.

Grechulevich, Vasilii. *O dolzhnostiakh roditelei i detei: Dve besedy, govorennyia na Malorossiiskom iazyke.* St Petersburg: V tipografii Aleksandra Iakobsona, 1859.

Grechulevich, Vasilii. *Propovedy, na Malorossiiskom iazyke, Protoiereja i Kavalera Vasiliia Grechulevicha.* St Petersburg: Tipografiia K. Kraiia, 1849.

Grechulevich, Vasilii. *Propovedy na Malorossiiskom iazyke.* 2nd revised edition. St Petersburg: Tipografiia A. Iakobsona, 1857.

G. T. [pseud.]. "O narodnosti v religioznoi zhizni." *Osnova,* no. 4 (1861): 128–42.

Halicz, Emanuel, and Miller, Il'ia Solomonovich, eds. *Dokumenty komitetu centralnego narodowego i rządu narodowego 1862–1864.* Wrocław: Wydawnictwo Zakładu im. Ossolińskich, 1968.

Hatchuk, Mykola. *Ukraïns'ka abetka.* Moscow: Universitets'ka drukarnia, 1861.

Horbunov, N. *Shcho robytsia u vozdusi i shcho z toho treba znaty zemlerobu. Pereklad na ukraïns'ku movu Y.M.R.* Kyiv: V tipografii gazety "Kievskii Telegraf," 1875.

Hrabianka, Hryhoryi. *Hryhorij Hrabianka's The Great War of Bohdan Xmel'nyc'kyj.* Introduction by Yuri Lutsenko. Harvard Library of Early Ukrainian Literature, vol. 9. Cambridge, MA: Distributed by the Harvard University Press for the Ukrainian Research Institute of Harvard University, 1990.

Iakushkin, Pavel. "Putevyia zametki." *Osnova,* nos. 11–12 (1861): 88–121.

Iashchenko, A. "Z narodnikh ust, VI. Moskal' Kyrylo." *Osnova,* no. 1 (1862): 28–38.

Iashchenko, Leonid. *Hramatka za dlia ukrains'koho liudu.* Moscow: Drukarnia Katkova, 1862.

"Iasnaia-Poliana. Dva slova o novom iavlenii v dele narodnogo vospitaniia." *Osnova,* no. 8 (1861): 122–4.

Iefymenko, P. "O malorossiianakh v Orenburgskoi gubernii." *Osnova,* no. 9 (1861): 189–93.

"Istoriia rusov ili Maloi Rossii." *Chteniia v Imperatorskom Obshchestve Istorii i Drevnostei pri Moskovskom Universitete,* nos. 1–4 (1846), *materialy oteschestvennyia,* 1–261.

Istoriia rusov ili Maloi Rossii. Moscow: V universitetskoi tipografii, 1846.

Ivanov, A. *Rozmova pro nebo ta zemliu. Z de-iakymy odminamy i dodatkamy. Pereklav na ukraïns'ku movu M. Komarov.* Kyiv: Tipografia M.P. Fritsa, 1874.

Ivanov, A. *Rozmova pro zemni syly: Z de-iakymy dodatkamy ta odminamy pereklav na ukraïns'ku movu M. Komarov, knyzhka druha. (z maliunkamy).* Kyiv: Tipografia M.P. Fritsa, 1875.
"Italianskii zhurnal 'Rivista Europea.'" *Kievskii Telegraf*, 7 March 1875.
Iuzefovich, M., and P. Ivanishev. "Otvet Kievskoi kommissii dlia razbora drevnikh aktov na obvineniia nekotorykh gazet i zhurnalov." *Osnova*, no. 10 (1861): 65–91.
Iuzefovich, V.M. "Tridtsat' let tomu nazad." *Russkaia starina*, vol. 84 (1895): no. 10, 169–202; no. 11, 344–78.
Ka-pa [pseud.]. "Moi vospominaniia." *Osnova*, nos. 11–12 (1861): 62–74.
"Kharakteristika russkago i pol'skago zakonodatel'stva o krepostnom prave po otnosheniiu k Malorossii." *Osnova*, no. 1 (1862): 1–27.
Kiev i ego predmest'ia: Shuliavka, Solomenka s Protasovym Iarom, Baikova Gora i Demievka s Sapernoiu Slobodkoiu po perepisi 2 marta 1874, proizvedennoi i razrabotannoi Iugo-Zapadnym Otdelom Imperatorskago Russkago Geograficheskago Obschestva. Kyiv: po rasporiazheniiu g. Kievskago, Podol'skago i Volynskago General-Gubernatora, v tipografii Imperatorskago Universiteta Sv. Vladimira, 1875.
"Kiev, 6 fevralia 1875 g. Malorusskoe literaturnoe dvizhenie v 1874 g." *Kievskii Telegraf*, 7 February 1875.
"Kiev, 21-go fevralia 1875 g." *Kievskii Telegraf*, 22 January 1875.
"Kievlianin za Shevchenko." *Kievskii Telegraf*, 14 March 1875.
Konys'kyi, Oleksander. *Arykhmetyka abo shchotnytsia: Dlia ukrains'kykh shkil.* St Petersburg: V tipografii P.A. Kulisha, 1863.
Konys'kyi, Oleksander [Oleksander Perekhodovets', pseud.]. "Lyst z dorohy." *Osnova*, no. 10 (1861): 145–8.
Konysk'kyi, Oleksander [Oleksander Perekhodovets', pseud.]. "Z Poltavy. (1 Ianvaria 1862)." *Osnova*, no. 2 (1862): 52–4.
Koroliuk, Vladimir, ed. *Obshchestvenno-politicheskoe dvizhenie na Ukraine 1856–1862.* Kyiv: Vydavnytstvo Akademiï Nauk Ukraïns'koï RSR,1963.
Kostomarov, Nikolai. *Bogdan Khmel'nitskii.* 2nd expanded edition. St Petersburg: D.E. Kozanchikov, 1859.
Kostomarov, Nikolai. "Cherty narodnoi iuzhno-russkoi istorii." *Osnova*, no. 3 (1861): 114–65.
Kostomarov, Nikolai. "Dve russkie narodnosti." *Osnova*, no. 3 (1861): 33–80.
Kostomarov, Nikolai. "Getmanstvo Vygovskogo." *Osnova*, no. 4 (1861): 1–66; no. 7 (1861): 67–114.
Kostomarov, Nikolai. *Istoricheskie proizvedeniia: Avtobiografiia.* Kyiv: Izdatel'stvo pri Kievskom gosudarstvennom universitete, 1989.
Kostomarov, Nikolai. "Iudeiam." *Osnova*, no. 1 (1862): 38–58.

Kostomarov, Nikolai. "Mysli o federativnom nachale v drevnei Rusi." *Osnova*, no. 1 (1861): 121–58.

Kostomarov, Nikolai [Ieremiia Halka, pseud.]. "Na dobra-nich." *Osnova*, no. 2 (1861): 44–8.

Kostomarov, Nikolai. "O pozhertvovaniiakh v pol'zu izdaniia knig nauchnago soderzhaniia dlia iuzhnorusskago naroda." *Chernigovskii listok*, no. 3 (1863): 19–20.

Kostomarov, Nkolai. "O prepodavanii na iuzhnorusskom iazike." *Osnova*, no. 5 (1862): 1–6.

Kostomarov, Nikolai. "Otvet na vykhodki gazety (Krakovskoi) 'Czas' i zhurnala 'Revue contemporaine.'" *Osnova*, no. 2 (1861): 121–35.

Kostomarov, Nikolai. "Pravda moskvicham o Rusi." *Osnova*, no. 10 (1861): 1–15.

Kostomarov, Nikolai. "Pravda poliakam o Rusi." *Osnova*, no. 10 (1861): 100–12.

[Kostomarov, Nikolai]. "Ukraina." *Kolokol*, no. 61 (15 January 1860): 499–503.

Kostomarov, Nikolai. *Ukrainskie ballady*. Kharkiv: V unyversitetskii drukarni, 1838.

Kostomarov, Nikolai [Eremiia Halka, pseud.]. *Vitka*. Kharkiv: V unyversytetskii drukarni, 1840.

Kostomarov, Nikolai. "Vospominanie o dvukh maliarakh." *Osnova*, no. 4 (1861): 44–56.

Koz'min, Boris P., ed. *Politicheskie protsessy 60-kh g.g.* Moscow, Petrograd: Gosudarstvennoe izdatel'stvo, 1922.

Kukha, Ia. "Voronyi kin'." *Osnova*, no. 10 (1861): 21–5.

Kukharenko, Ia. H. "Chornomors'kyi pobut na Kubani mizh 1794 i 1796 rokamy." *Osnova*, nos. 11–12 (1861): 1–40.

Kulish, Panteleimon. *Chernaia Rada: Khronika 1663 goda*. Moscow: Tipografiia Aleksandra Semena, 1857.

Kulish, Panteleimon. *Chorna Rada, khronika 1663 roku*. St Petersburg: Tipografiia A. Iakobsona, 1857.

Kulish, Panteleimon. "Divoche sertse." *Chernigovskii listok*, no. 1 (1863): 3–6; no. 2 (1863): 13–15; no. 3 (1863): 21–3; no. 4 (1863): 28–30.

Kulish, Panteleimon. "Drugoi chelovek." *Osnova*, no. 2 (1861): 56–104.

Kulish, Panteleimon. "Duma pro Savu Kononenka." *Chernigovskii listok*, no. 3 (1863): 20–1.

[Kulish, Panteleimon]. *Hramatka*. St Petersburg: V tipografii P.A. Kulisha, 1857.

Kulish, Panteleimon. *Istoriia vozsoedineniia Rusi*. 3 vols. Moscow: Obshchestvo "Obshchestvennaia pol'za," 1874–7.

Kulish, Panteleimon [Khutorianin pseud.]. "Kakiia rukovodstva udobnee upotrebliat' pri pervonachal'nom obuchenii krest'ianskikh detei?" *Chernigovskii listok*, no. 26 (1861): 202–4; no. 27 (1861): 210–12.

Kulish, Panteleimon, ed. *Khata*. St Petersburg: P.A. Kulish, 1860.
Kulish, Panteleimon. *Khmel'nyshchyna*. St Petersburg: P.A. Kulish, 1861.
[Kulish, Panteleimon, under pseudonym]. "Lipovye pushchi: Nachalo romana, naidennago v bumagakh pokoinago D. P. Khorechko." *Osnova*, no. 5 (1861): 1–25.
[Kulish, Panteleimon]. "Lysty z khutora. Lyst I." *Osnova*, no. 1 (1861): 310–18.
Kulish, Panteleimon. *Mikhailo Charnyshenko, ili Malorossiia vosemdesiat let nazad*. 3 vols. Kyiv: V universitetskoi tipografii, 1843.
Kulish, Paneleimon. "Obzor ukrainskoi slovesnosti." *Osnova*, no. 1 (1861): 159–234; no. 3 (1861): 78–113; no. 4 (1861): 67–90; no. 5 (1861): 1–33; no. 9 (1861): 56–68; nos. 11–12 (1861): 1–11.
Kulish, Panteleimon. "Perednie slovo do hromady: Pohliad na ukraïns'ku slovesnost'." *Khata*. St Petersburg: P.A. Kulish, 1860: vii–xv.
Kulish, Panteleimon. "Peredovye zhidy." *Osnova*, no. 9 (1861): 135–8.
Kulish, Panteleimon. *Povist' pro ukraïns'kyi narod*. Lviv: Litopys, 2006. Reprint of P. Kulish, *Povest' ob ukrainskom narode. Napisal dlia detei starshago vozrasta P. Kulish*. St Petersburg: V tipografii Imperatorskoi Akademii Nauk, 1846.
Kulish, Panteleimon. *Povne zibrannia tvoriv*. Edited by Hryhorii Hrabovych [George Grabowicz] et al. Kyiv: Krytyka, 2005–.
Kulish, Panteleimon. *Tvory v dvokh tomakh*. Kyiv: Naukova Dumka, 1998.
Kulish, Panteleimon. *Ukraïna: Od pochatku Vkraïny do bat'ka Khmel'nyts'koho*. Kyiv: V universitetskoi tipografii, 1843.
Kulish, Panteleimon. "Ukrainskie nezabudki." *Osnova*, no. 9 (1861): 1–48.
Kulish, Panteleimon. *Zapiski o iuzhnoi Rusi*. 2 vols. St Petersburg: P. Kulish, 1856–7.
Kulyk, Vasyl. "De-shcho z Poltavy (do redaktora)." *Osnova*, no. 9 (1861): 175–82; nos. 11–12 (1861): 99–107.
Kvitka-Osnov'ianenko, Hryhoryi. *Malorossiiskie povesti, razskazannye Gritskom Osnovianenkom*. 3rd edition. Kyiv, St Petersburg: Odesa: P.I. Bonadurev, 1913.
Lashniukov, Iv. "Sostoianie istoricheskoi nauki u zapadnykh slavian." *Chernigovskii listok*, no. 1 (1861): 6–8; no. 2 (1863): 15–16.
Lasocki, Wacław. *Wspomnienie z mojego życia*. 2 vols. Cracow: Nakładem gminy miasta Krakowa, 1933.
Lazarevs'kyi, A. "Malorossiiskiia istoricheskiia poslovitsy i pogovorki." *Chernigovskiia gubernskiia vedomosti*, no. 38 (1853).
Lazarevskii, Al. "Rasskazy iz istorii levoberezhnoi Ukrainy XVIII veka." *Chernigovskii listok*, no. 13 (1863): 101–4.
Lazarevskii, Al. "Zametka na pis'mo g. Dobrotvorskago." *Chernigovskii listok*, no. 9 (1863): 72.

"Letopis' samovidtsa o voinakh Bogdana Khmel'nitskago i o mezhdousobiiakh, byvshikh v Maloi Rossii po ego smerti. Dovedena prodolzhateliami do 1734 goda." *Chteniia*, no. 1 (1846–7): *materialy otechestvennye*, i–ii, 1–72; no. 2 (1846–47): *materialy otechestvennye*, 73–138.

Levchenko, Mykhailo. "Pro Konotip." *Osnova*, nos. 11–12 (1861): 7–9.

Levchenko, Mykhailo."Zametka o Rusinskoi terminologii." *Osnova*, no. 7 (1861): 183–6.

Lindheim, Ralph, and George S.N. Luckyj, eds. *Towards an Intellectual History of Ukraine: An Anthology of Ukrainian Thought from 1710 to 1995*. Toronto, Buffalo: University of Toronto Press in association with Shevchenko Scientific Society, Inc., 1996.

Litopys Samovydtsia. Edited by Ia. I. Dzyra. Kyiv: Naukova Dumka, 1971.

L. M. "Talant; Fiziologicheskii ocherk." *Osnova*, nos. 11–12 (1861): 75–87.

Lubenets [pseud.]. "A evrei shinkary delaiut svoe delo." *Kievskii Telegraf*, 7 March 1875.

Makarov, N. "Vospominaniia o N. A. Markeviche." *Osnova*, no. 1 (1861): 293–7.

Maksimovich, Mikhail. "Filologicheskie pis'ma M. P. Pogodinu." *Russkaia beseda*, no. 3 (1856): nauky 78–139.

Maksimovich, Mikhail. *Nachatki ruskoi filologii; Kniga pervaia: Ob otnoshenii ruskoi rechi k zapadnoslavianskoi*. Kyiv: V tipografii Feofila Gliksberga, 1848.

Maksimovich, Mikhail. "Pis'mo o galitsko-russkoi slovesnosti." In *Galichanin, literaturnyi sbornik izdavaemyi Iakovom Fedorovichem Golovatskim i Bogdanom Andreevichem Deditskim*. Book 1, part 1. Lviv, 1862.

Maksimovich, Mikhail. *Sbornik ukrainskikh piesen*. Kyiv: V tipografii Feofila Gliksberga, 1849.

Maksimovich, Mikhail. *Sobranie sochinenii*. 3 vols. Kyiv: V. Tipografii M.P. Fritsa, 1876–80.

Maksimovich, Mikhail. *Ukrainskie narodnye pesni*. Moscow: V universitetskoi tipografii, 1827.

Markevich, Nikolai. *Istoriia Malorossii*. 2 vols. Moscow: V tipografii Avgusta Semena pri Imperatorskoi Mediko-Khirurgicheskoi Akademii, 1842.

Menchyts', Volodymyr. "Z spomyniv." *Ukraïna*, no. 3 (1925): 66–7.

Metlinskii, Amvrosii, ed. *Iuzhnyi russkii zbornyk*. Khar'kiv: V universitetskoi tipografii, 1848.

Metlinskii, Amvrosii, comp. *Narodnyia iuzhnorusskiia piesni*. Kyiv: Izdanie Amvrosiia Metlinskago, 1854.

Metlyns'kyi, Amvrosyi [Amvrosyi Mohyla, pseud.]. *Dumky i pesny ta shche de-shcho*. Kharkiv: V universitetskoi tipografii, 1839.

Mickiewicz, Adam. *Dzieła*. 16 vols. Warsaw: Czytelnik, 1955.

Mikhalchuk, Kost'. "Avtobiohrafichna Zapyska." *Kyivs'ka Starovyna*, no. 6 (1994): 29–32.

Mikhal'chuk, Kost' [Mikhalchuk, K.]. "Iz ukrainskogo bylogo: K vospominaniiam B. S. Poznanskogo." *Ukrainskaia zhizn'*, nos. 8–10 (1914): 70–85.

Mykhalchuk, Kost'. "Nevidomyi avtobiohrafichnyi Lyst K. Mykhal'chuka. (Z arkhivu Iv. Steshenka)." *Ukraïna* 24, no. 5 (1927): 59–69.

Myrny, Panas. *Tvory*. 5 vols. Kyiv: Derzhavne vydavnytstvo khudozhn'oï literatury, 1960.

Nechui-Levyts'kyi, Ivan. *Pershi kyïvs'ki kniazi Oleh, Yhor, Sviatoslav i sviatyi Volodymyr i eho potomky*. Kyiv: Tipografia M.P. Fritsa, 1876.

Nechui-Levyts'kyi, Ivan. *Tatary i Lytva na Ukraïni*. Kyiv: Tipografia S.T. Eremeeva, 1876.

Nechui-Levyts'kyi, Ivan. *Ukraïnstvo na literaturnykh pozvakh z Moskovshchynoiu: Kul'turolohichni traktaty*. Lviv: Kameniar, 1998.

Nechui-Levyts'kyi, Ivan. *Unia i Petro Mohyla Kyïvs'kyi Mytropolit*. Kyiv: Tipografia M.P. Fritsa, 1875.

Nechui-Levyts'kyi, Ivan. *Zibrannia tvoriv u desiati tomakh*. Kyiv: Naukova Dumka, 1965.

"Nedorozumenie po povodu slova 'zhid.'" *Osnova*, no. 6 (1861): 134–42.

"Nekhitraia beztseremonnost' 'Kievlianina.'" *Kievskii Telegraf*, 28 March 1875.

[Neobachnyi, P. pseud.] "Znaidenyi na dorozi lyst," *Osnova*, no. 2 (1861): 233–8.

"Nevol'naia propaganda ukrainofilov." *Kievskii Telegraf*, 23 March 1875.

"Nezhin. (Korres. Kievskago Telegrafa)." *Kievskii Telegraf*, 10 January 1875.

[Nis, Stepan.] *Pro khvoroby. Iak ïm zapomohty*. Kyiv: Tipografia M.P. Fritsa, 1874.

Nomys, M. "Rasskaz o poezdke zaporozhtsev v Peterburg." *Chernigovskii listok*, no. 11 (1863): 82–5.

Ochakovs'ka bida: Kozats'ke opovidannia. St Petersburg: P.A. Kulish, 1861.

Olelkovych, Mytro. "Zhydivs'ka diaka." *Osnova*, no. 9 (1861): 73–8.

"Ot redaktora." *Ukrainskii zhurnal*, no. 1 (1824): 8–9.

"Otzyv iz Kieva." *Sovremennaia letopis Russkogo Vestnika*, no. 46 (1862): 4–6.

"Perepiska i drugiia bumagi shvedskogo korolia Karla XII, pol'skogo Stanislava Leshchinskogo, tatarskago khana, turetskago sultana, general'nago pisaria F. Orlika i Kievskago voevody, Iosifa Pototskago, na latinskom i pol'skom iazykakh." *Chteniia*, no. 1 (31 May 1847): *materialy otechestvennnye*, iii–iv, 1–68.

"Peterburgskii universitet." *Kolokol*, 1 July 1861.

Piskunov, Fortunat. *Slovnytsia ukraïns'koï (abo Iuhovoï-Rus'koï) movy*. Odesa: E.P. Raspopov, 1873.

"Pis'mo g. Lysenka v 'Golose.'" *Kievskii Telegraf,* 11 April 1875.

"Pis'mo iz Galitsii." *Kievskii Telegraf,* 6 March 1875.

"Po povodu aktov, otnosiashchykhsia do iugo-zapadnoi Rusi." *Osnova,* no. 3 (1861): 1–2.

Podolyns'kyi, Serhii. "In Defense of an Independent Ukrainian Socialist Movement: Three Letters from Serhii Podolynskyi to Valerian Smirnov." Edited by Roman Serbyn. *Journal of Ukrainian Studies* 7, no. 2 (Fall 1982).

Podolyns'kyi, Serhii. *Lysty ta dokumenty.* Edited by Roman Serbyn and Tetiana Sliudikova. Kyiv: Tsentral'nyi derzhavnyi istorichnyi arkhiv Ukraïny, 2002.

Podolyns'kyi, Serhii. *Vybrani tvory.* Edited by Roman Serbyn. Montreal: Ukraïns'ke Istorychne Tovarystvo, 1990.

Podolyns'kyi, Serhii. *Vybrani tvory.* Edited by Liudmyla Korniichuk. Kyiv: Kyivs'kyi natsional'nyi ekonomichnyi universytet, 2000.

Pogarskii, St. "O narodnom obrazovanii i o sredstvakh dlia izdaniia uchebnikov na ukrainskom iazyke," *Osnova,* no. 7 (1862): 13–18.

Pogodin, Mikhail. "O drevnem iazyke russkom (Pis'mo k I. Sreznevskomu)." *Moskvitianin* 1, no. 2 (1856): 113–39.

Polnoe sobranie zakonov rossiiskoi imperii. Sobranie vtoroe. 55 vols. St Petersburg: V tipografii II otdeleniia Sobstvennogo Ego Imperatorskogo Velichestva Kantseliarii, 1825–81.

"Pol'skii vopros u nas i v Poznani." *Kievskii Telegraf,* 10 February 1875.

"Pominki Shevchenka v L'vove i V'ene." *Kievskii Telegraf,* 16 April 1875.

Potebnia, Aleksandr [Oleksander]. *Dva issledovaniia o zvukakh russkogo iazyka: O polnoglasii i o zvukovykh osobennostiakh russkikh narechii.* Voronezh: Tipografiia V. Gol'dshteina, 1866.

Poznanskii, Boris. "Vospominaniia." *Ukrainskaia zhizn',* no. 1 (1913): 25–44; no. 2: 10–26; no. 3: 15–24; no. 4: 23–33; no. 5: 41–51.

"Proshchanie N. Iv. Pirogova s uchebnym sosloviem i gorodom Kievom." *Osnova,* no. 6 (1861): 108–33.

Reutt, Gustaw. "Do legionów (Z notatek rodzinnych)." In *W czterdziestą rocznicę powstania styczniowego 1863–1903,* edited by Bronisław Szwarce et al., 357–62. Lwów: Nakładem Komitetu Wydawniczego, 1903.

Rigel'man, Aleksandr. "Letopisnoe povestvovanie o Maloi Rossii i eia narode i kozakakh voobshche, otkol' i iz kakogo naroda onye proizkhozhdenie svoe imeiut, i po kakim sluchaiam oni nyne pri svoikh mestakh obitaiut, kak to: cherkasskie ili malorossiiskie i zaporozhskie, a ot nikh uzhe donskie, a ot nikh iaitskie, chto nyne ural'skie, grebenskie, sibirskie, volgskie, terskie, nekrasovskie, i proch. kozaki, kak ravno i slobodskie polki." *Chteniia,* no. 5 (1846–7): *materialy otechestvennye,* i–v, 1–100; no. 6 (1846–7): *materialy otechestvennye,* 101–219; no. 7 (1846–7): *materialy otechestvennye*, 1–108, no. 8 (1846–7): *materialy otechestvennye*, 109–201; no. 9 (1846–7): *materialy otechestvennye*, 1–147, 1–101.

Ryl'skii, Faddei [Ryl's'kyi, Tadei]. "Neskol'ko slov o dvorianakh pravogo berega Dnepra." *Osnova*, nos. 11–12 (1861): 90–9.

Sbornik postanovlenii i razporiazhenii po tsenzure s 1720 po 1862 god. St Petersburg: V tipografii morskago ministerstva, 1862.

Shapoval, Kuz'ma. "Z podorozhnyka." *Osnova*, nos. 11–12 (1861): 111–16; no. 1 (1862): 48–56.

Shcherbatyi, Vikhtur [pseud.]. *Pro hroshi*. Kyiv: Tipografia M.P. Fritsa, 1874.

"Sovremennaia iuzhnorusskaia letopis'." *Osnova*, no. 3 (1862): 100–40.

Shevchenko, Taras. "Dnevnik." *Osnova*, no. 5 (1861): 6–13; no. 6: 5–16; no. 7: 7–18; no. 8: 3–15; no. 9: 13–24; no. 11: 6–16; no. 1 (1862): 7–16; no. 2: 3–29; no. 3: 20–33; no. 4: 31–45; no. 5: 14–25; no. 6: 3–14; no. 7: 17–29; no. 8: 5–20.

Shevchenko, Taras. *Kobzar*. St Petersburg: P. Semerenko, 1860.

Shevchenko, Taras. *Povne zibrannia tvoriv u dvanadtsiaty tomakh*. Kyiv: Naukova Dumka, 2001.

Shevchenko, Taras. *Psalmy Davydovi, perelozhyv po-nashomu Taras Shevchenko*. St Petersburg: [P. Kulish], 1860.

Shevchenko, Taras. *Selections: Poetry, Prose*. Translated by John Weir. Kyiv: Dnipro Publishers, 1988.

Sheikovs'kyi, Kalynyk. *Shcho take Ibn-Dastova "Rus'."* Kyiv: K.V. Sheikovs'kyi, drukarnia E. Ia. Fedorova, 1870.

Sliusarenko, A., and M. Tomenko, eds. *Istoriia ukraïns'koï konstytutsiï*. Kyiv: Pravo, 1997.

Sokhan, P., ed. *Kyrylo-Mefodiïvs'ke tovarystvo*. 3 vols. Kyiv: Naukova dumka, 1990.

"Sovremennaia iuzhnorusskaia letopis'." *Osnova* 3 (1862): 100–40.

"Sovremennoe ukrainofil'stvo." *Russkii vestnik* 115, no. 2 (1875): 850–65.

"Spravka dlia kievskago otdela slavianskogo blagotvoritel'nago komiteta." *Kievskii Telegraf*, 7 February 1875.

Sreznevskii, Izmail. Review of "Slowanskij Nàrodopis..Zestavil P.J. Šafarik." *Zhurnal Ministerstva Narodnago prosveshcheniia* 38 (1843): VI.21–2.

Sreznevskii, Izmail. *Zaporozhskaia starina*. 3 vols. Kharkiv: Izhdiveniem Izmaila Sreznevskago, 1833–8.

"Stolichnaia i provintsial'naia periodicheskaia pechat' na Iuge Rossii." *Kievskii Telegraf*, 2 January 1875.

Storozhenko, Oleksa. "Zakokhanyi chort." *Osnova*, no. 2 (1861): 14–40.

[Stronin, Oleksander]. *Azbuka po metode Zolotova dlia Iuzhno-russkago kraia*. Poltava: V gubernskoi tipografii, 1861.

"Svedenie o chisle prodannykh deshevykh izdanii na ukrainskom iazyke." *Osnova*, no. 10 (1861): 155–6.

Svod zakonov Rossiiskoi imperii, izdanie 1857 goda. 15 vols. St Petersburg: Tipografiia Vtorogo Otdeleniia Sobstvennoi Ego Imperatorskogo Velichestva Kantseliarii, 1857.

Svydnytsk'kyi, Anatolyi. *Tvory.* Kyiv: Derzhavne vydavnytstvo khudozhnoi literatury, 1958.

Svydnyts'kyi, Anatolii. "Velykden' u podolian," *Osnova,* no. 10 (1861): 43–64.

[Święcicki, Paulin]. "Na gruzach: Powieść w dwóch tomach przez Teofila Szumskiego." *Sioło,* vol. 2 (1867): 153–64.

Syroczyński, Leon. *O życiu młodzieży kijowskiej przed r. 1863 przez czlonka ostatniego zarządu Trojnickiego.* Lwów: I Związkowa Drukarnia, 1884.

Syroczyński, Leon: *Z przed 50 lat: Wspomnienie bylego studenta Kijowskiego uniwersytetu Leona Syroczyńskiego.* Lwów: Nakładem autora, 1914.

Trots'kyi, Mykola. *Iak teper odbuvatymet'sia voienna sluzhba.* Kyiv: Tipografia M.P. Fritsa, 1874.

Trudy etnograficheskо-statisticheskoi ekspeditsii v zapadno-Russkii krai, snariazhennoi Imperatorskim Russkim Geograficheskim Obshchestvom. Iugo-Zapadnyi otdel. Materialy i issledovaniia, sobrannyia d. ch. P. P. Chubinskim. 7 vols. St Petersburg: Imperatorskoe Russkoe Geograficheskoe Obshchestvo, 1872.

"Tsenzura v tsarstvovanie imperatora Nikolaia I-go." *Russkaia starina* 35 (February 1904): 433–43.

Tyshchyns'kyi, Oleksandr [Lesia-ii, pseudonym]. "Iz Gorodnetskogo uezda Chernig. gubernii (25 iiulia 1862g.)." *Osnova,* no. 8 (1862): 46–51.

Tyshchyns'kyi, Oleksandr. "Zashchitniku golubichskoi shkoly." *Osnova,* no. 10 (1862): 78–81.

Tyshchyns'kyi, Oleksandr [Lesia-ii, pseudonym]. "Z Horodnians'koho povitu." *Osnova,* no. 2 (1862): 57–8.

Tyshchyns'kyi, Oleksandr [Lesia-ii, pseudonym]. "Z Horodnyts'koho povitu Chernih. hub. (15 hrudnia 1861)." *Osnova,* no. 1 (1862): 59–62.

"Uchilishcha, obrazovavshiiasia na iuge v poslednee vremia." *Osnova,* no. 6 (1861): 93–6.

Ukrainets, kniga 1. Moscow: Mikhail Maksimovich, 1859.

Ulozhenie o nakazaniiakh ugolovnykh i ispravitel'nykh. St Petersburg: V tipografii Vtorago Otdeleniia Sobstvennoi Ego Imperatorskago Velichestva Kantseliarii, 1845.

Ustrialov, Nikolai. *Izsledovanie voprosa kakoe mesto v Rossiiskoi istorii dolzhno zanimat' Velikoe Kniazhestvo Litovskoe.* St Petersburg: V tipografii ekspeditsii zagotovleniia gosudarstvennykh bumag, 1839.

Velichko, Samoil [Velychko, Samiilo]. *Letopis' sobytii v Iugo-Zapadnoi Rossii v XVII-m veke,* 4 vols. Kyiv: Vremennaia Komissiia dlia Razbora Drevnykh Aktov, 1848–64.

[Velikorossianin O-ov.] "Ukraintsy v Saratovskoi gubernii." *Osnova*, no. 9 (1861): 185–8.

"Vnutrenniia izvestiia." *Kievskii Telegraf*, 27 January 1875.

Vovchok, Marko [pseudonym of Maria Vilinska]. *Narodni opovidannia*. St Petersburg: P.A. Kulish, 1858.

[Vovk, Khvedir.] *Pro zviriv: (Po Bremu). Zlozhyv Iastrubets'. Mniasoïdy abo khyzhi zviri 1. Vedmedi*. Kyiv: Tipografia M.P. Fritsa, 1876.

"V poslednei (dekabrskoi) knizhke 'Trudov' I. V. ekonomicheskago obshchestva." *Kievskii Telegraf*, 15 January 1875.

"Zasedanie komissii po snariazheniiu etnografichesko-statisticheskoi ekspeditsii v Zapadno-Russkii krai, 6go maia 1869 g." *Izvestiia imperatorskogo Rossiiskogo geograficheskogo obshchestva* 5, no. 5 (1869): 241–2.

"Zhurnal komissii po snariazheniiu ekspeditsii v Zapadno-Russkii krai. 27go noiabria 1871g." *Izvestiia imperatorskogo Rossiiskogo geograficheskogo obshchestva* 8, no. 1 (1872): 4.

"Zhurnal obshchego sobraniia IRGO. 12go marta 1869 goda." *Izvestiia imperatorskogo Rossiiskogo geograficheskogo obshchestva* 5, no. 2 (1869): 104–7.

"Zhurnal zasedaniia Otdeleniia Etnografii. 21go fevralia 1869 goda." *Izvestiia imperatorskogo Rossiiskogo geograficheskogo obshchestva* 5, no. 3 (1869): 179.

"Zhurnal zasedaniia Soveta IRGO, 30 ianvaria 1869 g." *Izvestiia imperatorskogo Rossiiskogo geograficheskogo obshchestva* 5, no. 1 (1869): 13.

Zhytets'kyi, Pavlo. "Z istoriï Kyïvs'koï ukraïns'koï hromady: Promova na Shevchenkovyh rokovynakh." *Zapysky naukovoho tovarystva imeni Shevchenka* 116, no. 5 (1913): 177–89.

RESEARCH LITERATURE

Anderson, Benedict. *Imagined Communities: Reflections on the Origins and Spread of Nationalism*. 2nd edition. London: Verso, 1991.

Andriewsky, Olga. "The Russian–Ukrainian Discourse and the Failure of the 'Little Russian Solution,' 1782–1917." In *Culture, Nation, and Identity: The Ukrainian–Russian Encounter (1600–1945)*, edited by Andreas Kappeler, Zenon E. Kohut, Frank E. Sysyn, and Mark von Hagen, 182–214. Edmonton, Toronto: Canadian Institute of Ukrainian Studies Press, 2003.

Andrusiak, Taras. *Shliakh do svobody (Mykhailo Drahomanov pro prava liudyny)*. Lviv: Svit, 1998.

Antonovych, Marko. "Z istoriï hromad na rubezhi 1850–1860-kh rokiv." *Kyïvs'ka starovyna*, no. 2 (1998): 32–45.

Baraboi, A.S. "Kharkovsko-Kievskoe revoliutsionnoe tainoe obshchestvo 1856–1860gg." *Istoricheskie zapiski* 52 (1955): 239–52.

Barsukov, Nikolai. "Russkie paleologi sorokovykh godov." *Drevniaia i novaia Rossiia* 16, no. 2 (1880): 259–90.

Barsukov, Nikolai. *Zhizn' i trudy M. P. Pogodina*. 22 vols. Moscow: Tipografiia M.M. Stasiulevicha, 1888–1910.

Beiersdorf, Otton. "Kijów w powstaniu styczniowym." In *Kraków-Kijów: Szkice z dziejów polsko-ukraińskich*, edited by Antoni Podraza, 73–130. Cracow: Wydawnictwo Literackie, 1969.

Bernshtein, M.D. *Zhurnal "Osnova" i ukraïns'kyi literaturnyi protses kintsia 50–60-kh rokiv XIX st.* Kyiv: Vydavnytstvo Akademiï Nauk Ukraïns'koï RSR, 1959.

Bilenky, Serhiy. *Romantic Nationalism in Eastern Europe: Russian, Polish, and Ukrainian Political Imaginations*. Stanford, CA: Stanford University Press, 2012.

Bilenky, Serhiy, and Viktor Korotkyi. *Mykhailo Maksymovych ta osvitni praktyki na Pravoberezhniï Ukraïni v pershiï polovyni XIX stolittia*. Kyiv: Vydavnychyi tsentr "Kyïvs'kyi universytet," 1999.

Brooks, Jeffrey. *When Russia Learned to Read: Literacy and Popular Culture, 1861–1917.* Princeton, NJ: Princeton University Press, 1985.

Buda, Serhii. "Do biohrafiï S.A.Podolyns'koho." *Za Sto Lit: Materialy z hromads'koho i literaturnoho zhyttia Ukraïny XIX i pochatku XX stolittia* 5, 192–200. Kyiv: Derzhavne vydavnytstvo Ukraïny, 1930.

Buda, Serhii. "Ukraïns'ki pereklady revoliutsiinoï literatury 1870-kh rokiv." *Za Sto Lit: Materialy z hromads'koho i literaturnoho zhyttia Ukraïny XIX i pochatku XX stolittia* 3, 50–65. Kyiv: Derzhavne vydavnytstvo Ukraïny, 1928.

Butych, I. "M. I. Kostomarov i tsars'ka tsenzura." *Arkhivy Ukraïny*, no. 6 (1967): 60–70.

Chernukha, Valentina Grigor'evna. *Pravitel'stvennaia politika v otnoshenii pechati: 60–70-e gody XIX veka*. Leningrad: Nauka, Leningradskoe otdelenie, 1989.

Daly, Jonathan W. "On the Significance of Emergency Legislation in Late Imperial Russia." *Slavic Review* 54, no. 3 (1995): 603–30.

Danylenko, Andrii. "The Ukrainian Bible and the Valuev Circular of July 18, 1863." *Acta Slavica Iaponica* 28 (2010): 1–21.

Dei, Oleksyi Ivanovych. *Slovnik ukraïnskykh psevdonimiv ta kryptonimiv (XVI–XX st.)*. Kyiv: Naukova dumka, 1969.

D'iakov, Vladimir, ed. *Vosstanie 1863g. i russko-pol'skie revoliutsionnye sviazi 60-kh godov: Sbornik statei i materialov*. Moscow: Izdatel'stvo Akademii Nauk SSSR, 1962.

Dolbilov, Mikhail. "The Stereotype of the Pole in Imperial Policy: The 'Depolonization' of the Northwestern Region in the 1860s." *Russian Studies in History* 44, no. 2 (Fall 2005): 44–88.

Dudko, Viktor. "Auditoriia zhurnalu 'Osnova' (1861–1862): Kil'kisnyi vymir." *Kyivs'ka Starovyna*, no. 6 (2001): 73–85.

Dudko, Viktor. "'Rannii' Oleksandr Tyshchyns'kyi: Storinky zhyttia i tvorchosti." *Siverians'kyi Litopys: Vseukraïnsk'kyi naukovyi zhurnal* 10, no. 6 (2006): 76–83.

Dudko, Viktor. "Statti dlia zhurnalu 'Osnova' (1861–1862), zaboroneni tsenzuroiu." *Kyivs'ka Starovyna*, 1997, no. 5 (317): 71–102.

Dudko, Viktor. "Zhurnal 'Osnova' u zhandarms'kykh materialakh." *Spadshchyna: Literaturne dzhereloznavstvo. Tekstolohiia*, no. 2 (2006): 7–45.

Eroshkin, Nikolai. *Istoriia gosudarstvennykh uchrezhdenii Rossii*. 3rd revised and expanded edition. Moscow: Vysshaia shkola, 1983.

Fishman, David E. "The Politics of Yiddish in Tsarist Russia." In *From Ancient Israel to Modern Judaism: Intellect in Quest for Understanding. Essays in Honor of Marvin Fox*, edited by Jacob Neusner, Ernest S. Frerichs, and Nahum M. Sarna, 4 vols., 4: 155–71. Atlanta, GA: Scholars' Press, 1989.

Gellner, Ernest. *Encounters with Nationalism*. Oxford, UK, and Cambridge, MA: Blackwell, 1994.

Gellner, Ernest. *Nations and Nationalism*. Oxford: Blackwell, 1983.

Głębocki, Henryk. *Kresy imperium: Szkice i materiały do dziejów polityki Rosji wobec jej peryferii (XVIII–XXI wiek)*. Cracow: Arcana, 2006.

Grabowicz, George G. *The Poet as Mythmaker: A Study of Symbolic Meaning in Taras Shevchenko*. Cambridge, MA: Harvard Ukrainian Research Institute, 1982.

Hillis, Faith. *Children of Rus': Right-Bank Ukraine and the Invention of the Russian Nation*. Ithaca and London: Cornell University Press, 2013.

Hnip, Mykhailo. "Do istoriï hromads'koho rukhu 1860 rr. (Zapyska A. L. Shymanova)." In *Za Sto Lit: Materialy z hromads'koho i literaturnoho zhyttia Ukraïny XIX i pochatku XX stolittia* 5, 170–82. Kyiv: Derzhavne vydavnytstvo Ukraïny, 1930.

Hnip, Mykhailo. *Hromads'kyi rukh na Ukraïni v 1860-kh rokakh. 1. Poltavs'ka hromada*. Khar'kiv: Derzhavne vydavnytstvo Ukraïny, 1930.

Hrakhovets'kyi, D. "Pershi nedil'ni shkoly na Poltavshchyni ta ikh diiachi (1860–1862 r.r.)." *Ukraina* 29, no. 4 (1928): 51–71.

Hroch, Miroslav. *In the National Interest: Demands and Goals of European National Movements of the Nineteenth Century: A Comparative Perspective*. Translated by Robin Cassling. Prague: Faculty of Arts, Charles University, 2000.

Hroch, Miroslav. *Social Preconditions of National Revival in Europe: A Comparative Analysis of the Social Composition of Patriotic Groups among the Smaller European Nations*. Translated by Ben Fowkes. Cambridge: Cambridge University Press, 1985.

Hrytsak, Iaroslav. *Narys istorii Ukraïny: Formuvannia modernoï ukrains'koï natsiï XIX–XX stolittia*. 2nd edition. Kyiv: Heneza, 2000.

Ivanova, Liudmyla Heorhiivna, and Raisa Petrivna Ivanchenko. *Suspyl'no-politychnyi rukh 60-kh rr. XIX st. v Ukraïni: Do problem stanovlennia ideolohiï*. Kyiv: Mizhnarodnyi instytut linhvistyky i prava, 2000.

Kalleinen, Kristiina. *Suomen kenraalikuvernementti. Kenraalikuvernöörien asema ja merkitys Suomen asioiden esittelyssä*. Helsinki: Painatuskeskus, 1994.

Kappeler, Andreas. "Einleitung." In *Die Russen: Ihr Nationalbewusstsein in Geschichte und Gegenwart*, edited by Andreas Kappeler, 6–17. Cologne: Markus, 1990.

Kappeler, Andreas. *Russland und die Ukraine: Verflochtene Biographien und Geschichten*. Vienna-Cologne-Weimar: Böhlau Verlag, 2012.

Kappeler, Andreas. "The Ukrainians of the Russian Empire, 1860–1914." In *The Formation of National Elites: Comparative Studies on Governments and Non-Dominant Ethnic Groups in Europe, 1850–1940*, edited by Andreas Kappeler in collaboration with Fikret Adanir and Alan O'Day, vol. 6, 105–32. New York: New York University Press; Aldershot, Hants, Eng.: Dartmouth, 1992.

Katrenko, A.M. *Ukraïns'kyi natsional'nyi rukh XIX st.*, pt. 2, *60–90-ti roky XIX st.* Kyiv: Kyïvs'kyi natsional'nyi universytet imeni Tarasa Shevchenka, 1999.

Khi-Sok, Džong. "M. P. Pogodin i Kirillo-Mefodievskoe obshchestvo 30–50-kh. gg. XIX v. o slavianskom edinstve (sravnitel'no- istoricheskii analiz)." *Voprosy istorii*, no. 7 (1996): 137–49.

Kieniewicz, Stefan. *Powstanie styczniowe*. Warsaw: Państwowe Wydawnictwo Naukowe, 1983.

Klid, Bohdan. "Songwriting and Singing: Ukrainian Revolutionary and Not So Revolutionary Activities in the 1860s." *Journal of Ukrainian Studies* 33/34 (Summer 2008–Winter 2009): 263–77.

Klid, Bohdan. "Volodymyr Antonovych: The Making of a Ukrainian Populist Activist and Historian." Ph.D. dissertation, University of Alberta, 1992.

Kohut, Zenon. "The Development of a Little Russian Identity and Ukrainian Nationbuilding." *Harvard Ukrainian Studies* 10, nos. 3–4 (December 1986): 559–76.

Kohut, Zenon. *Russian Centralism and Ukrainian Autonomy: Imperial Absorption of the Hetmanate 1760s–1830s*. Cambridge, MA: Distributed by Harvard University Press for the Harvard Ukrainian Research Institute, 1988.

Korniichuk, L. Ia. "Zhyttia i diial'nist' S. A. Podolyns'koho." In S.A. Podolyns'kyi, *Vybrani tvory*, 17–47. Kyiv: Kyivs'kyi natsional'nyi ekonomichnyi universytet, 2000.

Koroliuk, I.D., and I.S. Miller, eds. *Vosstanie 1863 g. i russko-pol'skie revoliutsionnye sviazi 60-kh godov*. Moscow: Izdatel'stvo Akademii Nauk SSSR, 1960.

Kotenko, Anton. "Do pytannia pro tvorennia ukraïns'koho natsional'noho prostoru v zhurnali 'Osnova.'" *Ukraïns'kyi istorychnyi zhurnal*, no. 2 (2012): 42–57.

Kotenko, Anton, Ol'ga Martyniuk, and Aleksei Miller. "Maloross." In *"Poniatiia o Rossii": K istoricheskoi semantike imperskogo perioda*, edited by Aleksei Miller, Denis Sdvizhkov, and Ingrid Schierle, 2 vols., 2: 392–443. Moscow: Novoe Literaturnoe obozrenie, 2012.

Koz'min, Boris. *Khar'kovskie zagovorshchiki 1856–1858 godov*. Kharkiv: Proletarii, 1930.

Koznarsky, Taras. "Izmail Sreznevsky's Zaporozhian Antiquity as a Memory Project." *Eighteenth-Century Studies* 35, no. 1 (2001): 92–100.

Kruhlashov, Anatolii. *Drama intelektuala: Politychni ideï Mykhaila Drahomanova*. Chernivtsi: Prut, 2000.

Lemke, Mikhail. *Epokha tsenzurnykh reform 1859–1865 godov*. St Petersburg: Knigoizdatel'stvo M.V. Pirozhkova, 1904.

Lemke, Mikhail. *Politicheskie protsessy v Rossii 1860-kh gg. (po arkhivnym dokumentam)*. 2nd edition. Moscow, Petrograd: Gosudarstvennoe izdatel'stvo, 1923.

Luckyj, George S.N. *Between Gogol and Shevchenko*. Munich: Wilhelm Fink Verlag, 1971.

Luckyj, George S.N. *Panteleimon Kulish: A Sketch of His Life and Times*. East European Monographs 127. Boulder, CO: East European Monographs, 1983.

Luckyj, George S.N. *Young Ukraine: The Brotherhood of Saints Cyril and Methodius in Kiev, 1845–1847*. Ottawa: University of Ottawa Press, 1991.

MacKenzie, David. "Russia's Balkan Policies under Alexander II, 1855–1881." In *Imperial Russian Foreign Policy*, edited and translated by Hugh Ragsdale, 219–46. [Washington, DC]: Woodrow Wilson Center Press; Cambridge, New York: Cambridge University Press, 1993.

Magocsi, Paul Robert. *A History of Ukraine*. Seattle: University of Washington Press, 1998.

Marakhov, G.I. *Sotsial'no-politicheskaia bor'ba na Ukraine v 50–60-e gody XIX veka*. Kyiv: Vyshcha shkola, 1981.

Mijakovs'ky, Volodymyr. *Nedrukovane i zabute: Hromads'ki rukhy dev'iatnadtsiatoho storichchia*. New York: Ukraïns'ka vil'na Akademiia Nauk, 1984.

Miller, Alexei. *The Romanov Empire and Nationalism: Essays in the Methodology of Historical Research*. Budapest: Central European University Press, 2008.

Miller, Alexei. *The Ukrainian Question: The Russian Empire and Nationalism in the Nineteenth Century*. Translated from Russian by Olga Poato. Budapest, New York: Central European University Press, 2003.

Moser, Michael. "Clerics and Laymen in the History of the Modern Standard Ukrainian Language." *Journal of Ukrainian Studies* 37 (2012): 41–62.

Nadtochii, Olena. *Rosiis'ka tsenzura i vydannia tvoriv Tarasa Shevchenka (1861–1916 rr.)*. Cherkasy: Brama, 2006.

Nakhlik, Ievhen. *Panteleimon Kulish: Osobystist', pys'mennyk, myslytel': Naukova monohrafiia*. Kyiv: Ukrains'kyi pys'mennyk, 2007.

Omel'chuk,V. Iu., Maryna Dmytrivna Boichenko, and Larysa Semenivna Novosolova, eds. *Ukraïnomovna knyha, 1798–1916*. 4 vols. Kyiv: Abrys, 1996–2002.

Pashaeva, Nina Magometkhanovna. *Ocherki istorii russkogo dvizheniia v Galichine XIX–XX vv*. Moscow: Gosudarstvennaia Publichnaia Istoricheskaia Biblioteka, 2001.

Pelech, Orest. "The Cyril and Methodius Brotherhood Revisited." In *Synopsis: A Collection of Essays in Honour of Zenon E. Kohut*, edited by Serhii Plokhy and Frank E. Sysyn, 335–44. Edmonton: Canadian Institute of Ukrainian Studies Press, 2005.

Pelech, Orest. "Toward a Historical Sociology of the Ukrainian Ideologues in the Russian Empire of the 1830s and 1840s." Ph.D. dissertation, Princeton University, 1976.

Pelenski, Jaroslaw. "The Contest for the 'Kievan Inheritance.'" In *Ukraine and Russia in Their Historical Encounter*, edited by Peter J. Potichnyj, Marc Raeff, Jaroslaw Pelenski, and Gleb N. Žekulin, 3–19. Edmonton: Canadian Institute of Ukrainian Studies Press, 1992.

Petronis, Vytautas. *Constructing Lithuania: Ethnic Mapping in Tsarist Russia, ca. 1800–1914*. Stockholm: University of Stockholm, 2007.

Pinchuk, Iurii A. *Mykola Ivanovych Kostomarov, 1817–1885*. Kyiv: Naukova Dumka, 1992.

Plokhy, Serhii. *The Cossack Myth: History and Nationhood in the Age of Empires*. Cambridge: Cambridge Univesrsity Press, 2012.

Plokhy, Serhii. *The Origins of the Slavic Nations: Premodern Identities in Russia, Ukraine, and Belarus*. Cambridge, UK, and New York: Cambridge University Press, 2006.

Plokhy, Serhii. "Ukraine or Little Russia? Revisiting an Early Nineteenth-Century Debate." *Canadian Slavonic Papers* 48, nos. 3–4 (2006): 335–53.

Pobirchenko, Nataliia. *Korotkyi biohraficheskyi slovnyk chleniv Kyïvs'koï staroï hromady (druha polovyna XIX–pochatok XX stolittia)*. Kyiv: Intelekt, 1999.

Pobirchenko, Natalia. *Pedahohichna i prosvitnyts'ka diial'nist' ukrains'kykh hromad u druhii polovyni XIX – na pochatku XX stolittia*. 2 vols. Kyiv: Naukovyi svit, 2000.

Potichnyj, Peter J., Marc Raeff, Jaroslaw Pelenski, and Gleb N. Žekulin, eds. *Ukraine and Russia in Their Historical Encounter*. Edmonton: Canadian Institute of Ukrainian Studies Press, 1992.

Prymak, Thomas M. *Mykola Kostomarov: A Biography*. Toronto, Buffalo: University of Toronto Press, 1996.

Remy, Johannes. "Government Promotion of Ukrainian Studies: The Careers of Izmail Sreznevskii, Osyp Bodians'kyi and Amvrosyi Metlyns'kyi, 1825–1855." In *Defining Self: Essays on Emergent Identities in Russia, Seventeenth to Nineteenth Centuries*, edited by Michael Branch, 254–69. Studia Fennica Ethnologica 10. Helsinki: Finnish Literature Society, 2009.

Remy, Johannes. *Higher Education and National Identity: Polish Student Activism in Russia 1832–1863*. Bibliotheca Historica, vol. 57. Helsinki: Suomalaisen Kirjallisuuden Seura, 2000.

Remy, Johannes. "National Aspect of Student Movements in St. Vladimir's University of Kiev 1855–1863." In *Skhid/Zahid. Istoryko-kul'turolohichnyi zbirnyk*, no. 7, 248–73. Kharkiv-Kyiv: Krytyka, 2005.

Remy, Johannes. "Otnoshenia Ukrainy s Rossiei v trudah Mihaila Maksimovicha 1850–1860-h godov." In *Etnichna istoria narodiv Evropy. Zbirnyk naukovyh prats*, Vypusk 9, 60–4. Kyiv: Taras Shevchenko University, 2001.

Remy, Johannes. "The Past of Poland-Lithuania in the Polish National Movement, 1830–1864." In *Statehood Beyond and Before Ethnicity: Transnational Perspectives onto Smaller States of Europe, 1600–2000*, edited by Linas Eriksonas and Leos Müller, Multiple Europes 33, 219–42. Brussels: P.I.E. Peter Lang, 2005.

Remy, Johannes. "The Ukrainian Alphabet as a Political Question in the Russian Empire before 1876." *Ab Imperio*, no. 2 (2005): 176–8.

Remy, Johannes. "The Ukrainophile Intelligentsia and Its Relation to the Russian Empire in the Beginning of the Reign of Alexander II (1856–1863)." In *Imperial and National Identities in Pre-Revolutionary, Soviet, and Post-Soviet Russia*, edited by Chris J. Chulos and Johannes Remy, 177–98. Helsinki: SKS, 2002.

Rennenkampf, K.N. "Kievskaia universitetskaia starina (Sobytiia v universitete Sv. Vladimira v 1860–1862 gg.)." *Russkaia starina* 99, no. 7 (1899): 36–55.

Rodkiewicz, Witold. *Russian Nationality Policy in the Western Provinces of the Empire (1863–1905)*. Lublin: Scientific Society of Lublin, 1998.

Ruud, Charles. *Fighting Words: Imperial Censorship and the Russian Press, 1804–1906*. Toronto: University of Toronto Press, 1982.

Saunders, David. "Mikhail Katkov and Mykola Kostomarov: A Note on Petr A. Valuev's Anti-Ukrainian Edict of 1863." *Harvard Ukrainian Studies* 17, nos. 3–4 (December 1993): 365–83.

Saunders, David. "Russia and Ukraine under Alexander II: The Valuev Edict of 1863." *International History Review* 17, no. 1 (1995): 23–50.

Saunders, David. "Russia, the Balkans and Ukraine in the 1870s." In *Russia and the Wider World in Historical Perspective: Essays for Paul Dukes*, edited by Cathryn Brennan and Murray Frame, 85–108. Basingstoke: MacMillan, 2000.

Saunders, David. "Russia's Nationality Policy: The Case of Ukraine (1847–1941)." *Journal of Ukrainian Studies* 29, nos. 1–2 (2004): 399–419.

Saunders, David. "Russia's Ukrainian Policy (1847–1905): A Demographic Approach." *European History Quarterly* 25, no. 2 (April 1995): 181–208.

Saunders, David. *The Ukrainian Impact on Russian Culture, 1750–1850.* Edmonton: Canadian Institute of Ukrainian Studies, 1985.

Savchenko, Fedir. *Zaborona ukraïnstva 1876r.* Kyiv: Derzhavne Vydavnytstvo Ukraïny, 1930.

Semenov, P.P., with the assistance of A.A. Dostoevskii. *Istoriia poluvekovoi deiatel'nosti Imperatorskogo russkogo geograficheskogo obshchestva 1845–1895.* St Petersburg: V tipografii V. Bezobrazova i Komp., 1896.

Serbyn, Roman. "The Sion-Osnova Controversy of 1861–1862." In *Ukrainian–Jewish Relations in Historical Perspective*, edited by Peter J. Potichnyj and Howard Aster, 85–110. Edmonton: Canadian Institute of Ukrainian Studies, 1988.

Serbyn, Roman. "La 'Société politique secrète' de Kharkiv (Ukraine), 1856–1860." *Canadian Historical Association: Historical Papers* 1973: 159–77.

Serbyn, Roman. "Zhyttia i diial'nist' Serhiia Podolyns'koho: Biohraficnyi narys." In Serhii Podolyns'kyi, *Lysty ta dokumenty*, 43–100. Kyiv: Tsentral'nyi derzhavnyi istorychnyi arkhiv Ukraïny, 2002.

Sereda, Ostap. "'Whom Shall We Be?' Public Debates over the National Identity of Galician Ruthenians in the 1860s." *Jahrbücher für Geschichte Osteuropas* 49 (2001): H2, 200–11.

Shandra, Valentyna. *Heneral-Hubernatorstva v Ukraïni: XIX–pochatok XX st.* Kyiv: Institut istoriï Ukraïny NAN Ukraïny, 2005.

Shevchenko, Maksim Mikhailovich. *Konets odnogo velichiia: Vlast', obrazovanie i pechatnoe slovo v Imperatorskoi Rossii na poroge Osvoboditel'nykh reform.* Moscow: Tri kvadrata, 2003.

Sheveliv, Borys. "L. I. Hlibov i tyzhnevyk 'Chernigovskii listok' u protsesi S. Nosa, I. Andrushchenka ta insh. 1863–1868 rr." In *Za Sto Lit: Materialy z hromads'koho i literaturnoho zhyttia Ukraïny XIX i pochatku XX stolittia* 4, 25–41. Kyiv: Istorychna sektsiia Vseukraïns'koï Akademiï Nauk, 1929.

Shkandrij, Myroslav. *Jews in Ukrainian Literature: Representation and Identity.* New Haven: Yale University Press, 2009.

Shkandrij, Myroslav. *Russia and Ukraine: Literature and the Discourse of Empire from Napoleonic to Postcolonial Times.* Montreal: McGill-Queen's University Press, 2001.

Simonov, S.S. "Studencheskoe dvizhenie v Kievskom universitete v XIX veke." Candidate of Historical Sciences dissertation., Kyiv Taras Shevchenko University, 1963.

Skabichevskii, Aleksandr Mikhailovich. *Ocherki istorii russkoi tsenzury (1700–1863 g.)*. St Petersburg: F. Pavlenkov, 1892.

Smith, Anthony D. *The Ethnic Origins of Nations*. Oxford: Blackwell, 1986.

Smith, Anthony D. *National Identity*. London: Penguin, 1991.

Smith, Anthony D. *Nationalism: Theory, Ideology, History*. Cambridge: Polity Press; Malden, MA: Blackwell, 2001.

Staliunas, Darius. *Making Russians: Meaning and Practice of Russification in Lithuania and Belarus after 1863*. Series "On the Boundary of Two Worlds: Identity, Freedom, and Moral Imagination in the Baltics," 11. Amsterdam and New York: Rodopi, 2007.

Sysyn, Frank E. "The Cossack Chronicles and the Development of Modern Ukrainian Culture and National Identity." *Harvard Ukrainian Studies* 14, nos. 3–4 (1990): 593–607.

Tabiś, Jan. *Polacy na uniwersytecie Kijowskim 1834–1863*. Cracow: Wydawnictwo Literackie, 1974.

Tolochko, Oleksyi. "Kyievo-Rus'ka spadshchyna v istorychnyi dumtsi Ukrainy pochatku XIX st." In V.F. Verstiuk, V.M. Horobets, O.P. Tolochko, *Ukrains'ki proiekty v rosiis'kii imperii*, 250–350. Kyiv: Naukova Dumka, 2004.

Tolochko, Oleksii. *Kievskaia Rus' i Malorossiia v XIX veke*. Kyiv: Laurus, 2012.

Tolochko, Oleksii, and Petro Tolochko. *Kyïvs'ka Rus'* . Kyiv: Vydavnychyi dim Al'ternatyvy, 1998.

Ul'ianovs'kyi, Vasyl', and Viktor Korotkyi. *Volodymyr Antonovych: Obraz na tli epokhy*. Kyiv: Tov. "Mizhnarodna finansova ahentsiia," 1997.

Vasilenko, N.P. *O. M. Bodianskii i ego zaslugi dlia izucheniia Malorossii*. Kyiv: N.P. Korchak-Novitskii, 1904.

Velychenko, Stephen. "Local Officialdom and National Movements in Imperial Russia: Administrative Shortcomings and Under-Government." In *Ethnic and National Issues in Russian and East European History*, edited by John Morison, 74–86. Houndsmills: Macmillan Press Ltd.; New York: St Martin's Press, 2000.

Velychenko, Stephen. *National History as Cultural Process: A Survey of the Interpretations of Ukraine's Past in Polish, Russian, and Ukrainian Historical Writing from the Earliest Times to 1914*. Edmonton: Canadian Institute of Ukrainian Studies Press, 1992.

Velychenko, Stephen. "Tsarist Censorship and Ukrainian Historiography, 1828–1906." *Canadian-American Slavic Studies* 23, no. 4 (Winter 1989): 385–408.

Venturi, Franco. *Roots of Revolution: A History of the Populist and Socialist Movements in Nineteenth Century Russia.* Translated by Francis Haskell. London: Weidenfeld and Nicolson, 1960.

Vozniak, Mykhailo. *Kyrylo-Metodiïvs'ke bratstvo.* Lviv: Fond "Uchitesia, Braty Moi," 1921.

Vulpius, Ricarda. *Nationalisierung der Religion: Russifizierungspolitik und ukrainische Nationsbildung 1860–1920.* Forschungen zur osteuropäischen Geschichte, vol. 64. Wiesbaden: Harrassowitz Verlag, 2005.

Walicki, Andrzej. *Russia, Poland, and Universal Regeneration: Studies on Russian and Polish Thought of the Romantic Epoch.* Notre Dame, IN: University of Notre Dame Press, 1991.

Walicki, Andrzej. *The Slavophile Controversy: History of a Conservative Utopia in Nineteenth-Century Russian Thought.* Translated by Hilda Andrews-Rusiecka. Oxford: Clarendon Press, 1975.

Weeks, Theodore R. "Between Rome and Tsargrad: The Uniate Church in Imperial Russia." In *Of Religion and Empire: Missions, Conversion, and Tolerance in Tsarist Russia,* edited by Robert P. Geraci and Michael Khodarkovsky, 70–91. Ithaca, London: Cornell University Press, 2001.

Weeks, Theodore R. "Jidiš ir lietuvių kalbos Rusijos imperijoje: Politia dviejų 'uždraustų kalbų' atžvilgiu 1863–1913 m." In *Raidzių draudimo metai: Straipsnių rinkinys,* edited by Darius Staliunas, 175–90. Vilnius: LII Leidykla, 2004.

Wendland, Anna Weronika. *Die Russophilen in Galizien: Ukrainische Konservative zwischen Österreich und Russland, 1848–1915.* Studien zum Geschichte der Österreichisch-Ungarischen Monarchie, vol. 21. Vienna: Verlag der Österreichischen Akademie der Wissenschaften, 2001.

Whittaker, Cynthia. *The Origins of Modern Russian Education: An Intellectual Biography of Count Sergei Uvarov, 1786–1855.* DeKalb: Northern Illinois University Press, 1984.

Yaney, George L. *The Systematization of Russian Government: Social Evolution in the Domestic Administration of Imperial Russia, 1711–1905.* Urbana: University of Illinois Press, 1973.

Yekelchyk, Serhy. "The Body and National Myth: Motives from the Ukrainian National Revival in the Nineteenth Century." *Australian Slavonic and East European Studies* 7, no. 2 (1993): 31–59.

Yekelchyk, Serhy. "The Nation's Clothes: Constructing a Ukrainian High Culture in the Russian Empire, 1860–1900. *Jahrbücher für Geschichte Osteuropas,* new ser., vol. 49, no. 2 (2001): 230–9.

Zaionchkovskii, Petr Andreevich. *Kirillo-Mefodievskoe obshchestvo (1846–1847).* Moscow: Izdatel'stvo Moskovskogo universiteta, 1959.

Zaitsev, Pavlo. *Taras Shevchenko: A Life.* Edited and translated by George S.N. Luckyj. Toronto: University of Toronto Press, 1988.

Zaslavs'kyi, Isai. "Kalenyk Sheikovs'kyi – etnohraf, folkloryst, movoznavets', vydavets'." *Kyïvs'ka starovyna,* nos. 1– 2 (January–April 1997) (315): 86–100.

Zel'dich,Iurii. *Petr Aleksandrovich Valuev i ego vremia: Istoricheskoe povestvovanie.* Moscow: Agraf, 2006.

Zhukovskaia, Tatyana. "Count Sergei Uvarov and the Cyril and Methodius Society: The Crises of 'Official Nationality,' 1830–1850." In *Defining Self: Essays on Emergent Identities in Russia, Seventeenth to Nineteenth Centuries,* compiled and edited by Michael Branch, 271–84. Helsinki: Finnish Literature Society, 2009.

Zhukovskaia, T.N. "S. S. Uvarov i kirillo-mefodievskoe obshchestvo ili krizis 'ofitsial'noi narodnosti.'" In *Otechestvennaia istoriia i istoricheskaia mysl' v Rossii,* edited by R. Iv. Ganelin, 196–207. St Petersburg: Nestor, 2006.

Zhurba, Oleh Ivanovich. *Kyïvs'ka arkheohrafichna komisiia 1843–1921: Narys istoriï i diial'nosti.* Kyiv: Naukova Dumka, 1993.

Index

www.ingramcontent.com/pod-product-compliance
Lightning Source LLC
LaVergne TN
LVHW040152080826
844660LV00014B/932/J